One Guard Out

The Original Lifeguards of
California's Wild North Coast

Ed Vodrazka

CONTENTS

MANY THANKS

The book you now hold is a product of contribution and collaboration from many individuals.

My deepest gratitude goes out to my elder lifeguard brother, mentor, wine aficionado, and fellow scribe, retired Lifeguard Chief, Michael Brousard. Your incomparable passion for the profession of lifesaving is further reinforced by the love and respect you share with the many lifeguards who have become lead actors in your own life story. Your fondness for the Sonoma Coast, coupled with your support and wisdom throughout the construction of this project were instrumental in its fruition. Without exaggeration, every page I penned in these chapters was written with your ears in my mind, and your soul in my heart.

Retired Lifeguard Aquatic Specialist Michael Martino, whom you will soon come to know, was one of the *"Originals"* on the North Coast. Mike charitably offered his personal accounts of several of the stories contained within. His original manuscripts, written some 20 years before this book's publication, have been preserved largely intact. An additional thanks to Mike for pushing me to continue refining my early manuscripts "like a finish carpenter."

Kudos to Rex Grady for having the foresight to fastidiously document the various rescues, fatalities, medical aids, and formative events that beset the original crew from their outset. Capturing them in print not only was vital to their preservation, but also provided the framework which guided my interviews with the lifeguards, allowing us to delve deeper and reveal their proper significance.

A thousand thanks to my friend and scholar Mike Tanghe, who, Lord knows, tried his best to educate me on the fundamentals of grammar, punctuation, and sentence structure. Any remaining deficiencies you might discover in any of those areas are wholly my fault – not his.

A special thanks to the skilled artisans who breathed life into this book; to illustrator Tim Gunther for creating the maps, to the formatting wizard, Jeremy Herman, for wrestling a few thousand words onto these pages in a readable arrangement, to Jenny Borroso at J20 Graphics for designing the stunning cover, and to my writing muse and kindred ocean spirit, Neva Sullaway for your unfailing support.

To Jennifer, Jade and Charlie, who allowed me the better part of a year "on sabbatical" to compile this manuscript, thank you for granting me that supreme indulgence. Perhaps in your old age, long after I am gone, you might share these stories with your own kids and grandkids.

Above all, my solemn thanks go out to the original crew of lifeguards themselves for their time, their candor, and their willingness to share their astounding adventures with us. My conversations with Osh McNulty, Dave Carter, Dave Schardt, Mike Martino, Scott Melvin, Jon Gulick, Kurt Loeffler, Steve Franklin, Brian Hickey, Bud Brown, and Don Straub were deep and evocative. I only hope the gravity of their exploits are adequately conveyed in my words.

Lastly, to all of my brothers and sisters who ever wore a pair of "reds" and swam out into the swirling seas to rescue a swimmer in distress; may God shine down on you and provide you with all blessings pure and abundant. Know that you made a difference

"Son, I can't wait until you get in the Marines... where you will be safer."

— Father of North Coast Lifeguard Jake Snyder...before he
became an F-18 "Hornet" Fighter Pilot.

FOREWORD

When people think of ocean lifeguards, they picture young men and women, fit and tan, running across the sandy beaches of Southern California, rescuing swimmers in the warm summer ocean waters of Los Angeles, Huntington or San Diego. The vast majority of ocean-loving Californians are unaware there exists a small band of lifeguards who patrol along the rugged Sonoma Coast. The ocean conditions and lifesaving methodology bear little resemblance to the duties of their fellow guards 600 miles to the south. You won't find any palm trees there. Nor bikinis, umbrellas, hot dog stands, or sunbathing. Similarly, there were very few surf spots. With the average water temperature hovering around 50 degrees, even the fish are different.

This story chronicles the origin of the Sonoma Coast State Lifeguard Service, and their five-year struggle to establish themselves as the primary ocean rescue service within the local Emergency Services community.

Resurrecting the stories from their formative years and bringing them back to life, captured in print has been an endeavor of pure joy for me. It's a project I have wanted to undertake since the last day I worked on the Sonoma Coast in 2002. To hold this book in my hand, provides me an indescribable reward.

As I write these words, 30 years have now passed since that

auspicious fall day when thee lifeguards first arrived on the Sonoma Coast and, in so doing, etched their names into lifeguard immortality. As they age, the ever-increasing risk was that the monumental events they endured during their formative years would fade from our collective memory.

I didn't want that to happen.

Their emergence, confronted with untold adversity, and their incomparable heroics in spite of those challenges, weave into a saga that begs to be shared. Like an elaborate tapestry, the significance of their collective experience exists in the form of numerous individual events which readers may find thrilling and inspiring. The setting, in that harsh environment where ocean and land joined their powerful forces, formed the dramatic backdrop where each lifeguard invested a part of themselves into the shared history of the North Coast Lifeguards.

These are the stories of the unsuspecting visitors who came to the Sonoma Coast to recreate and would find themselves beset with unexpected tragedy, usually involving the power and intensity of Mother Ocean. As the serendipitous hands of fate dictated, and the skills of the lifeguards mitigated, some of these victims would lose their lives while others would be saved, often in dramatic fashion. For those who were rescued, the personal stories of their calamities became a colorful part of their family archives. For those who did not survive, within a generation or two, their stories will have likely faded into a vague summary of the tragedy, limited to the general circumstances surrounding their death.

In my attempts to maintain historical accuracy and a preservation of truth, the details of these events, most often, were obtained directly from interviews with the very guards who immersed themselves into those harrowing scenes. Their offerings provide us with the most accurate and detailed accounts of these events, along with a unique set of insights and analysis that is theirs alone.

Similarly, the details and substantiations, which expose the lifeguards' personal attributes, foibles, and general strengths and weaknesses, were (almost exclusively) provided by either their own self-critique or the judgments of their peers. These were not always complementary. In pursuit of honesty and a conscious desire to avoid canonizing the guards or fluffing them into superheroes, for better or worse, I expressed those sentiments as candidly as was prudent - warts and all. In my estimation, their reactions to the often insurmountable stressors of working that stretch of coastline reflect their "humanness" and my hope is that the reader will forgive their inadequacies, and regard them with a level of respect and compassion they most certainly deserve.

Similarly, my renderings of their adventures are as accurate and free from flourishes or embellishments as possible because, frankly none are needed. The truth of their exploits, as you will soon see, was dramatic enough.

A noteworthy factor validating the veracity of these events was revealed when two different guards provided their separate recollections of a specific event. Repeatedly, and with an uncanny consistency, the detailed accounts they independently provided aligned perfectly. No incident better reflects that uniformity than the harrowing crash of the Sonoma County Sheriff's Rescue Helicopter in 1992. Despite the fact the two guards had not spoken about the tragedy for over 30 years, the individual narratives from Straub and Loeffler were strikingly consistent, including their recall of specific statements made by both the rescuers and their victims at the time.

Because ocean aficionados reading these stories will undoubtedly want to know, in describing matters of surf size, severity of injuries, and overall intensity of the emergent calls recounted, I discovered a fairly consistent disparity between the perspectives of laypersons on scene and the guards who were the actual rescuers on the calls. Lifeguards have a long history of downplaying the dramatic elements of their rescues, so if anything, the reader can safely assume with some level of confidence that the heroic aspects of these accounts, provided from the perspective of the guards, have actually been moderated *downward*.

This is the story of the emergence of the lifeguard service on the Sonoma Coast. It's a story about big surf and big rescues at a time and a place which brought out spectacular demonstrations of courage and fortitude among a small group of ocean pioneers who were tasked with reversing an abominable 50 year trend in drownings and fatalities on that wild and untamed coastline in Northern California.

It's my great honor to share their stories with you.

INTRODUCTION

As one of the first surfers to drop into the massive waves at Waimea, Eddie Aikau firmly established himself in the pantheon of the pioneers of big wave surfing. What most people don't know is Aikau was also the first lifeguard hired by the city of Honolulu to work on the perilous North Shore. Assigning Eddie to that eminent position was an excellent decision, as there was likely no waterman alive who held his level of expertise and skills in that local surf line. Aikau thrived in the role and estimates as to the number of rescues he made in his career hovered around 500. In a surprise to no one in 1977, Aikau was awarded the honor of "Lifeguard of the Year."

The following year, Eddie was aboard the ill-fated voyaging canoe known as the *Hokule'a* in an expedition hoping to reach Tahiti using only traditional means of navigation when it suffered a fatal breach and capsized. According to Will Kyselka, in his book *An Ocean Mind*:

"Swells were high, but the canoe had ridden out such seas before. However, this time it was heavily laden with food and supplies for a month's journey. The added weight put unusual stress on the canoe, making it difficult to handle. Turning off-wind eased the strain but it also caused the sea to wash in over the gunwales, filling the starboard compartments and depressing the lee hull. Winds pushing on the sails rotated the lighter windward hull around the submerged lee hull, now

dead in the water. Five hours after leaving Ala Wai Harbor, Hokule'a was upside-down in the sea between O'ahu and Moloka'I"

With the vessel swamped 12 miles from the shore, Aikau courageously decided he would venture off to get help. In order to paddle more efficiently and utilize his powerful arm strokes, he removed his life jacket. After a warm aloha send-off, Aikau dropped his board into the clear blue ocean and began the 12-mile journey to get help and save his ship mates. The crew watched as the great lifeguard paddled off in the open seas. Eventually, he faded off on the horizon, disappearing from view. Eddie Aikau was never seen again.

The following day, with the crew hypothermic after hanging onto the vessel all night, the *Hokule'a* was spotted by the last Hawaiian Airlines flight of the day out of Kona. The pilot circled once, then hailed the Coast Guard, and eventually all of the remaining passengers were saved. Tragically, the only person to die in the disaster was the heroic lifeguard / surfer who bravely paddled off into oblivion attempting to save the others.

A phrase in reverence to Aikau became well-known in both the lifeguard and surfing communities. The phrase was simple but captured the valor, skill, and heroism Eddie Aikau personified.

"Eddie Would Go."

~

On the familiar summer beaches of Southern California, lifeguards are generally not tasked with crossing vast expanses of the open ocean on a paddleboard. Their ocean environment is sectioned off by jurisdictional boundaries and their responsibilities are limited by their scope of duties. But conversely, they most certainly had to contend with challenging crowds. On the busy beaches of Newport or Santa Monica, where thousands of beach-goers pack themselves onto the sand and into the water, towers are placed within 150 yards of each other such that the lifeguard's area of responsibility (even with the compulsory overlapping) is rarely more than a 200-yard swath of water.

Yet on *every* rescue, *all ocean lifeguards* make a decision to "go" and enter the water to help someone who is struggling. For the overwhelming majority of rescues, the guard's skill level and the manageable ocean conditions remove any doubt or hesitation the lifeguard *would* go.

When a lifeguard sprints out to make a rescue, a cadre of their partners will monitor that rescue and, if necessary, can deploy back-up guards, paddlers, personal water craft or the rescue boat to assist the original guard. Thus, in multiple victim rescue situations at Zuma or Manhattan Beach, it's conceivable to have 6 or 7 lifeguards in the water to make certain all of the struggling swimmers are safely delivered to shore.

The overall management of any Ocean Lifeguard Operation is predicated on two overarching factors; the number of swimmers in the water, and the relative danger of the ocean environment.

While the North Coast crew certainly did not have to contend with the formidable crowds which frequented the urban beaches of Southern California, their overall acuity was heavily bolstered by the second factor...as the ocean conditions were *insanely dangerous*. The arriving lifeguards on the North Coast were greeted with the combined challenges of bitterly cold water, perilously large surf, and severely limited options for any kind of back-up response.

Still, the basic, universal credo by which *all* lifeguards abide, remained the same:

Everyone who ventured out into the ocean should survive.

Owing to the this new and rugged environment, the long-standing practices successfully employed by lifeguard agencies in Southern California would need to be significantly altered when the first guards reported for duty on the Sonoma Coast. In some cases, bold new strategies and methods of lifeguarding would need to be invented where no template existed.

Above all, a pervasive and disarming uncertainty, fueled by the fires of pessimism and lack of faith from the local Emergency Services Community, instilled an insidious doubt into every one of those guards, causing them to question their ability to perform (and even survive) while attempting to save lives in *those* conditions.

Facing those challenges, even the most skilled guards among them understandably hesitated when faced with that same decision whether or not, like Eddie Aikau, *they would go.*

In 1995, five years after the inception of the Sonoma Coast

Lifeguard service, at a general meeting in an office at Salmon Creek State Park, Doug Shoaf, one of the guards who arrived after the original crew, asked Lifeguard Supervisor Brit Horn, the simple but profound question which up until that point had never been officially voiced out loud. While Brit was reviewing strategies on how best to traverse the deadly and relatively common double over-head shore break at Goat Rock, Shoaf slowly raised his hand and, when acknowledged by Horn, specifically asked, "Are we obligated to go?"

When the question was posed, all eyes turned to Shoaf, then immediately back to Horn. It was a moment of profound significance in State Lifeguard history. In those five simple words, Shoaf had posed a question every guard on that coastline had likely pondered many times, yet none had ever found the courage to verbalize. The reason the guards were reticent about asking, was because it conveyed an associated admission of their personal limitations as watermen. It was an overt confession they all concealed inside themselves; that harbored elements of doubt and even *fear* in the performance of their duties. Of course they all knew they were mortal, and all of them had their limitations, but if someone was out there fighting for their very life, no one wanted to admit they *couldn't* or *wouldn't* go.

Horn's impending answer would dictate, in essence whether his small crew, working on that perilous North Coast were *required* to swim out in unspeakable conditions to attempt the rescue, even if it meant putting their own lives in jeopardy.

But Horn was blindsided and was not prepared to give an answer. The son of legendary big wave pioneer Kit Horn, Brit himself was a well-established big wave enthusiast. His skill set was beyond that of most earthly watermen, so for him perhaps the question never arose in his own mind. Brit, like Eddie Aikau, *would always go*. But as a supervisor and a mentor for his crew, Shoaf's question opened Brit's mind to the possibility of why they wouldn't or even *shouldn't* go. None of them were Eddie Aikau. Certainly they were all supremely talented lifeguards who had developed their water skills to a level few people on the planet possessed, yet they were also made of flesh and blood, working in an area which tested even the greatest watermen in the world. Each of them had made the decision to come to the North Coast to prove themselves in one of the most challenging lifeguard operations imaginable. And yet their previous success was no guarantee they might pay the ultimate price while attempting to make their next rescue, when the ocean devised some new and improved method to kill them.

For the record, Brit didn't answer the question. His personal credo (that he, as a lifeguard would ALWAYS go) was not a mandate he could force upon his subordinates, and he knew it. To absolve his crew of their guilt and any perceived shortcomings, Horn could have simply said, "If it's too dangerous, you don't have to go." But those words were never spoken. Thus, the question remained a rhetorical one, and each lifeguard was left to figure out an answer for themselves.

When a lifeguard enters the water to make a rescue, the phrase most often used to notify the dispatcher is *"One Guard Out!"* Regardless of the beach or the agency you work for; on every rescue, the first responding lifeguard is almost always alone. In essence, they choose to place themselves in harm's way to rescue an overwhelmed individual. Even on those well-staffed summer beaches of Southern California when back up units are readily on scene, that first guard swimming out to make a rescue, enters the water alone.

The most striking example of the lifeguards' ultimate autonomy occurred on July 6th, 2014 when Newport Beach Lifeguard Ben Carlson dove off the back of the rescue boat in huge surf to save a struggling swimmer. Ben was an incredibly well-respected and well-loved ocean guard with impeccable water skills. Yet, despite a full complement of several dozen partners working that day, Ben was killed while performing that rescue and no lifeguard there could save him. The rescue cost Ben his life and left his family, and an entire community of fellow lifeguards grieving.

Conversely, on the patrol pattern for the Sonoma Coast, a *full complement* of rescuers generally amounted to four, stretched over 31 miles of rugged coastline. If you happen to be the first guard to go, it is unlikely any back-up would arrive to assist you for quite some time.

There especially, that solitary responding lifeguard was truly "One Guard Out."

Ben Carlson Memorial Statue – Courtesy: Ben Carlson Memorial Foundation

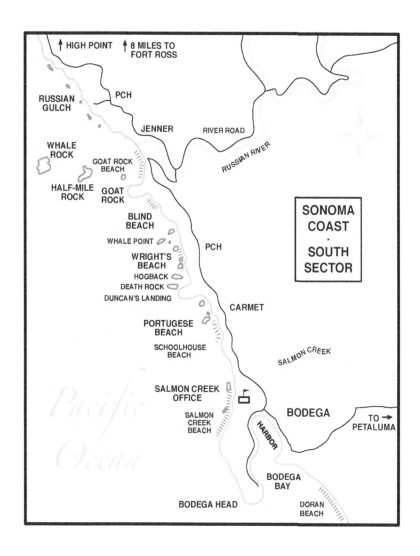

SOUTH SECTOR

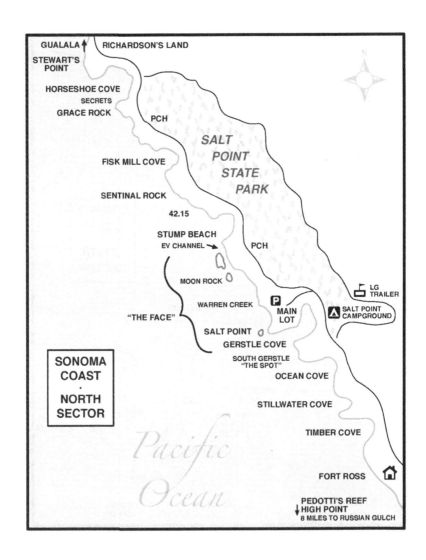

NORTH SECTOR

1

HUMBLE BEGINNINGS

The author getting anointed by a massive plume – Salt Point 1994

2 | ONE GUARD OUT

I had heard the Sonoma Coast District was starting their new lifeguard service back in 1990 and, like many of my compatriots, I was intrigued. Three members of their original crew of 11 (Bud Brown, Dave Schardt, and Jon Gulick) had come from my home district of San Clemente, and through them, for the next few years, occasional stories trickled back down to our beaches of San Clemente, San Onofre and Doheny. Most often, the accounts of their exploits were crazy daring adventures involving towering waves and incredible acts of valor. We sat and listened, completely enthralled, imagining ourselves swimming out on those death-defying rescues.

Like a few of my partners, I had considered transferring up to work that coastline out of a sense of curiosity and a drive to "challenge myself." But those thoughts usually vaporized from my mind just as quickly when I reminded myself I was not a decorated collegiate swimmer, I was neither strong nor imposing, and was only a mediocre free diver. Additionally, although I had been trained to work as a deck hand on the Surf Watch, my boating experience was negligible. Worst of all, being on the skinny side, I wasn't all that fond of being cold.

In the fall of 1994, I had just completed my 18th year as an Ocean Lifeguard. By then, I had reached the pinnacle of the schedule, and was able to hand-pick my assignments, choosing to work all of my shifts in the San Onofre Bluffs units (4501 and 4503). It was a dream schedule, with manageable calls, a patrol pattern across three miles of one of the most beautiful and sparsely visited beaches in the county, an hour-long surf break or soft-sand run every day, and a partner to hang with. Throw in a bag of sunflower seeds and I was all set. Although we had our share of challenging calls, many of my fellow rescuers admitted it was one of the best assignments on the West Coast. I wouldn't disagree.

But the male ego works in mysterious ways. Partially fueled by the same sense of challenge and curiosity of my predecessors, on a whim I called the Sonoma Coast Lifeguard Supervisor, Mat Fuzie to inquire about the theoretical possibilities of one day working there. Aware of the well-earned prestige granted to the lifeguards on the North Coast, I assumed open positions were rare, and my intention was to add my name onto some kind of list for future consideration.

Mat was pleasant on the phone while explaining a bit about the duties and the operations. But you can imagine my surprise when, despite never having met me, and with no formal interview, he agreed to hire me on the spot. I was blindsided with the offer and frankly, quite stunned. We chatted a bit more and I eagerly listened as Mat extoled some of the virtues of working up there. Realizing my excitement, and probably sensing my vulnerable mindset, Mat then ramped up the process, asking me if I could start the following weekend. The exhilaration of the moment and the intoxicating idea of working the wild North Coast left me giddy. Within five minutes of placing the call, I accepted the position.

Mat Fuzie – with a fresh batch of abalone – 1994

Amazed at my good fortune and my seemingly adroit negotiation skills, after hanging up the phone I began a spontaneous dance around the room celebrating the fact I was about to become a North Coast Lifeguard. After a few punches in the air and some inappropriate gesticulations, the realization kicked into my mind that Fuzie had just hired me despite the fact I hadn't really said *anything* about myself. Could it be, this fortuitous and spontaneous hiring might in fact have been a bit *too* easy for a reason? My joyous and inappropriate dance soon deflated into a short series of uninspired arm lifts, and soon after, now sitting, an insidious feeling of concern began to trickle into my mind. Moments later, now quite sober, I began to wonder if there might be some kind of a "catch" involved in working up there.

Regardless, in the fall of 1994 I transferred from the warm sands of San Clemente to work the chilly Sonoma Coast. It didn't take long for me to realize the "catch" existed, not in one specific element of the job, but rather in the entire *package* which came along with working there. This brand of lifeguarding bore little resemblance to the day-to-day assignments I had in San Clemente, and *SURPRISE!* Guys like me were NOT lining up to get their asses kicked by the cold, the wind and the huge surf on the North Coast.

But I made good on my commitment to Fuzie and in fact, my spontaneous decision to transfer there would parlay into a 7-year stint working the fall, winter and spring seasons. They generously allowed me to return to San Clemente to thaw out for the summers. I became one of the core lifeguards on the North Coast, soaking deep into the operation as well as the fabric of the community. My experiences there from 1994 to 2001 would form a foundation of memories which would become among the most dramatic, nostalgic, and profound of my entire 45-year lifeguard career.

But the story of the original crew on the Sonoma Coast is not my story. I arrived there 4 years after their inception. By then, only three members of the original crew were left. I offer my own introduction to the North Coast only to offer the reader a sense of trust that my perspectives comes from some level of experience. In guarding those waters and dealing with the insane surf, I developed a profound appreciation for the in-roads my predecessors had established long before I arrived. Plenty of mountaineers have climbed Mount Everest, but in 1953 it was Tenzing Norgay and Sir Edmund Hillary who were the first to forge up the previously unknown routes of that mountain. The subsequent trips were most assuredly impressive, but all of those brave souls who ventured up the side of Everest years later were bolstered and inspired by the fact that, thanks to Norgay and Hillary, they knew it *could be done.*

Those 11 pioneers paved the way for us and for the future guards who would follow. They created the original rescue strategies, assimilated into the rescue community, identified and mapped most of the dangerous rips and currents by trial and error, and most importantly, they proved that lifeguards COULD save lives up there. Without a doubt, we rode on their coat tails.

∽

I arrived on the North Coast on a cold, grey and blustery fall afternoon in 1994.

Back then, the town of Bodega itself was little more than a smattering of weathered grey buildings and seemingly abandoned shacks, overtaken with vines. I didn't see a soul outside. I knew this quaint but nondescript little town was the location where Alfred Hitchcock had filmed "The Birds" back in 1963; a black-and-white horror film I had seen as a spindly 5-year-old kid. I remembered the movie exceedingly well because it *scared the living crap out of me!* On that particular grey day, the cold weather, the wind, and the bleak landscape recreated the eerie setting of the disturbing movie, and as I ambled around the desolate town with my jacket zipped up to my neck, I instinctively glanced into the sky from time to time searching for predators. Apparently on that day, it was too cold, even for the birds to attack.

There didn't seem to be a great rush of people moving into this little enclave. As of 1994, gentrification had not yet creeped into the town of Bodega. Small houses were passed down from generation to generation, along with a family farm plot or a fishing boat.

Eventually, I headed back to the warmth of my van and continued on to the harbor which was the lifeblood of this little town.

Again I bundled up for a brisk stroll around the bay. On my half-hour orientation walk I saw no other living human being. This was not a "pleasure craft" and "cocktails on the sun deck" type of harbor. There were no college girls jogging around in white Nike's. It was an industrial-looking wharf, smelling of fish, rust, and diesel fuel. The whole place was a kind of monochromatic gray, as if the continual assault of fog, wind, and rain had managed to wash the color from everything...a place where color photographs of the area might be mistaken for black and whites.

Nautical debris lay scattered along the shoreline of the bay. Rusty hulls, coils of old weathered line, sailing masts; the kinds of worn antiques restaurant and bar owners used to decorate the plain sheetrock walls of their establishments in places like Corona Del Mar and Laguna Niguel to create an illusion of a rustic nautical soul in their otherwise sterile buildings. Among the boats and ancient debris in the industrial harbor, I felt inconsequential, and had the strange realization that if I died right then and there, my body would likely not be noticed for quite some time.

Seagulls stood on rusty skeletons of old boats, facing into the wind with their eyes half closed, patiently waiting for the wind to abate. They must have been used to it, as these winds were the norm every afternoon throughout the winter. This was not a familiar cold for a Southern California kid like me. It was a wet and windy chill which easily penetrated through my cotton clothes and found its way into my bones. It was a place where passing tourists in comfortable rental cars drove along the harbor road, peering out through their windows, while sipping warm coffee. The brave ones stopped and jumped out into the wind to take a quick photo before rushing back into their warm cocoon. With their skin red and tingling, they drove off, turning the dial on the heater up a notch.

On my way back to the van, I noticed a daring young couple sitting outside on the deck of the fish restaurant, generously bundled up like Arctic explorers, attempting to shelter themselves from the brunt of the wind behind a Plexiglas wall. They huddled there, directly under a gas heater, hurriedly spooning up mouthfuls of clam chowder from a shared bowl. Owing to the unique setting, I imagined they might remember that bowl of chowder for years.

Near the center of town a lone convenience store stocked a selection of cheap hard liquor and cigarettes, and despite being less than an hour from the heart of the wine country, offered few options for a quality Zinfandel.

Having to work this rugged coastline with huge seas, cold winds, and the continual spray of frigid water, the local fishermen had been tempered into a unique breed. They were old men with stereotypical white beards and callused hands who wore unwashed overalls and drove around town in beater pickups with various random engine parts in their truck beds. Some mornings they gathered to talk, sitting on their tailgates with a cigarette dangling from the corner of their mouths. No doubt the inhaled warmth of cigarettes provided them a sense of pseudo-companionship in their solitary cold world. I bet every one of them had several dozen dramatic sea-faring stories, all worthy of a Steinbeck novel, but their conversations likely centered on the more mundane issues of the day, like the current price of cod or their critique of 49ers offense. Having neither the temperament nor the inspiration to address issues of their own health and wellness, their bodies adapted correspondingly.

A couple miles up the road was the Salmon Creek Ranger Station. This would be my new home base. I caught up with Mat Fuzie before he left for the day. He was a large man with a pleasant demeanor. He welcomed me with a brief tour of the small office and issued me a new wetsuit, booties, gloves and a backpack. At some point in our conversation, he asked where I would be staying. It was only then I realized I had not asked for permission to sleep in my van on State Park property as I (and many others) had done for years in San Clemente. Sheepishly I asked if there might be an out-of-the-way place where I might park my van for the night.

"Up here" said Fuzie, "you can park damn near anywhere you want and stay for as long as you want."

With that bit of good news, I pulled in behind the maintenance shop and settled in. There would be no competition for places to park for the night.

By sunset, the place was desolate. Everyone, it seemed had left the chilly coastline to return to their warm homes in Sebastopol, Healdsburg, or Santa Rosa. With no street lights, the area was incredibly dark and moody, further intensified by the relentless wind which sporadically whistled in through invisible gaps around the doors of my van. Unprepared for the wind-chilling cold, I dug out every blanket and bedsheet I could find and bundled myself to stay warm. But my sleep was superficial and elusive that night, for in the distance I could hear the ominous rumbling...of surf. *Really big surf.*

In the morning I would become the newest member of the Sonoma Coast Lifeguard Service. I had no idea then, but I was about to embark on a 7-year run which would rock my world and expose me to more ocean-related drama, heroics, and tragedies than I could ever have imagined. I would join a team of committed individuals, carrying a torch handed off by our predecessors who had risen to the challenge and left their stories and trials behind for inspiration and guidance. By the nature of our work together, we would cultivate an indescribable, though deeply personal connection which would bond us forever as North Coast Lifeguards. Entrenched in the isolation and inclement weather, we would coalesce into a community of ourselves. The next 7 years on the Sonoma Coast would not only forever alter my perspectives on lifeguarding, but also on life and death itself.

∽

I walked into the Salmon Creek Office at 8:00 am. There were no cupcakes or welcome banners. This wasn't that kind of place. A few minutes later I met my new partner, Rex Grady. Rex threw me the keys to the 1-ton truck, proclaiming, "You're driving," and we were off for a full-day orientation to my new district.

As we pulled out onto PCH, I immediately noticed after already having been there for 16 hours, the wind was still blowing hard. I asked Grady what time wind usually laid down.

"Maybe August," he said.

I laughed out loud.

Grady didn't laugh at all.

Rex Grady was not your typical lifeguard. Although he was a gifted distance freestyler, the image he portrayed on land was that of the well-versed scholar and dedicated historian he was. Two years later, Grady would publish a definitive history on the region which included an accounting of many of the tragedies and sweeping events which helped shape the human history along the Sonoma Coast. Soon after the book was published, Rex became an attorney, and was subsequently invited to join the faculty of his law school. This wellspring of information, in the form of a lifeguard, would be my mentor. It was unlikely that there was another person alive who knew more about the collective aspects of that coastline.

The area between Bodega Bay and the Russian River mouth to the north had long since been cleared of trees to make space for cattle to graze. There existed a smattering of homes in the area inhabited by naïve souls who likely signed their escrow papers on a rare warm afternoon in August, not realizing they were about to embark on a long and intimate relationship with the wind. As we drove past those homes, we didn't see a single person. I joked to Grady that the occupants were likely huddled inside and probably shivering. Grady chuckled.

Rex directed me to pull into every little cove and beach access. At each desolate location we emerged from the warm truck and stood in the cold wind while Rex explained the significance of each particular site. The surf was running well-overhead and the spray, blown hard by the north-west wind, anointed us with a smattering of cold mist every 30 seconds or so. I struggled to take notes on the fluttering pages of my little flip pad. The importance of each location had often immortalized by some dreadful event which usually ended in a fatality.

Grady offered the guards' collective insights into the unique ocean hydrology of each landmark, highlighting the most viable access spots to enter the ocean, as well as the all-important down-current *escape routes* which I could utilize to extricate my victims (or myself) from the ocean. Each location provided a new rescue scenario in which I imagined myself climbing out over the rocks, timing my entry to coincide with the high-water surge of the waves, then diving into the frigid and uninviting surf. From there, the scenarios transitioned to swimming my victims south (exits were almost always south – due to the prevailing northwest swell) where I would deliver my imaginary victims safely to shore. Even the visualizations of these rescues were far more daunting than anything I had ever experienced before.

At Goat Rock we accessed the long beach and drove to the north end to check on a large group of harbor seals lounging near the mouth of the Russian River. Rex referred to the terminus of the Russian River as "The Pantry" casually explaining that sharks routinely patrolled there, often grabbing an unwary seal and occasionally leaving the partially dismembered carcass on the beach. He said with a chuckle that this was likely an unnerving realization for the rest of the harbor seal family. I added that it was an unnerving realization for *me too!*

The melancholy tour, and the mental stress of performing dozens of imaginary rescues in my mind, was quite sobering. The only saving grace was that there were no people anywhere, which, in my mind greatly reduced the eventuality I might actually need to rescue anyone at all. But soon people *did* start arriving. As they drove into the lots, I greeted them with a friendly wave, as I had always done in Southern California. Most of them waved back, but every so often, one of the drivers flipped us a bird. I was confused, having no idea who they were, or why they were pissed off at us. I had always viewed the lifeguards' primary role as "Purveyors of Goodwill" and getting flipped off by anyone was virtually unheard of in my Southern California lifeguard world. I wanted to know what he was so upset about, but Rex instructed me to "keep driving." Worse yet, within the next hour, several more random people repeated the same gesture. I was stunned. In my mind, people loved lifeguards. To add to the confusion, Grady seemed completely unfazed by these audacious acts of animosity, and after each instance, I noticed he added a hash mark to a running tally on the patrol log. Eventually, I asked him why the people were so pissed off at us.

Rex, looking out the window, muttered, "It's a long story."

I was beginning to feel the weight of the collective fatalism and the seemingly oppressive nature of the coastline. Just then, a pair of gray whales surfaced close to shore. Both were over 30' long. Grady smiled. Soon after, he directed my attention to the inland side of the beach. In the slow-moving waters of the Russian River at high tide, several fish jumped in the morning light. An hour later, I spotted an Osprey, the majestic fishing hawk, perched near a bluff-top. They were rare visitors to Southern California beaches and I pointed it out to Grady. Within minutes, Grady pointed out three others. Despite the fact Mother Nature had a reputation of being cruel to human beings along this coastline, the wildlife, at least, seemed to be thriving.

With people arriving onto the beaches, Grady had put his game face on. Although we had honed our careers in different districts, we had both earned some level of respect. Grady's style of guarding was infused with a mild, though near-constant sense of paranoia, which I found to be gratifying, because it was my style too.

Rex and I worked together almost exclusively for months. He seemed relieved to have a partner, and said I was an "easy guy to talk to." Grady was analytical and philosophical about lifeguarding and about life itself. He had a keen interest in the human condition and he was intrigued with my "colorful" life. Admittedly, my grass roots, simplistic, liberal-minded existence was, in many ways, antithetical to how Grady had been raised. And yet, we viewed our differences with a mutual sense of respect and intrigue which flowed both ways. Our conversations never lagged, and we both felt completely free to express our views on philosophy, pop-culture, music, women, politics, lifeguard personalities, human nature, and history. Within a month, we had come to know each other well. In that time, Rex also shared the details of the guards' previous rescues, and we scrutinized each one, like Monday morning quarterbacks, in hopes of strategizing improvements for the future rescues which were sure to come.

Later that week, Fuzie pulled me aside and confided that Grady had recently been first on scene to a fatality involving a child. Curious about the details, I later brought it up to Grady while we were driving. Rex bristled and descended into a quiet reticence. It was clear the event had affected him deeply. The uncomfortable silence lasted for several minutes, while Rex simply stared out the window. Eventually I broke the silence with an apology and Grady responded that the tragedy was still too raw in his mind to talk about.

We spent the bulk of our days at Goat Rock. For good reason. From a lifeguard's perspective, Goat Rock was one of the most challenging assignments on the West Coast. For the past 20 years, the number of fatal drownings which occurred there gave it the unwanted reputation as one of the most (if not THE most) perilous stretches of coastline in America.

GOAT ROCK

Goat Rock Beach (2019) – Photo: Drasko Bogdonovic

To any guard who has ever worked the Sonoma Coast, there are likely no two words in the English language which cause their gut to wrench more quickly than "Goat Rock."

Working Goat Rock was easily the most stressful and frustrating assignment in the district, and every guard who ever worked there had their collection of stories of nerve-wracking interactions with the public, and perilous, yet unglamorous shore-pounding rescues.

Goat Rock Beach possessed a unique combination of environmental factors which rendered it a potential death trap. With an unobstructed orientation to the Gulf of Alaska, the beach bore the full-scale brunt of the heavy winter-generated swells. From September to June the average size of the breaking waves was in 6-8' range, and it was not uncommon for that stretch of beach to get hammered by waves twice that size or even larger. Making matters worse, the ocean floor dropped precipitously just off-shore, such that the large waves would roll in, more or less hidden, then suddenly jack up and crash directly onto a berm which supported an angle of repose so steep, at times it seemed almost unnatural.

It was there I was introduced to an ocean term I had never before heard in my 18-year career as an Ocean Lifeguard. The "Sleeper Wave" (occasionally also altered to "Sneaker Wave") was a theoretical phenomenon the rangers spoke of liberally and the locals believed with unfailing confidence. According to the regional wisdom, these waves were unique because they seemingly "came out of nowhere" (hence the "sleeper" part) and were larger and more powerful than all of the conventional waves breaking at the time.

In 1989, John Coote, a submarine pilot for the Royal Navy published "The Norton Book of the Sea" in which he cites research on "freak waves" by England's National Institute of Oceanography. In his work, he theorized one in 23 waves is twice the size of the average wave, and one in 1,175 is *three times* the size. And, if anyone had the patience and time to notice, one in 300,000 is *four times* as large as the average. The study further claims the phenomenon of "significantly larger" waves is far more obvious when the average waves are already large, which was certainly the case on the North Coast.

Lifeguards are well-aware of the synergistic effects of combined swells converging on the coastline from different directions. Regardless, even after my 7-year tenure on the North Coast I never fully bought in to the phenomenon of a single wave which was dramatically different or more powerful than the others. In my mind, I perceived the "sneakiness" of the large waves as a by-product of the long lulls, when beach-goers were lulled into apathy, along with the human foibles of *indifference* and *ignorance*, both of which were in generous supply among the populace of people strolling along that coastline. Many, if not most of the people walking along the berm at Goat Rock Beach were oblivious to the power and intensity of the swells, and the only "sleeper" component involved in getting their asses kicked by the ocean came as a result of their own inattention to the world around them. Regardless, not to rock the boat, I went along with the "Sleeper Wave" concept, though I was never one to share the term as gospel.

Lifeguard Supervisor Bud Brown (whom you will soon meet) explained that the waves in Southern California break on the beach, whereas the waves along the Sonoma Coast break on the *continent itself.*

Goat Rock shore pound (2019) – *Photo: Drasko Bogdonovic*

Regardless of one's opinions on the existence of Sleeper Waves, the undeniable truth was this; large waves smashed down on that stretch of shoreline with a vengeance, snatching people from the berm with such alarming regularity that at times it seemed like the merciless ocean was *purposefully trying* to capture unsuspecting tourists. And when no victims were available, the ocean continued to pummel Goat Rock beach, obliterating the barren sands as if warning future beach-goers.

The most common method of the ocean's capture occurred when tourists engaged in the common game of "wave tag." They would run down the berm as the water receded, then race back up the berm as the next wave slammed back onto the shore behind them. Perceived as a thrilling game, the individuals (tragically often children) were unknowingly flirting with disaster. The sand on that steep berm was saturated with aerated water, which caused the victims to feel like they were running in quicksand. Those who fell, or misjudged the speed of the oncoming wave would be deluged in frigid water, then helplessly pulled down the steep berm by the powerful mass of the backwash, holding them low on the berm until the next wave engulfed them again. If they were wearing jackets, long pants, or shoes (which most were), the victims entered a nightmarish dream in which they became weighed down by their water-logged clothing, making their escape almost impossible. Subsequent waves would then slam them again and eventually they would be dragged out into the 10' deep trough where they could no longer touch the bottom. At that point it was only a matter of time before their body, shocked and overwhelmed by the frigid water, was forced to endure repeated dousings by the oncoming waves. Eventually they succumbed and drowned.

Lifeguard Steve Franklin, whom you will also meet shortly, said this of working Goat Rock:

"At Goat Rock, where I and my friends were the first lifeguards ever, I remember running down the beach but making slow progress because of the thirty knot winds blowing square into my face. A ten foot wave broke in deep water only fifteen yards off the steep shore (this is the phenomenon of Goat Rock). I saw the wave rush up the beach and bury a whole family, who had intended to only let the water touch their toes. I saw part of a kid's body rolling down the berm in the freezing, heaving white water, and, fully clothed with my gun on, I dove on top of him and held on. Miraculously, the rest of the family didn't get sucked down into the trough, where another wave with the same intensity would have broken on them and likely would have drowned them. Instead, it smashed them so hard, it washed them over the berm into the parking lot forty yards away."

Lifeguarding there was an incredibly frustrating ordeal. Seeing people close to the water, especially playing wave tag, the guards would run down to warn the potential victims. Often times the tourists viewed those warnings as overly officious, or completely unnecessary, as if the lifeguards were over-reacting to a perceived sense of danger which wasn't real. Thus, as one might imagine, despite the very real danger, and the long history of human tragedy there, gaining compliance from the pubic was a maddening and seemingly never-ending tribulation.

I had my first rescue at Goat Rock Beach the following Saturday. We had just warned a group of people about the dangerous backwash, and like so many others, they wandered away rolling their eyes and blatantly ignoring our warning. As if the ocean was in cahoots with us, moments later a huge wave appeared, knocked them off their feet, engulfed them, and dragged them down the berm. With no time to put on our wetsuits, Grady and I ran from the truck and assisted the visitors from the powerful pull of the backwash. Rex, obviously upset, later admitted he was secretly happy they got their comeuppance. It was shocking and poignant moment for me to see Grady's prophetic scenario materialize before my eyes.

～

My first swimming rescue occurred the following day. The Russian River mouth, near the north end of Goat Rock Beach, was another danger zone. Unsuspecting kayakers, completing their lazy paddle down the usually languid river, needed to exit the river before it picked up speed and dumped into the ocean. If they didn't get out in time, they would be deposited into the frigid ocean, often without wetsuits. From there, the current would often pull them out to sea, where they would find themselves fighting a losing battle against the powerful rip current. That scenario, which Grady warned me about, occurred all-too frequently, and in fact was exactly what happened to a middle-aged man from Stockton who, when thrust into the head-high waves, immediately swamped his kayak and began floundering 100 yards from shore. I pulled on my new wetsuit and swam out to him. After strapping him into the buoy, I towed him north until we were clear of the rip, then delivered him safely to shore. The victim was shaken up but seemingly appreciative. I then jumped back into the rip, swam out and towed in the man's kayak, again accepting thanks from him. In and of itself, it was a routine rescue, except that not more than 20 minutes later, Grady spotted *another man* in the same river rip and since I still had my wetsuit on, I was the logical choice to swim out. You can imagine my surprise when I reached the victim and discovered it was the *same guy* I had just rescued earlier. Apparently not fully processing the lesson about this powerful current, the man had re-entered the ocean in the same spot attempting to retrieve his discarded paddle. It was the only time in my career I ever rescued the same victim *twice* on the same day.

Later that week I met the rest of the guards in the North Sector including the jovial and like-minded waterman Dave Carter, the incomparable jack-of-all-trades Don Straub, and the veteran leader Osh McNulty. According to Grady, each of them possessed the pedigree of being phenomenal watermen and proven North Coast guards.

∾

The large surf we witnessed was especially humbling, as significant storm activity often brewed throughout the winter in the Gulf of Alaska, sending huge swells our way.

As a matter of comparison, the El Niño winter of 1983 generated one of the largest swells on record in Southern California. Wave heights reached 20' and battered the coastline for days. Several of the piers in Southern California (San Clemente among them) were badly beaten and partially destroyed. Lifeguards from Imperial Beach to Ventura laid awake at night, waiting to be called out at any time, fearing an obligation to rescue anyone who foolishly ventured out or got swept into those deadly seas.

But on the Sonoma Coast, 20' surf was common. In my first winter season on the North Coast, I witnessed over 30 *days* of 20-foot surf. In fact one day in January, while standing on the Bodega headlands, I witnessed the largest surf I would ever see in my career. The buoy readings were off the charts and solid 30' waves were lined up all the way to the horizon. At that size, there was no lull; just a continuous line of immense 30' waves breaking miles from shore. From that distance, the massive walls of crumbling water were surreal, and appeared to be moving in slow motion. I watched in awe for close to half an hour. Several of the sets easily reached 40', and a few likely topped 50'.

It was clear by then I had signed up for an assignment which far exceeded anything I had ever imagined. I had certainly expected it would be challenging, but trying to rescue someone from *that* ocean was utterly impossible.

∾

My first fatality came within 2 weeks of my arrival. Ironically, the tragic event occurred on land. As with many of the deaths on that coastline, the circumstances were not only unexpected but also bizarre. A 24-year-old rock climber had decided to "free-climb" (no ropes) the 40-foot bluff near Wright's Beach. Bystanders later reported he climbed nimbly with confidence and didn't seem to be challenged by the climb at all. For some reason which we will ever know, just as he reached the crest, his body fell the entire distance, landing on the beach below with an unnerving thud. Rudimentary CPR was initiated by a Good Samaritan until Grady and I arrived and took over compressions and ventilations. Although we had never worked a critical call together, Grady and I performed well as a team.

A fire crew arrived, then sheriffs units, State Parks Rangers, and soon after, a helicopter landed near-by. All of the arriving rescue personnel seemed oddly nonchalant, addressing each other by their first names. The flight medic stood by, seemingly in no rush to take over. So Rex and I continued with our CPR for several minutes more while the others stood by and watched. Then, at some seemingly random moment, the flight medic directed us to "Stop CPR." He reached down and performed a brief assessment of the victim's pulse, pulled open his eye lids to confirm the pupils were blown, and simply said, "It's over." He casually checked his watch and called out the *time of death* to no one in particular. An older looking fire fighter from Monte Rio Fire with a cigarette dangling from his mouth pulled a body bag from his truck and we helped him load the young man's body, still warm, into the thick black plastic bag. He zipped it up, and we carried the body across the beach and loaded it into his rig.

Within 20 minutes, all of the responding units, along with the sheriff's helicopter, had cleared the scene.

I was shocked at the stark and traumatic nature of the fatality, but moreover unnerved at the seemingly unaffected demeanor of the rescuers. Eventually, we got back into the truck but I didn't start the engine right away. I faced Grady directly and said, *"What the Hell kind of place is this?"*

Grady realized he owed the "rookie" more of an explanation. It was only then he began telling me the origin story of the Sonoma Coast Lifeguards. Over the next several shifts together, he would divulge many of the major events and tragedies the guards responded to since their inception, ultimately bringing us to the present. Rex's narrative would be a bald-faced retrospective, complete with the names and faces of all the heroes, victims, and villains brought together over the previous four years. He pieced together their great successes, their shame, their joys, their struggles, and their failures. And I listened intently as Rex Grady shared the incredible story of the emergence of the Sonoma Coast Lifeguard service.

2

THE SONOMA COAST

Cyprus trees overhanging PCH near Stump Beach (1995) – Photo: Vodrazka

I have heard from geologists you can get a rough estimate of the age of a mountain range by its texture. The soft rolling rounded mountains are the oldest, having been softened and eroded by the effects of wind, rain and time. The adolescent mountains are rough and jagged, with sharp outcroppings and dynamic pitches and falls.

I'm not sure how applicable it is in gauging the age of coastlines, but I always envisioned that the soft tapered beaches and weathered shores of Southern California suggested an elder coastline. Mature and settled, they reflect the influence of having been through a few millennia of the meteorological effects of wind and rain.

The calm of summer: Fisk Mill to Salt Point (1995)

In contrast, the Sonoma Coast reveals itself like a reckless teen, struggling in the transition between youth and adulthood. Feisty, dramatic, and often times unforgiving, the rocky coastline can also be cruel and sadistic. From late September through April the relentless ocean pounds the shoreline with swells generated from thousands of miles away, crashing onto the rocks and sending spectacular plumes of water 30 feet in the air. Then, in striking contrast, as if our adolescent ocean has gone into deep slumber, during the quieting of the storm season in Alaska in July and August, the surf along the coastline rarely reaches head-high.

We humans, in hopes of exploring this rugged and inspiring stretch of coastline, topple down ancient trees and build roads to allow our admission to these sacred places, but the idea we somehow *tame* this wild area is ludicrous. Every winter the rains batter against the windward hillsides and wash out sections of our feeble manmade roadways. The consistent 40-knot winds drive us to retreat from the open spaces, forcing us to seek warm shelter indoors. But above all, it's the ocean, our *Mother Ocean* who holds, below her surface, the most spectacular and untamed sanctuaries of wonder along the Sonoma Coast. And there they lie, her most precious treasures, protected by spectacular displays of surf, and unpredictable churning currents of water. Those courageous enough to enter her domain to marvel at her beauty, or to harvest the fruits of her bounty can be soundly tested, as she can be fickle, and moody as hell. And when she is angry, she can be downright vicious.

∾

The Sonoma County Coast spans close to 50 miles from the small town of Bodega Bay in the south to Gualala in the north. The entire coastline is traversed by the Pacific Coast Highway. On maps, the PCH appears as a simple and uncomplicated roadway, but in reality, owing to the robust terrain and the changing elevations, northbound drivers must navigate a long and circuitous route to reach the neighboring county of Mendocino.

The majority of the coastal land (31 miles of it) is owned by the California State Parks and managed locally by the Sonoma Coast District. Within the confines of this book, I will often refer to the district as the "North Coast" since, at the time of their arrival, it was the northernmost location lifeguards patrolled along the West Coast of the United States (subsequently, they have been established right up to the Oregon border).

Operationally, the Sonoma Coast District is divided into two Sectors, which differ considerably in terms of flora, geology, visitation patterns and the general activities of beach goers.

The mid-line between the two sectors is Russian Gulch.

THE SOUTH SECTOR

Winding through the South Sector, the Pacific Coast Highway traverses a path which seldom elevates more than 20' from sea level. Predominately jagged and rocky, the shoreline is speckled with several small, but picturesque pocket beaches where sand deposits, cumulatively eroded from mountains for eons, have been delivered to the coast by the ancient Russian River. The ocean, in turn, then collected and deposited those sands onto the shoreline by the action of the waves and tidal changes.

Other than a few scattered homes, built in seemingly random

locations, there is far more open space than evidence of human constructs in the South Sector. The vast majority of the ancient forests which once covered the land are gone, having been cleared by loggers and sent to the lumber mills over a century ago. Without the buffer from those trees, the northwest wind blows unrestricted across much of the area. The State Parks lists several hikes which extend inland from the coast, but they tend not to draw many visitors. It's that rough and untamed ocean, in all of her dynamic glory which people come to see.

By far the largest beach in the county, Goat Rock Beach lies at the terminus of the Russian River. Owing to the predominant swells coming out of the northwest, the majority of sand, delivered by this major waterway, is deposited to the south side of the river mouth. On the north side of the terminus, elevated a hundred feet or so above sea level, lies the quaint settlement of Jenner, where travelers often stop to admire the spectacular view of the coastline.

The Russian River itself is over 100 miles long, with a watershed encompassing 1,500 square miles of forests, agricultural lands, and urban areas within Sonoma and Mendocino Counties. The river attracts thousands of visitors who float, kayak, and paddle down the slow-moving river each summer.

In the winter months, the Russian River swells to epic proportions delivering unfathomable amounts of water to the sea, and often flooding the local river communities. The speed and intensity of the flow is sufficient to carry massive Redwood trees in its current and deposit them into the ocean where they eventually wash back onto the beaches. During the winter rainstorms, locals gather on bridges to watch the might Russian River flow beneath them and marvel at her tumultuous display of raw intensity.

Following the river upstream from Goat Rock, "River Road" parallels the waterway through several small towns, the most peculiar of which is undoubtedly Guerneville, an enclave which attracts a community of individuals seemingly seeking alternatives to the conventional lifestyles of the mainstream.

A turnoff in Guerneville leads to Armstrong Redwoods State Park; a true old growth forest which managed to escape the frenzied logging practices which altered the surrounding landscape a few generations ago. Continuing up River Road another 20 minutes or so will bring you into the Dry Creek Valley and the heart of the incomparable wine country of Sonoma.

Russian River terminus (1992) – Photo: Loeffler

THE NORTH SECTOR

Back on the coast, and continuing our northbound tour from Jenner, the road soon begins to climb precipitously hundreds of feet above the ocean, winding around some of the most harrowing yet spectacular sections of the entire 1,600 mile Pacific Coast Highway. The upper section is collectively known as "High Point" and is often prone to washout in the winter.

It's a drive not for the faint of heart, especially on the southbound lane, and occasionally drivers carelessly attempt to negotiate the challenging twists and turns far too fast (or far too buzzed) and plunge down the steep cliff-side to their death.

High Point road washout (1996) – Photo: Vodrazka

Lifeguards Loeffler and McNulty assist Henry-I crew in extrication (1992) – Photo: Scott Melvin

Continuing north, eventually the roadway descends back down into largely forested land with dramatic topography. Fort Ross, a preserved Russian settlement, is the first of several State Parks along the way.

Rainbow over Fort Ross Historic Park (1995) – Photo: Vodrazka

The forests are largely composed of Bishop Pine, Monterey Cypress, imported Australian Eucalyptus, and some remaining Redwoods. Inland, the species of Buckeye, Maple, Madrone, Tan Oak, and Bay trees dominate the landscape, with Alders and Willows gathering along the numerous waterways.

Moving east, away from the ocean, the land rises sharply in elevation to the coastal mountains near the tiny enclave of Cazadero. This mountainside captures Pacific storm clouds saturated with oceanic moisture as they come onshore in spring and winter, showering the area with copious amounts of rainfall. In fact, Cazadero tallies an impressive average of 85 inches of rain each year, and is reputed to be the second wettest location in California after the tiny town of Gasquet – population 685 - inland from Crescent City. If you can find a hotel room with a decent view, it's a great place to watch the incoming storms with a warm cup of coffee or a glass of Zinfandel.

Returning to the PCH, the northbound coastline alternates between State Parks' property, County Parks, Native American lands and plots of subdivided properties privately owned by some very fortunate individuals. On this rocky shoreline with no substantial river outlet to the immediate north, there are fewer sandy coves, and far more rocky terrain. Besides a couple of small family-run convenience stores, there are no options to buy groceries, get a meal, or fill the gas tank.

The majority of the remaining lands between the Russian River in the south and the Mendocino County Line to the north, near the town of Gualala, are owned and managed by the California State Parks. Although the various sections of parks' lands are separated, the bulk of their property exists under the umbrella of "Salt Point State Park." Just past the State Parks' northern boundary at

North Coast lifeguard at the Ocean Cove Store (1994)

Horseshoe Cove is the Richardson's Store, marking the beginning of the privately owned Richardson Ranch. The Richardson family has owned and managed their land since the mid-1800s. Incredibly beautiful and largely pristine, their property extends from the coastline far inland, and includes some areas of old growth redwood. The store is an iconic and historic landmark, and has changed little over the past 100 years. An account of the Richardson's history is included in the well-researched book, *"Neptune Wept,"* authored by retired State Parks Lifeguard Chief, Mike Brousard.

As an homage to the local dive culture in the area, the owner of the store, Arch Richardson began collecting trophy-sized abalone shells from avid divers many years ago. In order for an abalone to be legal for take, it must be at least 7-inches across at the longest length of its shell. Comparatively, in order to qualify an abalone as worthy of display in Arch's store, it must measure over 10" in diameter - which, I am told requires an abalone to live almost 40 years. Those deemed worthy are then diligently cleaned, soaked in muriatic acid, varnished, and proudly displayed on the store wall, documenting the date and the location (although often kept secret) the prized abalone was taken. More importantly, the tag also specifies the *name* of the diver who captured the treasured abalone, thereby immortalizing them into local history. In the unique and passionate world of abalone divers, the wall in Richardson's store is the equivalent of baseball's Cooperstown Hall of Fame.

~

From a lifeguard's perspective it was the surf conditions which set the stage for the dramatic ocean rescues in the Sonoma Coast District. As such, they attuned themselves closely to the ever-changing variables of water temperature, surf size, swell period, tidal fluctuation, and weather. Although all of these factors had an influence on rescues, undoubtedly the most important of these was the surf size.

The ruggedness of the district, the winding wet roadways, the harsh weather, and the rough seas combined to wreak havoc on the human species. The guards who patrolled that shoreline would become the first responders for isolated medical aids, major traffic casualties, and of course the numerous water-related emergencies which occurred there.

Although the two sectors differed by way of victim profile and topography, the common threads shared between them were the collective phenomenon of frigid water, cold wind, abundant rain, the aforementioned large surf, and of course the presence of human beings falling prey to nature's wrath.

3

FATAL DROWNING

An abalone diver walks past the body of fellow diver—staged for helicopter extrication

There's no way around it. Death is an inevitable eventuality for us all.

In the Buddhist tradition we are reminded:

All beings are born, they live for some time, then they pass away in accordance with the laws of nature.

In my seven years as a hospice nurse, I was present with many families when their loved ones took their last breath and were ultimately released from their bodies. I always viewed my inclusion at that most intimate and personal moment as a great honor, not unlike the privilege of being present for the birth of a baby.

With few exceptions, my hospice patients died with their families at their bedside and were loved until their last breath. Some served their country in war. Others provided for the families with long careers and personal sacrifice. Many had children who in turn brought them grandchildren. They had been cornerstones for their family and enjoyed a long and fruitful life with great reward. Then they died. You can call it "fate" or "God's will" but in essence, it was a proper and just ending to their life story.

But lifeguards don't deal with those kinds of deaths. We deal with traumatic death. Traumatic death is an entirely different phenomenon. Traumatic death is stark and cruel, tending to prey on younger victims who are yet to fulfill their destined course in life. Besides suicide, no one dies in trauma knowing this was to be their last day alive.

The recurrent scenario on the North Coast was that of an excited young man leaving his home to go abalone diving, unaware that the casual comment he muttered to his family upon leaving would be their last communication, and they would never see him alive again. The tragedy was further exacerbated in creating the awful juxtaposition of customary family roles, forcing parents into the soul-crushing task of having to bury their child.

As a coup de grace, if the traumatic death is by means of drowning, the tragedy plows another layer deeper. Unlike many other traumatic deaths which involve "freak accidents," when someone drowns, there is almost always a *voluntary decision* to enter the water, creating the unavoidable realization that the tragic loss of life was *entirely preventable.*

✍

The very nature of our profession forces us to deal intimately with issues of ultimate loss, pain, and tragedy. As social and empathetic beings, we are certainly not immune to the sufferings of our fellow humans. But in order to perform our duties to the best of our abilities, we must occasionally separate ourselves emotionally from the disaster at hand and somehow harden ourselves to the suffering of others. In theory, there is a perfect temperament for lifeguards to balance our feelings of empathy for our victims, while at the same time, adequately insulating ourselves from their pain. The latter issue is a continual challenge, and the prevailing wisdom among members of the EMS community is that we simply can't allow the victim's suffering to become our own. Manifest empathy and grief for the victims and their families not only hinders our abilities to perform on scene, but also gnaws away at our own well-being, dragging us closer to cumulative stress and burn-out.

Someone once coined a mantra we often remind ourselves when we are managing traumatic or disturbing events.

"It's not your emergency."

I always felt this simple but poignant reminder to all Emergency Services personnel was a little gem of wisdom. Despite the ultimate outcome for our patients and their relatives, in whatever horrific event we are trying to orchestrate, and despite the fact we may have just witnessed the victim's final moments of life on this planet, *our lives will carry on*. At the end of our shift, we will return home safely to be with our loving families.

As a coping mechanism, the phrase can be a useful tool for emergency personnel to cope with the acute stress while on scene. But on the North Coast, it was wholly inadequate as a panacea for dealing with the chronic residual stress which festered in the lifeguards' psyche. Over months and years, that stress gradually leached and coalesced deep in their souls. Compartmentalizing the stress and "dealing with it" proved to be a theory few of the North Coast crew ever successfully achieved. Beneath the façade of the uniform, they were human beings with varying degrees of emotional barriers, compassion, and coping mechanisms to insulate themselves from emotional trauma. In interviews with the original crew, I was wholly surprised that most of them confessed to being intensely affected by the heartbreaking events they valiantly attempted to mitigate. Reluctantly, in preservation of their own mental health, many of the guards were ultimately forced to leave the North Coast, and, as a shocking aside, most of them never guarded again.

~

On the beaches of Southern California impediments to drowning have evolved to a point where fatal drownings are truly exceptional events. Lifeguard Headquarters have been erected on some of the most populous beaches, providing exceptional vantage points to monitor swimmers and dispatch rescuers as needed. Towers are positioned along the crowded beaches, and are well staffed throughout the summer months when the crowds arrive in full force. Lifeguards are well-trained and utilize modern rescue equipment, vehicles, and radio communications, all designed to facilitate the rescue of besieged swimmers quickly, often times just as they begin to struggle. Rescue vessels patrol outside the surfline on the busiest beaches keeping an eye on the hundreds of swimmers from the unique vantage point of the water itself. In fact, swimmers in Southern California are often monitored by guards from the moment they enter the water until they exit, and rescuers stand at the ready to self-deploy should the swimmers find themselves in situations in which they become overwhelmed.

But on the Sonoma Coast, those safeguards in the prevention of drowning simply didn't exist. Compounded by the aforementioned challenges of huge surf and cold water, a picture soon begins to emerge of profound vulnerability and exponential risk to anyone who enters the ocean there. The consequences become predictable, and stories of fatal drownings, recounted by locals and verified by statistics and coroner's reports, have been regular occurrences along the Sonoma Coast for as long as anyone can remember.

The human spirit craves adventure. People came to the Sonoma Coast to bask in the beauty and the power of that coastline, and often traversed the fine line between the *thrilling* and the *deadly*. Ironically, as we have eluded to, it was their failure to respect the ocean's power, or simple ignorance which formed the foundation upon which the profession of lifeguarding is based. Just as good citizens become tempted to break laws, justifying the police force, well-meaning thrill seekers will, knowingly or otherwise push the limits of safety and get themselves into trouble, thereby justifying the lifeguards.

Realizing this, they accepted their fundamental mission was to intervene when people crossed that line.

~

In the State Lifeguard Rookie Academy, instructor Eric Dymmel used to embark on a half-hour story intended to shed light on the aftermath of fatal drownings. In my opinion it was the single most powerful message we presented to the hopefuls. As he wove his way through the story, every trainee sat riveted, hanging on every word.

The story centered on a beloved 10-year-old boy, born with physical challenges. His uncle had taken him to Castaic Lake for what should have been a fun-filled summer day. But unfortunately, while the boy was happily floating on his body board in 10 feet of water, the uncle left him unattended for a time. At some point the boy lost his grip on the board and quietly slipped under the water. No one, including the guard, witnessed the event. After an undoubtedly terrifying struggle, the boy succumbed and drowned.

The aftermath of the drowning was far-reaching. The uncle, who loved the child as his own, was emotionally devastated and understandably racked with guilt. After delivering the horrible news to his sister that her son had died, he was ostracized from the family in hate. The shame he felt burned like a continual fire in his soul which he tried to put out with alcohol. It didn't work. He would eventually become an alcoholic, and soon lost his job. Never forgiven for his egregious sin by the family, his life began spiraling downward to a place from where there was no return.

For the mother, there was a hole in her heart where her son used to live. Her grieving would never end. Her remorse gradually faded into a dull ache, but would be rekindled every holiday, every birthday, and especially every anniversary of that awful summer day. The boy's brother and sister grieved as well, having lost their much-loved brother.

Near the end of Dymmel's presentation, he reached under the table and pulled out a large framed black and white print of arguably the most famous drowning photograph of all time. Taken in the early 1950s by

Los Angeles Times staff photographer Paul Calvert, the image captures an immortal moment in time as Lifeguard Chief Myron Cox stands with his dive mask in hand, facing a distraught mother with his arms extended in an imploring gesture. The woman has already turned away from him, her face buried in her hands in grief. Behind Cox, the body of her deceased daughter lays lifeless on the sand, stiff with rigor mortis.

Dymmel then asked every rookie in the room to imagine themselves in that position, adding *"in that single moment of inattentiveness, that mother's entire life was taken from her. Her daughter was gone, along with all of the future memories. There would be no prom, there would be no wedding day, and there would be no grandchildren. All because the lifeguard failed to do their job."*

For every lifeguard trainee, that was the prescient moment they came to understand the true essence of lifeguarding. It was a revelation of the sacred responsibilities assigned to every kid who puts on a pair of reds and assumes their watch over any given body of water. In that moment, the gravity of what it meant to be a lifeguard settled into the deepest part of their being.

<hr />

For lifeguards, the word "drowning" is synonymous with failure. If you strip down the duties of a lifeguard to a single point of function, there would be little debate that *they prevent drowning*. All guards understand that accountability intimately and internalize it deeply.

Unlike many other types of traumatic death in which cardiac arrest ensues rather quickly, fatal drowning is an extended process in which the victim passes through a series of steps beginning with their struggle in the water, and ending with irreversible cardiac arrest. Having the unique set of both the *physical* as well as the *medical* skills to intervene and "interrupt the drowning process" anywhere along its course is a valuable commodity in saving victims. But of course the lifeguard has to *be there* to intervene.

Clearly, there is a vast difference between drownings which occurred in "guarded water" as opposed to those which occur in "unguarded water." Drownings which happen under the dominion of an on-duty lifeguard can immediately suggest culpability and/or negligence. But each situation must be scrutinized individually, and quite often there are factors which mitigate, if not completely clear, the guard of blame. Along the North Coast, as a case in point, their "guarded water" spanned for a distance of over 30 miles. Thus, one might logically infer that any fatal drowning occurring miles away from their location would certainly excuse that guard of fault, thereby releasing them from any peripheral damage or guilt.

But lifeguards working in remote locations (like the Sonoma Coast or Catalina Island), with large patrol areas, have the ultimate choice on where they decide to station themselves. Some will post up in the areas with the greatest number of swimmers or the most dangerous locations, while others prefer to keep moving, covering wide sections of the coastline, stopping only briefly to make cursory assessments of any situation at the time. In this way, one can see that lifeguarding is a bit like gambling. When guarding over large areas of water, try as they may, there's no guarantee the guard will be in the right place at the exact moment their victim finds themselves in trouble.

Furthermore, with their bare-bones crew of perhaps three or four on-duty guards, they were still the primary responding unit to those drownings calls, thus they took on the unenviable and nerve-racking tasks of diving for and recovering the body, attempting resuscitation when appropriate, coordination of transfer of the remains, and counseling the grieving family members. Distinctions between "guarded" and "unguarded" drownings provided little solace to the myriad of stressors they endured in having to manage those calls. Clearly, *every drowning was a tragedy* with repercussions affecting many lives. Of course these were devastating events for the surviving family members, but people rarely considered how profoundly *all drowning events affected the guards themselves.* No outsider can begin to understand how harrowing and stressful it is to coordinate a body recovery - let alone one in the calamitous conditions of the North Coast, or to deal with the emotional fall-out when it's all over.

As for culpability and blame, one can attempt to rationalize these issues, but labeling the call as an "unguarded drowning," and formally absolving them of ultimate responsibility for those deaths provides little solace for the lifeguards' lingering feelings of remorse and even guilt.

After clearing the scene of an unguarded fatal drowning, they invariably allowed their minds to drift into the painful realm of "what if." Inevitably, they would roll back the clock in their imagination and replay the event, considering what the outcome *would have been* IF ONLY they could have arrived on scene ten minutes earlier, or worse yet, if they had simply turned north instead of south, twenty minutes prior. Despite inherently knowing these tragedies were never their "fault" directly, and ascribing responsibility for the misfortunes to the whims of fate, these are the kind of guilt-provoking questions which can gnaw at a lifeguard's conscience for years, even when all of the rationalizations support the fact those tragedies were not their cross to bear.

Any Ocean Lifeguard who works for a decade or more will undoubtedly perform hundreds of ocean rescues. Among them will be several, if not dozens in which they *know for certain* they saved the victim's life. But while lifeguards will generally forget many of their great rescues, they *never* forget the drownings. Drownings have a way of burning deep into a guard's soul, where they continue to smolder for years and often decades.

Although easier said than truly internalized, it's important for them to be reminded that on a strikingly high number of calls, they *were* in the right place at the right time and they did save many lives.

DROWNING and FREEDIVING

Physiologically, as human beings, we're constructed with a design leaning heavily towards fragility and vulnerability, as every cell in our bodies requires a near-continuous supply of fresh oxygen in order to simply survive. Separation of any human from their oxygen source will quickly alter their brain function enough to render the person unconscious. Denial of oxygen for a mere 20 minutes or so is generally sufficient to bring about their ultimate death.

For that reason, humans don't often voluntarily isolate themselves from their life-giving supply of oxygen, yet this is exactly what free-divers do when they submerge themselves under water without the aid of a scuba tank or gills. After a relatively short period of time (compared to other aquatic mammals), the diver must unconditionally return to the surface in order to access the unlimited supply of oxygen-laden fresh air in our atmosphere, and rejuvenate their bodies. If, on the other hand, a diver encounters any sort of "issue" which hinders their return to the surface, they have perhaps 30 seconds to solve the problem before the rising CO_2 levels in their bloodstream, combined with their decreasing oxygen levels, will render them unconscious. Losing consciousness at depth (under the surface of the water), is a veritable death sentence. In almost every instance, the coroner will document the cause of death as a *fatal drowning*.

It's been professed that free diving is one of the most dangerous sports in the modern world, based on the relative number of fatalities per participants. The North Coast Lifeguards largely supported that notion, being privy to the sobering historical statistics of fatalities in their district, coupled with their first hand experiences in calls involving a "diver in distress" or, worse yet, "diver down."

RESCUES

The practice of "interrupting the process of drowning" on the Sonoma Coast translated to making critical rescues. In that environment, this meant swimming into some perilous situations in which a person was often fighting for their lives. During those rescues, the lifeguard's lives intersected with those of complete strangers at the most critical moment of their entire existence, and they reversed the hands of fate. Through their actions they said, "No." Not on this day. Not in my water. Not on my watch. And they delivered them from evil. Amen.

In most cases, the victims would never know the guard's name, and they would never meet again. But they lived on as someone's sister or brother. Someone's child or someone's parent. They would one day graduate from college and later marry. Eventually they would have a family.

But it bears mention, and perhaps a moment of reflection – that from the auspicious moment when the paths of lifeguard and victim converged, the victim's life began anew. Plucking them away from their early death, every moment of the remainder of their lives, as originally planned in their grand personal choreography would then play out. And all of the countless joys and interactions of their existence happened...because the lifeguard responded and successfully performed their job.

The positive ramifications from those heroic rescues are obvious for the victim and their families, but what most people never know is how profoundly those rescues affected the rescuers as well. Every veteran lifeguard who works in the ocean environment has experienced the thrill of performing rescues in which they know for certain that, had they not been there, the victim would have died. The full realization of the gravity of these rescues usually doesn't settle in until the dust clears and they are left alone with their thoughts. But then, a warm glow inevitably begins to shine into their souls confirming why they chose to be lifeguards in the first place. Those moments are a validation of the cumulative hours they have invested honing their aquatic skills in the surf line. When it all comes together and the guard is able to use their God-given talent to save the life of another, there is no better feeling in the world. It is said there is no more noble pursuit in life than to save the life of another. As life-savers we are fortunate enough to be given the opportunity to taste the sweet nectar of that gift from time to time. In a wonderful and unexpected twist, eventually it is the lifeguard who realizes it is THEY who are the benefactors of these special rescues, and being put in a situation where they are able to save lives becomes the ultimate gift.

4

A HISTORY OF PERIL

Bystander Rescue – Photo unknown

Since the California State Parks owns the vast majority of the coastal land in Sonoma County, and most of the disastrous ocean-related events occurred within their jurisdiction, inevitably it was the State Parks Rangers who were the first responders to the majority of these events.

Tragedies abounded along that coastline for as long as anyone could remember. The huge surf, inclement weather, rough shoreline and the perilous roadways all contributed to regularly occurring horrendous accidents, sordid calamities, and frequent drownings. Even the volunteer fire department carried body bags as part of their basic equipment.

The locals had ostensibly resigned themselves to the fact these tragedies were inevitable, as the ongoing foibles of *human nature* converged with those of *environmental nature*. Stories in the local newspapers reporting awful deaths by various means along their coastline rarely generated much response from residents beyond a brief head shake and a turn of the page. The locals, it seemed, had become somewhat numb to these harsh realities, and habituated to the sounds of sirens breaking the silence of their otherwise peaceful coastline.

Similarly, many of the rangers, Sheriff Deputies, fire fighters and EMS personnel, toughened by the traumatic nature of the calls they routinely attended to, bore the façade of tempered practitioners, seemingly impervious to any intrusion into their soul.

But statistics relating to death within the State Parks jurisdiction, especially those of fatal drownings, gnawed at the conscience of State Parks managers, causing them to lay awake at night. Recent statistics exposed an alarming trend, highlighting the fact that fatal drownings were steadily increasing. In fact, State Parks records documented an alarming 57 ocean-related fatalities in the 10-year timeframe from 1980 to 1990 before the guards arrived. This equated to **a person losing their life in the ocean, on average, every 64 days**, easily qualifying it as the most dangerous stretch of coastline in the country. The mission statement of the California State Parks states in part that they would "*provide for the health, inspiration and education of the people of California...*" Allowing unsuspecting visitors seeking those exact rewards of health, education, and inspiration to drown in their parks with alarming frequency clearly did not support that mission.

The Chief Ranger of the district was a man named Brian Hickey.

He was a feisty, stout, red-faced manager who had worked the bulk of his career as a State Park Lifeguard. For Hickey, each newly reported drowning was like a dagger in his side. Like all guards, he too had been deeply conditioned to equate drowning with failure.

Brian Hickey (1990)

It was Hickey who committed himself to bring lifeguards to the Sonoma Coast. He teamed up with Aquatic Specialist Carl Drake, future Aquatic Specialist Alex Peabody, Orange Coast Superintendent Mike Tope, and Union President Mike Brousard to try and move a bureaucratic mountain; namely to persuade the state officials in Sacramento who, by the way, were never robust supporters of lifeguards in the first place, to allow him to create the first lifeguard service on the Sonoma Coast. Peabody would prove to be the perfect partner in their quest. He was clever, altruistic, and as tenacious as a bulldog, with a reputation of badgering oppositionists incessantly until they ultimately acquiesced and came around to his point of view.

After considerable wrangling, Hickey persuaded the Deputy Director of Parks, Jack Harrison to visit his district for a brief tour, knowing it would likely be his only chance to lobby directly for the funding to start the program.

Harrison arrived on a sunny afternoon with moderate surf and sparse crowds. Knowing in the deepest part of his lifeguard soul he was fighting to save the very lives of men, women and children who would otherwise drown there one day, Hickey delivered an impassioned proposal balancing arguments between passion and logic. He cited the deplorable drowning statistics, collected over decades. He shared personal accounts of futile CPR measures, dangerous body recoveries and the phone calls he had made to the next of kin, notifying them their loved ones had drowned. In short, he laid it all on the table.

Harrison, not an overly expressive manager, said little during the tour and several times Hickey noticed him checking his watch. Then,

while standing on the bluffs above Duncan's Landing, the ocean delivered what could only be explained as a miracle. Two young boys, aged nine and eleven, were playing on the wet sand, just below the berm with no parents in sight. The surf was overhead and crashing on shore with substantial force owing to the rising tide. With their backs facing the ocean, the boys were obvious safety contacts, and Hickey pointed them out to Harrison, attempting to explain the phenomenon of "sleeper waves" which have been known to drag victims into the ocean. Just as he completed the explanation, a huge wave cascaded onto the boys, slamming them off their

Lifeguards Alex Peabody and Mike Brousard prepare an abalone feast at Salt Point (circa 1995)

feet and engulfing them in a frigid wall of water, then dragging them helplessly in the backwash until they were flailing in the deeper water. Then, just as quickly, the next wave thrust them back onto the berm where they both were able to crawl to the safety of the dry sand.

Hickey looked Harrison squarely in the face. "Just like THAT!" he said, resting his case.

Having just witnessed the potential tragedy, Harrison stood speechless.

Realizing the ocean's perfectly timed display of fury had provided the consummate argument to staff the Sonoma Coast beaches with lifeguards, Hickey continued.

"You know Jack, I may not be able to make those kinds of rescues anymore....but I know some guys who can."

Shortly thereafter, Hickey's proposal to fund a lifeguard service on the North Coast was approved and fully funded without compromise. Thus, after many years of struggle and wrangling, in the fall of 1990, the Sonoma Coast Lifeguard service was born.

The architect of the program was Supervising Ranger Michael

Stephenson. Small in stature and noticeably humble, Stephenson spoke judiciously, with a precise and measured cadence which conveyed a reflective sense of intelligence coupled with a comforting sense of calm. Interestingly, his reserved and formal manner extended to both his professional and personal life. Although he was light-hearted and quick to laugh at a joke or relay a good story, to the staff and to his friends alike, he would always be "Michael," and never "Mike." Above all, it would be impossible to find anyone more universally loved and respected by the entire staff.

Stephenson's aquatic pedigree was outstanding, and perfectly suited to take the helm of the new lifeguard service. He had been a seasonal guard as well as a Rescue Boat Operator for many years at Newport Beach and a Permanent Peace Officer for the State Guards at Huntington. Overall, his collective work history was that of a supremely talented, well-respected, and even-keeled leader who succeeded in virtually everything he had put his hand to. He would be the perfect choice to lead the new lifeguards.

Hickey tasked Stephenson with the job of creating the infrastructure for the program and Michael quietly set about to do just that. He set up the command structure, then worked with the finance department to purchase vehicles, rescue equipment, and two rigid hull inflatables. He structured a budget to fund one Lifeguard Supervisor, two year-round Permanent Peace officers, two "Permanent Intermittent" Peace Officers (who worked 9-months), and six Seasonal Lifeguards. Stephenson's rank as Supervising Ranger would allow him to simply lateral across into the newly

"Ranger" Michael Stephenson (1996)

created position of Lifeguard Supervisor. He could then assume management of the Aquatics Program, returning to his lifeguard roots and becoming a part of their history.

To anyone familiar with the players and the background, assigning the Lifeguard Supervisor position to Stephenson would have been the logical choice. But in a twist of fate which would eventually lead to significant upheaval, the State Parks brass awarded the role to a charming, yet inexperienced lifeguard from San Clemente who had never been to Northern California, had a limited aquatics background, and virtually no experience with Rescue Vessels. The decision would place the likable newcomer in a precarious position in which he was almost pre-destined to fail.

Those close to Stephenson reported that he was crushed. Yet, being the class-act he was, he never complained about the decision and continued on dutifully in his role as the Supervising Ranger. He supported the new aquatics program from afar, and like a protective parent biting his lip while watching his child ride a bike for the first time, he stood back quietly and observed as the newly formed crew struggled to gain their footing on their new and often-times intense playing field.

But as the popular mantra, "Lifeguards for Life" suggests, once you become an Ocean Lifeguard you are always an Ocean Lifeguard. Michael Stephenson continued to carry his wetsuit, fins and rescue buoy in the trunk of his ranger sedan in the event he might one day find himself in a situation where someone needed the services of a lifeguard and none of the "official" guards were around. Given the perfect convergence of time and place, Stephenson would be ready to shed his ranger uniform, pull his wetsuit on, and swim out.

5

THE ORIGINAL CREW

The Original Crew (1991) – McNulty, Gulick, Martino, Loeffler, Brown, Melvin, Franklin, Straub, Carter, and Schardt (missing: Haug)

By virtue of the nature of their work, there is a built-in reverence which lifeguards hold for each other.

In our world, there exists a core grouping of fundamental aquatic skills which all lifeguards possess to varying degrees. Proficiency and mastery of those skills tends to be the measure by which we ascribe respect to those who earn a living in the surf line. Like professional athletes, we know each other's comparative strengths and weaknesses, and unspoken pecking orders naturally emerge based upon those proficiencies. Swimming, board paddling, surfing, free-diving, boating, and emergency medical skills are usually at the top of that list.

The investment of roughly three summers spent scrutinizing the ocean's moods, trickery and foibles, along with the habits and deficiencies of swimmers, is usually sufficient to develop enough cred to merit respect from the crew. By then, the average Ocean Lifeguard has made upwards of 100 rescues and are able to navigate through the pounding surf with grace, fluidity, mettle, and humility to retrieve struggling swimmers a dozen times per day if necessary. By then, they are trusted to function without supervision and they are usually pulled in tighter to the crew.

That respect, in my opinion, is the catalyst which allows them to bond. Those friendships can be greatly bolstered when the personalities of the guards mesh, allowing some crews to become remarkably tight. For the San Clemente district in the '70s and '80s, that was magically so. After an 8-hour day together, executing rescues and tending to medical aids after being dispersed into the various towers, jeeps, and dispatch stations; they showered off, swapped their rubber flip flops for a pair of leather ones and headed off into the night for *another* 8-hours of reverie together. In those years, the guards surfed together, dove together, played music together, drank beer, created elaborate meals, traveled to far-off countries, played poker, double dated, did construction on each other's homes, and eventually stood before dolled-up, mannerly crowds at each other's weddings. They rolled on the ground with each other's toddlers, and regaled the guards' growing children with stories and confessions about their parent's past, often (though not always) conveniently omitting the most outlandish ones. And ultimately they stood before a church full of their grieving peers, reading their own words from sheets of notebook paper, trying to summarize the totality of their fellow lifeguards' time on the planet, trying to convey to the world why we loved them so much.

But those special bonds are not always a given.

Lifeguard agencies are composed of disparate individuals who come together to exact a common purpose. While set up splendidly to form lifelong bonds in the seemingly ideal social milieu of saving lives on the beaches of Southern California, the depth of that camaraderie can be fickle and varies considerably by agency and district.

In cherry-picking who would be given a Golden Ticket to join the inaugural crew on the North Coast, in retrospect, the selection committee might have consulted a wedding planner, who could have considered issues of compatibility, temperament, political views, and hobbies before gathering them all to work together at one table. But of course, that didn't happen. Their choices were seemingly based on their pure foundational abilities to rescue people from the surf line. And rightly so.

They arrived carrying their pedigrees in hand and there was little doubt every one of them was exceptional in the water. But those abilities in the surf line were only part of their construct as humans and like the resident harbor seals at Goat Rock, they would be spending the majority of their time on dry land where they would unpack their various foibles and quirks and share them liberally with each other, for better or worse. By chance or by design, several of the guards had bold personalities and were not afraid to make their opinions known, which would add a dollop of Tabasco to the simmering stew of the Northern California Lifeguard experiment.

While the California Bear on their shoulder patch tied them to a common purpose, their differences were seemingly enough to preclude them from bonding in a San Clemente-esque sort of communal magic and harmony. Sometimes that happens. In a professional sense, their commitment to work together and cover for each other in the surf would remain the driving principle to accomplish their goals, and in that sense they never faltered. Their time there, working shoulder to shoulder in that intense, humbling, fretful, magical, awful and wonderful place, would forever bond them in events which may boggle our minds. Unfortunately those shared experiences proved elusive in creating the lifelong bonds many others in their shared profession enjoyed.

Members of the original team were plucked from the State beaches of Southern California. In retrospect, it might seem that the major prerequisite for inclusion into this elite crew was having exceptional swimming prowess, since all of them were brilliant swimmers. But their general waterman skills likely played an equally important role in securing a spot on this elite team, as every one of those original guards was well-accomplished on paddleboards, boating, diving, surfing, and body-surfing.

Their arrival on the North Coast was not unlike the settling of the Wild West. Everything would be different there; the isolation, the biting cold water, the rocky coastline, the types of fish and wildlife, the lack of surf spots, the mentality of the visitors, the wet weather, and above all, the massive surf.

The starting lineup would soon distinguish themselves as confident and skilled watermen (and one waterwoman). They shared a desire to prove themselves on the wild frontier of the Sonoma Coast and wasted little time in doing just that.

～

The ranks and hierarchy on the Sonoma Coast would be the same as those for State Guards throughout California. The Peace Officers were collectively referred to as "Perms." They are fully-sworn officers with complete powers of arrest. They were issued 38-caliber, six-shooting revolvers, which they wore on their hip along with two extra speed loaders on their gun belts (for a total of 18 rounds). They also carried a Remington 870 Shotgun in their patrol truck. Instead of "reds" and a t-shirt, they wore long pants and boots, and cop-type shirts with a shiny badge on the left chest. Beneath their uniform shirts, they were protected by a bullet-proof vest.

But under those long blue pants, every one of them wore a simple pair of "reds." And being lifeguards, they always carried a full complement of rescue gear, including 5 mm wetsuits with hoods, booties, fins, rescue buoys, throw lines, and medical gear, along with a paddleboard on the roof.

I once heard a wise man say, "If you try to do two things at once, you will do both of them poorly." If you are wondering how a Permanent

Lifeguard manages to concurrently and effectively orchestrate the duties of two seemingly contrasting jobs (law-enforcement and lifeguarding), you would not be the first. In fact, many perms themselves are confused as to "which role" they should focus on each and every day. Districts throughout the state have struggled to define what the priorities and demands should be for their officer/lifeguards. The short answer is the Permanents' role in each district tends to adapt to "whatever is needed" for their particular area. Highly urban areas such as Huntington and Lake Perris expect their officers to function almost exclusively as cops, while other districts expect their officers' priority to be on lifeguarding.

Owing to the aforementioned history of drowning, the rural nature of the Sonoma Coast District, the fact that they were recruited there to be lifeguards, and the well-established reality that rangers and Deputy Sheriffs had successfully handled the law enforcement calls for years, a logical person might assume the Perms self-imposed priorities would weigh heavily towards saving lives. Furthermore, one might surmise that if they *strayed* from that concern, they would be re-directed back to re-focus on lifeguarding....but, as we are about to find out, things didn't quite work out that way.

THE PERMANENT LIFEGUARDS

Norman "Bud" Brown
Lifeguard Supervisor 1
(San Clemente)

For an African-American kid, born and raised in Leavenworth, Kansas, who admitted, as late as college, he was afraid of sharks and had never in fact, swam in the ocean, Bud Brown was certainly an unlikely candidate to become an Ocean Lifeguard on the beaches of Southern California. Yet, in retrospect, his entry into lifeguarding, as improbable as it may have been, was just the first in a *series* of surprising advancements, each of which more remarkable than the previous one. His rapid rise into the State Lifeguard echelon so defied the odds, it stunned even his most ardent supporters including the tight circle of fellow guards who knew him best. Truth is, it surprised Bud Brown too.

Bud Brown had always been an enigma. As a transplant to California, his family had pulled their roots in Kansas and boldly replanted themselves in the starkly white municipality of Mission Viejo. When they arrived, his father, a generational military man, sat the family down at the kitchen table and asserted that after he had served his country for many years, they *deserved* to live there to enjoy the fruits of his labor. His speech was bold and inspiring, and the kids were sufficiently on board.

Away from the kids, his parents were more reticent. As adults, having endured the sting of racism for many years, they were prepared to deal with the consequences of their audacious move, but in this chapter of their struggle, they realized they would be immersing their son, by no choice of his own, into his own set of racial challenges.

But Bud was a construct of qualities and traits which would greatly ease his assimilation into this new community. His character, both disarming yet universally endearing, was anchored in a persona of humility, which drew people in. His new high school was racially insular, but the majority of students, having witnessed the turbulent '60s as children, likely found in Bud, an opportunity to "do the right thing" and readily welcomed him into their social folds.

But beyond the superficial interactions, his father continually reminded him that living in the white world - Bud would be reminded *every day* that he was black, and any gains he achieved would need to be justified with unquestionable talent and diligent work, removing any doubt that he had *earned* those rewards.

The racially provocative social experiment Bud was thrust into, for better or worse, brought him under a level of scrutiny and attention he admittedly would never have experienced had they stayed in Leavenworth. Realizing he "was not in Kansas anymore," Bud smartly parlayed his hand, taking advantage of opportunities he created, as well as those which were graciously presented to him. A less confident man black man might have hidden from view and lived in the shadows, but with his charisma and savvy, Bud Brown, far from avoiding the spotlight, jumped directly into its flare, capitalizing on the attention, and parlaying it into success.

Separate from the poignant race issue, uprooting *any* family with high school children and immersing them into a new locality is a bold move with potentially significant consequences. The common adolescent issues, grounded in *social acceptance* and the tenuous transition into adulthood are both *universal* and *universally challenging*, even without the added experiment of relocating them during, arguably, the most formative time of their lives. In contemplating their move out west, and plopping him squarely in the white world of

Bud (sitting) with brothers Roger and Charlie (1976)

South Orange County, Bud's parents trusted Bud would be able to navigate his way through the struggles of adolescence, while concurrently dealing with the additional travails of racial prejudice.

Clearly cut from the cloth of the iconic trail blazers before them, their decision to take that leap of faith was based on their tremendous confidence in their children's ability to integrate themselves and navigate their way in this new lifestyle in South Orange County.

And Bud would soon prove them right.

Bud Brown (upper left) with family in Mission Viejo (1980)

∼

As if purposefully attempting to buck the stereotypes of the day, and despite being a *lightning fast* runner who could have distinguished himself on the track oval or the football field, Bud chose to continue with competitive swimming, joining "The Nadadores" which, by most yardsticks was the premier swim club in California, if not the nation. Thus, while Bud was swimming sprints across the pool, a few lanes over were future world record holders, Brian Goodell, and Jessie Vassallo (who coincidentally lived down the street from the Browns), as well as the renowned Babashoffs.

Capitalizing on his inborn skills as an orator and his ability to charm seemingly any audience, Bud entered San Diego State, majoring in Persuasive Speech and Inter-Cultural Communications. It was a natural choice. Not only did he thrive in the curriculum, the curriculum thrived in him. He emerged with refined proficiencies as (in no particular order) a debater, a story teller, a salesman, and a charmer.

In 1980, the State of California was immersed in the Affirmative Action program, actively seeking to recruit and promote individuals in traditionally under-represented classes of society, and lifeguard agencies across the state were tasked with "expanding the horizons" of their *very white* and *very male* work force. Within that milieu, Norman Brown was a prime candidate. While at a college swim meet, Bud was approached by a recruiter with the Los Angeles County Lifeguards, and invited to try out for a position with them. Bud immediately laughed it off, since, as he admitted to the recruiter, "I have never even swam in the ocean before." Months later, at another meet, he was approached by the State Parks' Aquatic Director, Carl Drake who, in making a similar sales pitch to the perspective lifeguard, touted instead the lifeguards' *alternative lifestyle* and the fact that the ranks of the State Guards were populated with "adventurer seekers" who wandered to the far corners of the world each off-season on exotic voyages, funded entirely with the money they made from guarding all summer. It was the perfect approach to reach the future vagabond. A few months later, Bud showed up at the try-out swim at Carlsbad, thereby altering the trajectory of his life.

For Bud, the orator, the interview was child's play, and he was sent to the Lifeguard Academy in May of 1980. Competing with a small class of 17 rookies, all of whom were surf rats who had spent innumerable hours in the ocean, Bud finished dead last. Regardless, he was awarded his first pair of reds and was sent off to report for duty at the "Pendleton Coast," a district correctly rumored to be a veritable "Shangri La" for guards. Although several African-Americans had broken the color barrier before him, Bud would be the first to work the beaches of San Clemente, San Onofre and Doheny.

Brown was well-received by the veteran crew, and immediately assimilated onto the team. He later stated, "I was welcomed into the crew and overwhelmed with kindness."

After quickly overcoming his fear of the ocean, the vast aquatic world, as it had for all of us, became his playground. He spent several years working the towers, and soon developed excellent skills in the surfline.

He was bumped up into the unit shifts and was often chosen by his peers as one of their favorites to ride with. His demeanor, as a supremely easy-going guy with a great sense of humor, blended perfectly with the soulful crew. His soft-spoken style, along with his pensive and analytical conversations and unique perspectives on life, were endearing to the crew. Riding together in the units for a full summer of 8-hour shifts, he and his peers covered every topic imaginable, including racial relations, their contrasting upbringings, girls, football, surfing, girls, family, travel, girls, philosophy, and countless lesser topics too numerous to list. It was there we all came to know Bud on a deeper level, and for me personally, he soon became one of my close friends. Although he was good in the water, he was even better on land, and his interactions with the public, especially with teenagers, were nothing short of magical.

North Coast Lifeguard Dave Schardt once said of Bud, "Man, he was a talker. He could sell you on just about any topic and sound convincing. His greatest gift was his ability to relate to kids, but he could charm just about anybody and captivate an audience like no one else."

The Perms at San Clemente, capitalizing on Bud's ability to influence and inspire young people, gave him a wide-berth to work on a project he created which he called the "Youth Awareness Program." His idea was to bring inner-city kids who, despite living within a 30-minute drive of the coastline, had never been given an opportunity to experience the ocean environment. After laying the groundwork and logistics, he began the program in earnest and developed it into a great success. The "Ya-Yas," as his compatriots referred to it, soon attracted

*Bud Brown and the author doing
"The Hambone" at San Onofre
(1981) – Photo: John Drucker*

the attention of some key bureaucrats in Sacramento, along with plenty of well-earned recognition for Bud.

Riding on the wave of his success, Bud applied for a position as a full-time Permanent Lifeguard. With the promotional process based solely on an oral interview, and Bud's well-matched skills as a raconteur, Bud found his name at the top of the hiring list and accepted a position in the Peace Officer Academy.

Assigned a position at the Orange Coast, Bud would begin his new career patrolling the State Beaches of Huntington and Bolsa Chica. His assigned Field Training Officer, tasked with educating Brown on the complex world of law enforcement, was a man named Kurt Loeffler. Loeffler challenged the new young officer and became uniquely privy to his strengths and his weaknesses; a fact that would prove to be significant some years later.

Coincidentally, at the same time, the new State Parks Director had initiated a "Ten Point Program" which, consistent with the Affirmative Action program, focused on attracting under-served populations to the State Parks. Needing someone to implement the program, Bud was the obvious choice and after only a brief time "in the field" learning the ropes as an officer, he was often pulled away to work with members of various committees in support of the Director's program.

As the doors continued to swing open for Bud, he boldly walked through them all. Working out of the Southern Service Center, the young guard was soon rubbing shoulders with some of the most influential and elite members of the State Parks' brass. He became a member of the Employee Equal Opportunity Commission. He also became part of the recruitment team. He attended every Interpretive Training Program he could find, and soon began teaching them. He sat on committees and offered input directly to the decision makers in Sacramento. Utilizing his skills as an orator, he gave presentations to school groups, community service organizations, State Parks managers, and influential members of the community. He became a Harassment Coordinator, as well as a Counselor. With each new speech and each new assignment, like a boy scout collecting merit badges, Bud gathered recognition and clout. In 1988 he was awarded the "Take Pride in California Award" followed by an honorable mention from First Lady Barbara Bush in a similar National Award. The recognition and praise far exceeded anything he could have imagined.

Despite the fact the patch on his shoulder still said "LIFEGUARD," his connections with the ocean and his Huntington crew soon began to fade off into the distance. Thus, while his fellow new officers were learning the fundamental skills and tactics necessary to function as Peace Officers, Bud was off glad-handing with appointees of the Governor.

When asked if the "Affirmative Action Program" had helped him in his career, Bud admitted it most certainly had. His unplanned entry into the world of State Government could not have been timed more perfectly for a man of color, yet he was quick to add that, as his father had indoctrinated in him, he felt a tremendous burden to *prove himself worthy* of those rewards stating, "In my mind, I had to be 75% better than anyone else, to justify my successes and silence my doubters." Apparently he did just that, since the accolades continued to come.

Despite being one of the younger candidates, and having less experience as an officer than the other candidates, Bud applied to become a Lifeguard Supervisor, a ranking only a few in California held at that time. In an attempt to "level the playing field" of the promotional process, as was the case with all promotions within the State Parks' system, the evaluation process was not scored on the traditional merits used in the private sector - such as years of experience, or subject matter expertise - but rather entirely on the candidate's performance on a single oral interview. Thus Bud Brown, happily gliding along on the silver road of success, found himself sitting before yet another interview panel comprised of a "home crowd" of individuals he had worked with at the Service Center. Despite their high expectations for him, Bud delivered a dazzling interview which captivated them all. He was placed in the first rank.

And so it was, when the historic announcement rang out through California that the State Parks would be hiring the first Supervising Lifeguard on the wild Sonoma Coast, Bud Brown was at the head of the line with a smile on his face and a Golden Ticket in his hand.

The position would not be his for the taking, since his potential competition would include all of the existing Lifeguard Supervisors in Southern California, who by virtue of transfer, had equal right to interview for the position.

Yet, rather remarkably, after hearing the stories about the huge surf, the shark attacks and the recurring drownings, every one of them declined the opportunity to transfer there, and when the interview roster was released, only two names appeared on the list. Michael Stephenson and Bud Brown.

The contrasting credentials and skill sets between the two candidates were noteworthy for the simple reason they were almost diametrically opposed. While Bud had little or no supervisory experience, Michael had plenty. While Bud had earned every conceivable merit badge imaginable from the State Parks, Michael had few. Bud had almost zero boating experience, while Michael had plenty from both Newport and Huntington. Michael, who was humble to a fault, was not an impassioned public speaker, and not one to readily tout his virtues. Meanwhile Bud, as mentioned, thrived in the role and had few reservations about laying on the charm.

In the end, despite having far less experience as a *lifeguard* or as a *supervisor*, it was Bud Brown who stunned the district and was awarded the job.

In his new role, he would oversee a diverse collection of veteran, hard-nosed lifeguards from across the state, all of whom had distinguished themselves in their respective districts. The added challenge for Bud was that several of the guards not only had considerably more ocean experience than he had, but also had reputations as being outspoken and oppositional. Bud's ultimate job was to meld them into a cohesive, efficient, and functional unit, and to assimilate the lifeguards into the community as a bonafide rescue agency. For Bud Brown, it would be a seemingly impossible goal.

∾

Kurt Loeffler
Lifeguard Permanent
(Huntington)

The first of the perms to be hired quite literally stood out in the crowd. Standing just short of 7-feet tall, the dark-haired and verbose Kurt Loeffler was an imposing figure. If you picture an elongated and slightly less manic Jim Carey in both looks and demeanor, you're getting close. Kurt began his career in 1982 at Huntington Beach, generally considered among the state beaches to be the most challenging lifeguard assignment in Southern California. It was there Loeffler made a name for himself, logging hundreds of rescues and treating similar numbers of medical aids.

Officer Loeffler poses with City cops at the Huntington Beach jail (1987)

In 1986, Loeffler was selected to enter the Peace Officer Academy and was assigned to work back at his home beach of Huntington for three years before he requested a lateral transfer to the newly created position on the Sonoma Coast.

Consensus among his peers was that Loeffler was a quick-witted guy who rarely buffered the content of his musings to match the make-up of his audience. He could be brash, head-strong, acerbic and polarizing at times, but he was also freakin' hilarious, which not only endeared him to the team, but also helped them to bond. When questioned about Loeffler, Osh McNulty said, "Given any kind of audience, Loeffler would 'light it up' with his own brand of irreverent shtick. During CPR and Cliff Rescue training sessions, the instructors made feeble attempts to rein him in, but were rarely successful, as Kurt would inevitably steal the spotlight and we would laugh our assess off." The comedy routines ran rampant and no member of the staff was safe. Inevitably Kurt became the prime suspect when the District Superintendent, sitting down to address his staff, emitted a resounding fart (from a strategically placed whoopee cushion) and was forced excuse himself to his staff. He was also suspected during First Responder training when the students opened their manuals and discovered Playboy photographs had been interspersed amongst the pages.

Unfortunately, Loeffler also brought with him a provocative style of law enforcement, forged and tempered at Huntington. According to one of his partners, "Kurt was brilliant – he would engage people who were breaking the law and mentally spar with them, cleverly allowing them to talk their way deeper into guilt. He was really good at it - always outsmarting them. Sometimes he poked people simply to get a reaction." In the urban setting of Huntington, being an assertive officer was viewed not only as appropriate, but also necessary. But to some of the others, his approach was unnecessary and counter-productive. The local residents, with whom he would feud fervently, were far less diplomatic in their critique of Loeffler. To many of them, to put it mildly, he was viewed as the authoritative "Bad Cop" incarnate.

Scott Melvin
Lifeguard Permanent
(Huntington)

Scott Melvin was the veteran among the group, having starting his lifeguard career in 1978. A powerful backstroker and water polo player for Edison High, Scott grew up on the beaches of Huntington, which is often somewhat flippantly referred to as "Surf City." As a child of six, he began his love affair with the ocean and soon became a skilled water-kid, then waterman. As a guard, he would work the same surf breaks and beaches he was weaned on and he too would make a name for himself. Eventually Melvin became a deckhand on the Surfwatch vessel, working with the legendary Mel Tubbs. Together their tally of rescues would dwarf those of the other guards.

Like Loeffler, Melvin was an immediate "presence" on the coastline, standing 6'4" and weighing in around 240. The cigar smoking Melvin admittedly "took no crap from anyone" which, as a law enforcement officer, could be seen as an asset or a detriment, depending on which side of the law you happened to find yourself.

Not only did he and Loeffler work together at Huntington, they, along with bassist Dan Kneafsy and lead singer Spencer Gilbert were uniquely bonded as members of an all lifeguard band known as "White Trash." Their exodus north was met with profound regret from their small but loyal fan base.

It was Loeffler who first informed Melvin about the new lifeguard service beginning along the Sonoma Coast, adding that he had been selected to be part of the inaugural crew. Unknown to Kurt, after hearing Loeffler's stories and seeing his excitement, Melvin also applied, and he too was granted a transfer to the Sonoma Coast. Thus, he and Loeffler would be the first of the 11 guards to arrive for duty and would share a house together in Petaluma. They would also continue their musical pursuits in the Bay Area with a new band called "Sacrifice Choir."

"White Trash" rocking Huntington – Kurt Loeffler (guitar), Spencer Gilbert (vocals), Dan Kneafsy (bass), Scott Melvin (drums) (1985)

Oisin "Osh" Mcnulty
Permanent Intermittent
(New Jersey Via San Diego)

"Osh" McNulty with "Philo"
(1996)

Osh McNulty was arguably the pick of the litter. A clever, yet humble man, he had graduated from Rutgers with a bachelor's degree in Chemical Engineering; which likely didn't contribute many transferable skills to his position as an Ocean Lifeguard. Ironically, this future West Coast lifeguard icon began his storied career on the Jersey shore, where he logged his first five years as a Seasonal.

McNulty was a stellar athlete, infused with a competitive fire which earned him success in his early days of lifeguard competitions. He was thin, tall and wiry, allowing him to excel in the traditional lifeguard events of running and swimming. His physique and strength also allowed him to excel in the less-traditional sports of rock climbing and wind-surfing, where he also flourished.

Arriving in California, McNulty was readily hired to work the San Diego Coast District, where he guarded another two years as a Seasonal. He entered the Peace Officer Academy in 1988, and not only came away with a new career, but also a future wife in Ranger Karen Broderick.

McNulty & Karen Broderick (1988)

Osh too was assigned to work Huntington and put in his compulsory two years of service before he was eligible to transfer. Coincidentally, his timing was perfect and he was also picked up to work the Sonoma Coast.

With his black curly hair and a perpetual bushy moustache, Osh, at various times reminded me of Jim Croce, Frank Zappa, or, if I am being honest here, a '70s porn star.

Happy to escape his previous assignment at Huntington, McNulty jumped at the chance to transfer to the Sonoma Coast, yet compared to the other 10 members of the original crew, he knew virtually nothing about the structure of the coastline, the nature of the job duties, the clientele, or the weather. Perhaps his naiveté was a blessing.

McNulty would outlast them all by a long shot.

In describing Osh McNulty, Brian Hickey was lavish in his praise, referred to him quite simply as "The answer to my prayers." I think many others would agree. McNulty was the personification of the "generalist" lifeguard. When the surf was up and the aquatic conditions called for it, he proactively raced between the hot spots in aquatics mode and, when necessary, would stash his gun belt and make rescues. When the aquatics were covered and the surf laid down, he did law enforcement, consistent with the job title. Seeing an alarming trend in abalone poaching, McNulty dedicated

McNulty (1996) – Photo: Vodrazka

himself wholly to busting poachers, and became damn good at it. In fact, within a few years, Osh would establish himself as a bit of a celebrity in the courts. The sheer number of citations he wrote for poaching dwarfed those of all of the local Fish and Game wardens combined. Additionally, while safely hidden behind rocks and bushes, he scrutinized and documented the specific illegal actions of the poachers' so meticulously, his citations were virtually bullet-proof. He rarely bothered with the divers who were grabbing one or two over limit. Instead he would focus on the flagrant offenders; guys taking abalone for another diver, high grading, or even guys coming down at night to dive for abalone under the cover of darkness.

Years later, McNulty would receive a Commendation from the Sonoma County courts for single-handedly citing hundreds of poachers.

From the Fish and Game Department, he would also win "Officer of the Year," despite the fact he didn't even work for Fish and Game. His years of dedication and loyalty to resource protection provided an unparalleled service to the community and an incomparable gift to the abalone populations along the entire coastline.

Steven Franklin
Permanent Intermittent
(San Diego)

Steve Franklin (1992)

The fifth and final Peace Officer Lifeguard on the North Coast arrived in the form of Steve Franklin. As an avid surfer from San Diego, you might conjure up an image of Franklin as a laid-back, easy going, mellow dude. Franklin was nothing of the sort. In fact, he was as intense and tenacious as any guard I have ever met. Between the four summers he worked as a Seasonal on the San Diego Coast beaches, Franklin, for a time, pursued a path towards becoming an attorney, and like many who "dabbled" in law, his years of legal study fortified a resolve in him which seemingly drove him to defend every perceived threat to any principle he even remotely believed in. That same resolve also precluded him from backing down from any fight he felt was noble (which, as it turns out, happened to be plenty of them). This level of tenacity might have served him well in a courtroom, but in life it tended to draw Franklin into an ongoing series of disputes and legal issues in both his professional and personal life.

As a graduate from the Peace Officer Academy, Franklin was assigned to the Sonoma Coast directly and would be mentored and trained by Loeffler. As a new officer, Franklin would be thrust into the dirty work of law enforcement; handling the most stressful calls, dealing with drug addicts, vagrants, career criminals, and various deviants. But

Franklin arrived freshly inundated with a robust passion to uphold the laws of the land by way of citation and arrest and did just that.

Franklin was never a collegiate swimmer. As a testament to his own validation of "worthiness" to join the Sonoma Coast team, months before he arrived, and without being asked to do so, he put himself through a self-imposed 1,000 yard freestyle time trial to see what kind of shape he was in. He logged a decent 11:17 and sent the results to Bud Brown to assure him he was ready for the challenge. For a surfer, the time was decent, but would fall short of several other guys on the force who, despite also being past their swimming prime, were faster (namely Loeffler, Schardt, Martino and McNulty).

As one might surmise, working the Sonoma Coast was not an easy assignment for a guy like Franklin, but there was never any debate among his partners that he was conscientious, tenacious as Hell, and supremely vigilant. Right out of the gate, the seemingly fearless Franklin let his presence be known by making several high profile rescues.

While the intensity of the job infused a significant amount of stress into all of the guards, many of them agreed that the pressures and anxiety hit Franklin the hardest. And although his partners were fully capable of swimming out and backing him on his spectacular rescues, no one, it seemed, had the appropriate skill set to help mitigate the emotional chaos which would soon begin to plague him on land.

～

THE SEASONAL LIFEGUARDS

The *Seasonal Lifeguards* were the front line warriors. Although they too enforced the rules and regulations, their primary focus was in saving lives in any way possible. They trained to swim out in large surf to effect rescues on struggling victims, they piloted the rescue boats, they descended off cliff faces with rescue gear, they assessed and provided medical aid for the sick and injured and, when necessary, performed CPR (Cardiac Defibrillators were not yet available). Often patrolling with the Perms, they also assumed the initial command and management of the traffic accidents, major medical aids, ocean emergencies, and a myriad of critical situations.

But beyond doubt, it was in the aquatics realm where they shined brightest as the first line of defense against any and all threats to human homeostasis.

But the Seasonals were just that. *Seasonal* employees. Keeping them on the payroll year-round would have necessitated the state provide them with a more generous benefits package, which the state chose not to do - even for their long-serving loyalists. Thus, their yearly work schedule was limited to a 9-month term, followed by a mandatory 3-months off. They garnered a meager paycheck for ¾ of the year without health benefits and only a rudimentary pension, then were essentially placed on a 3-month unpaid vacation leave, during which time they could "recover" from the stresses of the job, while at the same time, try to find some other viable means to pay their rent. Several of them worked as day-laborers doing construction.

Ironically, for a single kid in his 20s with limited responsibilities, the schedule, if not the salary or the benefits, was ideal. Most of them would scratch out some extra shifts during the year which they parlayed into an extra month off. They would then venture off on 4-month long surf trips, visit their families, take college classes, or come up with any number of reasons to distance themselves from the Sonoma Coast.

Don Straub
Lifeguard Seasonal
(San Diego)

Don Straub (1995)

For those of you who may have read my first book "Stories from Sea Level," you might remember Don Straub as the charismatic Medal of Valor recipient who, along with Dave Carter was able to save the stricken vessel, the La Ola in horrendous conditions. As you soon will discover, in chronicling of the North Coast Lifeguard history, Straub readily emerges as one of the featured players, and a larger-than-life character who will weave his way through much of the book and perhaps into your soul.

To understand him at depth, I have taken the liberty of reprinting his introductory narrative largely unchanged since it reflects my best rendering of this most colorful and charismatic guards, and sets the stage for the many swashbuckling adventures he will soon be featured in.

Among those who knew him, when the name *Don Straub* was brought up, the most common epithet which came out of people's mouths was "bad ass." I don't think Don minded that either. Fellow guard Jon Gulick described him as *"a character who was larger than life."* Without exaggeration, an entire book could be filled with Don Straub stories alone. Yet in a profession which tended to attract its share of colorful characters, Straub stood alone as one of the most charismatic, intense, talented, and storied lifeguards I have ever met.

Originally from Texas, Don spent his youth as a bonafide cowboy, breaking horses at the famous King Ranch from the age of 13 until he came to California at age 20. He stood 6'1" and was scrappy as all hell. He had a muscular build, honed by years of manual labor. He was a decent surfer, with a style predictably long on power and short on grace. He had a commanding stroke in the water, and in his heyday, swam a blistering 46:00 in the 100-yard free, which was pretty big smoke back in 1980.

Curiously, he arrived at San Diego with a thick slow southern drawl, which immediately set him apart as an anomaly and quickly endeared him to the others. Thriving on his uniqueness as a true cowboy, in his rookie season he entered the Del Mar amateur rodeo, likely the only State Lifeguard ever to compete in *any rodeo*. Years later, with his drawl still prevalent, he started riding in the units, and the other guards made fun of him for speaking "too slow and too cowboy" on the radio.

Don was committed to the profession and learned the ropes quickly. He was promoted to a lead role and operated the units in the shoulder seasons of the spring and fall. And there, on the San Diego Coast, Don guarded for 13 seasons, establishing himself as a trusted leader.

Straub was easily the most experienced and best-suited member of the initial crew of lifeguard imports from Southern California. It was likely his boating experience which attracted the attention of Bud Brown. Needing a mainstay to run the boating program, Don was an obvious choice. His grandfather was a Salmon fisherman and Don had grown up on boats. In fact, at the time he received the offer to work on the Sonoma Coast, he was living on his 32' Westsail, moored in Oceanside Harbor. He had also trained to pilot Rigid Hull Inflatables, and had sailed around the world as the first mate on the 60' yacht, *Maranoa*.

Don's *official* resume would have also included the fact he knew his way around mechanics and had worked as a construction foreman, an EMT and a cliff rescue instructor.

Don Straub (circa 1982)

His *unofficial* resume would also have included the more colorful facts that he was once a Chippendale's stripper, held leanings towards the Reggae lifestyle, and had been arrested for attempting to smuggle a large amount of marijuana into the country from Mexico.

Don was also a fighter. Literally. For a time he put his brawn and agility to use as a professional kick boxer. He started out as an amateur in Oceanside and eventually had earned enough wins to qualify as a pro. His debut was at the San Diego Sports Arena in 1980, when he was placed on a "smoker" card, which was a 5 round professional bout before the feature fight. Originally pitted in a contest with a fighter of similar weight and experience, at the last minute they substituted in Mark Zacharatos, a fighter, to Don's dismay, who was ranked fifth in the world and was preparing to fight for the world title.

In a show of support for their cowboy / kick boxer, his fellow guards rented a bus, loaded in a couple kegs, and headed down I-5 to the Sports Arena to watch the match. By the time they arrived they were noticeably heated, which, in that venue, as it turned out, was completely acceptable. When Don entered the ring, the guards commenced to *raise the damn roof* and amazingly, supported by their alcohol-driven enthusiasm, Don won the fight. The win propelled Straub into a top 10 ranking and an instant career. From that point on, he got plenty of fights and on April 1, 1980, he fought for the IKBA world title. Although he didn't win, he finished his career with a respectable record of 26-4 with 12 knockouts.

Having a professional fighter on the lifeguard staff was sometimes handy. Amidst the liberal social generation of the late '70s and early '80s, lifeguard parties often escalated into legendary events, and if you are lucky enough to find a guard still alive who attended any of them, it probably wouldn't take much prodding to get them to tell you their first-hand account. With scores of people attempting to get in, inevitably, some "hard dude" would show up uninvited and refuse to leave. When that happened, the younger guards would invariably run to get Don and, in a recurring scenario which played out often enough for the guards to gather in anticipation to watch, Don would greet the guy politely and ask him to leave. If he didn't (which was exactly what everyone was hoping for) Don would then hand his beer to someone and bait the guy by warning him he *"didn't want to have to hurt him"*, but he *would* if he didn't leave immediately. Of course the hard-dude, not wanting to lose face amidst the growing crowd, and fully expecting the customary gradual build-up of bluster and posturing, would refuse to leave. The nanosecond the guy offered ANY kind of punch, Don would block the blow then throttle him between the eyes with a single lightning-fast punch that everyone in the room (except the hard-dude) was fully expecting. The guy would fall to the ground and a few self-deputized guards would then proudly drag him out to the front lawn while Don retrieved his beer. Having worked the San Diego Coast for many years, I've asked plenty of the veteran guards who knew Don well about these altercations and they all agreed they were frequent occurrences. They also agreed that Don never lost a fight.

Straub was Bud's #1 draft choice, and was offered nine months of full-time work each year along with a seasonal lifeguard "residence." Don accepted the position without the benefit of seeing the residence, or even visiting the county. Regardless, two weeks later, he loaded up the trunk of his 12-year old Toyota Corolla with a few essential supplies, and headed north with his girlfriend Pam and their baby daughter Tiana to see their new home for the first time.

The drive was long, but they were able to make it to Sonoma County by nightfall. Descending from High Point along the precarious Coast

Highway, they meandered into a thick blanket of fog which obscured everything that existed outside the beams of their headlights. In her hand Pam held the scribbled directions to their new "residence" but in the dense fog, they drove right past every landmark and road sign until they realized they were hopelessly lost. By then it was very late and fatigue had gotten the best of them. Finding a wide spot just off the roadway, they pulled over and slept in their car.

With the first light of day, the fog had lifted and only then did they realize that they had parked within 20 yards of the Salt Point State Park entrance; the home base for the North Sector lifeguard operations. Sufficiently oriented, they drove south until they pulled into the "state residence area" at a place called "Arky Camp," a small non-descript camping area with a permanent bathroom and basic kitchen facility. Set amidst a small clearing the in the forest, the camp served as a base for seasonal archeology teachers and students who visited Fort Ross to participate in excavations in hopes of finding archeological remains of from the original Russian settlers who built and inhabited the fort.

And there, in the light of day, sat Don's new home; a pale yellow, dilapidated 19' travel trailer, sitting on two flat tires and adorned with well-established garlands of moss. Pam attempted to peek into the windows, but since they appeared to have not been cleaned in her lifetime, it was impossible to see inside. Don tried the door, which was unlocked. They entered tentatively. Needless to say, their initial impression fell short of their expectations, and no one had bothered to notify them the resident rat population would be included at no extra charge.

It would be the humblest of beginnings for the young family. But after their first fitful night of sleep in the trailer, they woke with a vengeance, evicted the rats, sealed up the intrusion points, and carried on with a week-long clean-up of the place.

Soon, they would breathe new life into the little trailer, and the unique solitude of Arky Camp became quaint and homey. Pam decorated the environs with driftwood, rocks, and abalone shells. With an endless supply of firewood, every night involved a campfire and a glass of wine. Don supplied most of their protein needs with a daily catch of Ling Cod, Cabazon, Rock Fish and Sea Urchin so fresh, the transition time between swimming and landing on the barbeque grill was often less than 30 minutes. And of course they enjoyed plenty of the local delicacy, California Red Abalone. The tough white meat of the huge mollusks, when pounded with a mallet, transformed into the most tender, exotic, delicately-flavored ocean sustenance imaginable. Don pounded them into steaks and fried them in garlic and butter. He coated filets in bread crumbs. They baked it. They shredded it and made abalone soup. They sliced it into strips and put it into pasta. The variations, it seemed, were endless.

With healthy populations of exotic Chanterelles, Boletes, and Prince Mushrooms growing in the woods around them, they took full advantage. Thus, although by most measures of modern society, Don and his family were living a lifestyle as near to the earth as vagrants, their nightly diet would have been the envy of any 5-star restaurant in San Francisco, New York, or Paris.

Eventually joining them there, sleeping in his truck, would be Steve Franklin. Living there together each night, and sharing the wild adventure of guarding the North Coast every day, Franklin would soon form a special bond with Don and his family.

~

For better or worse, Don was cut from the cloth of the elder generation of "he-men" lifeguards. But on that coastline, amongst a rural community of hard-nosed outdoorsmen, Don was, in every way, their equal. The locals would eventually discover this "lifeguard" could fire up a chainsaw to clear a downed tree from the roadway, or get under the hood and adjust the carburetor of a local's stalled truck, or even help to build a community garage. Seeing him navigate the rescue boat with skill and confidence inside the surf line was something *none* of them had ever witnessed before. At their best and especially at their worst, the guards would be constantly watched, and the locals took notice when they did things right. Straub would be the first lifeguard there whom the North Sector locals came to appreciate, and their respect helped greatly in the guards' assimilation into the community. In essence, drafting Straub to work the Sonoma Coast was like drafting Mickey Mantle onto your baseball team, and probably the single best move Bud Brown made. While the South Sector guards would be forced to endure years of scorn and resentment from the community, the North Sector guards were able to garner a sense of credibility far sooner, and in due course, even developed a bit of a swagger.

Dave Schardt
Lifeguard Seasonal
(San Clemente)

Schardt with abalone (1993)

One might assume Dave Schardt was selected to work the North Coast based on his swimming prowess. In 1982, at his collegiate final, he swam a blistering 4:27 in the 500 yard free. Beyond that, Schardt was able to maintain a respectable level of speed in the water long after his official swimming career was over.

But Schardt's swimming, as it turned out, would not be his greatest asset to the program. What really set him apart was his infectious and near-constant *positivity*. People who knew him well universally loved him. And who wouldn't? The guy was perennially happy. He could have lost the winning lottery ticket and you would never know it. Schardt walked around 365 days a year with a giddy expression on his face as if some beauty queen had just given him her phone number.

As a testament to universal appeal of Dave's smile, one day in the late '80s I was driving through downtown Sacramento and lo and behold, I looked up and saw a full-sized billboard with an 8' tall head-shot of none other than Dave Schardt plastered on it; and yes he was wearing that ridiculous lottery smile. The billboard ad was for some insurance company and had a caption under Dave's head which said something like, *"This guy is happy with American Insurance, you could be too!"* Nice to know - even the American Insurance Company found Dave's face endearing.

But of course his charm soaked far deeper than just his countenance. Dave Schardt was high on life. In San Clemente, he would show up to the shop after almost every shift and proclaim, *"Eddie! Man, the body surfing is great right now...let's go!"* So I'd grab my fins and we'd run down the hill only to find the surf was only waist high and blown out. Regardless, with Schardt involved, we'd go out anyway, and always had a good time goofing around. Drafting Dave to join the team was a great move to buffer the tension and stress brought on by the job, and to keep the guards' spirits up.

Raised in Walnut Creek, Schardt was also the only Northern California native in the bunch, and likely knew more than the others about the frigid waters of the North Coast. Seemingly impervious to the cold, he used charm and magical powers of coercion to convince the crew to get in the water every day; not a small feat when the water was 51 degrees and the winds were howling at 30 knots.

Schardt would serve as the ideal counterbalance to the jostling alpha

Dave Schardt (1993)

males who, at times, were prone to bickering.

Dave remembered his early days working there. *"I heard they were going to start a lifeguard program on the North Coast and I was determined to be a part of it. That coast was rugged, exciting, cold and sometimes downright nasty! This was a new type of guarding for me where we worked independently almost all the time with little or no back up. I had heard about the death statistics and knew it wasn't a matter of 'if' but rather 'when' we would deal with ocean tragedies. Most guards in Southern California don't see death in their short careers. But guarding the Sonoma Coast, we all knew we were going to be involved in saving people who are looking into the eyes of death...and at some point we would be recovering bodies. There was just no getting around it."*

Audrey Haug
Lifeguard Seasonal
(Lake Perris)

Audrey Haug (circa 1992) – Photo: Unknown

The lone female on the original crew, Haug started lifeguarding in 1984 and had worked her entire career at what was likely the most "opposite" work location to the Sonoma Coast in the entire State Park system; Lake Perris. But she was tough as nails and had solid credentials. Having gone to school in Humboldt, Audrey was also familiar with cold water and showed no hesitancy in attacking the surf.

She was also a Rescue Boat Operator and had her master diver scuba certification. She had been lavishly recommended by her supervisors and lived up to their billing. Her medical skills were exceptional, having run on plenty of major medical calls in the urban jungle of Lake Perris.

Joining a team comprised entirely of audacious males might have been intimidating for a lesser guard, but Audrey stood toe to toe with every one of them and held her own. She had confidence and strong opinions about how a lifeguard operation should run and had no reservations about expressing her beliefs.

Mike Martino
Lifeguard Seasonal
(San Diego)

The first thing which comes to mind when describing Martino was his pure and seemingly natural swimming style. He was smooth and deceptively fast. Many years later, I accepted an invitation to do a workout with him, and spent the entire hour getting quietly, though politely hammered into submission. The next time he invited me, I knew better and came up with some transparent excuse as to why I couldn't make it. For decades after his time on the North Coast, he won the annual re-check swim in San Diego, among other lifeguards who were 20 years his junior. In 1990, Martino was in the swimming prime of his life and likely felt invincible.

Mike Martino (circa 1992)

During the off-season from lifeguarding on the San Diego coast, Martino, in pursuit of a stable income and long-range security, accepted a position as an English teacher at Mount Carmel High School. On his day off, he happened to run into Steve Franklin at sporting goods store. Franklin, immediately began "geeking out" to his fellow lifeguard/surfer about his pending positions opening on the Sonoma Coast. Martino, not wholly invested in his role as a teacher, sat and listened intently as Franklin, with unvarnished enthusiasm, extoled the virtues of the job, the wild coastline, the challenging surf and the fact that they would be saving lives in conditions unlike any he had seen before. In short, he implored Martino to join him. Their chance meeting was one of those fork-in-the-road moments that would completely alter Martino's path in life. Capitalizing on near-perfect timing, Martino secured a recommendation from his Lifeguard Chief, made a few phone calls and was accepted to be part of the original crew. Within a week he resigned his teaching position and began the process of relocating to the Sonoma

Coast. The decision would set him on a path that would propel him along the ladder of the success within the State Parks hierarchy – eventually landing a position as the Aquatic Specialist – the highest ranking lifeguard in the state system.

Martino was raised in a conservative household, which infused into many aspects of his life. Young and admittedly a bit naïve at the time, Martino came to the North Coast seeking the promise of a challenge and he most certainly got one. Despite having logged five years of service on the San Diego coast, he would arrive as the youngest member of the crew. But Martino was clever, well-spoken, and interested in soaking up every aspect of lifeguarding. He learned quickly from the elder guards and they correctly saw great potential in him. In fact, they trusted the young guard enough to station him as the primary lifeguard at Goat Rock; no doubt one of the most challenging assignments on the West Coast.

In retrospect, it would have been almost impossible to find a better suited guard to direct the daily operations there. For one thing, along with his thick curly brown hair, Martino happened to have piercing china-blue eyes, which seemed to captivate members of the public and likely helped charm them into compliance with his enforcement of the regulations. One of his partners later admitted the charming Martino had an uncanny way of "getting people to listen to him" when others ran into opposition. Secondly, Martino was a rocket in the water, and those swimming skills were put to use almost immediately by making plenty of rescues. In scrutinizing statistics from those early years, it was Martino who consistently logged the highest totals of aquatic rescues.

As was the norm for most lifeguards of his generation, Martino was undeniably poor and arrived thrilled with the promise of getting 9-months of guaranteed work each year. Yet, needing to find a place to stay and not having a van (or even a car) to sleep in, he secured a small apartment in Sebastopol. Then, out of a combination of necessity and self-challenge, he rode his bike on the 40-mile round trip commute to the coast each day.

Martino proved to be a diligent guard and a hawk on the water. He soon became a stalwart in the South Sector, etching his name into lifeguarding history with a series of high profile rescues. Jon Gulick remembered Martino as "A super lifeguard – really strong in the water –

and extremely bright." By the time he hung up his North Coast wetsuit to become a Peace Officer, there was no doubt Martino had saved several lives on the Sonoma Coast.

Additionally, as an amateur historian, even at his young age, Mike was perceptive enough to realize the creation of this fledgling lifeguard service, whether successful or not, might one day be seen as a momentous and truly historic undertaking in the larger world of lifeguarding and ocean safety. With that in mind, he (and later Rex Grady) diligently began documenting all of the crew's rescues, medical aids, fatalities, and associated significant events. Those original documents provided an essential framework for this book, and Martino's overall contribution to its fruition can't be overstated.

Martino making a safety contact at Goat Rock (circa 1992)

David Carter
Lifeguard Seasonal
(Huntington)

Dave Carter (1992)

As with Straub, the introduction of Dave Carter was pulled from "Stories from Sea Level."

Dave Carter was a heart-centered surfer who grew up in the Los Angeles area. He became a lifeguard in 1986 and like Loeffler and Melvin, learned the trade by pulling swimmers out of the rip currents at Huntington.

Carter was an inherently cheerful guy who sought a peaceful existence in the world. In search of a like-minded community, he attended college at Humboldt State. In his time near the Oregon border, he soaked into the laid-back culture and the vibe of the poets, musicians and simpatico environmental studies majors.

When he caught wind about the establishment of the Sonoma Coast Lifeguards, he submitted his name for consideration and was selected to join the crew. Like Schardt, Carter was in the water almost every day and it didn't take long for Dave to prove himself as a worthy partner to the others. Also like Schardt, his demeanor and overall vibe would be a perfect balance for some of the more hard-driving members of the team.

Carter's long and lean frame was topped with shaggy long locks of sun-streaked blond hair. The length violated the State Lifeguard grooming standards, but guarding up north, and having greater issues to worry about, no one really cared. In their isolation from the rest of the lifeguard world, the guards were essentially free to grow their hair long, and even report for work unshaven - which was unheard of in the lifeguard operations of Southern California. Carter's appearance and attitude personified the laid back style of a Southern California Lifeguard, and beneath the facade was the soul of a religious studies student, who at the time was actively considering entering the seminary. Carter could speak with an impressive level of expertise about Christianity, Jainism, Buddhism, or likely any other "ism" you could come up with. But being well-rounded, he was never one to advocate for any doctrine or specific religion. His added goatee completed the persona of a modern day coastal prophet, and Carter soon inspired the affectionately coined nickname of "Boy Jesus" from the crew. And it stuck.

Dave was a true lifeguard. He loved the water. He loved surfing. In rescue situations he showed no hesitation regardless of the size of the surf. Like Schardt, he would do his part to buffer some of the bold personalities and served a vital role as a peace-keeper in times of unrest, which, as it turns out would be more often than expected. Dave was well-suited to the role and became an unofficial mediary between the guards. In retrospect, the State Parks should have given him bonus pay for his services as a counsellor.

Interestingly, when Carter was a rookie at Huntington, it was Michael Stephenson who sent him on his first rescue with the poignant and often used phrase, *"You might want to go on that."* On the North Coast, Carter would be reunited with Stephenson, who had been one of his notable mentors. Three years after his arrival in Sonoma, while he and "Ranger" Stephenson were scrutinizing a possible routine rescue at Salt Point, Carter looked to Stephenson with a huge grin and said, *"You might want to go on that."* After a mutual laugh, Stephenson actually did suit up and made the routine rescue – if nothing else, just to complete the joke.

Working the front lines, almost immediately Carter would find himself involved with several major rescues. One of them would immortalize him in the annals of lifeguarding forever.

Jon Gulick
Lifeguard Seasonal
(San Clemente)

I first met Jon Gulick, of all places, in a swim class at Sacramento Junior College. Both of us signed up with the same intention of getting some pool miles in for a nominal fee. Jon and I hit it off immediately and would eventually become life-long friends. He was a soft-spoken carpenter raised in Redondo Beach, and an avid surfer. He stood six-foot and bore an uncanny resemblance to Clint Eastwood, especially if you coaxed him to squint.

I suggested he try out to work San Clemente in the summer of 1990, which he did. Working with him that season would be one of the fondest summers of my career. His zeal for

Jon Gulick with longboard at Trail #1 – San Onofre – (1993) – Photo: Vodrazka

surfing was so infectious, he persuaded me to paddle out almost daily and I rode more waves that summer than any other before or since.

Jon possessed a profound and wonderfully endearing appreciation for people. He was genuinely interested in their lives and their hobbies. The ongoing joke was that he would tell me about some "incredible" person he had come to know. He would extol their virtues and build them up with bold assertions of reverence, then when I finally met them, I usually found them to be utterly "average" human beings. But that example tells you a lot about Jon. He loved and truly appreciated people like no one else I've ever known. He was the kind of guy who breeds no enemies. He was a true role model for us all of us – and still is.

Living close-by in Davis, Jon and his girlfriend Gretchen became mainstays at the frequent gatherings my girlfriend and I hosted in our home in Sacramento, and he and I soon grew to be incredibly close. A now-legendary speech, amalgamated from various legendary lifeguard entities over the years contains a stanza touting the solidarity and lifelong kinship formed by guards as a result of the nature of their shared profession. In part it states, *"Lifeguards will dance at your wedding...and they will be there at your death bed."* As proof of the validity of that sentiment, not only did I dance at Gulick's wedding, but I also served as his best man, and would eventually become a godparent to his children.

Gulick – on foot patrol with rescue pack - North Sector (1992)

After that single summer at San Clemente, Gulick landed the final vacancy, joining the original North Coast crew. Owing to his lack of experience, Brown took a risk on hiring Gulick, but it was an educated risk since Jon was living in Northern California at the time, and was one of the only guards who was familiar with the ocean environs of the Sonoma Coast. Being an adventurous sort, he had already explored the coastline, scouting out all of the possible surf spots. He had also become a skilled abalone diver. His knowledge of that stretch of ocean was a tremendous asset to the newly formed North Coast Lifeguards, some of whom had never free-dove before, or surfed in cold water.

Jon held his own on the front lines with the more experienced seasonals and soaked right into the Bohemian, vagabond, ocean-loving lifestyle.

He remembered his time there fondly stating, *"I thought Salt Point was a magical area. We surfed or dove together almost every day. I couldn't get over how many abalone there were along that stretch of coast. Even though lots of people dove there, we could still get a limit of 4 legal size abs right out front on a single breath. Spearfishing was also super easy. Those cold water fish were pretty slow and we could get fish and abalone for dinner in 20 minutes. We even made our own fish smoker using a metal box we found behind the shop and an electric frying pan we found at a thrift store."*

In the two years Jon served on the North Coast, he would be involved in many heavy calls, and would make his own unique contribution to the program.

~

In the process of compiling the stories for this book, I had several long talks with Don Straub. I asked him about the overall mettle of the original crew. The mere fact they chose to move north and accept that work assignment validated a sense of daring in every one of them which was beyond reproach. But working shoulder to shoulder, the nature of their work would expose their strengths and weaknesses. In time, their foibles, quirks, and flaws, as well as their hidden skills, valor and ability to overcome adversity, would surface and assimilate into the totality of their worth as lifeguards and their character as human beings. Some of the relationships formed there would last a lifetime, while, for reasons still a mystery, several of the guards would leave, and essentially vanish from the lifeguard community completely.

But while they were there, in that magical convergence of space and time, they accepted an unsaid responsibility to protect each other first, and at all costs. The connecting fiber, which weaved through all of the heavy calls and precarious situations you will soon read about, was a continuum of *ultimate trust*, knowing regardless of the circumstances, they had each other's backs. In that regard, every one of them proved worthy.

In the words of Straub, *"Being up north and working with those guards, if I was dying in 20 foot surf, I always knew my partners would come for me. Some of them, intelligently, might initially hesitate. They would call for " Henry-I" (the rescue helicopter) and stand by to see how things would work out. But eventually, if necessary, every one of them would swim out to bail me out of a tough jam. Making big rescues in big surf, especially off the boat, we realized early on that we ourselves were our only real back up. This wasn't San Diego Coast where you swim out on a rescue and everybody and their brother responds to back you up."*

In a critical and retrospective review of those first five years, after countless hours of interviews with those guards, and scrutiny of their formative rescues and medical calls, one factor shined clear and bright. After pulling on their wetsuits, standing alone on the shore, beholding victims who had somehow managed to get themselves into various terrifying and potentially deadly situations in the sea, every one of those guards keyed the radio mic and uttered the same three words phrase before scampering down the rocks and swimming out into the uncertainty of the unfolding rescue.

"One Guard Out."

There was never a time when even one of them chose not to go.

Lifeguard Nate Buck descends below a 14' wall of water (1996) – Photo: Tom Neth

6

A BOLD ENTRANCE

Lifeguards Scott Melvin and Kurt Loeffler (1990) – Photo: Unknown

On an August morning in 1990, Kurt Loeffler and Scott Melvin, the first two field guards to report for duty on the North Coast, were scheduled to arrive at the Sonoma Coast District Office to sign their paperwork.

Coming from Huntington, one of the largest State Park districts in California, Loeffler and Melvin were accustomed to being somewhat lost amidst the multitude of 250 *other* State Parks employees in their jurisdiction. The Sonoma Coast, on the other hand, was a far more modest district; so small and quaint in fact, every person who wore a State Parks uniform knew each other.

Like adopting two new children into a family, the arrival of *any* new employee on the Sonoma Coast was an event in and of itself, but the buzz amongst the state parks office staff - that they would be welcoming the *first lifeguards* on the North Coast - had been brewing for months. Unlike the existing rangers, maintenance workers, environmentalists, park aides, and office staff members, these two men represented a new type of employee, and like it or not, they were an oddity. The four women who attended to the tasks of collecting time cards, processing purchase orders, and issuing paychecks had never met a Southern Californian Lifeguard before, and understandably they were curious to see if the incarnation of these mysterious men matched the preconceived image in their minds; one fabricated almost entirely on the handsome actors portrayed on "*Baywatch.*"

Hickey had done his best to dispel the age-old stereotypes that Ocean Lifeguards were nothing more than scantily-clad, muscle-bound, free-loving hippies with a propensity towards a party-lifestyle and carousing with girls. "These are Peace Officers," he contended, "reputable men who had ascended to a level of reverence and honor in their communities by upholding the law and administering to the needs of the general public." Although Hickey's testimonial was believable, understandably the office women still wanted to see for themselves.

The District Office was a small rustic building set amongst a settlement of quaint historic structures in Duncans Mills, at the site of an old railroad stop. Behind the tiny store and a small café, stood the yellow painted wooden office building where a small group of State Park managers and office personnel tended to their duties each day.

Loeffler and Melvin had every intention of arriving on time, but this was before the days of the internet, cell phones, or GPS units, and they were not entirely sure where the tiny enclave of Duncans Mills actually was. Not wanting to "suit up" in their cop-gear before going on duty, they threw their uniforms, gun belts, and bullet-proof vests into the trunk and drove off to the nearest gas station to purchase a roadmap. Standing next to the gas pumps, they scrutinized the best route to reach Duncans Mills and, upon reaching an agreement, sped off.

Unfamiliar with the winding roads, and the rural topography of Sonoma County...and feeling compelled to stop and check out several of the cool sights along the way, at some point they realized they would arrive painfully late to their first day of work. Meanwhile, the four women, brimming with excitement for their impending arrival, kept peering through the large bay window, searching for any sign of the guards so they could notify the others.

As it turned out, the office staff would have no problem identifying them as they pulled into the gravel lot rather hot, skidding to halt some 30 minutes late. Someone called out to the others and a dozen or so faces appeared in the window.

To the city-raised, Southern Californians, they probably felt like they were in the remote wilderness, which is likely why they decided that it would be appropriate to "get suited up" in the parking area, not even remotely aware that the team of fellow employees they were about to meet for the first time, were watching them just 20-yards away.

Immediately confirming every stereo-type ever consigned to lifeguards, while at the same time embedding irreversible images into the tender minds of the office staff, then proceeded to strip down naked, shining their bare white butts squarely in the direction of the staff, two of whom, in a matter of minutes, would be sitting alongside them and guiding them through their transfer paperwork.

After a moment of shocked disbelief, the entire group erupted into laughter.

Above the ruckus of the collective laughter, one women then boldly yelled:

"THE LIFEGUARDS ARE HERE!"

7

CHALLENGES

On state beaches across Southern California, the rookie guards' first day on the beach is a ritual known as the "Rookie Tour." The young guards are loaded into the bed of a truck and are driven along every stretch of beach in their district. Stops are made every few minutes so the elders can point out the unique features and subtle nuances of each section of beach; the locations where inshore holes tend to form, the favorite sand bars where sting rays tend to congregate, the usual surf spots along with their fickle tendencies, the troughs and channels where the rips tend to pull the strongest, and the gathering places where underage teenagers secretly guzzle beer from red cups.

Similarly, on a dreary day, clouded in fog and gloom, it was Chief Ranger Hickey who greeted his newly arrived Permanents and set off with them on his own guided orientation tour of the Sonoma Coast District. Hickey's excursion, infused with alternating themes of dread and melancholy, quickly began to sound more like an on-going speech intended to convince them NOT to work there. His descriptions of the various locations were punctuated with unique stories and vignettes, none of which did much to lighten the mood.

While looking out at Bodega Head, Loeffler noticed a little point break far below them that looked appeared to be a decent wave, and wondered out loud why no one was surfing there. Hickey quickly explained the area was one of the "sharkiest" areas in the county, adding that just recently, a crab fisherman, while setting his traps, was greeted by a massive White Shark which shot up from the depths of the ocean in spectacular fashion, attacked one of his two-foot long floats, and swallowed it whole.

"Understood," said Loeffler. "No surfing there."

Later, at Duncans Landing, watching the waves breaking some 30 feet below, Hickey recalled that one day the surf was so large there, a Honda Civic, parked where their patrol truck now sat, was hit by waves with such force that it was pushed across the entire lot, some 25-yards away. The guards, spitting out sunflower seeds with their hands in their pockets, nodded pensively, imagining how huge a wave would have to be to crest the 30-foot bluff and still have enough residual power to physically move the car.

His descriptions of the distinctive topography of each area, along with the ocean's unique hydrology were further dramatized by the daunting statistics and gory details of all of the fatalities which had occurred there since 1950.

To a lifeguard, chronicling the death toll was like repeating a mantra of failure, and as they arrived at each new setting, the guards stood on the rocks, and somberly peered into the churning water. The heartbreaking reenactments of those fatalities played in their minds, as they imagined the horrible circumstances by which those people had died. Bodega Head had 11 deaths; all of whom had been swept off the rocks and into the frigid water. Salmon Creek had 7 deaths; mostly swimmers who were pulled out to sea in strong rip currents. Another 9 people had been swept off the rocks and drowned at Duncans Landing.

As the tour continued, so did the death toll. Wright's Beach had 17 drownings. The Russian River mouth at Jenner had claimed 6 lives. The tour ended at Goat Rock which, Hickey remorsefully admitted, was the undisputed leader in fatalities. An astonishing 32 people had lost their lives on that ¾ mile stretch of beach. Some had been climbing on Goat Rock itself and had been washed into the ocean by large waves, but most unsuspecting victims had been engaged in nothing more adventurous than strolling along the wet sand, when they were knocked off their feet by a large wave, dragged into the inshore hole and overcome by the pounding shore break.

Hickey further explained - the ocean was not selective in choosing her victims. With equal ferocity she claimed young and old, athletic and frail, male and female. The only consistent demographic was the victim's naïve and sometimes blatant disregard for the power of the ocean. At Goat Rock, Hickey confided that they were still reeling from one of the most tragic events in recent history. In the exact spot they were standing, a grandmother lost sight of her three-year old grandson momentarily and he was swept into the sea. In an act of desperation, she entered the water attempting to save him. Witnesses stated that almost instantly, both of their bodies were swallowed by the sea. Two bystanders entered the water to try and save them, and narrowly avoided losing their lives as well. In fact, State Parks' statistics documented the startling prevalence of "bystander drowning," and the heartbreaking truth that 14 of the fatal drownings involved Good Samaritans who courageously entered the violent ocean attempting to save someone and lost their life in the process.

Sadly, Hickey expounded, the recent event was not unusual, and if you change a few faces and ages, similar scenes had played out at Goat Rock like a nightmarish recurrent movie for a generation or more.

The other common victims in the South Sector were the fishermen who, determined to access remote fishing areas, climbed out onto the cliff-side rocks, fully exposed to the massive surf crashing just below them. Their lack of appreciation for the power of the ocean played out in dramatic fashion when a rogue wave engulfed them in a wall of water and washed them into the ocean. In the frigid water, with their clothing weighing them down, it was almost impossible to stay afloat. The pounding surf prevented them from climbing back onto the rocks, so their only chance for survival was to swim to some safe beach, but owing to the remote area they had chosen to access, few were able to reach the shoreline alive.

A fisherman tempts fate – North Sector (1992) – Photo: Loeffler

As if the cold and inhospitable ocean wasn't enough to force the guards to reconsider their decision to work there, while they stood near Goat Rock, Hickey returned to the topic of sharks, adding the rather sobering fact that the waters directly off shore were notorious for them, and in fact experts in the field often came to that very area to study them. He added that shark stories have a tendency to get exaggerated with graphic and inflated drama, but up there, the stories needed no hyperbole, as sightings of large sharks were quite common.

Soon after, as Hickey nonchalantly explained a few more entry points and exit locations the guards could use to rescue their victims, it was inevitable that disastrous scenarios began playing in the lifeguards' minds, visualizing themselves swimming out in that inhospitable ocean - and coming face to face with some massive deadly predator.

By late afternoon the South Sector tour was completed. For those keeping score, the death toll ended at 94 lives lost.

The following day, they would tour the North Sector and the death count would resume once more.

The victim profiles in the North Sector were largely dominated by abalone divers. Regulations stated that any diver procuring abalone from the bottom must do so without the aid of SCUBA or any other underwater breathing apparatus. Thus their new clientele would be "Free Divers" whom they would soon come to know quite well. Unlike the South Sector victim who were unexpectedly swept into the ocean and found themselves immediately fighting for their lives, the typical North Sector diver, wearing varying layers of neoprene, tended float around on the ocean surface for a while. Although they planned on being in the ocean, most of them had no intention of leaving the relative calm of the inside coves and crannies. The majority were divers with limited skills, who entered the water hoping to come across the rare abalone in less than 8' of water.

As mentioned, in order to stay alive, the free-divers' return to the surface was a recurring challenge requiring nothing short of 100% success after every dive. Conversely there were plenty of "issues" which could hinder their safe ascent. One of the most notable of these was the kelp. Bull Kelp was so prevalent in the North Sector that many divers strapped holstered dive knives to their lower leg for quick access in the event they found themselves tangled in the thick strands below the surface. Unfortunately the tenacious strands of kelp had a tendency to get caught in *any type of device* or implement attached to the divers. In a cruel irony, several divers drowned as a result of their knife holsters becoming hopelessly snagged in kelp.

Divers also got stuck in caves, got their hands pinned under abalone, became tangled in their spear gun line, or got spiked by poisonous fish. They also committed plenty of errors in judgment, compromising their safe return to the surface by diving too deep, staying down too long, or being rendered unconscious from shallow water black out.

But by far, the greatest threat to divers was the punishing and seemingly ever-present surf.

A Free Diver contemplates his entry – North Sector (1991)

Without a doubt, the surf was the diver's worst enemy. In order to access the safe deeper water, the divers had to pass through the shallow and rocky environment of the impact zone. If they timed their entry poorly, or took too long getting out in between sets, they were destined to get slammed by the waves, and battered back onto the rocks, often times with grave consequences. The lucky ones lost only their gear. The unlucky or unskilled were often punished with some degree of bodily harm. Occasionally that impact was severe enough to render them unconscious. On calm days, the guards would often dive in the popular spots to collect various pieces of dive gear found on the bottom, all of it jettisoned by hapless divers involved in some previous struggle with Mother Ocean. Eventually, the lifeguard dive locker held an impressive stockpile of dive gear, and the guards could choose from a wide selection of the latest dive masks, fins, snorkels, abalone irons, and weight belts. Needless to say, they never had to purchase any dive gear for themselves.

The large surf also created powerful rip currents. Unlike the sandy beaches of Southern California, rips along the rocky coastline are often difficult to identify. On the distant sandy beaches of Huntington or Carlsbad, the customary upwelling of sand on the inside is carried in the outflowing rip current, providing trained guards with a relatively obvious milky-brown demarcation. Conversely, rips on the rocky shoreline contain little or no sand, thus they lacked the customary delineation and were referred to as "clear-water rips." Unsuspecting divers often found themselves defenseless in the pull of these strong rips. Many were not strong swimmers, and clung tightly to their abalone float tubes, which were basically inner-tubes with a mesh covering. With their arms occupied and only a weak kick, they were severely limited in their ability to propel themselves against the strong flow.

The "rock pickers" were at an even greater disadvantage. They wore tennis shoes and slithered around the kelp covered rocks at low tide, searching under hidden ledges to find a rare legal abalone. Since they had no intention of swimming, if they happened to get washed into a rip (which occasionally happened), they were forced to flounder in the ocean, praying someone would come rescue them.

Rock Picker

The structure of the rocks along the coastline was a random and continuous obstacle field; harsh, jagged and unforgiving, punctuated by sea stacks and wash rocks which became the focal points for the large breaking waves. Even underwater, unwary divers were often pounded into submerged rocks by the force of incoming waves.

Even the skilled and well-conditioned diver who managed to avoid all of these pitfalls still has to dive down anywhere from fifteen to thirty feet to reach the bottom while holding their breath just to begin the search for a legal-prized abalone.

The original guards were facing a great unknown. They had heard the war stories and the pessimism and knew in the coming months, the winter swells would arrive. The day was coming when, facing daunting conditions and a struggling victim, they would have to swim out into those violent seas, entering an aquatic world more intense, colder, and less forgiving than anything they had ever ventured into before. Yet every one of them had proven themselves as capable ocean rescuers and were confident in their skills.

Before they arrived they increased their training regimen exponentially, preparing themselves for the challenges certain to come. There will likely always be a healthy level of peer pressure amongst lifeguards and in this case it served them well, since no one wanted to be the lifeguard who had to "tap out" of a rescue, admitting they couldn't (or wouldn't) go in.

But the smoldering and overarching truth, left to muddy that confidence was the simple fact that...

No lifeguards had ever successfully swam out to make rescues there before.

Hickey had anticipated their apprehension and breeched the subject they all were quietly wondering, tipping his hand in the process. He confessed, "A lot of people feel we are crazy to bring you guys up here to patrol the coast. Their reasons are varied, but the most common one is simply because it's never been done before. I want you to know - although I personally feel confident you will succeed, there are many others who are convinced you will fail. I can't say with certainty you *will* be successful, but I do know *this* for sure...*if you guys can't make these rescues, no one can.*"

It was a great speech and it hit them squarely in the chest. Hickey knew his target audience and his message tapped into their sense of altruism and their competitive fire.

Hickey's lifeguards were ready to rumble.

8

TAKING THE FIELD

Tourists view 12' surf rolling in at Windermere Point (1991) – Photo: Loeffler

The State Lifeguards have a generational history of understating their accomplishments and failing to capitalize on opportunities to showcase their skills and achievements. Predictably the North Coast Lifeguards arrival was so completely unheralded, most other agencies didn't even know the State Parks was implementing their program in Sonoma County. In fact, even the United States Lifesaving Association made no mention of their endeavor, and one is left to wonder whether they were even aware of the historic undertaking occurring in their common profession.

But in retrospect, their arrival on the Sonoma Coast was truly momentous. Whether they realized it or not, every member of the original crew would soon become a part of lifeguard history.

In late August of 1990, the Sonoma Coast Lifeguards "took the field" for the first time.

Led by Supervisor Bud Brown, Permanents Loeffler and Melvin began patrolling the coast, soon to be joined by Osh McNulty, and Steve Franklin shortly thereafter.

The starting front line Seasonals would be Straub, Haug, and Schardt, but soon their ranks too would be fortified with Martino, Carter and Gulick.

One can only imagine the sense of trepidation they felt as they patrolled along the coastline searching for some kind of "trouble," yet not being entirely sure what that trouble might look like.

Each of them was issued a brand new, day-glow blue and yellow, '80s style, 5 mm thick wetsuit with attached hood. They were also given booties, gloves, and a backpack to carry it all. Since their Southern California swim fins would not fit over their booties, they were tasked to purchase over-sized fins; any brand of their choosing.

Realizing the standard State Lifeguard uniform (red trunks, white shirt, and navy blue jacket) was inadequate in that cold environment, the Perms were approved to wear pilot-style jump suits with a single zip down the front. The idea was brilliant and soon after, permission was given for the Seasonals to wear them too. The jump suit was warmer, covered their legs while walking through brush, and as a bonus, made them look like "Top-Gun" pilots. More importantly, it facilitated "stripping out" in seconds to get their wetsuits on. Of course they all wore their reds underneath. Most of the guards wore the jump suits daily and had their names embroidered on the chest patch, allowing them to blend in with the Sheriff Deputies and Flight Medics.

They would use the same style of Peterson rescue buoys they had been accustomed to down south.

The guards were released into their new environment to patrol the coastline in search of a new kind of victim; someone in the South Sector who, as the statistics suggested, would be swept out to sea by the shore-pounding surf. The North Sector guards began scrutinizing divers, trying to familiarize themselves with the numerous ways in which they could get themselves into trouble.

In true North Coast fashion, their first major call would be neither.

9-8-1990
THE GREAT WHITE WELCOME

As if a welcome note from Poseidon himself, their first major call would be a dramatic shark attack, occurring not at Goat Rock, or at Salt Point, but rather at a seldom visited area known as Russian Gulch, smack dab between the two sectors. The victim would be the seemingly immortal Rodney Orr. Although they had not yet met Rodney, he was already a fixture on the North Coast, and in time virtually all of them would come to know him well. His introduction could not have been more dramatic.

It was universally agreed Rodney Orr was a phenomenal free-diver. He had a beat up old paddleboard he used to access the deeper waters where he preferred to dive. Even at 49-years old, his bottom time (the amount of time a diver spends under water on each dive) was repeatedly around two full minutes, with only a short break to recover between dives on the surface.

Rodney stated he had been diving about 200-meters from shore when he saw several harbor seals (also known as "shark snacks") rapidly scatter. He had already collected his allotment of four abalone and was on the surface when the water instantly exploded around him. The shark grabbed Orr by his head and shoulders and thrashed him across the surface like a wet rag. Blood poured over his face, obscuring his vision but he distinctly remembered the unnerving sight of the *inside* of the shark's teeth as his face was actually *inside the shark's mouth*. The shark dragged him by his head and shoulders for at least 30 feet, and at some point he felt his body collide with his board. During the ordeal, Orr beat the side of the shark's head with his spear gun and ultimately the shark released him. Rodney then watched the predator descend and slowly fade out of sight.

Still bleeding and a quarter mile off-shore, with no one around in that desolate area, Orr kicked over to his board, and began the feverish paddle for land, all the while surveying the dark water around him, and praying the shark would not return to finish him off. Once safely on shore, he was able to better assess his wounds and felt confident that he would not bleed-out. But he also knew he would never be able to drive himself to the hospital. Having no alternative, dazed, shocky, and still actively bleeding from several areas on his face and neck, Rodney walked out to the roadway in hopes of flagging someone down. There he stood, with his face and torso covered in maroon blood, looking very much like a man *who had just been attacked by a shark*. One can only imagine the shocking sight he must have been for a southbound CHP Officer who rounded the corner at Russian Gulch and was confronted with a bloody, wetsuit-clad diver standing in the middle of the roadway, frantically waving for help.

The officer stopped and immediately requested the Sheriff's Rescue Helicopter to evacuate the stricken diver. Interestingly, neither the officer nor his dispatcher requested assistance from lifeguards, who were in the area and could have rendered medical care long before the helo arrived. Only later was it discovered that the reason for the non-call was because no one had bothered to announce the lifeguards' arrival to the neighboring agencies, so of course they were not plugged into the 911 system. In fact, most agencies didn't even know they existed and on later calls in which the lifeguards were first-on-scene, the arriving sheriffs often viewed them with confusion. A common greeting the lifeguards heard was "who the Hell are you guys?!"

Only by coincidence, Scott Melvin happened upon the scene just as the traumatized diver was being loaded into the helo. Orr was flown to Santa Rosa Community Hospital where he was treated for multiple lacerations and punctures to his face, neck, and shoulder. The wounds would eventually fuse into permanent scars which the charismatic Rodney Orr wore like an ultimate badge of honor.

As an addendum to the story, there are few people alive who can say they survived an attack by a Great White Shark. But what made this call *truly* remarkable was the fact this was Orr's SECOND attack. Yes, you read that correctly. In the small circle of fishermen, lifeguards, and surfers, the event would instantly raise Rodney's status to stratospheric proportions as being the *only person on the planet who had been bitten by a Great White Shark TWICE*. Subsequently, Rodney Orr would eventually become a fixture of "Shark Week" every year thereafter.

For the curious, the first attack happened on May 21, 1961. Rodney was just 20 years old diving for abalone with a buddy off their small boat at Tomales Point, an area now notorious for shark sightings. He was on the bottom, prying an abalone from the rocks when he saw the predator approaching. He tried to escape behind the safety of a large outcropping but he didn't make it. The

Rodney Orr – Recovering (1991)
Photo: Courtesy Rodney Orr

shark charged. Rodney raised his arm in defense, deflecting the shark's open mouth away from his chest. The shark grabbed him by his hip and Rodney had the wherewithal to start gouging at one of the shark's eyes. His counter-attack proved successful, as the shark released its grip on him. Rodney surfaced and immediately began nervously swimming towards the boat as the shark reappeared and began circling. A middle-aged couple who were fishing on a boat nearby saw both Orr and the shark on the surface and Rodney distinctly heard the woman yell the unnerving statement, "It's a shark. It's going to eat him!" Luckily, Rodney's buddy pulled him aboard the boat before the shark could strike again.

Never one to shy away from the spotlight, Rodney was only happy to share his shark stories personally with the new guards, including the long versions of both of them if you had the time. With minimal prompting he would even pull off his shirt and show you the scars.

9-22-1990
THE FIRST FATALITY

As if the shark attack wasn't dramatic enough, and counter to any scenario they could have expected for their commencement, before any lifeguard made a single rescue on the North Coast, they would be dealt their first fatality.

It was a Saturday, and coincidentally, Osh McNulty's first shift on the North Coast. Ranger Ashford "Woody" Wood was providing him an orientation to the local dive spots in the North Sector when a call came over the air for a "diver in distress" just south of Stump Beach. The area was a rough and remote section of coastline fully exposed to the northwest swell. Two men had been diving near Moon Rock when one of them noticed that his partner, a 24-year old man, did not surface from one of his dives. After a brief but frantic search, his partner spotted him lying face-down on the bottom in 20' of water with his weight belt still strapped to his hips.

Wood and McNulty arrived to the unnerving scene of a wetsuit-clad diver, struggling to drag the unconscious body of his friend over the jagged rocks while being battered by waves. The two rescuers completed the extrication and immediately initiated CPR on the lifeless diver while his partner watched in horror from a short distance away.

Unlike many of the fatalities which occurred on the coast, this diver was "freshly" dead. Having been recovered quickly, hope endured that there might be enough residual oxygen left in his heart and his brain to allow for him to be revived. Drowning in the *cold water* also increased his chances of survival, since the induced hypothermia preserved his vital organs. Thus, for this man, unlike many others, there was a chance. McNulty and Wood immediately began performing compressions and breaths. Cycles passed and they switched off roles. Periodically, Osh lifted the man's eyelids to assess whether they had constricted in response to the oxygenation, but each time he looked, they remained stubbornly fixed and dilated.

The Sheriff's Rescue Helicopter was summoned for an air evacuation. Wood and McNulty carried on with CPR continuously for 20 minutes with no sign of recovery until they arrived overhead, seized the victim and flew off to Santa Rosa General Hospital.

Unfortunately, a subsequent call to the hospital confirmed that the victim had been pronounced dead.

It was noteworthy that McNulty's tragic initiation to death on the North Coast had been thrust upon him within 4 hours of him going on-duty on his very first day of work there. In a statement capturing how little he understood about their crazy new work assignment, Osh later admitted, *"After that first CPR, I honestly thought every day was going to be like that."*

10-6-1990
THE FIRST NORTH COAST RESCUE

On the afternoon of October 6th, Audrey Haug was patrolling solo at Goat Rock Beach when three men, attempting to traverse the thigh-deep outflowing Russian River, were knocked over by the powerful flow of the river, pulled into the surf line, and quickly swept off-shore in the standing rip current.

Seconds later, beamed out across the State Park radio airwaves, the unmistakable voice of the only female lifeguard on the crew rang out with the immortal transmission they had been waiting to hear....

"Three victims just got swept out at the river mouth – One Guard Out"

The simple phrase, sent out across the airwaves, and heard by every State Parks worker on patrol that day, was significant...The first ocean rescue performed by a lifeguard on the North Coast was occurring.

Scott Melvin, patrolling some 15 minutes away near Bodega Head, hit his overhead lights and siren and began speeding north towards Goat Rock to assist. Loeffler and Schardt, patrolling in the North Sector, pulled their truck over and fell silent, leaning in toward the radio to monitor for any updates on her rescue. With no one on scene to provide updates, the airwaves remained silent.

Haug, working alone, dove into the river outflow, and swam out in the mouth of the rip through moderate surf, quickly reaching all three men and secured them on her buoy. Determining they were okay, swimming backstroke, she towed them south until they were to clear of the wide rip, then arduously towed all three back to shore unassisted.

The men, all moderately hypothermic but appreciative, denied any further medical evaluation and walked away with a new-found respect for the ocean.

Haug jogged back to her patrol vehicle, keyed her mic and stated *"Code-4 - guard returned"* thereby successfully completing the rescue. Some 20 miles north of her location, Loeffler and Schardt let out a cheer and shared a high-five in the cab of their truck.

Melvin arrived on scene in time to see the victims walking away on their own. Smiling widely, he pulled his vehicle up next to Haug's. A brief exchange between the guards ensued which focused more on the hear-and-now specifics of the rescue as opposed to the symbolic gravity of the historic event which had just occurred. As they de-briefed, Haug dried off and changed out of her wetsuit. With no press or associated hoopla, soon after, both guards simply went back on patrol.

In the grand scheme of ocean rescues, the save was routine. The surf was moderate, and the victims, though struggling in the cold water, were young and would likely have eventually been able to reach the shore on their own.

But the rescue marked a milestone for the guards. It was the first convergence of frigid water, North Coast surf, a lifeguard, struggling victims and a healthy dose of uncertainty....and it ended well, supporting the guards' self-assurance that it *could* be done, of course the immediate added caveat which sprang into their minds was *"at least in those conditions."* With the infamous huge surf of winter looming on the horizon, none of them were ready to tout their skills or get cocky.

But that first North Coast rescue by the lifeguards seemed to break the proverbial ice. The following day Dave Schardt rescued two divers at Salt Point. The next weekend Haug logged three more rescues at Goat Rock, and as the surf began to increase with the advent of fall, all of the guards began making rescues with some regularity.

On October 20th it would be Schardt again who rescued three men from an over-turned boat at the mouth of the Russian River.

Melvin's first rescue involved two kayakers who were swept out to sea in the spot where Haug had made her rescue at the Russian River mouth. He recalled, "It was pretty surreal, I had my overhead lights spinning on the truck when I swam out...and with the beach easily visible from the roadway above at Jenner, the lights attracted the attention of the passing motorists who stopped to watch. It was a lengthy rescue and by the time I had pulled in both kayakers and their boats, PCH was packed with onlookers. It was the largest audience I ever had for any rescue."

A review of the Activity Log for the month chronicles the fact that after Haug's initial rescue, a fairly consistent stream of rescues ensued. For the new North Coast lifeguards, it was *Show Time!*

They had plenty to learn. They studied every area of the coastline with a diligence reflecting the fact their own safety could depend on their knowledge of viable accesses into the ocean, the rocky shelters they might utilize from various swell directions, and most importantly, the down-current exit locations where they could escape from the sea when the large surf shut down their usual exits.

Their ongoing mental drills involved "what if" scenarios of various hypothetical situations, and the guards quizzed each other to identify the most plausible strategies for making their theoretical rescues, knowing that it would only be a matter of time before they became real.

Besides Straub, their collective experience with the IRB (Inflatable Rescue Boat) was only rudimentary. But they practiced diligently, experimenting with varying methods to perform rescues. In precarious areas inside the surf line where submerged rocks prevented access, they used throw bags to reach victims. Sometimes the deckhand swam off the boat with a line connected to the boat, harkened back to a variation of the old "belt and reel" method of rescue. But an unexpected problem quickly arose when they discovered the weight of the line tended to plow both rescuers and victims under water. To remedy this, and add flotation, they tried sending the deck-hand off the boat with a boogie board on some rescues. In that scenario, the operator would come in "hot" dropping off the deck hand with the board. The skipper would then return, throw the deckhand a line, and tow both victim and rescuer out. Amazingly it worked and became another viable method in their bag of tricks.

～

The rangers worked to orient and familiarize the guards with the entire coastline. Many of the coves, landmarks and dive spots had unofficial names which were old colloquialisms or slang terms, and the guards did their best to learn them all. But inevitably, emergency calls were reported in remote locations with vague regional names they were unfamiliar with. This forced the guards into the unnerving situation of driving back and forth along the Coast Highway with their lights flashing, waiting to be flagged down by any bystander who could provide them with a more accurate location for the incident, all the while knowing their victim was likely struggling somewhere out there.

Many calls were in remote locations with no vehicular access. In those situations, if the boat was unavailable or too far away, they ditched their truck, ran out to the edge of the bluffs, then scampered down narrow deer trails to reach a viable access point to swim out.

～

Compounding their challenges, in some of the more secluded areas, the guards often discovered their portable radios were "out of range." Thus, with some potentially dangerous aquatic situation developing before them, and their repeated requests for back-up unheard, they soon faced the sobering reality that they were truly on their own. With no alternative, they were forced to drop the radio and swim out alone to reach their victims in time. On those demoralizing rescues, they could find themselves swimming far off-shore and towing their victims on lengthy 30-minute rescues to reach shore, all the while scanning the shoreline in vain for back-up units which would never arrive. Knowing there would be no responding helicopter and no boat, the guards were then forced to put their heads down and begin the arduous task of swimming their victims back through the rocky impact zone to reach shore. After clearing the rescue, they often came to the dispiriting confirmation that no one was even aware they had swam out.

Another significant difference from guarding the beaches of Southern California was the lack of emergency medical back-up. A rudimentary volunteer fire department existed out of Timber Cove, and they were often called, but their team members were regular citizens, with regular jobs who had to be summoned from wherever they happened to be working that day. They then had to drive to the station to get the rig before responding to the scene. Even when they *did* show up on scene, they offered no advanced skills beyond an EMT level, which was on-par with most of the guards. It was not uncommon for a guard performing CPR in some remote area on that coastline, to carry on doing compressions for 40 minutes or more before *anyone* would come to their aid.

Timber Cove Volunteer Fire Crew – downed motorcyclist (1995)

Many of the original guards had never summoned a helicopter or set up a landing zone in their prior positions at Huntington or San Diego. But they quickly realized the utilization of Henry-I in getting their patients to definitive medical care often proved vital in their survival.

The bottom line was they had entered into a world of lifeguarding which was radically different from anything they could have imagined. The range and intensity of the rescues was sobering. Because they arrived before the advent of cell phones with video capabilities, it might seem rather surprising to young guards today, whose entire lives are chronicled and preserved in video, that the vast majority of these rescues were not filmed, and largely unheralded. Consequently, their stories only survived in the fading memories of those who were there and the victims whom they rescued. Thankfully, most of the seminal events which occurred during those formative years were captured in the Lifeguard Activity Log Book – and eventually further solidified in my interviews with the guards themselves.

They discovered early on that it was impossible to safeguard everyone along that vast coastline. But they also felt a glimmer of validation with the realization that they WERE saving lives. With each rescue, a bit of lifeguard goodwill went out to Poseidon. Their understanding of the district quickly improved. They learned the names and nuances of all of the coves and inlets on their patrol pattern. They came to know the most dangerous locations and they played the odds, positioning themselves where the highest probability of danger would likely be. They utilized their abilities to assess victims, honed by countless hours of scrutinizing weak swimmers back at their home beaches in Huntington, San Diego, and San Clemente and they leaned on that intuition to anticipate rescues.

And ever so gradually, they began to believe they *could* do the impossible; to safeguard an area of coastline which just about everyone (except the guards themselves) thought was impossible.

9

WELCOME TO THE NEIGHBORHOOD

Picketers gather at the entrance to Bodega Head to protest State Parks' fees (1991)

In retrospect, considering the thousands of rescues made in the 30-year history of guarding the Sonoma Coast, and the hundreds of lives which certainly have been saved, one might assume the lifeguards' arrival, back in 1990, would have been heralded with a parade, and a feast of abalone and ling cod hosted by the locals.

Far from it.

In an absolutely disastrous coincidence of bad timing, their appearance on the coast happened to coincide with the State Parks decision to begin charging fees to visit their local beaches. The residents obviously inferred the fee increase was designed to cover the cost of these new lifeguards, and many were understandably incensed they would have to begin paying to enjoy *their own* beaches which, up until the guards' arrival, and in fact since the dawn of time, had been free.

Bumper stickers and T-shirts appeared seemingly overnight proclaiming "FREE OUR BEACHES." The offending agency, The California State Parks, was viewed as a money-hungry oppressor with no right to claim sovereign rule over these wild beaches. To the residents, these beaches belonged to the local flora and fauna which, interestingly in their view, included themselves.

They also viewed the State Parks as a vulnerable adversary. Since their staff were tasked with *public service* and were paid, at least in part, by the local citizenry in the form of state taxes, the State Parks managers were obligated to listen to the locals' contentions and objections. Their unification against the oppressive State Parks was swift, potent, and virtually unanimous.

Californians - especially the Northern sub-culture - have never been known to shy away from any nobly-intentioned environmental protest and it didn't take much prodding to mobilize their troops in opposition to this perceived tyranny.

Worse yet, a small but vocal sub-group of locals were "eco-activists" by nature. Despite the irony the State Parks philosophies were ostensibly in line with their own as far as preservation of the natural resources, these individuals jumped on the opposition bandwagon en masse, and added their fervent tenacity to stir the pot more vigorously. Their contention, albeit it extreme, was the mere presence of the guards on the beaches was a detriment to the local wildlife, and that the tire tracks left by the guard's patrol vehicles were scarring the aesthetics of the beach. In meetings with Brian Hickey, when he showed them the objective statistics about the guards' successful rescues, and the declining numbers of drownings, their response was, *"We would rather see people die than have jeep tracks on the beach."* With that as their opening salvo, Hickey and the other managers likely reasoned it was impossible to negotiate with lunatics.

Banded together, the opposition forces mobilized into potent protest groups. They exercised their First Amendment rights by making posters and stationing themselves at park entrances, and encouraged arriving visitors NOT to pay the fees. Although the true adversaries of their wrath were actually the decision-making bureaucrats in Sacramento, those individuals - who had the power to change the policy - rarely left their offices. But the lifeguards did, and were forced to drive past the protestors a dozen times a day. As one might expect, those same guards, positioned firmly at the bottom of the totem pole, became the prime targets of the protesters vitriol.

A reasonable person might assume that in the face of this powder keg of social discord and unrest, the Peace Officer Perms would "lay low" and do their best to patronize the swarming crowds while waiting for the fervor to settle a bit. Essentially, they did the opposite, choosing instead to figuratively grab a few large sticks and begin battering the hives.

As eluded to, the roles and duties of generalist State Park Lifeguard Peace Officers are customarily modified to the better align with the vibe and needs of the park they are assigned to. Officers working in the urban areas like Huntington are asked to adapt their work assignments to lean heavily on law enforcement. Other officers, who might be assigned to some quaint seaside town in Northern California, like Bodega Bay for instance, might choose to focus less on law enforcement.

Apparently the arriving officers from Huntington never got that memo. Despite the already strained relationship with their new clientele, the officers emerged out of the gate and began writing citations to anyone who so much as bent the law.

This, to no one's surprise, pissed off the locals even more. When cited, and despite the fact the citations were valid and justified, the "victims" commiserated and complained amongst themselves about the *egregious wrongs* thrust upon them, and began to coalesce into an ever-expanding base of opposition. In their shared rage, they eventually arrived at the only logical conclusion as to why these new "gun-toting lifeguards" felt compelled to desecrate them in such a malicious way...they were spawned from the devil himself.

Of course the Seasonals had nothing to do with the fee increase OR the citations, but the logo on the side of their truck displayed the same familiar State Parks' Bear as the one pasted on the Permanent's trucks, so they were guilty by association, and similarly type-cast as demons.

∾

Lost in all of this, was the irony that these reviled Southern California transfers were bringing a wealth of rescue experience, along with a genuine and altruistic desire to help, to a dangerous coastline which desperately needed their services. And yet, they found themselves hated by the very people whom they came to serve.

Back on their home beaches of San Clemente, Huntington, and San Diego, the lifeguards enjoyed a level of esteem, often bordering on *adoration,* from the locals. Their image, as Ocean guardians had become a fundamental and iconic part of beach culture, as essential and recognizable as brightly colored surfboards, lime green bikinis and the soundtrack of Good Vibrations. Their beaches, their towers and their jeeps routinely appeared on TV commercials, and their rescues were often seen on the 5:00 o'clock news. Alas, they soon learned that the local populace of Northern Californians, frankly, didn't care much for *anything* which came out of Southern California, including lifeguards, with all of their associated beachy hoopla.

This was Sonoma County where very few of the residents surfed. Many arrived at the beach alone, bundled against the cold winds to be inspired by the rugged cliffs and the pounding waves. Others came in groups to beat drums and celebrate the equinoxes and the quarterly solstices. Most of the women never even owned a bikini.

Mike Martino remembers, *"One group of west county women celebrated what they called 'Oceansong and Earthdance'. These women would sit in a circle with paper bags lit up by candles in the sand, then shake rattles and play drums for an hour. They would hold hands and sing songs under an oak tree near the beach chanting invocations to*

Mother Earth. It was a safe bet to assume no part of their invocation included men in trucks driving across the sands of Sonoma County's beaches interrupting their vibe to warn these earth mothers of the dangers of chanting too close to the large surf."

To make matters worse, the antiquated and largely negative stereotypes of lifeguards, which had finally burned down to embers during the '80s, was being stoked back ablaze by the new TV sensation, *"Baywatch"* which, in yet another unfortunate twist, had just starting airing the year before their arrival. The show's not-so-subliminal underlying themes, seemingly rooted on unbridled sexuality, only confirmed the public's perception they were young, testosterone-driven, surfer-type men who idled their days away soaking up the sun, flexing their muscles, and rubbing sun tan lotion on the backs of bikini-clad girls. The locals wanted no part of these misogynistic playboys working on their beaches and being paid with their tax dollars.

Animosity brewed hot among the locals and soon the entire lifeguard staff experienced something they had never felt back on their home beaches in Southern California.

They were hated.

12-20-1990
THE SANTA INCIDENT

Differing variations of the following incident have been offered by both sides through the years. As you will soon see, it's a story vulnerable to exaggeration. In researching the event, I began with a narrative written by Mike Martino, which was later supplemented with an interview with Kurt Loeffler himself, who, as you are about to find out, was the focal point of the incident. I feel confident this version of the story is a true representation of what actually happened on that fateful day in late 1990, just outside of Bodega Bay.

On the first Saturday of December, protestors manned picket lines at State Parks entrances with signs reading, "FREE THE BEACHES," in continued protest of the new fees. Meanwhile, the Bodega Bay Grange Hall had scheduled an appearance by Santa Claus and his female assistant, Jelly Belly to help the children celebrate *"Bay Days."*

As was the established tradition in this fishing enclave, Santa's arrival into town would not be by sleigh, but rather by boat. At the dock, Santa and Jelly Belly would then transfer into the bed of a pick-up truck and be driven through the town of Bodega Bay with the accompanying sound track of joyous, though somewhat distorted, Christmas songs blaring from a large boom box in the truck bed. Once they reached town, they would meet the children at the Grange Hall.

Along the route to their destination, Santa and Jelly Belly swelled with holiday spirit, eager to deliver hope and good cheer to all of the good little boys and girls.

At some point, the pick-up truck happened to cross paths with a State Park Patrol vehicle. Lifeguard Kurt Loeffler, riding with ranger Steve Edinger, saw the oncoming pickup with Santa and Jelly Belly standing in the truck bed.

As the pick-up approached, Loeffler extended his long arm out of the window and motioned for the truck to stop, which they did. Staying inside the patrol vehicle, Loeffler yelled out "All of your passengers in the bed must be seated!"

The driver, Charles Greene, nodded his understanding and Jelly Belly complied with the order, sitting on the truck bed as they drove off, however Santa, obviously feeling more naughty than nice, utterly ignored the directive and defiantly remained standing.

It's not known how much thought or foresight went into Loeffler's next move, but officers generally don't appreciate getting "blown off" when they give a law-breaker the courtesy of a verbal warning as opposed to a citation. For Loeffler, that sentiment apparently applied universally to all law-breakers, including middle-aged rotund men dressed in Santa Claus costumes.

The events of the next ten minutes would become deeply dyed into the fabric of local history in Bodega Bay, and the previously strained relationship between the locals and the new lifeguards would descend to an even deeper level of resentment and hatred. Despite all of his heroic rescues and medical aids; despite the hundreds if not thousands of people he had helped as a guard, Loeffler's "confrontation" with Santa Claus would prove to be the single most infamous moment in his career and the twisted truth of the "Santa Incident" tends to be the Loeffler story which comes up most often.

Loeffler fired up his overhead blue and red lights and performed a vehicle stop on Santa's Sleigh (which, as it turns out, happened to be a 1981 Isuzu Trooper).

Greene, assumedly in the role of Rudolph, complied by pulling the ~~sleigh~~ Isuzu off to the side of the road. Loeffler and Edinger exited their vehicle and walked over to greet them.

Loeffler asked Greene for his driver's license and the registration for the vehicle. While Greene retrieved his license, Santa (since it was HIS sleigh), climbed out of the truck bed, opened the passenger side door, and retrieved the registration from the glove box.

Loeffler looked at the driver's license and the registration, and said to Mr. Greene, "Your passengers have to be seated in the back of the truck while you are driving. If you hit the brakes, they could be thrown from the truck. You understand Charles, don't you?"

Edinger then echoed, "It's just a safety issue, Charles."

Greene said, "I understand. I used to be a reserve officer."

"Good," responded Loeffler, "I don't want to cite you, but you will have to keep your passengers seated on the bed of the truck until you get to the town. We're all adults here. Do you understand what's expected of you, Charles?"

"Yes officer, I do."

With that, Loeffler returned the documents to Green and the "sleigh" pulled away, heading toward the eagerly awaiting crowd in Bodega Bay.

Less than five minutes later, another ranger radioed Loeffler, informing him that Santa was again standing in the bed of the pick-up as the truck drove past the cheering crowd. Luckily, by then Loeffler and Edinger were well on their way north and decided not to pursue the issue further.

It's hard to imagine an event which would be more vulnerable to embellishment than this one. The local citizenry, actively seeking any evidence of perceived heavy-handedness of law enforcement in their community, had been given the Golden Goose. The mean-spirited "gun-toting" Loeffler had used his police powers to accost not only *any* citizen of Bodega Bay, but the lovable character known throughout the world as the personification of generosity, kindness, and goodwill. For the love of God, Loeffler had *harassed Santa Claus.*

News of this travesty exploded through the normally sleepy town.

For anyone who has ever played the game of "telephone," the result might not be surprising. The game involves passing a story along to a series of people, then comparing the end story to the original. In almost all cases, the ultimate narrative, often replete with stark omissions and added flourishing, often bears little resemblance to the original.

Similarly in this case, the story passed through coffee shops and boat docks, gas stations and schools, picking up steam and colorful fortifications and embellishments along the way. And with every re-telling, Kurt Loeffler was damned a little deeper. The press, eager to capitalize on the event, yet choosing NOT to interview Loeffler himself, printed the exaggerated versions, documenting a greatly enhanced conflict in which Loeffler was shouting at Saint Nick with his Billy-club drawn. The title in one local paper simply read, "*Lifeguard Arrests Santa Claus.*" One columnist quoted Jelly Belly as claiming Santa had been forced to "*contemplate the choices of civil disobedience and the children of Bodega Bay.*" No one it seemed, had bothered to acknowledge that the vehicle stop was not only justified, but actually a courteous verbal warning provided as an act of safety.

Eventually, in the fog of war, the *exaggeration* became the *story itself*, characterizing the vehicle stop as a flagrant and outrageous abuse of power. The citizens and activists now had new and potent ammunition for their letter writing campaign, and the people of Bodega Bay largely believed the inflated hype.

Loeffler, when asked to comment on why he had performed a vehicle stop on Santa Claus, calmly clarified the seemingly obvious fact, "*Santa Claus is a fictional character...the entity standing in the back of a moving vehicle was a human being.*" As far as Loeffler was concerned, he was paid to keep the public safe, which he did with diligence. Consistent with his peace officer's oath of allegiance, if he saw a safety issue, he was going to address it. No one in the community, it seemed, viewed his actions as a courtesy to prevent the man (who was not a fictional character) from being injured. Compounding all of this for Loeffler, the State Parks managers reportedly offered him little in the way of support or counsel for his decision to perform the vehicle stop.

In retrospect, Loeffler stated "*Never doubt the power of the press because it worked wonderfully. Their reporting solidified the prevailing public opinion against the lifeguard program, creating an atmosphere of mistrust, with me as their poster child."*

~

Through all of the early turmoil and confusion, in their first five months of existence, the lifeguard service logged 3,110 safety contacts, warning beachgoers of the dangers at the shoreline. Additionally, the guards made 164 cliff contacts on people who were illegally climbing in closed areas. They had handled 5 major first aids, made 3 cliff rescues and performed 13 aquatic rescues.

The challenge before them was to continue to learn the coast and to continue to save lives. The guards reasoned that given more time, eventually the citizens were sure to see the value in their work.

Meanwhile, from the local's perspective, "The Santa Incident" only solidified the sentiment these new lifeguards were nothing more than power-hungry cowboys, and they wanted them gone.

Capitalizing on the dubious start to the program, the local newspaper ran a subsequent article about the new lifeguard service titled, *"Facing a Tidal Wave of Resistance."* Photos accompany the piece including one of Scott Melvin wearing his gun, and Don Straub making a safety contact on a family at Goat Rock. One of the opening lines of the article starkly summed up the public sentiment stating *"To some beachgoers they (the lifeguards) are as welcome as a decomposing whale."*

The lifeguard's climb, to dig themselves out of the deep hole of antipathy would be a steep one.

~

The guards' favorite dining establishment for the guards in the South Sector was Lucy's Bakery in Bodega Bay. Without exaggeration it was the only business where they felt welcomed. Willard Lucy had once worked as a seasonal maintenance aide for State Parks. He stayed out of the fray of the protests, and always treated the guards with respect. The guards responded in kind by frequenting his bakery every chance they could get. Willard's dad, Bud Lucy, had been a veteran in World War II, Korea, and Vietnam, so along with his morning coffee and Danish,

Loeffler always made sure to thank Bud "For serving our country." It was a simple gesture the family never failed to appreciate.

～

While the Lucy family provided a quiet, behind the scenes admiration for the guards, there was seemingly no one in town willing to offer them any support publically.

Except one lone devotee.

Barry was a 20-year old young man, living with his loving family in Bodega Bay. Born with Down syndrome, he had been blissfully insulated from the stream of negativity directed towards the guards. In fact Barry had glommed onto the guards from the first moment he saw their patrol truck driving along the highway with their red lights and the paddleboard on the roof. When he found out they swam out into the ocean to rescue swimmers in distress, their reputation as real-life heroes was solidified in his mind.

Although Barry loved all of them, his personal favorite was Dave Schardt. The perpetually jovial Schardt was an excellent choice, who always had time to share a few stories with Barry and ask him about his action figures and his dog. Barry never quite mastered the pronunciation of Dave's last name, and referred to him fondly as "Dave Shark." No one bothered to correct him.

Several times a day, Barry's excited face could be seen peering out of the window of the family car while they meandered along the Coast Highway as the spirited fan was on a constant search for the lifeguard truck. His parents supported his passion and would often drive him around for no other reason than to try and the find them. Anytime they spotted a State Parks vehicle, they would stop and Barry would excitedly yell out, "Is Dave Shark working today?"

Eventually, all of the guards came to know the family's car and, if it passed it on the roadway, they would raise an arm out of the window to wave, of flash the overheads lights, expecting to see the exuberant smiling face of their biggest fan in the back seat, waving back passionately as they drove past.

Collectively, the guards grew to universally love their lone supporter. Barry's demonstrative expression of goodwill was like a salve for the emotionally beaten crew. Ironically, that young man never knew how much his expressions of joy had lifted their spirits.

Never once did Barry let them down.

THE SONOMA COUNTY SHERIFFS

As if the public scorn directed at the new lifeguards wasn't bad enough, they would also encounter immediate opposition from the primary law enforcement and medical response team on the Sonoma Coast; namely the Sonoma County Sheriffs. For as long as anyone could remember, they had been the de facto ocean emergency response agency in the county, and for some unknown reason, news of the lifeguards' arrival on their coastline was perceived as a threat to their dominion.

A sheriff's deputy standing over a deceased diver – awaiting Henry-I

In retrospect, it's hard to imagine why they would *not* have welcomed any entity which might be able to assist them in the harrowing task of making rescues in huge seas and the abhorrent obligation of recovering dead bodies. But their opinion seemed to be that these unpleasant jobs were *their* unpleasant jobs, and quite frankly, they didn't need any help.

Rumors had been percolating for months that these Southern California Lifeguard transplants were coming to work the Sonoma Coast, and they rightly assumed that none of the arriving guards had ever worked an extraordinary North Coast day with 15-foot surf, 49 degree water, and dozens of abalone divers venturing out into the ocean. When they were told these guards were planning on *swimming out* to make rescues without the aid of a helicopter, it solidified the fact these naïve young guards had no idea what they were getting themselves into.

The sheriffs methods of rescuing swimmers, by hoisting them out on a static line, secured to the belly of a helicopter had never before been challenged, and in their established culture, well-meaning rescuers who ventured out into the ocean to aid victims almost immediately became victims themselves, further complicating the rescues and unnecessarily risking the lives of their own staff who were then tasked with having to extricate *them* from the ocean as well.

Although there wasn't a single deputy on their force who knew *anything* about the capabilities of Ocean Lifeguards, none of them seemed willing to offer them the benefit of the doubt, and collectively, they made no secret of the fact they did not want them there. Additionally, in conversations with the State Parks Rangers, word soon leaked out that many of the Deputies were actually hoping they would fail and leave in shame with their tails between their legs.

Henry-I

Sonoma County Sheriff's Rescue Helicopter – " Henry-I" (1991)

In the phonetic alphabet used on emergency radio channels, "H" was "Henry" which is why the designation for the Sonoma County Sheriff's Rescue Helicopter had always been " Henry-I."

The guards were forced to be diplomatic with the sheriff officers. Although the sheriffs couldn't perceive of any valid need for lifeguards, the lifeguards most definitely needed the sheriffs. Admittedly the sheriffs' abilities to swim out and effect rescues in the surfline was essentially zero, but they had, at their disposal, the ultimate tool in Henry-I, which was a true lifeline in the extrication of victims (and potentially lifeguards) from horrendous situations. If the guards could swim out and stabilize a victim, they could then wait for Henry-I to arrive, and combining their services, there was a far better chance of the event ending as a "rescue" and not a body recovery.

The lead pilot for Henry-I in those days was Tom McConnell. Tom was an expert pilot, having honed his skills flying Hueys in the Vietnam War. Tom was also a true gentleman, with an American folk hero persona; part Chuck Yeager and part Jimmie Stewart. When the guards arrived, Tom was in his 40s and had already been flying rescue missions for the previous six years. As one might imagine, in his time, McConnell had witnessed more than his fair share of human drama.

There was little doubt that flying into through the narrow gorges and dangerous terrain of the Sonoma Coast, in the unpredictable weather, was a hazardous assignment. That fact was alarmingly clear to the Sheriffs since two of their recent helicopters had crashed in 1977 and 1980. In both tragedies, their pilots had been killed. One might assume that the knowledge of those catastrophes might have haunted McConnell as he struggled to keep his bird horizontal while getting blown about in the formidable winds, but the veteran pilot seemed undeterred. He admitted that flying in inclement weather and volatile winds could be challenging at times, but quickly added, "At least no one is shooting at us."

Before he had arrived, the standard rescue technique was to use a winch to lower a basket to the scene, with a crew member seated at pilot's side, calling out signals to him. But McConnell soon devised an innovative, though unorthodox system which was far quicker to set up. He would land the bird near the incident, and while the deputy/medic was laying out the 100' rescue line, McConnell would remove the pilot-side door from the helicopter. Once in the air, he didn't need a spotter. He simply leaned out from the cockpit to watch the action play out below, guiding the rescuer to the victim himself.

Pilot McConnell with Franklin (1991)

McConnell rose above the petty bickering. If he too believed the lifeguards would fail, he kept those sentiments to himself and was always cordial towards them. For that, the guards were thankful. If they could have chosen just one deputy to support their mission, it would be the skilled Henry-I pilot who might one day be called upon to lift them free from hell.

For the next eight years, the sounds of McConnell's rotor blades cutting through the misty air overhead provided a comforting realization they could hand off their panicked patient, and forego a long and often arduous swim to return them to shore.

From the time the lifeguards arrived in 1990 until his ultimate departure in 1998, Tom McConnell would pluck several hundred victims from their care in every situation imaginable. And if the guards requested, after dropping off the victim, Tom would return outside and offer a "courtesy lift" to the tired lifeguard, quickly liberated them from whatever quagmire they found themselves in, and adroitly lowering them within yards of their warm, dry patrol vehicle.

～

Early on, Don Straub met face to face with one of the sheriff officers who was conversing with ranger "Woody" at the time. Tensions were palpable and they soon got into a debate about the lifeguards' capabilities. Surprisingly Woody sided with the sheriffs, agreeing with the prevailing sentiment that the guards would never be able to cope with the cold water and large surf. The underlying disparagement was that they had no idea what they were in for.

Straub was incensed. To acclimate themselves to the brisk water, the North Sector guards had been swimming the 300 yard Gerstle buoy every morning. On an impulse, Straub proclaimed, "Hey, tomorrow morning we're going to swim the Gerstle Cove buoy, why don't you guys come and join us?" The deputy laughed out loud before he realized Don was serious.

Straub then rallied a few of the guards, and remarkably, a group of officers actually showed up. They informed the guards they were going to "get ready" and started putting on their wetsuits and pulling out their boogie boards. Meanwhile, the guards dropped their sweats and were already in their speedos. The officers looked at them in disbelief and one of them said, "You're not going to swim the buoy like that!?" To which Schardt boldly proclaimed, "Sure we are, it's only 52!"

The guards hit the water. By the time the officers had gotten their wetsuits on, the guards had already completed the 300 yard swim and gotten out.

In fact, the guards swam the Gerstle buoy regularly, just as a matter of principle and to prove to their detractors that they knew nothing about the resolve of lifeguards. They were determined to prove that they COULD swim out in that cold angry ocean to execute rescues...and by God, they WOULD make those rescues!

～

A month later, with tensions still strained with the sheriffs, Straub and Schardt were on a long rescue at Secrets - at the south end of Horseshoe Cove. By then, the guards had already made plenty of rescues and on several occasions had delivered the victims back onto dry land before Henry-I had even arrived overhead. But on this rescue the victims had been pulled far from shore in a substantial recurring rip. Straub and Schardt eventually reached the victims, strapped them in, and had begun the long and arduous swim back towards shore when Henry-I landed and set up their static line. Unfortunately Tom McConnell was not working that day, so the pilot was an officer they didn't know.

The chopper lifted, arrived overhead and lowered their deputy / rescue swimmer in the water next to them. After an exchange of pleasantries, the rescuer accepted the first of the two victims, then returned shortly thereafter to grab the second one. Of course the guards were thrilled to pass off the dead weight of the victims, before they embarked on their return swim to shore.

While swimming in, they were surprised when the chopper again returned. Smiling and seemingly friendly, the deputy offered them a "free ride to their patrol vehicle," which they both gladly accepted as a means to save some energy and to take in the amazing view.

The following morning, much to their horror, a photograph appeared in the Santa Rosa newspaper featured Don Straub, hanging under Henry-I with a caption which read "Sonoma County Sheriffs Rescue Lifeguards."

Straub was livid. If they had known him better they would have realized they had chosen the wrong guy to shame. He called the sheriffs immediately and laid into them. Suffice to say he questioned their professionalism, their ethics, and probably made a few disparaging remarks unfit for print which did nothing to salve their already strained relationship.

The sheriffs were unapologetic, stating that they *did* rescue the lifeguards and the photo was proof of that rescue. Straub was furious and offered a zesty rebuke stating, "We were offered a ride! We didn't need you! In fact we were generous enough to allow you to be part of OUR rescue! We could've towed those guys ourselves, but we were nice enough to give you the rescue to bolster your statistics!"

Despite subsequent attempts from peace makers on both sides to smooth things over, including several visits with their commanding officer by Brian Hickey and Bud Brown, the damage was done and the scars from that event would take years to heal.

One thing for certain, the lifeguards' arrival in *both sectors* appeared to be cursed from the outset.

MELVIN'S RACE with Henry-I

The crew found themselves in a continual struggle to prove their abilities to the sheriffs. The guards leaned heavily on the fact that Henry-I was housed in a hanger somewhere in Santa Rosa, miles from the ocean, and boldly asserted they could beat Henry-I to the victim on almost any rescue. The sheriffs countered that once airborne, their helo travelled a hell-of-a-lot faster than any swimming lifeguard, and vehemently disputed their claim.

As an astute reader might already infer, the challenge, although never formally agreed to, *was on!*

One of Melvin's first rescues came on a sunny and warm day on the Sonoma Coast, a unique phenomenon, according to Melvin, that seemingly occurred "about 3 days per year." The dispatcher notified him of two Boogie Boarders who had been swept out in a large rip current at Salmon Creek, adding that Henry-I had already been dispatched to the call.

The problem for Melvin was that although making a rescue on two Boogie Boarders was squarely in the wheelhouse for any guard, he was patrolling near Goat Rock at the time, a distance of over 8-miles away.

Not wanting to get "snaked" by Henry-I, he fired up his overhead lights and siren, and drove like a wild man until he arrived on scene. With people on the beach standing and pointing, he pulled on his wetsuit and, despite the fact the surf was only running about head high, he spotted the two victims far from shore in a ridiculously long rip current. Melvin later stated "they were so far from shore it was crazy...it would be hard to estimate the distance, but it was easily two full buoy swims (1,000 yards) from shore."

With no paddleboard, having to swim on a lengthy rescue like that, the guards usually fall into a long-distance pace so as not to exhaust themselves, especially since both victims had floatation, but knowing Henry-I was coming, Melvin was far too amped up to restrain himself. He tore in the water as if the victims were 50-yards away and actively drowning.

After swimming under the waves, he regained his stroke cadence and raced off-shore in the mouth of the rip, directing himself to his victims. Then, around 500 yards from shore, and with a considerable distance yet to cover, he began to hear the unmistakable, though faint thumping sound of a helicopter. Scaling the unbroken waves, he occasionally spotted his victims, and could see they were floating high in the water, in no immediate danger, yet with the helo coming, Melvin plowed ahead full sprint.

With 200 yards left to go, turning his head with every breath, he could distinctly hear the thumping getting louder and knew they were approaching. Again, he continued his frantic pace, not daring to waste any time by stopping.

Already exhausted, his last 25 yards was a ridiculous flat-out sprint, and just like a swimmer racing an adversary in an adjacent lane, only after he reached the victims did he turn and look up into the sky. The sight of Henry-I overhead, still 100 yards away, solidified the undeniable fact that he had beaten them fair and square in this rather ridiculous race.

As they circled overhead, Melvin, deeply gasping in air-hunger, tapped his wetsuit-clad head with his fist, and, screaming with delight like a madman, yelled out, "CODE-4 SUCKERS! MY RESCUE!"

In retrospect it might have been a dubious gesture. The chopper could have easily plucked his victims from his care and quickly delivered them to shore. But after his spirited display, they instead simply spun to the east and jetted clear of the scene, leaving Melvin and his two victims alone, facing an arduously long swim to get them back to shore.

Even more noteworthy, only after Melvin's defiant interaction with the chopper was over did he direct his gaze to his victims (a father and son). Despite their significant distance from shore, they floated comfortably on their boards, seeming as content as if they were bobbing in a backyard swimming pool. Ironically, at the same time, it was the lifeguard who was hyperventilating from his swim.

The father stared at Melvin with a look of concern until Scott asked him what was wrong.

"Are you okay?" asked the father, appearing genuinely worried.

"What do you mean?" gasped Melvin, obviously shattered from the swim.

In an odd reversal of roles, the dad continued, "Man, your face is kind of purple and you seem like you are really exhausted. Maybe you should take some deep breaths and calm yourself down...You'll be all right."

After choking down a hefty helping of pride, Melvin did exactly that.

And in a few minutes, having accepted his lesson in humility, yet still secretly gratified with his victory over Henry-1, he began the lengthy endeavor of towing them back to shore.

10

LIFEGUARD JOURNAL: 1991

Bud Brown - Traffic Collision with injuries – Jenner (1991) – Photo: Loeffler

Brian Hickey had a lot of skin in the game. He had invested a significant aggregate of time, effort, and most importantly his lifeguard soul into the creation of the program. A folder stuffed with State Parks records and press articles clearly documented the tragedies and deaths which had been an obvious concern for State Parks officials for over 40 years. Yet with each added drowning, their collective response failed to establish any kind of viable drowning prevention program. They posted warning signs. They put out press releases documenting the deaths and imploring the public to "NEVER TURN YOUR BACK ON THE OCEAN." Still the drownings continued. Over and over, they hung their heads and repeated the defeatist mantra *something really should be done about this,* though no one quite knew what it was they should do - Until the ex-Lifeguard Hickey arrived, rolled up his sleeves and set himself on a dogged pursuit of bringing lifeguards to the North Coast.

Knowing the common drive and altruistic nature of lifeguards, Hickey knew they *could* flourish and become an instrumental part of the EMS community. His crew were a solid group of lifeguards, all of whom had the requisite skills to make a difference.

He knew that his guards would be entering uncharted waters (both literally and figuratively) and his primary concern was for their safety. After attempting to plan for every eventuality, the great unknown, well-beyond his control, would be the private reckoning between the guards and the moody ocean herself - to determine whether they could survive in those seas.

Yet after all of the lobbying, the meticulous groundwork and logistics, the purchasing, the hiring, and the piloting through the cumbersome struggles, their emergence was almost immediately hamstrung by two issues which no one (including Hickey) could ever have seen coming.

The first was his new peace officers' heavy-handed administration of the law onto the local citizenry. The second was the State Parks' disastrous decision to begin charging day-use fees at their beaches, devastatingly ill-timed to coincide with their arrival. Both issues would throw a proverbial wrench into their well-laid plans.

2-17-1991
"ONE GREAT RESCUE"

Steve Franklin arrived a few months after the others as the 5th Permanent. To say it was not an ideal atmosphere to start his North Coast law enforcement career would be an understatement. Public animosity had peaked, and anyone wearing a LIFEGUARD patch on their shoulder and carrying a gun was viewed with abject scorn. The idealistic and enthusiastic Franklin would begin his tenure on the Sonoma Coast in a collective vortex of hate.

Welcoming his new officer, Hickey confessed that things were not good. Franklin listened intently, getting briefed on the stream of negative events which had damned the guards so deeply. By then they had made 19 significant rescues but none of them would unequivocally validate their worth. Especially so since the press, focusing instead on the fee increase, all but ignored them.

Still, Hickey truly believed they *could* right the ship, and ended his fatalistic "State of the Union" confession to Franklin with a declarative statement that what they truly needed was "***one great rescue***" to get the people's attention and open their eyes to the value of his guards. To Franklin who, by nature, was already an incendiary-type guy, Hickey's inspiring statement was like a rallying cry. By the time Steve had left Hickey's office, he was vibrating with excitement. He promised Hickey they would deliver that "one great rescue," and secretly, Franklin hoped *he* would be the guard to do it.

Unbeknownst to the two men, as they were exchanging pleasantries in Hickey's office in Duncan Mills, a fisherman from Alameda had fallen into the water in a remote area south of Blind Beach, and was in the process of drowning. With no one there to witness the event or call for help, the lifeguards were never notified.

The following morning, Steve Franklin reported for his first full day of work. Fittingly, it was a cold, sleet filled day with horizontal rain blowing hard out of the northwest. Dressed in long johns under his uniform, a bullet proof vest, trousers, uniform shirt and a thick jacket, Franklin didn't feel much like a lifeguard. As Steve was preparing the Ram Charger for duty, the dispatcher notified him that a panic-stricken woman had just reported a dead body floating in the water south of Blind Beach.

The Sonoma Coast's welcome gift to the new Lifeguard Peace Officer would be the body of the missing fisherman. Like McNulty before him, Franklin's orientation to the perilous nature of the job would be thrust upon him on his first day of work, and in Franklin's case, his very first call.

Michael Stephenson met Franklin in the parking lot. Standing outside their vehicles in the wind and intermittent rain, the two men pulled on their wetsuits and entered an ugly ocean, tattered with whitecaps by wind. They began their search along the rocks in the south area of Blind Beach and it wasn't long before they discovered the grotesque body of the fisherman.

Bodies of drowning victims recovered from lakes and pools have a certain look to them. Their bodies, weightlessly suspended in a water, are preserved and protected, unblemished with bruises, wounds, or the usual purplish tint of dependent lividity. Often they looked like stringy-haired wax figures – too white and lacking expression to even look human.

In contrast, bodies pulled from the ocean bear the scars of the incessant actions of the waves. Even small waves, rocking a deceased individual back and forth along the sandy bottom for a day or two will exact a surprising amount of damage. On that day, submerged in the surf line with a moderate 6-foot swell running, in just 24 hours the ocean had battered the man's body far beyond recognition.

Franklin was overcome with revulsion, but Stephenson maintained a sense of dutiful calm, helping Steve to deal with the most unpleasant of tasks. The two men wrangled the man's stiff remains into a body bag, then towed him to shore, before carrying him across the rocks to the parking lot, passing a few mortified early morning walkers. With no place to "hide" the body out of public view, the men unceremoniously laid him on the cold wet asphalt next to their truck and Franklin stayed with the bagged human in the rain for over an hour until the coroner arrived.

3-18-1991
MARTINO'S ARRIVAL

The newest addition to the seasonal crew would be Mike Martino in early 1991. His arrival was met with significant rains and large surf, neither of which succeeded in keeping people away from the coast. Scott Melvin was assigned to give Martino his orientation to the district. At each stop Scott pulled the cigar he was smoking out of the ashtray and relit it before they got out of the truck to survey the various locations. When they returned to the vehicle, Melvin gently placed the cigar back in the ash tray and let it burn out. As if bestowing some wise revelation, or perhaps delivering a cryptic metaphor for life itself, Melvin faced the young Martino with his eyes squinted and slowly whispered, "You never snub a cigar out, Mike, you just let it fade out slowly."

By then, every guard knew the locations and circumstances of the recent tragedies, and Melvin recounted them with Martino, as well as the past disasters, just as Hickey had done with him. The stories of tragedy and death would taint each location with an ominous and unforgettable stain which Mike would remember for decades; the spot where Audrey made the first rescue, the location of the body recovery the previous week, the spot where the grandmother and her three year old grandson had been swept to their deaths, the reef where Rodney Orr was struck by the Great White, and of course, the spot along the roadway where Loeffler pulled over Santa's sleigh. Each new story added another element of gravity, or humor, or tragedy, eventually enriching the coastline with a sense of significance.

3-29-1991
PREVENTATIVE LIFEGUARDING

Making heroic rescues in the chilling water was quickly proving to be achievable, but a far better approach was to *prevent* rescues from occurring in the first place. That philosophy, of seeing dangerous conditions developing early and removing the people from the situation, had long since been indoctrinated into the practices of the Southern California lifeguards. In LA County they called them "Prevents" while the State Guards referred to them as "Safety Contacts." Regardless of the terminology, these proactive measures were especially useful on the North Coast. Keeping unwitting people from being swept into the ocean was obviously good for the victims. Truth be told, it was good for the guards too.

One of the great examples of preventative lifeguarding would involve Martino in his first week while on patrol in the South Sector. On an otherwise uneventful morning, he pulled into the Duncan Landing parking lot. Below the bluff are two large rocks. The northernmost rock is known as "Hogback." The southern outcropping is called "Death Rock." For years, both of these rocks have enticed unsuspecting tourists, unfamiliar with the dangers of the area, to climb onto them and subsequently get swept into the ocean by powerful waves. By the fatalistic name of the latter, you can imagine the results. In an attempt to keep people safe, the State Parks erected warning signs and fencing to prevent people from climbing out onto them. But of course, many people view State Parks warning signs as trivial suggestions which don't pertain to them. Some barely glanced at the signs before climbing over the fence and scampering down the face of the rocks.

That particular morning signaled the arrival of a long period, well-spaced swell. With buoy readings of 12' at 20 seconds, the lulls were extended and the sets of waves were spaced out considerably. Seeing a car parked in the lot with no one around, Martino got out of the patrol truck and walked over to the edge of the bluff. Sure enough, a family of six had climbed over the fence, descended down the rocky face and had managed to climb out onto Hogback. From the bluff edge, Martino immediately yelled down to them, advising them to climb back up. Seeing they had been "caught" they complied with his order. Minutes later, the whole family had managed to climb back up the rocks where Martino greeted them near their car. Just as Martino initiated his explanation of why it was dangerous to be on the seemingly safe rock, and as if choreographed with the ocean itself, out of the corner of his eye, he saw a massive set rolling in and asked them all to turn and watch. In that instant, a powerful, 8-foot wall of water engulfed the entire rock, submerging it completely. The normally talkative Martino stopped speaking and let the ocean provide the lesson. The two women in the group held their hands over their mouths and everyone one in the group fell silent with eyes wide open. Instinctively, the father gripped the hand of his young son a little tighter. There could have been no more dramatic example of the ocean's fury. Every one of them stood there stupefied, taking in the violent scene and imagining themselves washed into the maelstrom of the ocean. The wave retreated, clearing the way for a second one which repeated the same display.

Martino stood with them bearing the same stunned expression. The ocean's lesson for him, too, was an epiphany.

But on this occasion Martino would *not* have to swim out. Dozens of rescue personnel would *not* arrive in their trucks with their lights flashing. The newspapers would not document the event. There would be no helicopter flying in and no surviving family members wrapped in wool blankets crying. But there was little doubt that lives were saved on that otherwise innocuous morning. He looked at the family as a whole and wondered which of them, standing before him now, would have been swept to their death.

Thankfully, because that lifeguard did his job, no one had to find out.

4-1-1991
OPENING DAY - 1991

For every Ocean Lifeguard working on any beach in America, the 4th of July is their "Super Bowl." The guards peruse the July schedule the moment it posts to find out where they will be working on the 4th. Like inspecting a baseball starting line-up, they scrutinize which guards have been assigned to the various units, the adjacent towers, and the relief spots on their beach. The busiest towers are doubled-up and every position is conscripted to be able to best accommodate the huge crowds. For a guard to call in sick on the 4th of July is tantamount to desertion.

On the North Coast their "Super Bowl" is April 1st. Although that date may be of little importance to anyone else, to scores of recreational divers, it meant *everything* as it marked the Opening Day of the abalone season. In the pre-dawn darkness every April 1st, the roadways lined with hundreds of vehicles winding their way to Salt Point from San Francisco, Fresno, Los Angeles, Sacramento, and Reno to be among the first to charge into the fertile waters, diving for abalone which had been unmolested for the five months of seasonal closure.

For many years, the sheriff's helicopter (staffed with a paramedic) was staged in the Salt Point maintenance yard the night before the opener. On the morning of April 1st, they would fly along the coastline actively searching for rescues. It was the only day of the year they worked in a *proactive* role. Flying above the divers was a sobering and effective tactic, not unlike having an ambulance circling around the infield of the Indianapolis 500, and it served to reign in some of the opening day exuberance and recklessness of the divers, forcing them to consider their own safety (if not their own mortality).

In that harsh and dangerous environment, most divers inherently realized they were on their own. If they got themselves into trouble, they were forced to figure out some way to rescue themselves. They knew if they couldn't solve their issue, their chances for survival were thin. Even if they *were* lucky enough to have someone on shore who would hear their cries for help and call 911, which in itself was rare, they still needed to hang on in whatever predicament they found themselves in for at least 30 minutes before Henry-I could get there. In reality, more often than not, the divers in distress would be overcome by waves and by the time the chopper arrived, they had already drowned. It was a recurrent scenario which had played out over and over for many years.

Before the lifeguards' arrival, opening day was pure hell for the ranger staff. There were numerous rescues to be made and only three of the rangers (Ashford "Woody" Wood, Bill Walton, and the ex-lifeguard Stephenson) were divers themselves. Although Wood and Walton knew that dangerous coastline as well as anyone, they were also wise enough to know their limits. Neither of them were lifeguards and smartly refused to risk their lives to rescue over-zealous divers who had ignored their safety warnings. They patrolled feverishly, bellowing safety warnings through their PA's imploring rock pickers and divers in dangerous areas to re-locate or exit the water. Some listened. Some didn't. In critical situations, posed with a diver in distress in large surf, they often called for Henry-I, relaying the location and number of victims, then nervously stood by the truck watching the drama play out and hoping the helicopter would reach the diver in time. On more than one occasion, both Wood and Walton bore witness to the tragic scenes of divers struggling helplessly, then submerging to their death before Henry-I could arrive. Days later, when the surf laid down, it was these same rangers who donned their scuba gear and retrieved their bodies. Needless to say, Walton, Wood, and Stephenson most certainly paid their dues on the Sonoma Coast.

But April 1st, 1991, marked a new day. A momentous day. From the perspective of the casual observer, the stage may have appeared to be the same as in previous openers. The campgrounds were filled to capacity, and cars were parked in every little turn out along the coast highway. Fish and Game wardens were scattered along the coast, along with dozens of Search and Rescue volunteers clad in bright orange vests. Every available State Parks employee was on duty. But there was something manifestly different on that day. Because *that* day, would be the first Opening Day in history in which *lifeguards* would be patrolling the Sonoma Coast.

"Aquatic" Rangers Ashford "Woody" Wood, Bill Walton, Michael Stephenson

The decade-long fight to bring them there was over. The equipment had been purchased. The vehicles were staffed. The boat was fueled up. All that remained was to see if they could succeed in their assigned role. All of the debates and the arguments had led to this day. The groundwork to bring them there had been laid with lofty claims and promises of their abilities to save lives. But no one, including the guards themselves, knew if they would make any difference at all.

A group of seven guards (Brown, Loeffler, Melvin, McNulty, Straub,

Martino, and Schardt) would patrol the 15 miles of the North Sector and do their best to keep the divers alive. The public would not only be their customers, but also their audience.

Schardt and Martino were so pumped up, they admitted they couldn't sleep the previous night. The guards were aware of a well-timed swell which would greet them that morning - adding a colorful element to the potential drama. They were on-duty before dawn, and already divers were entering the water. The guards dispersed themselves along the coastline in three pairs, and Don Straub launched the 4-meter inflatable out through Gerstle Cove, running solo.

Just as the sun rose, the action started. Unlike rescues in Southern California where guards routinely swam out to check on bathers or to offer trivial assistance, the North Coast guards adapted their tactics such that they would not swim out for "preventative" rescues, but rather only enter the water if the situation was serious. For that reason, virtually every rescue made on the North Coast, from that very first year and continuing today, would be considered a significant event until confirmed to be otherwise. Hearing the call of any guard swimming out would generate an immediate Code-3 response to their location. The back-up guard would then monitor the status of the rescue and determine if they too needed to swim out to assist. Alternatively, if the surf was too large for the first guard to safely return to shore, the guard in the water would signal to their partners on shore requesting the boat to pick them up, or a helicopter extrication. The over-riding and unquestionable responsibility from day one, in accordance with the primary gospel of every EMT program was, above all else, to dutifully provide for the safety of themselves first, their partners second, and their victims third.

"The Face" is the mile-long section of rocky, exposed and unprotected coastline which extends north from Gerstle Cove to Stump Beach. Due to the concentration of divers and rock pickers along that stretch, Straub focused his patrol pattern there, racing back and forth. In the past, divers who had been pulled off-shore in wide clear-water rips had occasionally been rescued by fishing boats which happened to be in the area, but no one had ever seen any vessel shooting INSIDE the rocky surf line to make rescues. Like a cowboy riding a wild bronco, Don found himself in his own aquatic heaven. He was reckless. He was crazy.

He was spectacular. His first rescue was on a diver who was stuck in a rip and screaming for help mid-way along The Face. With a sizable crowd of captivated onlookers watching from shore, Don flew inside the surf line, yanked him onto the boat, and spun the agile IRB around, avoiding the rocks in the process before throttling full-speed toward the outside with his victim clinging precariously onto the pontoon. To the delight of the crowd, he then crested dramatically over a solid 8' wave, reaching the safety of the outside water, then sped south and dropped the diver in the safety of the Gerstle Cove. Not more than 20 minutes later, he returned to retrieve another diver in virtually the same spot, and rescued him too. A third call came in just farther north at Warren Creek, and Don was able to pull yet another victim onto the boat. On Opening Day in 1991, Don Straub singlehandedly had performed three substantial rescues before 9:00 am.

"The Face" breaking 20'+ in 1998 - Tom Neth and Hoon Kim – Photo: McNulty

Later, tempting fate, Straub got cocky. Osh McNulty was on shore at the time and remembered the event as one of the most spectacular moments of the year. The boat was running well and Don was in his element. Fueled on adrenalin at the zenith of his entire lifeguard existence, he raced inside during a brief lull to check on a diver, but the diver was too slow in getting onto the boat. A clean-up set was building on the outside which was far bigger than anything they had seen that morning, and Don had waited too long to make his escape. He would be caught inside. Unlike the Southern California beaches where an IRB can escape upcoast or simply run up onto a sandy beach, this was the rocky and unforgiving coastline of Salt Point. The inside water was a virtual mine field of pinnacles, bull kelp and outcroppings. Countless obstacles lay hidden just under the surface. The shoreline itself was all rocks, so beaching the IRB was not an option.

Don made an instant and immortal decision that, in retrospect, was the only one possible. He turned away from the diver and gunned the throttle full-speed heading directly into the building 10-foot wave. The boat accelerated as the wave began to crest. Don had committed and there would be no turning back. The crowd of divers on shore, who had been watching the madman and his heroics all morning began screaming and pointing. The collective thought amongst all who were watching was, "How the hell is he going to get out of this?" McNulty too stood on the shore with his fingers interlaced on the top of his head helplessly watching the event play out muttering, "Oh my God..." then, "No Don...no Don....NOOOOO!!!"

Don accelerated and struck the wave squarely just as it was breaking. According to Osh, "Don hit the lip of the massive wave full throttle, and the boat shot straight up, high into the sky...I mean STRAIGHT up...perfectly vertical...it was a 50/50 moment and we held our breath expecting the boat to flip backwards. But the boat landed hard on the stern, engine first, then bounced back up, slightly forward and righted itself. Straub was hammered hard on his landing, but he had stayed on board....He made it...that bastard made it by a second." The crowd on shore erupted into a spontaneous cheer for this crazed aquatic gladiator. Moments later Don had the engine re-started and was back on the throttle, zipping across the surface as if nothing had happened. When the set passed, he returned inside to pick up the exhausted diver, who this time wasted no time in climbing aboard. It was an amazing start to an epic day.

Later, Osh boarded the boat, serving as the deck hand, and no doubt tempered some of Straub's recklessness.

Just after 10:00 AM, they received an ominous call of a "diver in distress" in a remote area north of Fisk Mill Cove known as "Grace Rock." Diving in distant areas can reward the diver with plenty of large abalone, but unfortunately those same areas are difficult to access for rescuers and the boat was instrumental in reaching the victim quickly. Straub opened up the throttle, and McNulty held on as the two guards bounced over the waves. Salt spray stung their eyes as they searched the coastline for the struggling man.

Martino and Melvin were flying along the roadway to the same call, with their lights on and their siren blaring. They were flagged down by a person waving frantically on the side of the road, directing them to the Fisk Mill area. They turned off the main road and navigated along a rutted and muddy path through waist high grass to get to the bluffs. When the trail ended and they could drive no farther, Martino jumped out of the Ram, grabbed the resuscitator and his rescue gear, and ran towards the bluff. There on the rocks below he spotted McNulty already giving ventilations to the lifeless wetsuit-clad victim, while a woman bystander was performing chest compressions. Mike immediately scrambled down the cliff to help.

The two guards fell into an automated rhythm of compressions and ventilations with the added therapy of supplemental oxygen. The diver's chances of survival may have been bleak, but if he was going to die, the guards would know they had given him every chance of survival.

Melvin brought down more supplies. He switched out the oxygen bottle as the two guards continued.

After 5 years of lifeguarding, with the associated training refreshers, Martino had only practiced CPR on plastic manikins, yet within two weeks of his arrival on the North Coast, he found himself performing chest compressions on a lifeless human body for the first time in his life.

They worked furiously but succinctly. Time passed. The cycles of CPR ensued. The two guards diligently continued on. Melvin offered to relieve them but they demurred, having taken a sense of ownership of this young man's fate.

Martino, in the prime of his life, was pumping like a machine, locked in his rhythm. As the successions of CPR continued, the realities of life and death began to enter into his mind. Mike had always been a spiritual man, and he wondered if this might be the exact moment when the young man's spirit, carried in the shell of this body for the past 27 years, slipped away to some unknown realm. To the rest of the world, this event would not register even a blip on their radar, but to this young man in their care, these moments were the most crucial of his entire existence.

Eventually, seeking to orient himself to the larger world around him, Martino lifted his gaze from the victim and surveyed the horizon. There he saw Don, circling outside in the boat. He looked up farther and saw two seagulls gliding in flight overhead. He saw the remnants of a broken wave splash gently against the diver's legs, moving them slightly and momentarily giving them the appearance of life.

Then out of the sky, he heard the sound of helicopter blades whop whop whopping through the air. A moment later a medic descended on the static line. The medic called for a stop in compressions and the guards obliged while he adeptly intubated the patient. He then called for compressions to resume and the guards started once again.

They continued to work on the diver for some time. Standing next to them was a Sheriff's Deputy and the diver's friend who silently watched in disbelief as the guards made every effort to try and save him. Then, a few moments later, the medic "called it" and the rescuers simultaneously stopped and sat back on their heels. Only then did Martino look at the diver's face for the first time. He noticed the details and the texture of his pale skin, and his peaceful countenance, as if he was somehow just sleeping. He studied the young man's fingers...just an hour before, fueled with oxygenated blood, they functioned with skilled dexterity. Now white and still, curled in a loose fist, their representation of death was unmistakable.

The moment was interrupted by the medics who then covered his body with a yellow plastic tarp. His dive partner, with head bowed, began crying. Standing alone, his shoulders shook and the tears poured from him.

Together, the rescuers loaded the body into a Stokes basket and a few minutes later, Henry -1 was again hovering above them. The guards backed away, as the patient, now tended to by the medic, rose from the rocky ground, lifted by the powerful helicopter. The backdrop above the helicopter was a high ceiling of fog which had lifted 200' above the ground where it persisted. From the perspective of the rocky ground and the shoreline, Martino and McNulty watched the diver ascend into the sky as if he was being drawn up to heaven itself. Martino had participated in the man's final struggle to the very end. He looked up and saw gaps in the fog allowing views of a blue sky with white wisps of clouds. More seagulls flew above. It was such a beautiful day. "Good luck," he said in prayer.

A few words were exchanged, acknowledging the efforts of the rescuers and it was over. Osh gathered his fins and buoy and swam back out to the boat to resume his patrol with Straub.

Back in the patrol truck, Melvin noticed an odd-looking abrasion on the back of Martino's hand.

"What happened there?" he asked.

"I don't know," Martino answered. Mike hadn't noticed, but in doing CPR for countless cycles, he had completely abraded a small section of skin from the back of his left hand, leaving it completely raw. As if by divine intervention, the wound would not heal well, and would eventually form a permanent scar. Whether by design or not, it would serve as a life-long reminder of that day. That diver. The tragic end of his young life. And the valiant effort Martino had given in his attempt to save the young man on his first CPR.

~

Later that day, Martino swapped out with Osh, joining Straub on the boat. For the rest of the day the guards checked on dozens of divers and assisted several to shore. In the afternoon, when the cold winds had increased and the ocean surface was a blanket of white-caps all the way to the horizon, even the heartiest of divers had gotten out, showered up, and were likely enjoying their first well-earned beer. Yet Straub and Martino were still out on the patrol boat. Just as they were considering coming in, a huge gray whale surfaced within ten feet of the boat and the guards decided to follow the leviathan. The sight of the massive whale bending to breathe on the surface was inspiring and humbling. Sharing the ocean environment and communing with whales and dolphins was an experience which never grew mundane. The two guards, reluctant to leave their giant visitor, continued to follow it for half an hour before finally returning to the boat ramp to call it a day.

On the shoreline, an ancient Monterey Cyprus extended its gnarled, moss-covered branches out over the bluff edge of the rugged coastline. Martino looked out over the wild seas he had just left. The surface was tattered by the wild winds, and the ocean had succeeded in expelling everyone from her water. The vast ocean, extending as far as he could see, once again was wild and perfectly free, with no evidence of man's influence. Only rocks, and clouds and surf and sky, bathed in the effects of the elements. On the shoreline, the twisted pines and the tall grass, the cliffs and the sandy coves; they all seemed aligned in natural harmony. It was no wonder the divers had come there. It was more than just the diving which brought them to this beautiful wild place. More than the abalone. It was there, in that very spot, still reeling from his first fatality, a poignant thought entered into Martino's mind.

"It was a wonderful place to die...but it was a far better place to be alive."

To the thousands of divers who would continue to arrive through the season, the guards would do their best to keep them all alive. Yet there were so many of them, arriving each day with reckless enthusiasm, eager to descend into the fickle ocean, and so few rescuers to protect them.

Yet the guards believed at their core that they *could* save them. Utilizing their experience and their judgment, they could dissuade them and coerce them, and when necessary, direct them away from the awesome power of the surf. Failing that, they could use their God-given skills to physically enter those same seas and deliver them back to the safety of the land.

Virtually every guard entered the water at least twice that day.

There was no doubt in any of their minds that lives were saved.

In many ways, Don's reckless heroics and his brush with catastrophe that morning was a perfect analogy for what the young and brash lifeguard service would become. In the subsequent years they would perform some of the most heroic rescues in lifeguarding history, but they would also make poor decisions and push the limits of prudence. Pervasive conflicts would fracture morale and cause a debilitating rift amongst the crew. The stress and intensity of the job, combined with the isolation and the dark wet winters would slowly but relentlessly erode the spirit of the original crew, such that most of them would be gone in less than three years.

But on *that day*, with the first Abalone Opener in the books, the guards looked favorably toward the future. Many more rescues would be made. The lifeguards' entrance onto the larger stage of the Sonoma Coast was nothing short of magnificent and a large audience was there to bear witness to that fact.

The North Coast Lifeguard service had arrived.

UNDERSTANDING FREE-DIVERS

Free Diver – North Sector (1992) – Photo: Loeffler

Abalone diving was not an easy pursuit. The guards dealt with divers who had varying degrees of proficiency, which they categorized as beginners, novices, and veterans.

The majority of abalone divers rarely progressed beyond the rudimentary skill level of beginners. Some of them persisted and were eventually able to get a few legal abalone. For them, that achievement was a great reward.

The beginners group was the largest in numbers, but also the easiest to deal with. Because they were impressionable, they sought advice from the guards and heeded the guards' warnings. When they were re-directed to safer waters, or told that conditions were too dangerous to dive, they complied without challenge or argument. Their mistakes were usually errors of naiveté and ignorance. But as one might expect, they were rescued more than those with better skills.

Conversely, the veteran free-divers were, by far, the smallest group. These were individuals who had developed exceptional skills in the water. They had bottom times of over a minute (often two minutes) with minimal surface recovery time. They dove remote areas, deep and fertile with abalone and fish. Generally they were humble and compliant with the laws. The guards rarely ever had any issue with these divers.

The novices were, by and large, fine human beings who loved the sport and strived to improve in a responsible way. They took their fair share of abalone and did so legally and responsibly.

But within the novice category was a sub-group of divers which the lifeguards dealt with most often and most negatively. They were an interesting breed of human. These were men (always men) who had allowed their developing skills in the water to inflate their egos to a dangerous level. These were men who looked into the mirror and saw themselves as *exceptionally skilled hunters*. They carried themselves with a swagger and an arrogance which made them challenging, if not impossible to counsel. They were the ones who took unnecessary risks in pursuit of getting the largest abalone, and often paid the price for their irreverence to the power of the ocean.

Recognizing a member of this dangerous sub-group was not difficult, as they often identified themselves by a mantra which would soon become an ongoing inside joke to the lifeguards for decades to come. It was a line most often proclaimed with an intent to convey a validation that their aptitudes as accomplished divers had progressed to a level of expertise so advanced - they were beyond counsel, and had in fact become magically impervious to the huge surf which *lesser* divers were forced to contend with. The line was this...

"I've been diving here for 20 years."

It didn't take long to realize the phrase more accurately represented an unintentional confession that their skills in the water might be questionable, and they were likely to take unnecessary risks. Ironically, claiming they had *"been diving here for 20 years"* became a warning they needed to be monitored closely.

It should be noted that, as with other sportsmen, the true veteran divers felt little need to prove themselves to anyone, thus ironically, even those who *had actually been diving for 20 years or more* rarely ever mentioned it.

The ridiculousness of the "20-year" statement came to light when the guards heard it proudly declared by divers who were preparing to kick out during times of huge surf and deplorable dive conditions, as if the diver was somehow immune to the perils of the 15' seas and the pounding shore break they were about to enter. It also suggested they might possess some kind of special X-ray vision which would allow them to see clearly through the churned up silt and debris hammered off the bottom by the huge waves which limited the visibility to mere inches for the "lesser divers" who perhaps had only been diving there for "10 years."

The "20-year Club" claim validated nothing more than an inferiority complex, questionable skills in the water, an overabundance of testosterone, or a combination of all three.

When the surf was pounding the coastline, any truly experienced diver, with several hundred dives under their belt, would have taken one look at the angry ocean and driven off to get breakfast.

In the subsequent years, after having to swim out and rescue an assortment of members of the "20-year club" *who had JUST been warned earlier*, the guards became bolder in their assertions that they should NOT be kicking out that day. But since they were not legally empowered to *prohibit* divers from entering into those perilous conditions, they were forced to utilize alternate methods of psychological chicanery to convince them not to go in.

To the lay person, some of the tactics employed to coerce the divers to abort their dubious plans to venture out might seem a bit extreme, but one has to keep in mind that the guard's intentions were true. After getting blown-off by the cocky divers, some guards were known to pull out a cervical collar and, with a straight face, ask the divers to "try it on" to get their size dialed in, so as to expedite their extrication process in the event they became paralyzed. Even more audacious, some guards would ask to see their driver's license and actually copy down their pertinent info. When the diver asked why they needed the information, the guards nonchalantly explained - it provided a jump start on the process, should they need to notify their next of kin. All of this, mind you, done with a straight face and serious demeanor.

Regardless of their unorthodoxy, truth be told, these methods, and other similar tactics, proved to be *exceptionally effective* in gaining compliance. Their fatalistic warnings of impending doom, delivered by Ocean Lifeguards working on that coastline, worked wonders in purging the hot wind from the divers' inflated egos, and allowed a smoldering sense of fear to begin percolating into their minds. To set the hook, once the delivery had been made, the guards bid them well and left the scene. Now very much alone, with no one standing by to watch them, the growing sense of doubt continued to work its magic. Most often, the diver would stand on the bluff, looking back at the surf with a new, reality-based frame of reference, picturing themselves getting heaved up onto the rocks by the surf. The guards, of course had never *actually* left the scene, but rather had driven a cove away, parked the truck, then hiked out to a covert vantage point with binos watching to see what the guy would do, while preparing themselves to make the rescue if need be. Almost always, the diver would get back in his truck and leave. These "mental manipulation rescues," likely numbering in the 100s, never made it to the stat sheets.

Admittedly their seemingly never-ending attempts to convince divers NOT to go out - if we are being honest here - carried an equally beneficial goal of *preventing them from having to venture out* in those hellacious seas to rescue those divers. Facing one's own mortality is not something most humans often encounter, yet on the North Coast, within the parameters of their work life, fearing for one's life was a reality that every guard experienced. That drive for self-preservation was an incredibly strong motivator to master techniques which would successfully dissuade divers from entering the ocean on those bad, bad days.

Another rather interesting and fairly consistent demographic which parlayed into rescues and drownings was the distance divers had to travel to reach Salt Point. It was exceedingly rare to rescue any of the locals, but the guards made plenty of rescues on divers from San Francisco, Fresno, and in particular, the environs of Sacramento. They affectionately referred to these guys as the *"Four-Hour Club"* in reference to the four-hour drive it took them to get there. After the lengthy trip, brimming with high hopes of getting abalone, when greeted with lines of 15 foot surf extending to the horizon, many divers in the "novice" category were foolish enough tempt fate and ventured out anyway.

~

As much hype as the opening day received each year, it was easy to forget that the divers continued to flow into the parks for the entire week of the new season; especially the first weekend. In '91, that first week was nothing short of epic.

As if enraged that the lifeguards had stolen so many divers from her rips on the opener, the ocean responded with a substantial swell, peaking at a powerful 17' at 18 seconds for three days before settling in around 10' at 13 seconds. Coves and little bays which once were safe harbors, were closed-out with waves breaking across their mouths. Months earlier, divers had reserved their vacations to coincide with the opening of the abalone season, and those same divers continued to arrive with every intention of going in.

GERSTLE COVE

The Gerstle Cove Reserve is an underwater sanctuary, bestowing every creature which happens to wander or grow within its boundaries with supreme immunity from the long established predator-prey interactions with abalone hunters, spear fishermen and poachers known to frequent the surrounding 20 miles of coast. The fish seem to know it too. Those who live in the reserve swim frolic around divers, as if flaunting their protected status.

Although no larger than perhaps a few football fields, Gerstle Cove is a popular locale for scuba divers, providing them a safe spot to "swim with the fishes" and commune with nature. Situated in the lee of Salt Point proper, the cove is almost entirely protected from the predominant N-W swells, thus both scuba and free divers, after walking down a short path, can flop into the water and can kick around aimlessly, gawking at the various species of fish and wildlife in relative peace, without having to traverse the impact zone and get beaten around by the surf.

Gerstle Cove and Visitor Center (1995) – Photo: Vodrazka

Scuba diving itself attracts a unique crowd of enthusiasts. Of course there are the stereo-typical adventure-seeking, environmentalist types, inspired by the likes of Jacques Cousteau, Lloyd Bridges, and James Bond. But there are plenty of others who most assuredly don't fit into that mold.

An interesting and unique demographic common to divers who frequented Gerstle in those days was that of being "portly" (or larger). One guy in particular weighed in at a rather astonishing 420 pounds. And the guy showed up regularly. A jovial sort, probably in his 30s, he was often seen in the parking lot, engaged in conversation with other random scuba divers.

The guards would watch him as he began the laborious undertaking of getting his huge custom-made wetsuit on. The process, which an average person could usually accomplish in a few minutes, was for him, an exhausting 30-minute undertaking, punctuated by a series of compulsory rest breaks. Seen from a distance, one might erroneously assume he was tussling with a giant black squid. Once he was securely encased in his black neoprene skin and further weighed to the earth with another 60 pounds of gear – including scuba tank, regulator, BC, mask, and fins, he then began his laborious march, waddling down the 100-yard walkway, huffing and puffing all the way to reach the water's edge. But every time that guy passed the lifeguard truck, he always managed to greet the guards with a smile and a wave.

Despite the seemingly "not worth it" ordeal, the man showed up often, and the guards, well aware of his condition, kept a close eye on him waiting for the day his overworked mitral valve would explode out of the side of his heart.

One day Straub approached the man and breached the subject all of the guards were wondering, asking him why he repeatedly bothered to put himself through this painstaking and exhaustive ordeal just to get a dive in.

The man responded with a wide smile. His explanation was enlightening.

"As you can see, I weigh over 400 pounds. It's probably hard for a guy like you to understand what life is like for a guy like me...every day, every moment of my life is a struggle. Even simple things you don't think about are hard for me. I am out of breath even resting. But when I am in the ocean, something magical happens...Gravity disappears – and I become weightless. I drift and float through the water as if I am flying in space. For those 40 minutes, I drift around like frikkin' Tinkerbell."

FELIX

In the world of the colorful characters living along the Sonoma Coast, Felix Macias stands apart as a true individual. A Native American from the Yaqui tribes of Southern Arizona, his father worked the steel mills in Chicago and Felix grew up on the notorious Southside. As soon as he was old enough, Felix high-tailed from Chicago and established himself along the Sonoma Coast, arguably the antithesis of his previous lifestyle. As

Felix Macias with abalone (1990)

gregarious and funny as any human I have ever met, Felix was not one to insulate himself from the rest of the world by the seemingly irrelevant fact that he was born deaf. In fact, Felix immersed himself in every aspect of culture, sports, social gatherings, and work, eventually accepting a job as a full-time supervising Maintenance Worker with the Sonoma Coast District. His generous heart, his humility, and that goofy sense of humor endeared him to entire crew, but Felix had a special affinity for the lifeguards. I suspect it had to do with their similar *joie de vivre* lifestyle, along with their own brand of irreverent humor. Soon they adopted Felix into their inner circle. In fact, as a testament to his respect for Felix, Loeffler eventually became conversant in sign language, just so he could communicate with Felix on a deeper level.

"All Abalone Are Deaf"

Felix became an accomplished abalone diver. In fact, he became so passionate about the sport, he wrote a book about it cleverly titled, *"All Abalone are Deaf."* The title alone gives you a little insight into his self-deprecating style of humor. The cover photo is even more hilarious. Since abalone divers are in constant competition to find the largest specimens and a 10" abalone will secure bragging rights forever, Felix capitalized on the competitive trend. The photo shows Felix, in his State Parks uniform no less, standing with his arms folded in pride, next to a super-imposed abalone shell which appears to be a ridiculous four-feet in diameter.

Felix was so active in the deaf community, a steady stream of visitors made the trip to the coast to visit him and his wife, Karan. But the group which came most often and in the greatest numbers were his "deaf dive club" buddies. Apparently, unbeknownst to the guards, there exists a large population of divers who are deaf. When one of the guards asked Felix why diving was so popular among the hearing-impaired, he revealed, "You know, in almost every world we live in, the hearing population have an advantage over us...but under water, we shine. While two of you guys try to converse there by gross gestures and grunts – we simply sign back and forth like any other time and express, in detail, exactly what we intend to say."

It was another "ah ha" moment of insight for the guards.

4-10-1991
AVERTING TRAGEDY at GOAT ROCK

Goat Rock - Ugly 10' shore break (1991) – Photo: Loeffler

Although the North Sector received almost all of the attention with the opening of the abalone season, the same swell which battered the divers at Salt Point hit the South Sector as well. Because of the discomfort in wearing a wetsuit all day, the usual practice on busy days was for the guards to wear their wetsuits "pulled up to the waist," keeping their shirts and jackets on their upper body.

That strategy proved to be shrewd when Loeffler and Martino made an impressive rescue in which a family of seven were snagged in the all-too-familiar scenario at Goat Rock. Oblivious of the danger, and walking too close to the water's edge, a massive wave slammed into them all, striking both parents chest high, and completely engulfing their children in a 5-foot thick wall of cold, sandy, and foamy water. The guards, who had coincidentally been driving toward the family to warn them to stay back, witnessed the huge wave swallow them up. The two guards sprinted from the truck. Martino, having his wetsuit pulled up to his waist, was able to pull it over his head while running. Loeffler, unfortunately, was not only fully clothed in long pants and boots, but also carried the added burden of his gun belt and bullet-proof vest.

As they approached, they witnessed the frenzied scene of the entire family being violently thrown up the sand berm. Then, amidst a strange silence from the shocked children, their bodies were being helplessly pulled back toward the trough with an almost equal ferocity. Martino sprinted into the waist-deep water and grabbed the first of the children, handing the young boy off to Loeffler who then plodded through the thigh-deep water in his boots to deliver the child to the dry sand. Frantically Martino snatched another child and again delivered her off to Loeffler who made a second trip up to the dry sand. The advance and retreat of the waves continued, carrying the remaining victims back and forth, but eventually Martino was able to rescue every one of them and pass them off to Kurt.

In the end, Loeffler, having been bowled over and smashed by the waves, was completely doused. But the guards' performance was nothing short of amazing – and in the span of perhaps two minutes, all of the children and both adults were safely delivered to dry sand. Standing on the crest of the berm with their hands on their knees, the two guards struggled to catch their breath after their unplanned sprint.

"Nice work out there Mike" praised Loeffler. Martino nodded and returned the praise, as the two lifeguards basked in the realization that they had just averted a tragedy.

One can only imagine their frustration when the mother approached them afterwards – instead of offering praise and thanks for saving the lives of her children, she scolded them because they refused to re-enter the ocean to retrieve a lost shoe that belonged to one of her sons.

That afternoon Loeffler would spend hours completely dismantling, cleaning and drying his firearm, along with every article of his Peace Officer gear.

4-12-1991
THE WEEK ROUND UP

At midnight on April 12th, the first week of abalone season was officially in the books. Seven straight days of surf had thoroughly tested the lifeguards. Rescues which would have been considered remarkable just one month earlier barely garnered mention. By week's end, every guard had performed several rescues and all of them had risen to the challenge. Privately they must have felt a burgeoning sense of confidence in overcoming the doubts from being untested. That said, their new found confidence was in no way an indication of apathy; they were fully aware the ocean had plenty more to offer.

By then, many of the locals in the North Sector had become intrigued by this curious and seemingly dedicated group assigned to watch over their ocean. In the South Sector that was not the case. In fact, on the top of each page of the patrol log, they began tallying the number of times they had been "flipped off" by random people each day. The hash marks were often in the double digits.

~

Three weeks after the opener, a personal letter from Frank Allison arrived at the district office, thanking the lifeguards for rescuing not only them, but their boat as well. He stated that while diving for abalone north of Russian Gulch, in heavy surf and high winds, their inflatable IRB lost power, and they, along with a similar boat in the same area, capsized and were blown to shore. The Coast Guard was summoned, but their policy prevented them from retrieving any vessels once they came aground.

In part, Allison's letter read *"...the two lifeguards arrived and immediately took command. In their small inflatable boat they maneuvered into heavy surf to make an incredible evacuation of both divers and safely recovered our boat."*

Lifeguards in general have a long history of minimizing their accomplishments, and apparently that trend continued on the North Coast. Despite the praise of their service in an obviously significant rescue involving two vessels, it should be noted - neither of the guards had even bothered to enter the rescue into the log book thus no official record of Allison's boat rescue even existed. It was 30 years later, in the course of researching this book that I finally got the story from Scott Melvin.

It was he and Straub who responded in the IRB. Both small inflatables had capsized in the substantial 40-knot winds, and four divers, clinging onto their boats, were forced to come ashore in the rocky area south of High Point, a considerable distance north of Russian Gulch. The Coast Guard *was* in fact on scene and circling on the outside, but as stated, they are unable to assist any vessels once they reached the surf line. Because the boats beached in a virtual no-man's-land several hundred feet below the roadway, it would have been logistically impossible for them to retrieve their vessels. In fact, they themselves would have had a considerable challenge to reach the roadway simply to evacuate themselves.

It was Melvin's ingenious idea to swim in, and attempt to perform a rather unorthodox reverse-direction rescue of both divers, swimming them OUT through the surfline to the awaiting rescue boat. After confirming that the divers felt strong enough to re-enter the surfline, one-at-a-time, Melvin towed each of them back out, and safely delivered them to the lifeguard IRB.

Melvin then returned to shore, retrieved the first boat, hooked his buoy to the bow and was able to tow it back through the considerable surf and hellacious winds to reach Straub and the two divers. He then completed an encore performance for the second boat. The combined rescues would take almost two hours, but once the vessels were reunited with their owners, the guards towed both boats, along with the divers and their gear, back to Timber Cove and safe harbor.

5-27-1991
BOY JESUS

In the spring of 1991, Dave Carter arrived ready for work on the North Coast. His easy-going style was a welcome attribute to help balance and mitigate the potent anxiety a few of the guards carried. Not the least of these was Steve Franklin. The contrast in demeanors between the two men could not have been more profound.

On May 27th, Carter would make his first rescue. Coincidentally, he was riding with Franklin at the time when they received the call of a diver in distress in a remote area south of Horseshoe Cove. As mentioned, at that point in their existence, every member of the lifeguard service, eager to prove their collective worth, responded "balls-to-the-wall" to every rescue, attempting to beat Henry-I to the scene. Carter flipped on the overhead lights and siren and raced northbound along the Coast Highway well above the posted speed limit. But for the high-strung Franklin, it wasn't fast enough. As they turned off onto the dirt road leading out to the remote area near Grace Rock, Franklin repeatedly yelled at Carter to *"Drive faster!"* The truck bounced hard along the gutted road, and traversed through a shallow creek. Since this would be Carter's first major rescue, he was already sufficiently "amped up" and didn't really need any additional hype from Franklin, yet the perm continued spitting orders at him from the passenger seat.

When they reached the bluff, they jumped out of the truck and spotted the diver floundering offshore, but immediately before them was a sheer 30-foot vertical drop to the rocky shoreline below. In a statement Carter remembers vividly, Franklin, seemingly obsessed with getting to the victim immediately, yelled at Carter to "GO!!!" Risking insubordination but preserving his life in the process, Carter chose *not* to jump off the cliff and instead ran south, with Franklin trailing on his heels. Carter eventually found a thin goat trail, scampered down to the rocks below and swam out, performing his first successful rescue on the North Coast - and beating Henry-I by a long shot.

6-1-1991
FALLING FROM the SKY

In early June, McNulty and Straub were dispatched to *"a vehicle in the tide pools at Stump Beach."* While responding to the call, Osh was initially confused and asked the dispatcher to confirm the location since Stump Beach was accessible only by foot, and protected by 40' cliffs on both the north and south ends. While awaiting clarification from the dispatcher he casually mentioned to Don, "The only way a car could have gotten down to Stump Beach is if it had *flown in."*

Apparently that's exactly what happened.

No one was there to witness the dramatic event the previous night when the car cascaded off the north side cliff and splashed into the ocean below. The early morning walkers didn't notice it either until the tide had dropped low enough for the chassis and tires of the upside-down vehicle to become exposed, and a hiker, spotting the unusual site, called 911.

Abandoned vehicles were not uncommon in remote areas along the Sonoma Coast. Some had been stolen then ditched. Others were events of insurance fraud. On one occasion a vehicle was rolled off a cliff as a result of a domestic disturbance. But it was certainly rare to find any vehicle in the ocean.

Although the guards didn't know the circumstances of this call, and despite the fact that no APB had been issued for anyone missing, as a matter of policy, McNulty and Straub were tasked with "clearing the vehicle" to make sure no one was in it.

They arrived on scene and hiked out with their water-gear in their packs. The car was resting on the bottom in the surfline with waves breaking over it, so initially it was difficult to spot, but occasionally the retreating backwash allowed the chassis to become exposed above the water line.

They suited up, grabbed their dive masks and fins, and started kicking out to inspect the vehicle.

Of course, being in the surf line, it was surgey as hell, limiting their under-water visibility to less than a foot. Thus, the guards were forced to feel their way around the vehicle to orient themselves and identify the front, then the driver's side door.

Once established, it was Straub who would "clear" the driver's compartment, so they could return to shore to begin planning for the vehicle extrication. He took a breath and dove down in the turbulent and murky water. As he pushed his head into the driver's window, through the sediment and surge an object slowly came into view. It was striped black-and-white fabric waving in the surge. He pushed his face closer to get a better look. Initially he thought it might be a pillow, but through a separation in the fabric he saw something which looked white and solid. After pulling himself farther through the window and entering into the driver's compartment, leading with his face to see, he reached in and probed the object with his finger. What he felt was the unmistakable and gut-wrenching sensation of *cold flesh*. Don, not having anticipated on finding a body in the car, screamed under water, instantly yanking himself out of the tomb of the passenger compartment. His underwater profanity-laced yelling continued as he ascended and, once clear of the water, became clearly audible. Amidst the barrage of colorful expletives, Osh was able to pick out the words "HE'S STILL IN THERE!"

Floating on his buoy on the surface, negotiating the small waves, it took Don some time to gather himself. But eventually, the two guards formed an impromptu plan. Interactions with dead bodies was unpleasant enough, and generally, emergency personnel limited the amount of physical handling of bodies to a minimum. But this case was unique and would require more manipulation and wrestling. Over the course of several dives that would result in far more familiarity with the body than they had planned on, they were eventually able to extricate him from the vehicle. Once on the surface, they strapped him into Don's buoy and began kicking him to shore. Neither guard spoke during their most unpleasant ordeal.

Later reports from the rangers confirmed the man, hell bent on ending his life the previous night, drove south along the Coast Highway, crashed through the split rail fence on the roadside, bounced along through a couple hundred yards of rough brush, then flew off the cliff on the north side of Stump Beach, dropping 40' to his death in the ocean below.

6-9-1991
GULICK'S ARRIVAL

Less than a month after Carter filled in the penultimate position, Jon Gulick arrived, becoming the final member of the inaugural crew. On the morning of his first shift, he swam out to deckhand for Straub on the rescue boat to get his orientation to the operation. They were watching two abalone divers just outside of Gerstle Cove when one of them suddenly began yelling for help.

Gulick on foot patrol (1991)

Straub maneuvered the boat into position and signaled Jon to go. Gulick dove into the water with his rescue buoy and fins and quickly reached the struggling diver who was suffering from exhaustion and cramps. Gulick then towed him to the rescue boat and the two guards assisted the appreciative man on board. Thus, Gulick made his first rescue on the North Coast less than 3 hours after the beginning of his first shift there.

It would be the first of many more rescues for the soft-spoken carpenter.

6-15-1991
THE BANDALERO ROCK PICKER

On an early morning in June, the North Sector received an ominous report of an "unconscious diver."

Just before dawn, a rock picker with only rudimentary swimming skills, ventured out at Pedotti's Reef near Fort Ross at low tide, joining several dozen other pickers who were scavenging under the rocks in hopes of finding a legal abalone.

When the call came over the radio, four guards responded, with Franklin and Melvin in the patrol truck, and Straub and Carter in the rescue boat. The response of four guards, all of whom were in the vicinity at the time, greatly increased the possibility of successfully resuscitating the unconscious diver. But as Franklin and Melvin approached the reef, all hopes for a timely arrival were dashed when they were confronted with a parked 4x4 Suburban completely blocking their emergency access to the scene.

Having no alternative, Melvin, already in his wetsuit, jumped the fence with fins and buoy and set off on a half-mile run down "Cardiac Hill" (so named for its steepness), with Franklin following close behind with the resuscitator. This was a few years before portable AED's were part of their gear.

Reaching the shoreline, Melvin quickly located the witness, another wetsuit-clad rock picker, who stated he heard the victim "screaming for help" and spotted the man struggling. As he was running to the scene, the man's screaming stopped and he looked up in time to see the victim slip below the surface and not come up.

In an act of bravery, the witness then swam out to attempt to save the drowned diver, but having only rudimentary swimming skills himself, and fearing for his own life, he was forced to return to shore.

Melvin quickly explained he would need the man to show him the exact spot where the victim went down and coaxed him to re-enter the water with him to isolate the location. Trusting the lifeguard, the witness agreed. Melvin then clipped him in his rescue buoy and, in the most unorthodox of tactics, began *towing the witness off-shore*. Melvin swam backstroke, monitoring the man's directions, and at some point, as if divulging the location of some buried treasure, the witness motioned Melvin to stop and pointed straight down, seemingly confident they had reached the exact location where he had seen the diver disappear below the surface.

Melvin removed the strap from his shoulder and left the witness safely floating on his buoy. Then, with the visibility near zero, he began a series of surface dives in 10' of water. Unable to see more than a single foot in front of his face, he kept his arms fully extended in front of him, so as not to collide with the unseen rocks. Trusting his witness, Scott was confident he was in the right location and in a race with time, he anxiously began groping along, blindly feeling for the man's body.

Even though he expected to find the body, Scott still "freaked out" momentarily when his hands gripped an unidentifiable appendage. But in a testament to his mettle, fearing he might lose the body if he ascended for a fresh breath of air, Scott grabbed hold of the dead diver with both hands.

Attempting to kick him to the surface, Melvin immediately felt an incredible amount of resistance and soon realized the diver was grossly over-weighted.

By then, Straub and Carter had arrived. After dropping the boat anchor, they swam over to assist Melvin who was struggling just to keep the diver's body on the surface. Despite the efforts of all three to release the victim's weight belt and facilitate his delivery to shore, the ends of his jerry-rigged belt were tied in a complex knot, forcing the guards to tow him in with the belt still in place. With Carter and Straub kicking feverishly to support the weight of the deceased diver and keep him afloat, Melvin towed the entire group (including the mortified witness) to shore.

Franklin received the body, pulled him onto the flat ground and together with Straub, began performing chest compressions and ventilations.

The non-swimmer had been picking abalone from the rocks wearing an ancient wetsuit and tennis shoes. Instead of purchasing a standard weight belt, the man had strapped two sections of rope across each shoulder "Bandalero style," each of which held a various collection of weights. Unfortunately, weighing only 110 pounds he had grossly overestimated the amount of weight (later determined to be 25 pounds) needed to off-set the floatation of his wetsuit and allow him to gently submerge below the surface. He was knocked over by a wave, and pulled out by a moderate rip current into an area of deeper water. While screaming for help, he fought valiantly, bobbing and kicking to keep his face above the surface while being pulled down by the mass of his collection of weights. Ultimately he was unable to overcome the ballast, and sunk to the bottom. Others, including his family on shore, looked on in horror but no one jumped in to save him. None of them knew how to swim either.

Despite their best efforts, too much time had elapsed. The Medic descended from Henry-I shortly afterwards and pronounced the man dead.

The guards were understandably livid that their emergency response had been delayed by the illegally parked truck, and Melvin questioning the people on scene to determine who was to blame.

In a sad twist of fate, the man's family informed him that the truck belonged to the dead diver himself. In blocking the emergency access, he had unintentionally blocked the rescuers from saving him.

To compound matters, during the rescue attempt, the CHP, responding to an earlier complaint of the vehicle blocking the emergency access, and already arranged for the vehicle to be towed. Thus, the family, having no means of transportation, were given a ride to Guerneville by Melvin. As one might imagine, the 30-minute drive, with the family sobbing the whole way, was one of the most maudlin events the lifeguard ever had to endure.

With over 30 miles to patrol and perhaps 4 or 5 guards covering the water, it was obvious the guards couldn't be everywhere at once, but as they learned the coastline and the hot spots, more often than not, they *were* in the right place at the right time. Their patrol patterns took on a proactive role, warning people about the potential dangers and advising them of safer alternatives to whatever questionable activity they were involved in. The north guards began anticipating trouble long before the divers even realized they were in a perilous situation. And their *proactive* strategy was working.

Of note, these face to face *proactive* and preventative measures were, up until then, almost universally unknown to the various rescue entities along the Sonoma coast. Their responses had always been *reactive* strategies wherein they were called *after* someone had already gotten in trouble. To the guards, the best rescue is always the one which never has to happen. Before they arrived, the only proactive measures employed were their posting of warning signs about the dangers of the coastline and surf, which were largely ignored. The lifeguards' presence offered a revelatory new approach in *actively preventing rescues*, a strategy no one in Sonoma had seemingly ever considered.

Thus, in their ongoing metamorphosis to maximize efficiency and prevent the majority of rescues and drownings, the guards were constantly vigilant, on the move, patrolling, anticipating, warning, and as necessary, effecting the rescues.

7-3-1991
TWO DIVERGENT WOMEN

The following narrative is an abridged version of an account gleaned from Mike Martino's unpublished manuscript, documenting two contrasting encounters which occurred on the same day.

As one might expect, with a growing surge of public sentiment against them, the South Sector crew became wary and even a bit skittish when any member of the public approached them. On an otherwise routine day, Franklin and Martino were coming off of Goat Rock Beach when they were approached by a woman dressed in a long colorful dress. Both of her arms were adorned with an impressive assortment of hand-made jewelry. She wore bangles, jade rings, brightly painted nails, multi-colored bead necklaces, and several belts of chain. As she approached, it was Franklin, ever the lifeguard, who mentioned that if she fell into the water, she would immediately sink to the ocean floor.

Appearing to be in her late forties, she carried herself in a lofty sort of way, as if she had tapped into the secrets of some new age enlightenment. Nearing their truck, her gait adopted a stern sense of purpose. Then, while still some distance away, though closing quickly, and with no discernable sense of higher enlightenment at all, she yelled harshly to them.

"Hey – I want to talk to you!"

Franklin stopped the truck and observed the colorful woman heading their way. "I wonder what she wants?"

The woman reached their patrol truck and rested her bangled arm on the glass edge of the partially lowered window. "I think," she said in a terse and accusatory tone, "you should stop driving on the beach. Those tracks look horrible."

"Well ma'am," Franklin said, "as you can see, we are lifeguards, and we drive on the beach so we can talk to all of these fine people, and warn them about the ocean currents and waves. You might not realize it, but many people have lost their lives on this very beach and we are trying to prevent more people from dying here."

Martino, ever the peace maker, piped in from the passenger side, "And we don't drive over there" pointing to the Blind Beach side which was completely unmolested by tire tracks.

"I just think," said the jeweled woman, "there should be some wild places left on earth, free from tires, and dripping oil, and man."

"There are plenty of those places" said Franklin. "But this is a State Park and people come here to recreate. We provide the service of offering safety information and we occasionally even make rescues when necessary."

The woman began to get angry. "I am sick of seeing tire tracks on the beach. I want wild untamed places, and I don't want you to drive on the beach anymore!"

By this time Franklin was getting angry. Martino intervened to try and placate her. "Look, like I said, we never drive on the Blind Beach side. If you just walk 100 yards around the bend and you won't see many people. And although we try to keep the tracks to a minimum, perhaps it might help you to look at them as "tracks of love." They help us get to people faster and prevent people from dying here."

Now pushing her face in through window, significantly violating their personal space, she said, "I don't care. Sometimes people have to die!"

Franklin, never one to back down from any noble debate, could restrain himself no longer.

"Now hold on a minute here ma'am. You yourself drove your car down here to the beach today, and now you are clamoring to keep these beaches inaccessible for people? And you have the nerve to say it's alright if people die on this beach. What are you, crazy?!"

"Listen here mister!" she spouted, "You better watch your attitude. I don't appreciate being spoken to like that."

"Well, excuse me," mocked Steve, "But we can't waste any more time talking with you. We get paid to keep people alive whether you agree with that or not."

The woman backed away from the window, incredulous at Steve's rude behavior. Franklin pulled away slowly, and Martino looked back at the woman. Her hands were on her hips and her face was contorted in a nasty scowl of vitriol.

The jewelry woman had set a bad tone for the day and the ill-will continued. Other beach patrons seemed to have it out for them as well that morning, and the guards shared an unnerving feeling that everyone on the beach was glaring at them. Seeking an asylum from the human race, they drove out onto the middle of the mile-long beach and hunkered down. But their respite didn't last long.

"Hey, Steve," Martino said pointing north. "Here comes another one."

Steve looked north along the beach. There, in the distance they saw a woman holding a shoe box. She was walking directly towards them with a gait and carriage which clearly conveyed that she wanted to talk with them.

"Great," Martino said, "Another irate Sonoma County psycho. She's probably got a bomb in there."

Steve laughed for second then suddenly stopped, wondering if she might. "Do you think maybe we should take off?"

It was too late. "Excuse me," said the woman. "I have something for you." She handed the box to Steve through the open driver's side window. Steve delicately took the unknown gift into the truck, being careful not to shake it.

"Thank you?" he questioned, not yet daring to open the box.

"I'd just like to thank you for being here," she said.

Franklin and Martino both turned to one another simultaneously with eyebrows raised.

"I made you some cupcakes," she explained.

Both stunned by this unexpected act of benevolence, they stammered out a simultaneous "thank you," not quite sure what to make of their new benefactor.

"My name is Karen Stockdale," said the woman looking down. She paused, struggling to speak.

"In 1985 I lost my son David on this beach. He was climbing on that rock over there." She was pointing to the north side of Goat Rock, a place they had made innumerable safety contacts since they first arrived. "He and his friend Todd were climbing on the rock and a wave swept David into the sea. David was being knocked against the rocks and his friend Todd jumped in to help him. Todd gripped David's hand for a second, but lost his grip and David was gone. I've never seen him since." She paused, looking down again. The tears began to flow and her shoulders began to lightly shake. Looking back at them she summoned the courage to complete her story. "Every year I come here to throw a wreath in the water and to remember my son."

The guards were shocked. Immediately their hearts opened with a surge of empathy for this soft-hearted mother.

"I just wanted to thank you for being here. I was so glad we finally have rescuers like you on this coast to help keep people safe. I just wish you had been here back then."

"I do too," said Steve, choking up a bit.

There's often an uncomfortable silence when a stranger unexpectedly reveals something so intimately personal, but in this case there was none. The volition behind her heartfelt offering of cupcakes provided a gift far greater than she could ever have imagined. They were instantly linked in a common purpose, and although they had not been there to save her son back in 1985, their goal was to be there from now on and to save all future mothers from the anguish she has had to endure.

In Karen Stockdale, they had found an ally who understood and appreciated *why* they patrolled the beach, and the horrendous and devastating effects of every fatality. Her story completely eradicated any rationality to the ludicrous idea that *"sometimes people have to die"* and the citizenry should somehow be okay with that.

As humans, we all share the common fate of eventual death, but if traumatic death could be prevented by a sharp eye, or a friendly warning, or if necessary, by swimming into the very maw of the sea to rescue a human being who is struggling for their life, then no, people didn't have to die on these beaches. Not in that way...and not on their watch.

Martino and Franklin enjoyed those cupcakes, especially so knowing they were made with love.

And every year, Karen Stockdale returned to Goat Rock to remember her son. Over the years, all of the guards came to know her and even began to expect her arrival each July. The guards viewed her as one genuine and reliable supporter who understood their mission and valued their service. Those visits never failed to bolster the morale of the crew and paid dividends in rekindling their passion to save lives.

7-14-1991
CARTER and GULICK - FIRST CPR

On an otherwise pleasant July day, Dave Carter was on patrol with Jon Gulick in the North Sector. By then Carter had been working on the North Coast just shy of 2 months, while Gulick was still in his first month. The abalone season had entered its summer closure. The surf was small, and the two men were enjoying a break from the stresses the abalone divers created. Having time, they stopped to visit with Sylvia and Bob, a kindly old couple who spent many summer days scuba diving in the Gerstle Cove Reserve. Bob and Sylvia had no interest in taking game. They were simply gentle souls who shared a profound passion for the undersea world. To them, Gerstle Cove was their Shangri La.

On that day, Bud Brown was playing tour guide to a group of New Zealand exchange lifeguards, showing them their areas of responsibility along the coast. Carter and Gulick were able to meet their kindred brethren from a world away and shared a few laughs with them. These were the first New Zealand guards Gulick had ever met. Coincidentally, within ten years, Gulick would move to New Zealand and become one of the country's leading ambassadors for traveling lifeguards from around the world.

In the afternoon, Carter and Gulick were driving north along the Coast Highway when they received a call of two scuba divers in distress at Gerstle Cove. While they sped to the scene, Gulick suited up in the front seat. As Carter pulled the truck onto the access road above the cove, the guards saw the gut-wrenching scene of an elderly woman, struggling to pull her lifeless husband toward shore. Carter immediately recognized the woman as Sylvia.

CPR in progress - Medic with Stephenson, Carter and Gulick

Gulick raced down the ramp and swam out, reaching the victims first. Sylvia, struggling mightily to keep her husband afloat, was distraught and exhausted. Evaluating her husband, Jon confirmed he was not breathing and started delivering rescue breaths while kicking his victim towards shore. Carter, having donned his wetsuit, arrived seconds later, clipped into Gulick's buoy and began towing both Jon and the victim towards shore, while Jon continued giving breaths. While the two struggled to keep the victim alive, rescue crews from the volunteer fire department, Sheriff Deputies, and Henry-I were summoned.

Once on shore, Carter and Gulick immediately began performing CPR. It would be the first CPR in the careers of both guards, and this one would be even more intense owing the fact that they knew their victim. Stephenson overheard the call and arrived to assist the guards. A newspaper photographer happened to be in the area and captured a rare, but heart-wrenching photograph of the guards performing CPR with the victim's wife sitting just above them watching helplessly. Despite the guards' involvement in many other CPR calls, his photograph was the first known image of the North Coast Lifeguards engaged in CPR.

Henry-I arrived and the victim was flown off for definitive care. But his lifeless body never took another breath. Bob would never again descend into the beautiful underwater world he loved so much. The guards were left to try and comfort his distraught wife, who as one would imagine, was inconsolable.

After the call, Carter took on the unenviable task of gathering all of the deceased diver's gear and bringing it to the victim's daughter. He tried in vain to adequately express his condolences, as she had just learned, minutes earlier, that her father was gone. Even the soulful Carter could not find the appropriate words to provide her with any solace.

8-1991
THE ONE YEAR ANNIVERSARY

As the one-year anniversary of the lifeguard service approached, the realization of their successes were severely tempered by the ongoing struggles and resultant stress, and there was little cause for celebration.

An old guard once famously said, *"Lifeguards are not paid for what they do, but rather what they might have to do at any moment."* That discernment was particularly true on the North Coast.

It was no mystery that the eradication of drowning on the North Coast was a tall order. Many, if not *most* of the Sonoma rescue agencies felt it was a goal far too lofty to aim for, and the guards knew that bets aligned heavily against their success. The perilous conditions, the limited staff, the personal risk and the passionate desire to prove the oppositionists wrong created a level of stress amongst the guards that, at times, was unbearable.

Never knowing where or when the next emergency would occur, they needed to be ever-ready to perform in order to validate their existence, with human lives hanging in the balance. As a result, they had to operate at a heightened sense of vigilance at all times.

And heightened vigilance creates more stress.

Many of the best guards watch the water with a mild sense of paranoia. That low-grade paranoia has been shown in numerous studies to create more acute awareness, resulting in earlier detection of trouble, thus earlier responses to critical incidents. But that same stress eventually corrodes their mental and physical well-being.

Physiologically, stress causes the sympathetic nervous system to fire in our "fight or flight" response. Adrenaline pumps through the blood stream and the body responds by increasing the heart rate, dilating the pupils, and most notably, increasing the blood pressure in preparation of the perceived need to either run from an aggressor or to attack them. If a lifeguard then spots a rescue and swims out, the exertion of performing the rescue provides a physical release of the stress.

But lifeguards don't make rescues constantly, so they end up sitting and waiting, with the aforementioned symptoms incessantly brewing, and the anxiety continuing its slow burn.

One can only imagine what the stress levels were like for those original guards. The daily staff of three or four were responsible for covering an extensive area of the coastline and there was rarely an opportunity for an adequate respite.

While patrolling the wide expanse of the Sonoma Coast, they endured a constant and nagging suspicion that something bad might be happening *someplace else.* For that reason, if the people in their area were relatively safe, they were ever on the move, searching for more dangerous situations which warranted their presence; a pair of beginning divers heading out to a rough area in the North Sector, a group of teenagers climbing the rocks at Blind Beach, a recent breach of the river mouth, a dive class kicking out in rough seas at Stump Beach, or a large family playing wave tag at Goat Rock. The moment any of these situations was remedied, the guards were off to find the next potential issue, all the while hoping it wasn't too late. In essence, they were constantly fighting a losing battle to be everywhere at the same time.

Since there was rarely an opportunity to "burn off" the stress, they, like baseball managers, discovered some solace in chewing sunflower seeds or tobacco. Busying themselves with seeds, provided an oral occupation and a mental pre-occupation which helped to mitigate the stress. The North Coast guards went through a LOT of seeds. Similarly, some of them actually smoked cigarettes and cigars. Martino, the son of an alcoholic father, and keenly aware of the risk that he might follow that path, allowed his 20-mile bike ride to be his source of de-stress – and it certainly worked for him.

But for many of the others, when they signed off each night, after eight hours of mental duress, the quick and easy fix to douse the sympathetic fire in their brain was to quench it with a unit-dose depressant in the form of a beer (or three). You don't need to be a neurosurgeon to acknowledge that it works quite well to alleviate anxiety. Just ask any North Coast Lifeguard. Of course, those pacifying habits engrain quickly, and as one might imagine, alcohol consumption soon became a crutch for some of them, creating its own set of detrimental issues.

SCENE SAFETY

Scene Unsafe – Photo: Bogdonovic

In all job sites in the US, "Workplace Safety" is regulated by OSHA. Yes, the Occupational Safety and Health Administration reigns supreme in making sure employees are not subjected to conditions which may place them at risk, or compromise their health or wellness.

Violations of workplace safety can elicit substantial fines, and even promptly shut a business down.

Similarly, the tenet of "Scene Safety" is *the* predominant and foundational principle which permeates every practice taught in all *Emergency Services Providers* textbooks in print today. In any situation where a rescuer realizes that their safety may be jeopardized, universally accepted protocols state that they should immediately retreat and "save themselves" first. Although this strategy throws a wrench in the portrayals of every "hero" movie ever made, the reasoning behind it is sound. If the rescuer becomes injured or incapacitated, he or she can offer little in the way of help, and, worse yet, they add another *victim* to the situation for the other rescuers to have to contend with.

For the North Coast crew these two related principles would seemingly pertain to them since they were both *employed in a workplace*, and *responded to emergencies*.

But that's about as far as the enforcement of that line of reasoning goes.

There is a publication (presumably read by an infinitesimally small number of safety nerds) called *"The Emergency Management Guide to Preparing and Protecting Personnel in Emergencies Handbook."* I will confess up front that I haven't read it, nor have I even held one in my hand, but I'm gonna go out on a short limb here and assume that it is veritable bible that spells out the foundational guidelines for keeping employees in the emergency services field safe and secure. Although it seems almost comical to mention, in reality the challenging ocean conditions which these "employees" routinely ventured into were often not only *unsafe*, but *downright deadly* for the average human being. I laugh to myself when I imagine the thought of an OSHA representative who stopped by on a routine day in November and witnessed lifeguards swimming out into 14' seas in 50 degree water. No doubt he would have a hard time finding justification for their actions in the good ol' *"Emergency Management Guide to Preparing and Protecting Personnel in Emergencies Handbook, 1991 edition."*

If we are being honest here, actual compliance with the OSHA safeguards, even tweaked with ridiculously wide tolerances, would have prevented the guards from being able to perform their jobs at all.

Additionally, we should also keep in mind that the *Seasonals* among the ranks were provided no health insurance. Besides the bureaucratically challenging system of Worker's Compensation, they had little to fall back on if they were injured. I doubt it gave them much solace that the State *did* provide a *death benefit* of $5,000 to their next of kin, should they happen to be killed on a rescue. The specificity of that amount, interestingly, gives you some insight as to the value the California State Parks consigns to the lifeguards. Each of their lives was worth no more than the dented 12-year old Toyota Corolla that Straub arrived in.

Ultimately, the solution to appease the seemingly unresolvable conflict between performing their jobs and adherence to OSHA safety standards, as well as the basic principles of EMS workers, was simply *to ignore all of it*, and continue swimming out in atrocious conditions anyway.

This is not to suggest they were reckless. The lifeguards themselves, in a predictable adaptation to ensure their own safety, grew to trust each other emphatically. This reliance on their partners was something they rarely spoke of, yet everyone inherently knew. The harsh conditions in which they were forced to perform created an unquestionable loyalty and commitment to each other. When they swam out, they knew their partners had their backs. Without exaggeration, on many occasions, their partner's coordination with Henry-I, providing hand signals of oncoming waves, responding with the boat, or swimming out as a back-up guard, served as instrumental measures in getting the initial guard out of a major bind with their hides still attached. It was not an exaggeration to say that at times, they truly *trusted each other with their very lives*.

When asked about it, Straub explained, *"The real reason we could risk it all was because we knew our partners had our backs. In those early days, on many gnarly rescues, I knew Osh was on shore. He probably didn't realize there was any impact of him being there, but he was there for me and I knew it. That gave me confidence to dive into the madness."*

~

While the Permanents in the South Sector (Melvin, Franklin, and Loeffler) continued to take heat from the public, they discovered quite unexpectedly that many of the law enforcement calls they were responding to in their rural community were as heavy as anything they had dealt with previously in the urban world of Southern California. Although the focus of this book is not on the Law Enforcement aspect of their jobs, it bears mention that the nature and intensity of the calls they responded to were beginning to get under their skin.

Franklin later recalled:

"Sonoma County had the highest rates of AIDS-related violent suicide in the state. Also, the place was riddled with weird drug-related, park vicinity murders and rapes. Thinking about this, a flood of memories came to me. The time I had to cut an AIDS-suicide victim down from the tree where he had hanged himself. Another time, I responded to a shooting, came through the bushes with my gun drawn, and saw a giant woman beating on a prostrate man with a bullet hole in his forehead screaming 'You son of a bitch...we were going to get married!' I had to kick the gun out of the way, cuff her, and then start CPR on him. Turns out, he had just been paroled from San Quentin and was dying from AIDS.

Another time, Loeffler and I responded to a call of a shooting. When we arrived, we found no gun but a victim laying on the ground. When we pulled back the hood of his sweatshirt, we discovered most of his head had been blown off. While searching for the weapon (a shotgun which had been thrust into the bushes by the kick-back), an aggressive dude came out of the bushes near the roadway and approached us with his hands behind his back. We drew down on him and demanded he show us his hands. He did, but kept walking towards us aggressively. We holstered, jumped him and cuffed him, while he resisted the entire time. We later found out the guy kept a scanner in his car, and responded to emergencies, then intentionally interfered in the scene enough to get arrested, giving him fodder to then sue the agency. At the time he had a case pending against the fire department. We arrested him anyway. It was the only time in my career I wanted to beat up a guy, but I didn't."

≈

Eventually Melvin, realizing the deleterious effects the law enforcement was having on both the community and himself, decided he would taper back on the number and intensity of his contacts. In so doing, he managed to successfully ease himself somewhat out of the limelight.

Franklin, on the other hand, being a newer and idealistic officer, seemingly felt an overwhelming responsibility to enforce *all* of the laws *all* of the time and picked up the bulk of the slack Melvin had left. Remarkably, in a district which employed a dozen law enforcement officers, including the rangers, in the first year of the lifeguard service, officers Franklin and Loeffler alone were responsible for over half of the staggering 800 citations written in the district. That daunting statistic might suggest they had completely pulled themselves from the aquatics realm to focus solely on writing citations. Not true. In fact, the two hard-driving Peace Officers were also involved in 63 out of the 93 documented rescues, dismissing any the notion that the gun-toting Perms did not pull their weight in the ocean.

In fact Loeffler's reputation as an intuitive and skilled lifeguard surfaced early on, and he soon became a mentor for the Seasonals. Martino cited Kurt as his main role-model in coordinating the aquatics in the South Sector. On one occasion Kurt insisted that they carry two paddleboards on an otherwise benign day. Sure enough, by day's end, they utilized both boards to perform an off-shore rescue of two victims off the Russian River outlet. As a caveat, Martino also cited Loeffler as the reason he would eventually become a Peace Officer himself.

On August 28th, 1991, the *Bodega Bay Signal* interviewed Hickey on the status of his program. Hickey, yet again, explained to the readers how dangerous the coastline was, and reiterated the virtues of his crew. But this time, near the end of the article, Hickey surprisingly opened his heart and eluded to the fact that the stress and emotional turmoil from the public scorn was taking a toll on his guards.

"Morale in the district is taking a beating. In the past, Park Rangers have been viewed by the populace as benign servants, custodians of the environment, friends of Smokey the Bear, but says Hickey, 'the current attitude towards us is making things really tough on our people.' Though reluctant to discuss in detail, he admits that Park personnel and their families have been harassed in supermarkets and schools."

To add to Hickey's concerns, by this time, two of his veteran, salty Permanents were beginning to see through the veil of charm their Lifeguard Supervisor had successfully parlayed on his rise up the State Parks ladder. To Franklin and Loeffler, all of the flashy accolades, glad-handing on committees, and recognition as a prodigious orator were paltry substitutes for Bud's lack of field experience. Thus, while Bud was seeking a similar kindred relationship he had been weaned on from the San Clemente crew, his efforts to bond with his North Coast crew were largely (and often times unfairly) viewed as patronizing and insincere. To them, behind his veil of charm, laid a thinner veil, and behind that one, only smoke and mirrors.

Ironically, at the same time his crew's respect for him was beginning to crumble, unbeknownst to them, Bud was diligently "working the crowd" behind the scenes on their behalf, meeting with the sheriffs, touring reporters through the district, attending nightly meetings with local civic groups and fielded the complaint calls those same Perms were generating with some regularity. Many of these meetings with outside entities were, to say the least, unpleasant encounters and his previously effective, tried and true methods to find rapport and middle ground with others, simply weren't working with these people. At one point he came to the stunning revelation that a significant number of locals actually hated him and his lifeguards, and he found himself asking himself the bombastic question *"How can these people hate me? I am a lifeguard!"*

Worse still, because Bud, thus far, had been unable to achieve any tangible results, his pride prevented him from letting his staff know he was actively fighting for them. Thus, although Hickey knew and acknowledged what he was doing, his staff never did and, like sitting in the proverbial pinch of the hourglass, Bud Brown was fighting a losing battle on both ends.

⌒

Undeniably, his veteran crew was a tough group to supervise and some would say Bud was destined to fail no matter what course he attempted to steer. In retrospect, he admitted his greatest fault at the time was his *"immaturity,"* which might explain why, he often refused to listen to input from them, despite their considerable real-world aquatics experience. According to them, owing to the harsh environment, the extended backup times from allied agencies, their lack of intra-agency training, and their limited resources, Bud's operational plans, designed from lifeguarding models used in Southern California, were simply not feasible in the wild west of the north, and to make matters worse, his guards were not willing to give him the benefit of even trying them. Eventually they would further pull their support from him and deliberately drag their feet in executing his orders, often stopping just short of insubordination.

After hours of interviews with all of the players in this saga, and hearing all of the arguments between Bud and his vocal oppositionists, it eventually struck me that *all* of those involved were guilty on one major account; *They forgot they were fighting the same fight.* The insane stressors to their psyche which they all shared (relentless public scorn, grotesque medicals, drownings, daunting rescues, massive surf, lack of recognition from the sheriffs, isolation, etc.), could have been opportunities to *commiserate and empathize* with each other, which they did - to some degree - in the patrol truck between calls, but inevitably they allowed those pressures to spurn disdain and overshadow the fact they were *lifeguards first, with a unified mission.*

On a personal note, early in his tenure on the North Coast, Loeffler had begun a sales pitch to his girlfriend back at Huntington, extoling the beauty and tranquility of the Sonoma Coast (while at the same time failing to mention the isolation and the rain), and he eventually convinced her to move up and live with him in the state residence. For the first year, the wonder and beauty of the area drew them closer and they were soon married. For Kurt, having a loving companion to come home to would help him cope with the heaviness of the calls. But soon after their nuptials, the solitude and quiet morphed into loneliness and isolation, and before long, their young marriage was on the ropes, piling on yet another layer of stress for Kurt.

In retrospect and overview, it's disappointing that Bud refused to accept guidance from his staff and admit his limitations...and it's equally disappointing that the original guards couldn't cut each other a bit more grace and forgiveness. Despite their monumental individual and collective accomplishments and numerous undeniable acts of heroism, the workplace suffered from a degree of unrest which wouldn't subside until the roster changed.

9-8-1991
THE RESCUE of the LA OLA

Originally included as one of the 39 stories in my first book "Stories from Sea Level," Straub and Carter's monumental rescue of the La Ola, was a truly historic event, and in some ways was the first step in the process of securing credibility with the other public safety agencies and the community. As a critical component of the North Coast Lifeguard's inaugural year, and it deserves to be retold in that context.

On September 8th 1991, the ocean conditions were horrendous, even by North Coast standards. A significant long-period swell produced a relentless stream of massive waves, the tops of which were being tattered by 40-knot winds which had been blowing all afternoon. After working in the wind all day, Straub and Carter had been looking forward to signing off, getting out of the elements, and enjoying a beer.

They were returning back from the South Sector and had just crested High Point when they overheard a mayday call on Channel 16 directed to the Coast Guard. The skipper of the "*La Ola*" reported his vessel was taking on water and that it was almost over his engine. He stated he was heading south from the Fort Ross area. With a voice of resignation he confided he had already donned his survival suit, indicating that losing the ship was only a matter of time. He added he had only a single passenger with him; his small dog.

The mention of Fort Ross caught the attention of the guards since they were close to the area. Then, as Carter rounded one of the turns, Straub, from the passenger seat, actually caught a glimpse of the boat, about a mile south of Pedotti's Reef. The vessel was most often obscured behind the enormous white-capped seas and from their vantage point the boat looked woefully small and vulnerable. Straub knew it was her, based solely on the fact there likely was not any other vessel out in *those* seas for a hundred miles.

The guards continued north with their overhead lights still off. They were not responding to this call. They couldn't. They didn't have a vessel large enough to venture out into those conditions. This was a call for the Coast Guard who would dispatch their 47' Motor Lifeboat out of Bodega Bay, and Straub mentioned that even a boat of that size would be tossed around mightily in those seas.

"Oh Man..." said Straub remorsefully. "That poor skipper guy is getting his ass kicked right now."

Carter nodded empathetically. Their conversation paused.

Straub continued, "There is no way he's going to survive in those seas. The ocean is simply gonna swallow him up. What the hell is he doing out there on a day like this?!"

Another pause in the conversation ensued as they continued north. For a full minute neither of them spoke, but in secret, both of them were running through various scenarios in their minds. It was gut-wrenching for guards *not* to respond this call, yet the only available boat they had was their little inflatable. For them to deploy in their glorified dinghy in those seas would be downright crazy. In a few minutes they would be passing Fort Ross, where their inflatable was kept in the garage. They both knew that if they continued past the Fort, their decision would be final.

Attempting the rescue would be insane and Don knew it. In order to have a chance to save the skipper he would need Carter, but he also knew they would be risking their hides and he couldn't force Dave to go. Eventually it was Straub who broke the silence, looking directly at Carter. His impassioned plea rang out like a sergeant imploring his under-gunned troops into battle, while ignoring the danger. "Hey, that skipper is fighting for his life right now. And right now he's alive. We are lifeguards dammit, and we have been brought up here to save lives. I think we can get to him and save him. Do you want to do it?"

Without hesitation, Carter reached down and hit the lights and siren. *"HELL YES!"* he shouted.

Straub picked up the mic and notified their dispatcher they were responding to a vessel in distress somewhere off of High Point. He requested "everyone and their brother" to respond.

And so began one of the craziest rescue scenarios in the history of the Sonoma Coast.

The *La Ola* was a classic old 40' Portuguese salmon boat. It was all wood with a small cabin. The boat had been on the seas for over 60 years, passed down from father to son through three generations of fishermen.

An hour earlier, the *La Ola* was getting beaten about by the nasty conditions and the captain was forced to seek refuge in the relatively sheltered seclusion of Fort Ross Cove. Unfortunately, the skipper was unaware of the single massive rock hidden just below the surface near center of the cove. The *La Ola* struck it with enough momentum to cause a breach of the hull and she immediately began to take on water. He went below deck and saw his worst nightmare. The damage was significant and water was hemorrhaging in through the shattered wood.

He had fired up his bilge pump but soon realized it was unable to keep up with the steady flow coming into the hull. The *La Ola* was his livelihood. The skipper knew if he did nothing, the *La Ola* would sink right there in the cove. He could swim to shore and save himself, but he would lose everything in exchange for his life. The other option would be foolhardy; to try and make the 25-mile run to the nearest dry dock in Bodega Bay. He knew if he committed himself to the open ocean, there would be no turning back, and sinking in the inhospitable ocean would not only cost him the loss of his vessel, but also quite possibly his life.

His decision would be fateful. He turned the crippled vessel to the southwest and limped out of Fort Ross Cove, pushing the *La Ola* back into the same violent seas from which he had sought refuge. He took a heading in the failing light then brought the engines to full throttle committing himself to a desperate 25-mile run to Bodega Bay.

Immediately after leaving the protection of Fort Ross Cove, the vessel was hammered by the wind, and the huge seas caused the *La Ola* to sway precariously back and forth. Realizing his chances of actually making it were slim, the skipper donned his bright orange survival suit and put out the Mayday call on Channel 16 as a prayer for help. Then stubbornly, he carried on into the open ocean.

The Coast Guard dispatcher was understandably shocked to hear that any vessel was out in those conditions. He heard the skipper's call and immediately dispatched their 47-foot Lifeboat out of Bodega Bay. Within ten minutes the crew was on board and heading north, fighting against the prevailing winds in a race to reach the *La Ola* before she sank.

Meanwhile, the guards pulled into the garage and retrieved the only rescue boat they had. It was their simple four-meter rubber inflatable equipped with a single 30-horse motor. They quickly donned their full wetsuits (without booties) and with the help of a few bystanders they carried the inflatable through the wind to the rocky shoreline. Straub was yelling orders, not so much out of stress but rather to be heard over the wind, as they carried the boat over the rocks and into the water.

Carter was beginning to feel the effects of fear creeping into his mind, which quickly swelled into an overwhelming sense of apprehension regarding their impending launch into those seas. He looked to Straub for guidance, searching his face for any similar signs of reservation. But as Straub was busy readying the boat, his expression was stern and committed, with no trace of hesitation at all. Don's steadfast confidence provided Dave with the sense of assurance he needed, as he would undoubtedly be riding on Don's coat tails on *this* adventure. They walked the boat out into thigh deep water and jumped aboard. Straub yanked on the starter cord and with a puff of smoke the little Yamaha came to life, almost inaudible amongst the winds. Straub guided the bow seaward and the two men shared a "high five" as they motored out through the relatively calm waters of the cove. They both knew that for the next few hours they would be involved in some major swashbuckling...yet they were "all in."

They turned southwest, out into the open ocean in search of the *La Ola*. They had no lights and no VHF communication. In fact they even left their handheld radio in the truck since they reasoned they would most likely lose it in those seas anyway. Their only gear on board were the most rudimentary of rescue tools; a couple of Peterson buoys and their fins, all of which were clipped onto the sponson with carabiners.

The moment they cleared the protected cove, they found themselves in the full force of the 40-knot winds blowing hard out of the northwest, occasionally lifting the starboard side of the little inflatable. Straub navigated at an angle to the wind to keep the boat from flipping. He opened up the throttle and the little boat bounced across the surface, with Carter pulling up on the bow line to keep the nose of the tiny vessel from plowing into the base of the breaking waves. The wind blew continual dousings of freezing cold water onto the men as Straub's sure hand guided the boat out into the open seas. Both men held gripped the braided line strung across the pontoons and they bounced along as if riding on a grey inflatable bronco. Once they reached the open ocean, they began riding up the faces of monstrous waves, the tops of which were being haphazardly torn off by the high winds.

Carter remembers, *"We headed offshore in our little inflatable. Don was expertly piloting us over some massive waves. Then we descended down into these deep green valleys and into the troughs, before heading back up the immense walls on the other side. When we crested the tops of the waves, we got air and the little engine was whining like crazy every time the prop broke the surface. I would have been more scared, but at some point Don was laughing and told me to look back to shore. I did and I've never felt so small in my whole life."*

Straub remembered the last sighting he had of the *La Ola*, considered where they had launched their IRB, estimated the lumbering speed of the sinking ship, contemplated the swell and wind, then threw all of that information out and tapped into the intangible intuition of his mind, setting a course to find a sinking vessel they could not see.

Straub recalled the moment. *"We just punched out and I took a dead reckoning course, estimating the waves and the wind and where I thought she might be. We were jammin' hard and fast, and coming off the tops of some of these waves getting so much air, we were literally flying. A couple times we came off and had a 30 foot drop to the bottom of the trough. While in the air the boat started to flutter, lifting the bow up and causing the engine to land first, so at some point I had to stall a bit and slow down so we wouldn't flip."*

Like reckless cowboys, the pair carried on out to sea, scaling and descending waves as large as warehouses. Through it all Straub kept a death grip on the tiller with one hand, and held onto the pontoon with the other to avoid getting pitched off the side. With the wave spray pelting him in the face almost continuously, he laughed hysterically like a madman defiantly mocking his adversary's beating.

Several miles south and two miles off-shore they came upon the *La Ola* just as the sun was going down. She was laboring mightily with a belly half-full of salt water. Every time a wave picked her up and she started to surf down the face, the water in her hull would pitch forward, causing her bow to dig deep into the trough, and allowing the ocean to wash more water over the gunwales. By then she was lumbering so slowly, the following seas were overtaking her. Barely three miles into the run for her life, she was sitting so low in the ocean, that it was clear to everyone, including the skipper, she was never going to make it.

The guards pulled up alongside her and through the wind and the spray the skipper made eye contact with them for the first time. Seeing the two guards approaching in the distance in their little grey inflatable in *those* seas, the skipper later confessed he initially thought he was hallucinating.

Osh McNulty had also responded to the call, and had driven to High Point in an attempt to spot the vessel. From that optimal vantage point, Osh watched through binos at the drama unfolding two miles offshore. Just then Henry-I arrived in the area. They located the vessel and began giving a sort of play-by-play over the radio. Osh remembers, *"McConnell was the pilot on Henry-I. He was always so professional and even-keeled on the radio...monotone and brief. But on that call, he narrated the events like a sportscaster... 'The little inflatable is heading towards the La Ola...I think they see it...Yes they see it... The lifeguards are pulling up alongside right now... They are tying up to the boat... THE LIFEGUARDS ARE BOARDING THE BOAT...THEY ARE BOARDING THE BOAT IN HIGH SEAS RIGHT NOW!'"*

Straub and Carter boarded the boat but there was little they could do. Straub went below her deck briefly and came out reporting - things didn't look good. Having to yell above the noise of the engines and the howling wind, Don breached the subject with the skipper of gathering up the valuables and the little dog to prepare for the inevitable loss. The skipper, old and stubborn, like a caricature of himself, refused to leave the helm. The winds were blowing far too strong for Henry-I to pluck the skipper from the vessel, so McConnell could do little except to monitor from above. If the *La Ola* went down, it would be the guards alone who would have to attempt to rescue the skipper and his dog in the inflatable.

With all the water in its hull, the boat was squirrely and, as Straub later said "just not acting like a boat should act." Additionally, the inflatable, tied off on her starboard side, was getting soundly beaten by the surf, such that some of the lanyards were getting yanked out. The entire situation, for everyone involved, was dire.

Soon after, the Coast Guard Lifeboat arrived on scene. Unfortunately they were too large to come alongside the sinking vessel and risk a deadly collision by slamming into it. By then, the La Ola's hull had taken on even more water and waves were now washing over her stern.

Don jumped back into the inflatable and told Carter to untie him so he could pilot over to the Cutter. With the soft-sided inflatable, he could pull directly alongside their vessel. He gave the captain a quick status report and asked for a portable bilge pump. The crew obliged and lowered the pump onto the inflatable along with two gas cans and the first of three officers who wanted to board the La Ola. Straub then delivered the pump and the officer back to the La Ola. Together, the officer and Straub descended into the dim light of the hull and fired up the portable bilge pump. Moments later, water began to flow from the exit hose, and initially there was some sense of hope. But as darkness grew, it was clear they were fighting a losing battle, as the flow of water now pouring into the hull was greater than the bilge pump could remove.

To complicate the situation, the young Coast Guard officer was from the Midwest and had never been in seas like these. When he descended into the cramped cabin he was greeted with the provocative smells of an old man's domicile. The *meritage* of stale beer, cigarette smoke and diesel fuel took the officer out with a violent case of seasickness, and he soon became incapacitated. Don shuttled him back to the relative comfort of the Lifeboat. The two other officers, after seeing what their partner had just gone through, both decided to bow out, stating "No that's okay, you lifeguards can manage the call."

Straub then requested and received a second bilge pump from the Coasties. He and Carter carried it into the hull and fired it up. With both pumps working at full throttle, eventually the water level in the hull began to descend. A gradual sense of confidence settled on all three men, and within 30 minutes, the La Ola began, ever so slowly, to rise in the water. Hope soon began to grow that she might actually make it the remaining 20 miles to dry dock. Now in complete darkness, the skipper took a heading for Bodega Head, and continued full throttle with the two guards aboard, and the cutter leading the way.

Carter also remembers a magical detail about their run. *"With the two pumps working, we were able to relax somewhat. The vessel was dragging two ballasts behind her. It happened to be a night of red tide and the ballasts stirred up the phosphorescence brightly. Staring into the black water behind the boat, it looked like there were two brightly illuminated comets trailing long tails following us."*

But for Carter, the drama was not yet over. There was one element of the rescue he kept in confidence for many years. Few individuals ever knew about it, but McNulty was one of them. In researching the story, he made sure I asked Carter about it, and Dave came clean.

At some point in the night, amidst the huge seas and relentless winds, Straub asked Dave to retrieve something from the inflatable which was tied off the starboard side. Carter climbed down off the side of the *La Ola*, which by then had recovered considerably and was riding much higher in the water. As he descended onto the inflatable, Carter lost his footing and in that instant, three miles offshore in near total darkness, he fell from the boat and splashed into the blackness and frigid chill of the 49 degree water.

Amid the noise and the wind, no one heard him yell out. In fact, there is no doubt that no one would've realized he was gone for a very long time, and Carter would likely have had to swim the entire three miles, at night, in the most horrendous of conditions imaginable, simply to make it to shore in *no man's land*, on a desolate coastline, still many miles from any town. But amazingly, the man upstairs threw him a lifeline, literally, as Dave felt the momentary sensation of a rope dragging against his leg. It was the 12' section of rope they routinely trailed behind the inflatable. He grabbed it and held on to that rope as if his life depended on it, because it did.

Carter remembered that critical event, *"In desperation I reached out and managed to grab the rope. The vessel was doing far better by then and was making way so it was incredibly hard to hold on with my freezing hands while being dragged behind the boat. I instinctively knew if I lost my grip it could cost me my life, so I just held on and eventually was able to incrementally pull myself closer and closer to the IRB. But I bet it took me at least six or seven minutes to make it back to the stern of the inflatable. My arms were sore for days after. I pulled myself back onto the inflatable, then back onto the La Ola. As I had suspected, no one had even noticed I was gone."*

The skipper had radioed ahead to dry dock, and someone woke up the Harbor Master. Just after midnight the *La Ola* pulled into the harbor and directly into the dry dock slip, where she was hoisted out of the water to safety.

All told, according to the dispatch logs, the rescue had taken four hours and twenty minutes. McNulty met his guards there with blankets and a warm welcome before they embarked on the long drive back to their patrol vehicle at Fort Ross.

Carter and Straub would not get to sleep until 2:00 am, but both took their well-deserved rest, content in knowing they had just performed the rescue of their lives.

A week later, Chief Ranger Hickey received a beautiful letter from the captain, commending the efforts of Straub and Carter. The end of the letter stated in part...*"The Coast Guard later arrived with another pump and in the end my boat, my dog, and I were safely returned to port. Rough seas and high winds made the whole operation incredibly difficult. Without the skills and fast actions of lifeguards Straub and Carter, the outcome of this story would have been much different. I am in their debt and send them and you my grateful appreciation."*

Thirteen months to the day after the lifeguards arrived, Brian Hickey finally had his "big" rescue.

In retrospect, he could not have choreographed a more dramatic display of heroism. The elements of the rescue played out like a movie. With a backdrop of the dramatic high seas and the 40-knot winds, these two simple guards, equipped with no communication or navigational assistance, and only the most rudimentary gear imaginable, had the audacity to venture out in those hellish conditions and were able to effect the rescue, saving the vessel and her crew, using nothing but their God-given skills and a truckload of bravery.

Word about the rescue quickly spread throughout the North Sector community and the locals took notice. Soon, the story migrated into the coffee shops and boat docks of the South Sector as well.

The savvy Brian Hickey was ready to capitalize on the outpouring of recognition as the ultimate validation of his crew's worthiness and mettle. He waited for the tide of resistance and opposition to turn and, finally, for his guards to be welcomed into the fold as a vital and worthy part of the Emergency Services Community. But unfortunately, the wall of adversity built and fortified against the lifeguards for over a year proved to be surprisingly dense. Within three months, chatter about the rescue dwindled and Hickey came to the painful realization - even *that* rescue would not be the panacea he had hoped for. But he took solace in the fact that it did serve to chisel off the first few chunks from the wall, and if you looked really closely, some deeper cracks were beginning to show as well.

In June of 1992, in a small unpublicized ceremony in San Diego, The United States Lifesaving Association awarded Don Straub and David Carter the Medal of Valor for their efforts in saving the *La Ola* and her crew.

It should be noted that nominations for the Medal of Valor are submitted by the supervisory staff of their respective organizations. On the Sonoma Coast the general consensus was that making rescues in horrendous conditions was part of the mutually agreed job they had signed up for. Simply put, the bar which constituted an act of "heroism" was undeniably set much higher there. For the powers that be to acknowledge a rescue as being worthy of Medal of Valor status was, up until then, unprecedented.

Dave Carter and Don Straub receive the first Medal of Valor for the North Coast Lifeguards (1991)

It was the first Medal of Valor event awarded to the lifeguards from the Sonoma Coast, but in the ensuing years, they would perform many more rescues deemed worthy of that honor. To date, the small band of guards working that district have garnered more Medal of Valor awards than any other agency.

9-22-1991
THE STOLEN ICE CHEST CAPER

In the pre-dawn darkness of October 12th, a camper at Salt Point named Jeffrey Slade heard voices outside of his tent. Silently he pulled himself from his sleeping bag and emerged to find two men in the process of stealing his $13 ice chest. Until 5:00 pm the previous evening, the ice chest contained 12 bottles of Miller Lite, a 10-pack of Oscar Meyer hot dogs and a can of Skoal chewing tobacco. But by midnight, all that remained were a couple submerged bottle caps and two Miller beer labels submerged beneath two gallons of melted ice.

But the crooks didn't know that. They grabbed the ice chest and started heading toward their truck.

Mr. Slade, however, was not altogether on board with the plan of having his $13 ice chest released from his possession. In his pseudo-awake state-of-mind, he grabbed a long handled axe he had left by the fire pit and, wearing only his boxer shorts and his tattoos, headed towards the thieves to reclaim what was rightfully his.

The crooks started up their truck and, for some unknown reason they would soon come to regret, drove *toward* Slade, apparently not noticing the man was holding in his right hand, an implement of significant bearing. Slade, who up until five minutes prior had been enjoying a deep, Miller Lite induced sleep, suddenly found himself staring into the headlights of an approaching truck which, by his reckoning, appeared to be bearing down on him. Fearing for his life, Slade took an aggressive stance and lifted the axe over his head with both hands. The driver, no doubt surprised by the sight of the boxer-clad man illuminated in his headlights wielding an axe, stopped the truck just short of striking him.

Slade, inspired by the synergistic effects of adrenalin, combined with residual buzz of alcohol, decided at that moment to thrust the head of the axe into the hood of the truck several times in rapid succession, leaving several gaping, wedge-shaped holes in it. The culprits suddenly found themselves in a situation which had quickly escalated well-past any conceivable expectation they might have had for the evening's outing of light thievery. The driver threw the truck into reverse, thereby solidifying their juxtaposed roles as victims.

Unfortunately for the would-be thieves, Slade was not yet done. In a remarkable display of nimbleness and agility (considering his mental status), he ran to the truck and reached the door just as the driver was shifting out of reverse and into drive, in an attempt to flee the scene.

The answer to the question, "*Why men do what they do?*" is a riddle as old as time itself. The question is often a rhetorical one providing no gratifying answer. In this case, perhaps the ice chest held some sentimental meaning to the owner, beyond the $13 he had paid for it; possibly it was a gift from his beloved grandfather. Maybe he had some special plans for the remaining ice. But for whatever reason, as the driver slammed the accelerator to the floor and the tires spun wildly, throwing dirt and gravel 20' behind them, Slade took a final mighty swing with his trusty axe aimed squarely against the driver's side window, hoping to shatter it into a million little chicklets of glass.

Unfortunately for everyone there that night, the driver's side window was *open*. Slade lost his grip, and the axe flew into the driver's compartment like a weighted missile cast recklessly into an abyss with no specific target.

Slade then heard the unnerving and sobering sound of a loud thud, consistent with a direct hit on some human body part.

The bad guys, with hatchet in tow, sped away.

The extent of the injuries to one or both of them men was unknown. The responding lifeguard, called out from his state residence, was Kurt Loeffler. As part of his investigation, he contacted Santa Rosa General Hospital and gave them instructions to notify him if anyone arrived in the Emergency Room with a skull fracture, a detached mandible, or an axe-shaped dent between their eyes.

Loeffler also considered calling the local body shops around Santa Rosa in the morning to see if any trucks came in, punctured with somewhere between 7 and 10 axe-shaped holes on the hood which extending in a rather random pattern along the left quarter-panel. But since Slade declined to press charges, Loeffler let this issue rest.

Mr. Slade had lost his $13 ice chest and unintentionally had added his $17 axe to the thieves' booty. But he had the rare and twisted satisfaction of brutal frontier justice in absolutely annihilating the bad guy's truck, and quite possibly his face. Loeffler explained to Slade - without a victim he had no grounds to pursue assault and battery charges against him, and with a wink, informed Mr. Slade he was free to enjoy the rest of his stay in the campground.

But before leaving, Loeffler leaned over to Slade and whispered the question which most of the general populace of men probably would have liked to ask...

"How did it feel to wallop on the thieves like you did?" he asked with a prompting smile.

Slade stared at the ground expressionless, as if pondering the question for the first time. Then slowly he started nodding, and a wry smile came over his face.

"Pretty damned good," he said.

GOOFIN' OFF

Donning wetsuit and scarf, Martino takes the helm of the "Redwood Rocket"

As mentioned, the staff conflicts admittedly created some tension among the guards, but it should be clarified - those struggles and personality conflicts were limited to a few key players. The rest of the crew, especially early on, avoided choosing sides or entering into the fray. They genuinely liked and respected each other; sentiments which were most certainly bolstered by the nature of their work together, and they had a LOT of fun together.

Lest we forget, these guys were *lifeguards*, for God sakes; a group of individuals with notorious reputations as fun-loving, larger-than-life, thrill-seeking individuals who live their lives in bold colors on the larger stage of life. They were story-tellers, quick with a joke, living in the moment and investing in each day to the fullest. Like brothers, despite their conflicts, they hung out together after work. They dove together. They drank wine and created lavish seafood meals together. They surfed together and engaged in plenty of carousing and mischief.

Also like brothers, they teased each other ruthlessly, which often included the planning and execution of elaborate pranks.

Loeffler was the unchallenged king of comedy. He had a sharp tongue and a quick wit, and used both liberally among the entire staff.

His sense of humor pushed the limits of decency at times, but it also served as a salve to diffuse pent-up stress and certainly helped bond the guards together.

Straub too could tease his partners ruthlessly.

Case in point...

Straub and Franklin – Windy patrol in the IRB – (1991) – Photo: Loeffler

Steve Franklin would be the first to admit he was not much of a "boat guy." Now, one might think an experienced operator like Don might ease the rookie deckhand into his new role on the high seas, but Don didn't see it that way. The moment Franklin confessed his lack of experience, Don began to look for opportunities to exploit his new apprentice.

Just inside the park's northern boundary is a beautiful large inlet known as Horseshoe Cove. The south side of the bay has one of the few surf breaks on that stretch of coast. Few people knew about the break, hence the name given to it is "Secrets."

The two guards pulled the IRB into the cove one day, and came across a young couple free-diving. Neither one of them had any skills at all, so Don cut the engines and threw out the anchor line, and the guards settled in to scrutinize the divers' ineptitude. After about 30 minutes the girl had given up and was resting on her float tube, but her boyfriend was persistent, and kept making surface dives in vain attempts to score a prized abalone. Because he was such a pathetic diver, the guards found themselves stuck there, babysitting him.

At some point Franklin admitted he hadn't eaten before they left, and with that bit of information, Don hatched a plan. Unfortunately he couldn't initiate it until the knucklehead diver got out, and the guy was still stubbornly trying to get an abalone to impress his girlfriend. By then his lips were blue and he was shivering noticeably.

Don pulled the anchor and they motored closer to the couple, then engaged the diver, suggesting perhaps it might be time to give up and head back to shore. The kid, seemingly incensed and overtly defensive, proclaimed he was an "experienced diver" and attributed his lack of success for the past 90-minutes on the fact there were "No abalone down there."

Horseshoe Cove (1995)

Straub offered him a deal, suggesting he would give the kid an abalone if, in exchange, both he and his girlfriend would agree to kick to shore and go home. Surprisingly the kid's desire to have an abalone exceeded his need to protect his ego, and he agreed. Don grabbed his mask and an old weight belt from the gear hold, and eased off the side of the boat. In less than 30 seconds, he returned to the surface with an abalone which was a full inch larger than the legal limit, then kicked over and handed it to the kid. The couple were both thrilled and, keeping up their part of the deal, began to kick in.

Straub, knowing Franklin hadn't eaten and already knowing the answer, innocently asked him if he was hungry, to which Steve replied, "I'm starving!" Don then innocuously asked the follow-up question,

"Hey man, have you ever tried 'Uni?'"

"What's Uni?" asked Franklin.

"They're Sea Urchin eggs, Steve. It's a rare delicacy - super expensive - served in the fanciest restaurants in Tokyo."

"Wow, really? No, I never even heard of it before. Where can we get some?" asked Franklin.

Being able to sustain oneself from the ocean's bounty by fishing, foraging, or spearfishing was one of the fundamental skills in becoming a well-rounded Waterman, and part of that skill hinged on knowing the many varieties of foods available. So when Don disclosed that Uni was a supreme delicacy, and "super expensive," Franklin, eager to discover this new and exotic treat, took the bait.

"Well, I'm not sure, Steve. But I *have* seen a few in this very area before, and, if we are lucky, I might be able to find us a couple. Just hang out for a minute."

In truth, on Don's previous dive he noticed the bottom was literally covered with the invasive urchin, so he dropped back down, grabbed a half-dozen of them, then stalled near the bottom for over a minute to add to the drama before surfacing with both hands full. Franklin was beaming with excitement!

"Here, grab them from me" said Don, handing them over the gunwale to Franklin.

Back on the boat, Don then meticulously cracked around the ring of the shell with his abalone iron, then dropped the slimy, yellow, fishy concoction into his dive mask. He then demonstrated how to slurp it down in one big gulp.

Franklin eagerly followed suit, carefully cracking and slurping his first urchin and immediately busied himself working on another.

Meanwhile, with Franklin looking down, preoccupied with his new assignment, Don subtly began backing the boat at a 45-degree angle to the swell, causing the boat to start rocking irregularly, while at the same time allowing the idling exhaust fumes to waft over them.

No more than ten minutes had passed when Franklin, working on his 4th urchin, suddenly looked up from his task. His normally red face had taken on an interesting shade of pale and Don knew it wouldn't be long before his mission would be accomplished. For the coup-de-grace, Don cut the engine and let the boat turn parallel to the swells, causing the rocking motion to shift once again. In no time Franklin was laying over the sponson, puking like a frat boy.

∽

As a further testament to the wild cowboy that was Don Straub, one night, after a successful day of lifeguarding, while having a beer by the campfire with Franklin at Arky Camp, Straub heard the distinct rustling of something in the bushes. Neither of them knew what it was, but there was no doubt it was large and clumsy. Their conversation stopped mid-sentence.

Moments later, a massive wild boar trampled free from the brush with several piglets accompanying her.

Instantly, Straub yelled out, "WILD PIG!" as he bolted up from his chair.

Franklin too sprang from his chair, prepared to follow Don, fleeing to the safety of the trailer, or into his truck bed, whichever Don decided.

One can only imagine Franklin's confusion when, in the next

moment, expecting Don to run *AWAY* from the massive snorting animal and her brood, instead he watched Straub sprint *AFTER* them.

The pigs immediately scattered in retreat, back into the concealment and safety of the dense brush, and probably assumed their unplanned encounter with the humans was over. But Don, proving to Franklin he most certainly was a wild man, immediately vaulted into the tangled brush in hot pursuit.

Franklin stood there dumbfounded, thoroughly confused as to why Don would consciously engage in a pursuit of such a wild and intimidating animal. Worse yet, he feared the possibility that at any moment Don might yell out for him to enter in the fray to assist in some way.

A major commotion ensued deep in the brush. Amid the raucous sounds of breaking branches and Don's screams, were the bone-chilling squeals of what sounded like a hundred little pigs, followed by the clumsy rustling sounds of a major retreat up the hillside.

As if escaping from the jungle in some pre-historic movie, traipsing out of the brush emerged the wild cowboy himself, laughing triumphantly, with a squealing little piglet securely held under his arm.

Through all of this, Franklin had not moved, and stood next to his knocked over chair with his beer in his hand and his mouth hung open.

Straub then casually explained to the stunned Franklin, amidst the ongoing squealing, that pigs are sprinters, and have virtually no endurance. He added - if you chase them, they quickly tire and you can nab them. As if Franklin needed verification of this claim, Don extended the squealing piglet as proof.

Franklin, it seemed, was as freaked out as the little piglet, and concluded (as if there was ever any doubt), that Don Straub was, in fact, insane.

10-12-1991
SCUBA GIRL - TIMBER COVE

Wendy Howell was a 20-year old college student from Livermore who, from the time she was a little girl, loved everything which involved the ocean. As a child, her parents took her to the Monterey

Bay Aquarium regularly, which further solidified her passion for the undersea world.

For her 20th birthday she enrolled in a scuba course in hopes of being able to immerse herself directly into the ocean sanctuary, and marvel at the undersea universe without the insulation of glass.

In October of 1991, she set off with high hopes for a memorable adventure on her maiden dive.

After discovering the swell forecast indicated only modest surf, she teamed up with three friends and chartered a cabin cruiser which would deliver them to the fertile waters near Salt Point where she would finally be able to immerse herself into the wild and untamed ocean.

Unfortunately, when they arrived, the ocean conditions were atrocious for diving, as an unexpected yet pervasive red tide had settled in along the coastline, severely limiting the visibility to almost zero. The boat captain traversed along various coves and areas of the open ocean, searching for any pockets of clear water, but found nothing but a seemingly endless expanse of rust-brown colored water. Eventually he delivered the foursome to an arbitrary spot just north of Timber Cove, where he anchored the boat in a clearing, near the edge of a large expanse of kelp.

After prepping their gear and making the necessary safety checks, the divers paired up. Wendy would dive with her boyfriend, who reportedly had some level of proficiency and several dozen dives under his belt.

Unlike her training dives in the clean and chlorinated water of the swimming pool, as she descended toward the bottom, she felt like she was immersing herself into a sea of root beer. Almost immediately she realized that it would difficult, if not impossible to orient herself in this strange and heavily obscured aquatic world. Once her fins touched the sea bottom, she began kicking slowly, using the sea floor as her only guide to stay horizontal. Unable to see anything but dark brown water in all directions, the disorienting sensation, not unlike floating in complete darkness, began to stimulate a growing sense of anxiety inside in her. Frustrated that she could see nothing which wasn't immediately in front of her, to assess the visibility she slowly pulled her hand towards her mask and was stunned to realize that her fingers only come into view when they were less than a foot from her face.

Consciously trying to overcome her nerves, she continued on, and unintentionally entered into the kelp forest. Suddenly, what little light previously permeating though the murky water was blacked out by the thick kelp canopy overhead, which laid over the ocean surface like a blanket. Realizing her mistake, she attempted to retreat, but owing to her disorientation, she was unknowingly advancing even deeper into the underwater jungle. As the darkness thickened, invisible strands of kelp brushed against her body, and her visual field, seen through the 4" tube of her facemask, was now inundated with a barrage of swirling kelp fronds coming in and out of focus through the murky water.

A profound sensation of anxiety and claustrophobia boiled over inside of her. Having ascended away from the bottom, she was now unable to see or feel any stationary structures with which to orient herself, and was overcome with the maddening realization that she wasn't entirely certain which direction her escape path to the surface might be.

Unable to resist the growing sense of panic, she began hyperventilating and quickly consumed her remaining air. She began thrashing in terror against the invisible kelp which surrounded her, which only caused the strands to tangle and cinch around her tank, her fins, and eventually her body. At some point, hopelessly ensnared like a fish in a gill net, her strength began to fade...then she felt the alarming sensation of the air flow in her regulator begin to restrict. Still conscious, Wendy faced the terrifying realization that in a matter of seconds, her air supply would run out, and she would suffocate.

Her boyfriend, who had been preoccupied with his own attempts to orient himself, had become thoroughly distracted from his obligation to stay with her. As he kicked along the bottom searching for a clearer water, he suddenly realized he had lost contact with her, and began back-tracking to locate her.

With an ever-increasing sense of unease, after violating the critical rule of staying together, he started moving through the kelp and suddenly came across the shadowy figure of his girlfriend's body, hopelessly tangled in the kelp. He approached her tentatively. Through the murky water he was able to see her regulator hanging uselessly by her side. He pushed his mask closer to her face and through her faceplate, saw the alarming sight of her eyes wide open in a blank stare.

Resisting the urge to escape to the surface, he gathered himself enough to pull the regulator from his mouth and insert it into hers in hopes she might still be able to breathe...but he quickly realized it was pointless, as she was already unconscious.

Shot through with panic, he escaped to the surface and immediately yelled out to the boat captain that his partner was unconscious. The skipper immediately switched over to channel 16 and put out an emergency call of a *"DIVER DOWN OFF OF TIMBER COVE!"*

After taking a brief moment to gather his wits and several breaths of fresh air, the boyfriend settled into the reality that he alone must now act if she had any chance of being saved. He pushed his regulator back into his mouth and descended back down through the thick kelp.

In the haze of the murky water and thick kelp, he was fortunate to relocate her quickly. Struggling to remain calm, and without the aid of a knife, in the limited visibility he began to yank recklessly at the thick braids of kelp in an ever-increasing frenzy, and was able to disentangle the strands from around her tank, her neck, and her arms. He managed to drop her weight belt, then released the rest of her gear, which sank to the bottom. Now positively buoyant in her 7-mm wetsuit, he was then able to ascend through the thick canopy of kelp and reached the surface with her lifeless body.

While the skipper backed the boat toward them, the boyfriend, not knowing exactly what to do, gave her two full breaths, then assisted the skipper in loading her lifeless body into the transom of the vessel.

Fortuitously, Straub and Franklin were in the area, and had heard emergent call go out. Loeffler and Schardt, in another unit, also acknowledged the call and were also in route.

It was Straub and Franklin who arrived in the area first. They spotted the vessel anchored a quarter-mile off-shore just north of Timber Cove, but unfortunately with a steep 25' bluff between them and the water, there would be no easy access. Regardless, with no time to waste, they quickly suited up. Straub then pulled the paddleboard off the roof, secured the clip of his buoy to one of the handles, and quickly lowered it as far down the bluff face as the line would allow before letting it fall the rest of the way. Realizing they would likely need their portable resuscitator, Franklin grabbed one from the unit and ran south to find a viable goat trail to reach the water. Then, in one of the more unorthodox rescues ever completed, Franklin kicked out on his back, while *clutching the resuscitator in his arms*, successfully negotiating through a series of waves and making it outside the surf line with the clumsy apparatus.

Meanwhile, Straub had somehow managed to descend over the steepest part of the bluff, retrieved the paddleboard, and launched himself recklessly into the sea directly in the full force of the breaking waves. A sizable set greeted him and ejected him violently back onto the rocks, but somehow Don was able to hold onto the board and, on his second attempt, plowed through the waves and made it to the outside.

Clear of the breaking waves, Franklin then placed the resuscitator on the front of the paddleboard and Don began sprinting out to the vessel, with Franklin swimming behind him.

Soon after, Loeffler and Schardt pulled into Timber Cove and commandeered a small vessel from the boat launch. They too were motoring north to the dive boat.

Arriving first, Straub and Franklin found the unconscious victim laying on her back on the boat deck.

Her friends encircled her, wearing grave and pleading expressions, fearing their friend was dead. The boyfriend was administering mouth to mouth ventilations, but the victim's skin tone was a death-like shade of pale-blue. They cleared a path for the guards and Franklin quickly unzipped the resuscitator while Straub cut open her wetsuit and placed his fingers along her trachea to assess if she still had a viable pulse. That determination, which would be critical in guiding their course of action, was challenging with this hypothermic patient and the diminished sensation in Don's chilled fingers. But after several moments, Don looked to Franklin, "I think she had a fleeting pulse...double check for me, Steve." Switching positions, Straub completed hooking up the ventilation mask while Franklin delicately palpated her carotid artery. "Definitely," he confirmed. "She's got a pulse, although it's very weak."

With this bit of good news, the guards proceeded to focus on providing respirations for their patient who was not breathing. Straub held the oxygen mask over her mouth and nose, and tilted her neck back to open her airway while Franklin began squeezing the bag, filling her lungs with supplemental oxygen.

Loeffler and Schardt boarded the boat. While Straub and Franklin continued with their resuscitative measures, they wrapped the victim in a blanket. Loeffler, using the boat's radio, confirmed their location with the REACH Helicopter.

Straub and Franklin continued on for some time, periodically stopping to re-check the pulse to make certain she hadn't descended into cardiac arrest. But soon, the patient's cyanotic blue skin color began to fade and the guards realized they were making progress. At some point Franklin called for a stop and placed his ear next to the victim's mouth. "She's breathing!" he stated emphatically. Not only was her skin color returning to normal, she was *breathing on her own.*

Schardt switched out the resuscitative mask, replacing it with one which would support the victim's own ventilations. The small bag attached to the device could be seen gently inflating and deflating with every breath, assuring the guards that she was, in fact breathing on her own.

Together the crew monitored the victim until Henry-I arrived overhead. In that time the patient had continued to make significant progress. Her respirations had grown deeper and slower. Soon she began to cough and cry, though she still was unable to respond to Franklin's commands to open her eyes.

While hovering in the helo, Tom McConnell skillfully lowered his medic with a Stokes basket directly onto the deck of the small boat. Beneath the deafening noise of the massive helo, the victim was lifted from the boat and ascended into the open belly port of the aircraft. Seconds later, they turned and flew off to the Santa Rosa Hospital.

Upon arrival, the patient was whisked into the ICU where, as is the protocol for all drowning patients, she was placed in a medically-induced coma, intubated and secured to a ventilator to allow her lungs to adequately heal from her non-fatal drowning.

A month later, an emotional letter of thanks written by the victim's friend on her behalf arrived at the district office. Written testaments of thanks to the lifeguards were exceedingly rare, and in this case well-deserved. The physician who treated her attested to the fact that without their swift actions and vigorous resuscitative efforts, had she lived at all, she would likely have suffered irreversible brain damage. Instead, with the added beneficial factors of her youth, the cold water, and the boyfriend's efforts, despite the extended time of her submersion, and her brief visit to the "other side," she would eventually make a complete recovery.

Commodore helicopter pilot Tom McConnel, State Parks lifeguard Steve Franklin, Wendy Howell, Bob Maclean, Kimberly Palmiter, and Search-and-Rescue Team paramedic Lou Lupo pose in front of the helicopter that rushed Howell to the hospital last month.
Signal photo by Kathie Morgan

Sonoma Coast divers honor rescue team

The Press Democrat captured the reunion of rescuers with the victim.

Several months later, both Straub and Franklin were invited to attend the victim's birthday celebration in the Bay Area, and were joyfully reunited with their young patient. Additionally, for the next six years, Straub faithfully continued to attend her annual party. And each time he arrived, Don was introduced and heralded to her friends as *the reason* they were gathered to celebrate her life. As might be assumed, when someone endures a life-threatening brush with death, their appreciation for simply being alive can be deep and profound. For Don, seeing this young woman growing and thriving, provided an ongoing and tremendously gratifying reward for him as well. From a distance, watching her laugh and interact with her friends was a living validation of his original decision to pull up stakes and head north into the "great unknown" of the Sonoma Coast, to pursue his crazy passion as an Ocean Lifeguard.

THE WINTER of 1991

As expected, in late October the surf rose again. With buoy readings climbing daily, solid 15' waves hammered the coastline. A chill descended over the entire area, foretelling their imminent entry into winter. The guards patrolled with the windows of their trucks rolled up and the heaters on. In the North Sector the numbers of divers dwindled, yet the guards still searched for the tougher ones, willing to brave the elements and bone-chilling water during the coldest and roughest months for their prized abalone. These were guys who were more experienced, and truth be told, some of them could still get out into sheltered areas and get their abs safely, even with the surf breaking overhead. By then, the guards had met many of them and had even begun to recognize their vehicles.

As mentioned, it was the novice divers who were the biggest concern; especially in the winter months. Like wild teenagers trying to prove themselves, these young men were often reckless and took unnecessary risks. Some were toying with hyperventilation in order to extend their bottom times. They had discovered that blowing off higher levels of CO_2 on the surface before descending could extend their bottom times - which was true. But few were aware the practice was a major culprit in the phenomenon of "shallow water blackout" wherein a diver loses consciousness on their subsequent ascent. Using themselves as test-subjects, and most often diving alone, they repeatedly pushed the limits of prudence and, for some, their carelessness led to tragedy. Thus, shallow water blackout was always suspected as a possible mechanism of death whenever an experienced diver drowned with no other obvious cause.

The onset of winter hadn't so much curtailed the lifeguards' work, but rather altered their strategies. The guards in the North Sector patrolled the Coast Highway looking for trucks parked in areas known to be adjacent to dive spots. When they found a truck they suspected might belong to a diver, they hiked out to try and locate him in the ocean.

Of course the winter was also mushroom foraging season along the North Coast, and the pickers used many of the same parking spots, forcing the guards to try and decipher whether the car belonged to a diver or a mushroom picker. The most obvious clue involved the type of vehicle. A beater old pick-up truck was a sure bet to be a diver. Conversely, a Hyundai Sonata, VW Gulf, Mini-Cooper, or any white car suggested they were mushroom pickers. If there was a doubt, the guards would peer in through the windows to find further clues the owner might in fact be a diver. The usual evidence included piles of clothes, beer cans, extra dive gear, NRA stickers on the windshield, cigarette butts, and fishing licenses left on the dashboard.

10-29-1991
PROVEN RIGHT

Using the aforementioned strategy, on a day in late October with a decent swell running, McNulty found a truck parked in a remote location and reasoned it likely belonged to a diver who had likely headed out to dive the waters around Grace Rock. That entire area was fully exposed to the north-west swell, with no viable safe place to dive for quite a distance in either direction. Osh felt the hood of the truck and determined it was still warm, so he grabbed his pack containing all of his rescue gear and began briskly hiking out through the wet grass towards the distant roar of the waves in hopes of reaching the diver before he made the bad decision to kick out.

Osh got lucky. His proactive tactics paid off. As he reached the bluff and peered over the edge, sure enough, there was the lone diver on the rocks far below, preparing to go out. From above he watched the guy finish a beer and chuck the can onto the rocks. Osh then scampered down the goat trail to the water's edge. The diver, who had probably thought his long trek had sufficiently delivered him far from all trace of humanity, was understandably surprised when Osh greeted him on shore.

McNulty was a man of few words and the actual phrases he used are long forgotten, but it is safe to assume the general content of his conversation was something like, "Hey there, buddy. I see you're preparing to go out here. I just wanted to point out the surf is running kind of large right now, and the bigger sets are well-overhead. Frankly, it's pretty damn dangerous in this area, and the visibility is definitely going to be awful. I was hoping to convince you it might not be in your best interest to go out here today."

The novice diver, as so many did, misinterpreted Osh's erudite and well-meaning advice as an insult to his manhood. What he heard in Osh's polite warning was (and again I am paraphrasing here) was probably along the lines of, *"Hey a***hole. I just hiked out here to remind you that you are a candy-assed pansy. Only real men could get any abalone on a day like this, and since, as I just mentioned, you are a candy-assed pansy, there is no way you're gonna get any."*

Okay. That might be a slight exaggeration, but as I said, it was not uncommon for divers to take offense to the lifeguards' well-meaning warnings (this generalization did not apply to women by the way). Often times the guards, realizing there was no way to reason with them, had no choice but to retreat and leave them to their own undoing.

Realizing that the guy was incorrigible and dead-set on diving there, Osh wished him luck and retreated back up to the top of the bluffs and out of sight, so as not to force the diver to feel further challenged to prove him wrong.

Regardless, the moment the diver hit the water, Osh started gearing up and had ample time to comfortably don his wetsuit, booties, and even his gloves - which was rare. The diver's entry point was in the lee of a large rock, which allowed him some shelter from the oncoming swell, but it also exposed him to unseen currents and some dynamic hydrology which, of course, he had not anticipated. Immediately upon traversing past the inshore area he was pounded by several sizable waves and clung tightly to his ab float, while the ocean re-circulated him back into the impact zone, where he was immediately battered again. By then the nimble McNulty had already dashed back down the bluff trail and was on his way out to make the rescue.

The diver found himself mired in the swirling waters of some mysterious hydrology created when large swells channel in and around dynamic rock formations. With each passing wave the water surface rose and fell eight feet or more, and at times spun the man around without warning. He was utterly helpless. As if trying to deliver a lesson, the breaking waves pounded him further before dissipating into the deeper channel, thereby preventing him from riding them out of the impact area. Thus, he remained in the dangerous area, where the ocean held him, and soundly pummeled him.

Osh was familiar with the area and swam out through the clear water rip just to the north. The man clung to his ab float in desperation and didn't notice McNulty until he was right next to him. When the diver looked up, his eyes, behind the glass of his mask, were wide open and filled with fear.

Little conversation exchanged between the two men. Osh wrapped his buoy around him, then pulled him due south to escape the rip. Once free from the pull, he could have simply turned to shore and begun the long swim straight in. But Osh chose another plan...

Jon Gulick had responded to Osh's original call, and was standing on the bluff top monitoring the rescue, ready to hail Henry-I for the extrication to relieve McNulty of the lengthy return swim with the victim. By then Osh had already cleared the impact area. McNulty, spotting Gulick on the bluff, tapped his fist to his head, indicating to Gulick he was "Code-4" and didn't need help. Gulick returned the signal as an acknowledgement, then watched the lengthy rescue play out. Osh allowed the northwest swell to push the two men to the south, which was understandable, then curiously continued kicking them even farther south. Much farther. They continued in the down-current flow past several viable exit points until finally Osh turned toward shore and entered a small inlet. Gulick, confused as to why he had diverted his return so far south, ran back to the truck and drove along the highway to meet them.

This was McNulty's way of driving home a point. Upon reaching the shore, Osh had every right to berate the man soundly for his ignorance and disrespect, and a lesser guard would likely have thoroughly emasculated the knucklehead with an "I told you so" scolding, but Osh wasn't that guy. There was no lesson left to teach the man which the ocean had not already delivered with unmistakable clarity.

Gulick met them as they came up a goat trail to the top of the bluff, a solid ¼ mile from where the diver originally kicked out. Osh threw his fins and buoy into the truck bed for the ride back to his vehicle. As the diver started to load his own gear into the back of the truck, Osh calmly explained it was "Against their policy to offer rides to the public" which was not untrue, adding he would have to walk back to his truck. The once arrogant diver then began the long walk back carrying his hefty weight belt along with his cumbersome dive gear, hopefully reflecting on the lesson in humility.

11-30-1991
THE OCEAN TAKETH

Saturday, November 30th, marked the last day of abalone season. The surf, which was growing with each passing hour, became an ever-increasing concern.

A young scuba diver, perhaps 20 years old, was spotted outside the reserve at South Gerstle, and seemed to be struggling to reach shore in the large surf. Loeffler, using the truck's PA, called out to the diver to get his attention, then, standing next to the patrol vehicle, Loeffler gave him the universal "Okay?" sign, tapping his fist on his head. The young man quickly returned the signal, indicating he felt he was fine. Unbeknownst to Loeffler, both Straub and Dave Schardt had already contacted the same guy earlier on separate occasions. Schardt had spoken to him about the poor conditions as he was preparing to kick out, and Straub contacted him on the boat since he seemed clumsy and unfamiliar with his gear.

The diver successfully reached shore, and Loeffler approached him to provide some friendly counsel. The kid notified Loeffler he had been scouting out the area since he was planning on returning in a few hours to free dive for abalone, since it would be his last chance before the season closed.

In no uncertain terms, Loeffler advised him the surf, which was already unsafe, was forecast to increase in size and it might be best to "Call it a day," and abort any plans for free-diving. The diver acknowledged the warning and loaded up his gear, then drove back to the campground. The guards cleared the area and resumed their patrol on the busy Saturday, as other divers, in other areas, were rushing to beat the oncoming swell to get their last limit of abalone.

Less than an hour before sunset, with their work day all but done, the guards were ready to celebrate the end of their first abalone season when Dave Schardt's voice came across the radio reporting a missing diver at South Gerstle.

With his buddy watching from the bluffs, a free diver had kicked out and made several successful surface dives, including one in which he returned to the surface with an abalone and placed it in his float. Then, after a long rest on the surface, he descended back down. And never resurfaced.

The young diver was negatively buoyant, meaning that his weight belt was on the heavy side, such that when he went unconscious, instead of floating to the surface where there might be a chance for him to be spotted and saved quickly, he descended to the ocean floor, greatly complicating the rescue and all but guaranteeing his own death.

When the victim's partner could no longer see him, he frantically ran back and forth along the bluff to try and find him. When it was clear the diver had submerged, he called 911.

Loeffler arrived on scene to find Schardt hurriedly pulling his wetsuit on, while his buddy, gravely concerned, stood on the edge of the bluff and continued to stare at the ocean surface. In the fading light of dusk, Loeffler made a final radio call to notify the crew they were initiating a dive search, knowing they would respond and summon Henry-I as well. The two wetsuit-clad guards, armed only with fins, masks, weight belts and rescue buoys, then scampered down the short trail to the water's edge.

By then the expected increase in the swell size had materialized, and the guards had to time their entry to avoid getting hammered back on the shoreline rocks. They held their ground, watching a large set of waves roll through, breaking violently on shore and sending a plume of water into the sky. Just after the crescendo of the final set wave, they dove in side by side, riding the inertia of the backwash and kicking wildly to clear the impact zone.

Once outside, they began their hasty search, doing repeated free-dives in an impromptu grid pattern. They focused on the area where he buddy has last seen him, hoping to find the submerged diver on the bottom. The visibility was awful, and the faint ambient light on the surface didn't penetrate to the bottom, yet they continued to descend, with failing hopes of miraculously coming across the diver. In the haze of the turbidity and the darkness of the deeper water, the diver, clad in a black wetsuit, would be almost impossible to see, so they followed their outstretched hands on each descent, groping almost blindly for his body.

Ironically, the location the diver had drowned was an area well-known to the guards. Referred to as "The Spot," it was a short drive from the campground, and boasted plenty of sizable abalone, easily obtainable for a decent diver. Since the guards dove the area frequently, they were familiar with the access, the currents, and even the general topography of the bottom.

But, as any diver can attest to, diving at night is like entering some other unknown cosmos. When the light disappears, the features of even the most familiar locations take on a surreal and other-worldly quality. With the added complication of the poor visibility and the powerful surge along the bottom, their recovery efforts were greatly complicated.

Back up units arrived on shore. Rangers Stephenson, Walton, and Karen Broderick, along with Straub, peered through binos to try and locate the missing diver, while at the same time struggling to keep tabs on the two lifeguards in the fading light. By then, the victim's family had also arrived from the campground and it was Stephenson who met them and delivered the bleak news that things did not look good.

In the brief period between dives, while recovering, Schardt and Loeffler engaged in an ongoing conversation.

Schardt: "Hey Kurt - Remember that guy we talked to here earlier?" A 40-second gap in the conversation transpired while both guards dove and resurfaced.

Loeffler: "Yea, I do...Is this him?" Again another descent and a bottom search, followed by both guards' heads breaking the surface.

Schardt: "It is...and guess where he is from?" Both guards again descend, kicking along the bottom, while Loeffler ponders his eventual answer. By the time he ascends, Loeffler has his guess prepared.

Loeffler: "Don't tell me he's from Sacramento!?" Another descent, while Loeffler awaits the answer.

Schardt: "Yup!"

True to their well-established prejudgment, the Greater Sacramento area had provided yet another victim. By then, thirty minutes had passed. Not having gloves or taking the time to put on booties, the chill of the 50-degree water had rendered the guards' hands and feet numb, and the chill had penetrated to their core. They began shivering uncontrollably, though neither made mention of it.

Protocols dictated they would continue with the "Rescue" effort for one full hour, giving any drowning victim every conceivable chance for recovery and resuscitation. After one hour, their efforts would then transition to a "Body Recovery" operation, slowing the process and becoming more methodical. The darkness too was a significant factor which justified a decision to terminate the search efforts based on safety concerns for the guards. Yet, despite the unsafe diving conditions and almost zero light, they decided to continue on.

Far from the illumination of any shore lights, the two soon found themselves fully ensconced in darkness, being raised and lowered by unseen waves which passed them before breaking on the distant shoreline. From the vantage of the rescuers on land, despite their neon yellow wetsuit hoods, both guards had were now lost in the blackness of the night ocean. Even though they were well within range of a potential PA announcement from shore, any communication with them would be one-sided since *their* voices in response didn't stand a chance of being heard above the roar of the waves.

Just then, Henry-I arrived overhead.

Amidst the deafening noise of the chopper, the light shining down from the belly of the airship pierced through the night sky in a violently bright translucent column, illuminating a 20' circle on the ocean surface around them. Yet, all peripheral areas not directly targeted by the beam, remained shrouded in darkness.

They continued descending through the dim gloom of the murky water, essentially diving blind, and waiting for the moving light beam from the helicopter to reach their area. In the instant it did, their black and menacing world exploded into a blazing brightness rivaling that of the noon-day sun. But then, just as quickly, the beam of light would pass, and they were instantly thrust back into the darkness, once again blindly groping along the bottom, futility feeling for anything which might be a human body part, and helplessly waiting for the beam of light to return.

Eventually, after exhausting every conceivable means, and realizing the effects of hypothermia were beginning to cloud his thought process and judgment, Loeffler decided to "call it" and the two guards began kicking back towards shore. It was over.

Guided by handheld flashlights shining down from the State Parks personnel on the bluff top, the two exhausted guards negotiated their way over the rocks and escaped from the ocean. With State Parks' personnel staged in various locations along the bluff line, it was Stephenson whose voice came across the radio reporting to dispatch that both guards had safely returned to shore, adding that the search had been terminated.

Shivering and obviously hypothermic, they laboriously ascended the short bluff trail, stumbling on clumsy legs stiffened by the extended exposure to the cold. Reaching the top, they entered a surreal scene, illuminated by the headlights of a dozen emergency vehicles. The faces of familiar rangers and fellow lifeguards were intermittently illuminated by the spinning colored lights, like some outdoor disco. Stephenson assessed their overall condition and determined that despite their chattering teeth and impaired dexterity, their mental status was "passable" and he released them. Loeffler and Schardt then retreated to their patrol vehicles and began changing out of their wetsuits. This normally effortless skill, practiced hundreds of times, was now laborious and slow, hindered by the stiffness and persistent shivering. One by one, all of the vehicles eventually cleared the scene.

The young man's family, still praying for a miracle, stayed and held an impromptu vigil throughout the night. Some of them walked along the bluff-top path, shining weak beams of light out to sea while chillingly calling the victim's name out into the wind. With their hearts torn, there they stayed, diligently staring into the dark ocean as if their son would miraculously rise in a beacon of light to greet them.

Instead, they were tortured with the devastating reality that his body was out there somewhere, laying cold and alone on the bottom of that huge ocean, surrounded by nothing but the blackness.

The body recovery search resumed in the morning. By then, the surf had settled somewhat and the visibility had greatly improved with the light of day. Within an hour the guards located the diver's body in 20' of water. He, like so many other free diver fatalities, still had his weight belt on. Any desperate hopes the family had for a miracle were dashed when Straub loaded his body, stiff with rigor mortis onto the boat and delivered him to Loeffler and Woody at Gerstle Cove. Kurt immediately recognizing him as the same young man they had warned the previous day. Disappointed he had not heeded their warnings, they zipped him into a body bag and carried him to the parking lot to await the coroner.

Straub transports the body of the drowned diver through Gerstle (1991) – Photo: Loeffler

Through trial and error, in a single year, the crew had reached a level of proficiency in guarding the Sonoma Coast few would have ever expected. They trained incessantly, and the boat paid dividends.

In time, their coordination began to sync into a well-oiled machine. On busy days, the boat traversed the coast outside the surfline, while guards on foot hiked along the trails with handheld radios and their gear stashed in backpacks, evaluating divers from the shore. On these proactive foot patrols, the guards were known to cover incredible distances, occasionally hiking from Horseshoe Cove to Salt Point then back, a distance approaching 15 miles.

The guards in vehicles checked in at the various dive locations while one unit was assigned to each of the two major hot spots where the majority of the action took place (notably, Salt Point and Goat Rock).

From both land and sea, the guards provided an incredible service.

THE DIVE CONDITIONS LINE

One of the great tools the guards offered to the dive community was *The Dive Conditions Line.* The 40-second long phone recording provided divers with all of the vital information about the current and forecasted diving conditions. Updated early every morning, the recording included the swell readings (height and wave spacing), breaking wave height, wind, weather, and most importantly, the visibility in protected coves. It also gave the indicator readings of the 200 and 600 mile off-shore buoys as predictors of swell activity for the coming days.

Having a captive audience of divers each day, the guards ended each recording with the safety message, *"At the first sign of trouble or distress, remember to drop your weight belt."* The specificity of the message was an attempt to reverse the trend of divers who drowned unnecessarily because they failed to drop their belts. That single simple act, requiring less effort than pulling a rip cord on a parachute, would likely have prevented the deaths of many divers.

The "Dive Line" soon became an instrumental and trusted source of information for the dive community, and hundreds of scuba and free divers called in each day to find out whether it was worth their while to drive out to the coast. If the surf was ominous, the recording always added the recommendation that divers might find safer conditions in the normally protected coves at Fort Ross and Fisk Mill, though it was a well-known fact to veteran divers that the waters of Fort Ross and Fisk Mill were a poor consolation for taking game, since all of the larger abalone which once thrived there had long since been picked over.

Fisk Mill Cove offered protection from the northwest swell (1995)

The lifeguards' narratives on the recording sounded professorial and scientific, suggesting the guards had just completed analyzing data gleaned from complex scientific instruments and various gadgetry in their professional weather laboratory. In fact no such laboratory existed.

In truth, all of the recorded data was collected by the early shift guard who simply jumped in the patrol truck and made a speed run down the hill to Gerstle Cove. Along the way, he checked the surf - thereby getting the *breaking wave height*, and looked at the sky - for the *current weather*. The essential readings for *water clarity* and *visibility*, the most important factors for divers, were obtained by the rather unscientific method of simply peering down into the water of the cove and assuming a "guesstimate" of the visibility. On his way back up the hill, the guard then tuned their VHF radio to the 24-hour weather station to get the *forecasted swell readings*, and by the time he got back to the office, he was all set to do the recording. Thus, if they didn't stop to blabber with the Camp Hosts, all of the pertinent information could be gathered in ten minutes.

Once back at the lifeguard office, a glorified trailer, they took the machine off-line for a couple minutes while they narrated the newly acquired data onto the recording. Most of the guards, if not being grab-assed or mocked by other guards in the office while trying to recite the info, could capture a decent rendering in a single take. On the other hand, if another guard was there - especially if they had already gotten into the coffee - the teasing could be quite a challenge to overcome, it might require several takes to get it down.

The North Sector Trailer-Office (recording gizmo far right) (1994)

Immediately upon completing the update and setting it live, the counter started clicking away as the impatient divers began calling in. On weekends, it was not uncommon to log several hundred calls. Divers soon began to trust and rely on the information, and eventually, when the lifeguards reported that conditions were dangerous, the divers knew that it really was. Without exaggeration, the dive line not only saved many unnecessarily long drives, but may well also have saved lives.

JACKS of all TRADES

The terrain, the ruggedness of the coastline and the isolation created the need for the guards to develop a set of non-traditional skills to better serve the public. All of the guards learned how to repel down cliffs, and became proficient in performing cliff-rescues. They were certified to run chain saws and cleared the roads when fallen trees blocked the highway. They carried Slim Jims and responded to members of the public who had locked their keys in their cars, relieving the owners from having to call tow companies from Santa Rosa, and saving them hundreds of dollars. In fact, Gary, the owner of the local convenience store at Ocean Cove, began referring stranded drivers to the lifeguards for their lock outs, which helped to spread a bit of goodwill in the community.

The guards were proactive in seeking ways to help people in need. They spotted and responded to boats adrift with mechanical issues. The skippers were always surprised when the guards showed up in their IRB and often asked how they knew they were in distress. Most of them were unaware they were under the watchful eyes of the guards on shore. Often times, Straub or McNulty could fix their issue on scene, but if needed, the skippers gratefully accepted a tow to the Ocean Cove boat ramp.

All of the guards monitored divers for poaching and occasionally even the seasonals signed citizen arrest citations when they witnessed gross violations of the Fish and Game Code.

Martino began dispatching for the State Parks on his days off, which included running criminal histories and vehicle registration checks for all of the officers – which ultimately helped inspire him to become an officer himself.

Carter on the ropes (1992) – Photo: McNulty

The guards were stewards of the land, and educated the public, not only about abalone, species of fish, bird populations, and local flora, but also about the various edible mushroom species in the area, the local history of the coastline, the preferred local wineries, and, if you were interested, a bevy of lifeguard stories, philosophy, and life advice. All, of course, free of charge - and worth every penny.

Ever so slowly, good karma began to spread. In the North Sector, the guards began assimilating into the community; attending local events and even hanging out with some of their influential neighbors. Soon, sentiments from locals could be overheard at various boat ramps and dive spots acknowledging the lifeguards' prowess.

Above all, they became skilled at this new type of guarding. The sheriffs were right in their assertion that it truly *was* different than Southern California. In that ocean, a lifeguard couldn't simply charge into the water

Osh "Doolittle" McNulty (1994) – Photo: Unknown

blindly and expect to make a rescue. They had to monitor the surf for a time, scrutinize the swell direction, the spacing of the waves, the timing of the sets, and the viable access points where they could safely swim out. Above all, anytime they entered the water in large surf, they needed to have a plan for a viable *down-current* exit spot, and a *second* exit spot if the first one was shut off by the surf. Every rescue was more than a reckless launch into the sea. Each one required a plan.

The rocks alone posed a considerable challenge and no two rock rescues were the same. But there were also times when the rocks assisted the guards, shielding them from the brunt of the surf, and providing shelter to get their fins on.

Long rescues with no witnesses and limited backup necessitated clear radio calls with precise locations and a foretelling of what resources the guard might need ahead of time, since their last transmission might be all the information the responding guards would have to find them and coordinate their needs for a safe extrication.

And the guards learned some cool new tricks. Placing a plastic bag over their foot allowed their wetsuits to slip on quickly, so all of them kept a few Ziploc bags in their backpacks. On big days some of the guys even wore pantyhose under their overalls for the same reason. Leaving their wetsuits out on foggy nights "to dry" usually only made them wetter, and in the winter months, wetsuits rarely *ever* fully dried. By November, they began to emit a moldy stench which was difficult to get rid of, so they carried their wetsuits in the truck beds in an attempt to air them out.

The original crew learned a tremendous amount and performed nobly. They had come a long way from the sandy rescues in Carlsbad and Doheny where they simply ran down the beach, high-stepped through the waves, dolphined a few times, and swam out.

~

The first full abalone season was in the books. The opening day began with a fatality and the last day ended with another. But in between the bookends of death, the guards had made exceptional progress. They logged 144 rescues since the beginning of the program. Of course, it was impossible to accurately estimate the number of tragedies averted, but there was no doubt amongst them that lives had most definitely been saved.

If only the residents of the South Sector believed that.

12-10-1991
GOAT ROCK - CLIFF FALL

This original story was taken from a first-hand account provided by Mike Martino, who was the subject lifeguard in the narrative. It captures some of the frustrations the guards experienced in the South Sector, often from the very citizens they were trying to protect.

I continued my patrol of Goat Rock Beach and looking south, I saw three people on the western point of Goat Rock. The surf seemed as if it had grown, and I saw a wave smash down with such force the three men disappeared in the misty white spray.

I put on my wetsuit and called Dispatch. "I have three out on the far west point of Goat Rock. I will be entering the water from the north and swimming all the way around the rock. Send back-up and notify the sheriff's rescue helicopter. One guard out."

Ranger Edinger was already in the north parking lot, so he was able to keep an eye on me as I swam out to the far side of the rock. The surge pushed me, but I anticipated the undulations and made it around to the ocean-facing area quickly. I could no longer see the shore, only the massive bulk of rock before me. I was fully exposed to the incoming waves and almost overwhelmed by their power. Rather than being swirled and lifted, I was nearly thrown onto the exposed rock. I kicked as hard as I could and tried to get a safer distance away. Another wave smashed down, and I could clearly see the three "men" were teenaged boys, and they were soaked once again by the wave.

I yelled for the kids to "Get back!" They looked up, startled more by the sound of a human voice than by the crashing waves.

I tried again. "Hey, you guys get back! This area is closed! Get back!"

One of the kids yelled back at me. His hand to his ear, "What, man? I can't hear you."

I stroked closer to the wall and another strong surge began pushing me toward the rock. Again I kicked hard and yelled, "Get back! More waves are going to be breaking here. You need to move to where it's safe, and we'll have a helicopter come to help you off."

One of the kids yelled back in response, "Fuck that man! We're out of here!" Like scared deer they started scrambling along the rocks.

I kept yelling, but the kids did not listen. They followed the rugged ledge until they climbed themselves into a corner. They wouldn't go back, and the area in front of them was covered with the rising tide. Above them was a sheer wall. From the water, it was as if I could see their thought patterns. They looked at me frantically waving them back and yelling. They looked forward, and behind. Then, in a flash, they all began climbing up.

The rock looks vertical. "No, don't! Stay right where you are!" I yell. But the kids pay no attention to my pleas, and each boy climbs steadily higher. Swimming, I navigate around the westernmost tip of the rock, praying to hear the familiar thump of the helicopter blades, but I only see the boys climbing and hear the formidable power of the surf breaking between me and the rock. I realize the remoteness of my own situation as well.

The waves build in intensity and the swirling currents pick me up and let me go at their whim. I try to concentrate on the climbers, remembering this is my job and I try to forget my own predicament; these waves could dash me against barnacle strewn rocks, or a great white shark could pick this moment to defend his territory. The boys slow their ascent. They still climb, but the steepness of the cliff hinders them. They are a precarious eighty feet above the water. As I watch them, I feel the water next to me swirl as if an object is surfacing right next to me, and fear overwhelms me. Then the black shiny head of a harbor seal pops from below the surface and I splash in his direction, "Get away from me!" His intelligent eyes survey me. I can tell by his look I do not impress him, and he ducks back under the surface.

I look back to the climbers. Two have made it to the top, but the third is stuck. His body rigid with fear, and I can see the strain on his face. His friends look down to him. One laying on his stomach an arm reaching down. The other acting as an anchor holding the prone kid's legs. I see the terror in their eyes. They have already made it, but their clumsy friend is proving them wrong. Wrong to climb the rock, wrong to challenge the beast of the Ocean, and wrong to climb this sheer cliff.

I strain to hear the helicopter's whopping blades, but still there is nothing. There is a boy and the ledge and the fear. I do not want to be eaten. He does not want to fall. I do not want to die, and he does not want to die. These collective fears bind us together. Still there is no helicopter.

A stone falls from under his foot, then another, and another. The moment has finally arrived. Gravity and the laws of physics make the boy's decision for him. The prone friend's hand extends further, the anchor boy digs in, and my desperate hand reaches up from far below as if I can actually hold him in place. One cold, wet hand clasps another and a thin flesh lifeline is formed. I see the hands slipping, and the lifeline stretches and instantly my mind reels. The next scene plays out in my imagination moments before it happens.

In my mind, I see the fall and the impact, like a wet bag of cement striking the ground hard with no bounce. There is no movement; just impact and stillness. I can see myself swimming toward what was once a vibrant, disrespectful, law-breaking, life-loving, boy coaxed by his friends to tempt fate and to lose. I see my hands turning his limp body over, opening his bloodied airway and trying to force breath from my living body into his broken one. The commingling of my breath with his means nothing. His heart has stopped, and his body crushed. The visual damage on the outside pales in comparison to the trauma inflicted on the inside. There is nothing I can do. I can only swim the remaining shell of this boy back to shore....

Another rock slips down, jolting me back to reality. I see another hand shoot down. They grasp eighty feet above the rocks below. The boy kicks his feet, finds a foothold, and struggles up. He is safe. All three look down at me, my head covered in my neon wetsuit hood, and they laugh. With middle fingers extended, defiant with their renewed sense of rebellion, they yell "So long sucker! We made it!"

Their words sting.

I have nothing left to do but retreat. I retrace my path along the rock face on a ten-minute swim back to shore. By the time I get there, they are long gone. I get out of my wetsuit, and into my dry uniform. It is over.

I stuff the emotions of disdain and frustration deep into the core of my soul where they will periodically resurface every few years. But with each recollection, the associated emotions become more muted and distant. I climb behind the wheel of the Ram to resume my patrol. There are more people to watch.

There are always more people to watch.

12-20-1991
CARTENSKI and MELVINOVICH

One of the most bizarre medical calls I have ever heard came out of the North Coast and, as it so happens, involved two of the core lifeguards

featured in this book. Unlike most of the other stories offered, this one is
unique because it happened while the guards were off-duty. In order to
protect their innocence, the astute reader will notice I have cleverly
disguised their names to shroud their identities. As an additional
disclaimer, I hereby declare that all elements of this story are hearsay.

Crazy things happen to lifeguards.

After signing off one winter evening, Lifeguards Dev Cartenski and
Skeeter Melvinovich went to San Francisco to enjoy a concert. They
took Skeeter's 914 Porsche for the two-hour drive into the city. The
concert was great, and they enjoyed it, limiting themselves to two beers
each, in light of the long drive home.

Around 1 o'clock in the morning they left the city, but instead of
staying on the customary Highway 101 route through Santa Rosa to
River Road to return to the coast, they pulled off in Petaluma and drove
along the back roads through the farmlands towards Bodega Bay.

Cartenski estimated it was around 3 o'clock in the morning when
they were approaching the small enclave of Two Rock which was not
much more than a scattering of a few farmland homes. In his memory
they were going pretty fast, and in Dev's subsequent conversations with
Skeeter, recalled they were traveling upwards of 80 miles an hour.
Skeeter contended there was no way they could have been driving that
fast, based on the seemingly convincing fact that his car was incapable of
going over 60.

Regardless, at some point in the vicinity of nowhere, and somewhat
dulled from the monotony and desolation of the drive, they came around
a corner where, unfortunately, a man happened to be wandering
aimlessly, smack dab in the middle of the roadway.

The instant manifestation of the human being, directly in the path
of their car instantaneously shot a full-dose of adrenalin into both
guards. Cartenski yelled out. Skeeter reacted, locking up the brakes. But
it was too late. Just as the victim lifted his gaze, illuminating his face in
their headlights, the car struck him squarely with a sickening thud, and
the man's body bounced off the hood, shattering the windshield in the
process, before rolling off the hood and onto the roadway. Skeeter
immediately pulled onto the shoulder and the guards ran over to assess
the victim, fearing he might have been killed.

The victim, a Hispanic man in his 30s, laid lifeless in the fetal position. They called out to him and tried to revive him but he gave no response. As one of the guards began assessing his neck for the presence of a pulse, the man started groaning. It was then that both of the guards noticed the man also reeked of alcohol.

Curious as to why this man was wandering along that desolate stretch of roadway at that hour, Cartenski stood up to orient himself. Only then did he notice a pickup truck crashed in a ditch, not more than 100 yards away. The man it seemed, obviously drunk, had just been involved in his own accident. In a tragic, yet highly improbable scenario, after the trauma of crashing his truck into an open ditch, he had attempted to flee the scene when he was promptly struck by what was likely the only other vehicle on the roadway for miles.

In broken Spanish they implored the man to lay still, and explained they would summon help. Of course, this was a time when only millionaires had cell phones, and neither of them held that distinction. To make matters worse, they were truly miles from nowhere at an ungodly hour.

Then, as if their victim had been given some kind of magical elixir, he suddenly rolled over and pushed himself to his knees. The guards were stunned, yet also keenly curious to see how far his miraculous healing would progress. They backed off and allowed him to continue. The man then stood up and started stumbling around, very much alive, though mumbling to himself incoherently.

The guards, both trained EMTs, were then left to ponder whether his compromised lucidity was attributable to the initial crash, being hit by them, or simply from being drunk.

The softhearted Cartenski had noticed a pack of cigarettes on the dashboard of his truck and, figuring this man had been through enough trauma already, pulled one out and lit it for his patient. Still not interacting with them, the man accepted the cigarette, and sat back down in the same truck he had just crashed moments earlier. Unable to leave their patient, and with no other option, they decided to settle in and wait on the side of the road until someone happened to come by. They pulled their jackets from their car and wrapped their victim in a blanket they found in his truck.

The awkward wait with their drunk, non-communicative, mumbling, accident victim lasted about 30 minutes when finally, a set of headlights approached. They stood up and waved but as one might expect, the vehicle whizzed past them not wanting to get involved in what looked like a complicated situation. Another half-hour passed before a second set of headlights appeared and thankfully, the car stopped. The guards approached to greet the kind strangers, and there inside the car was the most unlikely of couples in this rural farming community. The man looked like a clone of Joey Ramon, dressed "to the nines" in a dazzling bright-yellow cowboy outfit, highlighted with a pair of Cuban boots and a bright white blazer with frills hanging from the arms. The woman was equally flamboyant with a beehive hairdo, wearing a bright blue sequined dress. Assuming they might be returning from some kind of costume party, yet not in a position to ask, Cartenski chose to ignore their outfits and concentrate on the matter at hand, asking if they could summon help. The colorful couple agreed to drive to their home, which they said was only a few miles down the road, to call 911.

Just before they left, the woman scrutinized the truck in the ditch which spurred a surprising and explosive reaction from her.

"THAT'S MY TRUCK!!!" she yelled.

She bolted out of the car to make sure, then quickly confirmed the rather remarkable fact that it was, in fact **her truck**! The victim soon found himself in the unenviable position of being confronted by a dolled up woman with a bee-hive hairdo and a shimmering blue dress who, as one might expect, was yelling at him - in fluent Spanish, mind you - at a volume and intensity which seemed to be doing a fairly good job of sobering him up, greatly exceeding any of the previously employed methods of communication employed by the lifeguards.

In the next several minutes, after a brutal verbal shellacking by the lavishly dressed woman, and some adroit and prickly questioning, the sequence of events started to fall into place.

The suspect admitted he had broken into their home with the intent to rob them. In the process, he spotted their liquor cabinet and removed a bottle of rum, which he proceeded to consume. Greatly "inspired" by the euphoric effects of the rum, while at the same time losing what little remaining judgment he had left in discerning right from wrong, he wandered into their garage and decided to steal their truck. In the midst of his getaway, driving with one-eye closed to keep the spinning to a minimum, he crashed the truck into the ditch. The rest came from Cartenski and Melvinovich who rounded out the story adding that after he emerged from the truck, the victim wandered into the roadway, assumedly in a slow-motion attempt to flee the scene, and immediately, was struck by their Porsche.

The owner of the truck asked the guards to stay with him, which they did, while she and her boyfriend went off to summon the authorities.

A short time later the dark night erupted into a spectacle, filled with official vehicles, flashing lights and emergency personnel. The fire crew and police both interviewed the lifeguards and, being honorable people, they told the truth about what had happened. The patient was treated and placed on a gurney, then loaded in the back of the medic unit.

Before they left the scene, all of the parties were gathered together and it was there the medic reported that the patient, besides being drunk, was doing remarkably well. He added the rather extraordinary revelation that he could find no evidence of injuries to the victim at all, adding that he was quite certain the victim had not been struck by the car. The guards looked at each other for a moment, both left to wonder whether the victim had somehow miraculously healed himself, or if in fact their car had actually come to a full stop before the drunk man fell onto the hood.

Regardless, the officer released them from the scene without so much as taking their names.

Before they left, Cartenski walked to the front of the car to check the one place they had not thought to inspect. Running his hand along the front bumper, he felt nothing out of the ordinary beyond some mild surface rust.

Minutes later, the two men drove home with their broken windshield and a hell of a story.

BREAKING up the BAND

Scott Melvin and Audrey Haug would be the first of the original crew to leave. By the winter of 1991, both had checked out for greener pastures. Citing the considerable stressors of working the North Coast, Melvin sought out and accepted a coveted position as a Fish and Game Warden. His last documented rescue as a lifeguard was in late November of 1991. He left with two Commendation letters, and despite performing numerous impressive aquatic rescues, both letters were for his role in medical aids. The first for a downed motorcyclist, and the second for his role in caring for a patient suffering a Myocardial Infarction.

For Audrey Haug, her exit was a promotion, as she had been accepted into the Peace Officer Academy.

THE ARRIVAL of ADAM WRIGHT

Filling Melvin and Haug's positions would be a bureaucratic challenge for the managers and would take some time. In the interim, feeling an immediate need to cover the aquatics, they shifted Steve Franklin to the South Sector and began the search to fill Haug's vacancy with another Seasonal Lifeguard. But convincing any new guard to come work there would prove to be a challenge. Plenty of Seasonals expressed interest in transferring to the North Coast, but their initial exuberance in working there often quickly dissipated when they arrived and saw the conditions for the first time.

Steve Franklin remembered;

"I was the Seasonal Supervisor in charge of rescue and enforcement for Goat Rock State Beach and Salt Point State Park. I couldn't recruit enough guards. They would drive up from Southern California, see what we did, then turn around and disappear forever."

It was clear that filling Melvin's spot on short notice would be a challenge. A state-wide memo went out indicating an emergent need for a lifeguard to transfer to the North Coast, and Adam Wright, from the San Clemente District, happened to be in the right place at exactly the right time.

Adam was an 18-year old throw-back hippie, who had ventured from his family home in Pasadena to pursue his college education with the like-minded granola crowd at Humboldt State. In choosing his classes, and being an avid student of world percussion, he once read an article from Buddy Rich in which the legendary drummer suggesting that *tap dancing*, of all things, had greatly helped him in his development as a drummer. So, in accordance with his mentor's assertion, Adam perused the college catalog and sure enough, found a *Beginning Tap Dancing* class and signed up. Adam was a natural and quickly became part of their ensemble. Their final performance would be held on the main stage at the college and a surprisingly large crowd gathered for the show. In the uncanny lifeguard cosmos of inter-connectedness, among those in the crowd that day happened to be Dave Carter, who recognized Adam as one of the local Arcata surfers he had seen in the line-up. Introducing himself after the show (which, by the way, was well-received among the local artisan crowd), Carter discovered that Adam was also a State Lifeguard and immediately suggested he contact Bud Brown and inquire about the recent vacancy on the North Coast.

The only problem with his plan was that Adam, having just completed his rookie season at San Clemente, was a veritable fledgling. Having only worked the towers, he had never treated a major medical, dispatched, or even used the radio. In fact, he had never even been in a patrol vehicle before.

Regardless, Adam's phone call to Bud coincided perfectly with Melvin's leaving. He then explained how he had met Carter at his tap dancing performance, and he was eager to work the North Coast. Despite his lack of experience, in a surprise move, Bud hired him. The Supervisor later confiding to Adam "The only reason you were hired is because you could tap dance."

Despite his deficiencies in experience, the diminutive, grass-roots, curly haired, sprout-eating, vegetarian, Yoga-practicing, throw-back hippie filled a unique demographic in the crew which no one else occupied. When the Earthsong Chanters and Tree-Huggers arrived with complaints about tire tracks on the beach, or the protection of some species of worms, Adam would be the one thrust forward to hold their hands, light some incense, chant with them, and gently mitigate their concerns.

The moment he arrived, it was quite obvious that he was not only incredibly young, but also unbelievably green. When Loeffler gave him his orientation tour, as a joke, while showing him the various landmarks and topography, he pointed to a large rock at Salmon Creek and, in a factual tone declared "That's 'Dildo' rock...make sure people stay off if it." When Adam didn't laugh, Kurt realized the kid probably didn't even know what a dildo was, and let the joke pass. His suspicion was abundantly solidified when, two weeks later, on his first solo patrol, Adam picked up the truck's microphone and broadcast boldly to the entire district, *"I'm going to make a safety contact on some kids climbing on Dildo Rock."* The State Parks Dispatcher, upon hearing his transmission, and realizing she *must have* misunderstood the young guard, gingerly asked him to repeat the location, at which point Loeffler bailed him out, stating, *"I am familiar with that landmark, I will go back him up."*

Wright near Jenner (1992)

The idea of Loeffler and Wright working together immediately poses a rather comical image to anyone who knows them both, since Wright, who stood about 5'4, was likely one of the shortest lifeguards in the department, while Loeffler (at 6' 10") was easily the tallest. Curiously, their physical differences paled in comparison to their lifestyles, their philosophies, or just about any social issue one might consider. Adam was a peace-loving, non-confrontational, vegetarian, hand-holding, Eastern Religion practicing dude who wore loose-fitting clothes, listened to Reggae, and could "ohm-out" with the best of them.

Loeffler?....Well...suffice to say, he was none of that.

Regardless, the inclusive hiring practices of the State Parks, appreciating a variety of skills, while tolerating a wide-range of personalities, and realizing the inherent value of *all individuals*, magically brought them together. And together they would serve the public, complimenting each other side by side.

Adam soon glommed onto Loeffler as his personal mentor, and Kurt provided the young guard with a one-man crash course on lifeguarding the North Coast.

Remarkably, Adam's greatest lesson would be dealt to him on their very first shift together.

On a rare sunny morning with no pending calls, the two guards were enjoying their drive along the scenic Coast Highway. Suddenly, for no apparent reason, Loeffler told Adam to put his wetsuit on, which he began to do while seated in the passenger seat. Searching the passing coves for anyone in distress, Adam saw no one and eventually asked what they were responding to.

Loeffler tersely responded, "Just do it."

They pulled out onto Goat Rock Beach and parked in the middle of the great expanse. The surf was manageable at only head-high, but recent storms had swelled the Russian River, and the fast-moving muddy river flowed off-shore in a powerful and impressive rip current. Even still, no one was in it. Peering through the binos, Adam searched the entire beach and the ocean as far as the horizon, thinking perhaps Loeffler was testing him to spot some kind of rescue. But there was nothing of concern.

Minutes passed and Adam's tension grew. Loeffler sat in silence, expressionless, offering nothing to appease the curiosity and rising stress in the new lifeguard. Secretly, Loeffler's desire to get to Goat Rock rested in the simple fact it was already 11:00 and Goat Rock was their best chance to get the young guard on his first rescue. But of course Adam didn't know that.

One can only imagine Adam's surprise when, as if Loeffler had tapped into some mystical power to prophesize rescues, two kayakers wearing nothing but swim trunks, appeared behind them, floating down the Russian River. Their attempts to get to shore and out of the powerful flow proved futile and in an instant they were thrust into the surf, swamped, and separated from their boats.

Loeffler called for Henry-1 to respond as Adam sprang from the passenger seat and began unhooking the paddleboard from the roof. One man was cast to the south and out of the predominant flow of the river, but the other man was helplessly being pulled off-shore.

Adam timed his entry and was able to paddle over the manageable waves. Once outside the surfline, he relocated his victim, who had already been pulled an impressive 200-yards from shore, and was still moving farther off-shore.

Adam put his head down and began a sprint paddle for the victim, eventually reaching him a significant distance from shore.

The man, a poor swimmer anyway, was further compromised from the effects of the cold water. No longer able stroke with his arms, he floated in a modified dog-paddle while being pulled backwards out to sea. By the time Adam reached him, he had little left. Adam hoisted him onto the board and allowed him to rest before he began the long paddle to shore.

After skillfully riding a wave with his victim the last 50 yards, the man fell off the board in knee-deep water and, with Adam's help, stumbled free from the ocean. Once safely on shore, after his 30-minute ordeal in the ocean, the victim was reunited with his buddy. Just then, Henry-I arrived overhead, but Loeffler waved them off. Seeing the sheriff's rescue helicopter overhead, the middle-aged kayaker came to grips with the sobering revelation that had it not been for this lifeguard, the helicopter would have been his only means of rescue, and he knew there was no way he could have stayed afloat long enough to survive.

Similarly, Adam Wright also experienced his own revelation. Thanks to the foresight and seemingly uncanny vision of his elder, Adam was able to perform his first life-saving rescue on the North Coast, barely three hours into his first shift.

There would be more to come for young Adam.

SPROUT HEAD in PURSUIT

From the perspective of the peace-loving Seasonal Lifeguard, transplanted from the tranquil shores of San Clemente, joining forces with the gun-slinging Permanents from Huntington, needless to say, was a bit of an adjustment. To put things into perspective, in Adam's brief career, the entire scope of his law enforcement duties had been limited to reminding a few people that their dogs were not allowed on the beach.

Conversely, as previously mentioned, the Lifeguard Officers on the North Coast took their law enforcement duties seriously, having already written hundreds of citations and logging dozens of arrests. Thus Adam, who would be on patrol with them in their marked Law Enforcement vehicle, was about to get indoctrinated into their world, whether he liked it or not.

Loeffler with the Jeep Cherokee (1991)

Dragging your Seasonals into the fray of law enforcement calls was simply not done in Adam's home district, but on the wild environs of the North Coast, all bets were off, and they were "deputized" with impunity. For some of them, this aspect of the job was viewed as "inspiring" and "exhilarating." Comparatively, for Adam, who had likely never done anything more aggressive than letting his quinoa overcook on occasion, it was utterly *mind-blowing*.

His most memorable law enforcement call came, predictably, while riding with Loeffler. Adam was driving the law enforcement vehicle, a Jeep Cherokee, along the Coast Highway with Kurt in the passenger seat, when a motorcyclist pulled in behind their vehicle. With Loeffler awaiting his next move, the motorcyclist, flagrantly ignoring the code-3 lights on the roof and the state park decals on their truck, whizzed past them in a blur of noise and testosterone, accelerating to twice the posted speed limit, and zipping wildly around the curves on the rural road.

Instinctually, Loeffler switched on the overhead lights and the siren.

"LET'S GET HIM!!!" yelled Loeffler.

Adam, not-at-all processing what Loeffler's concept of *"LET'S GET*

HIM" actually meant, and yet at the same time fearing the worst, continued on for several seconds at a comfortable 35 mph, awaiting further clarification from Loeffler which, as he correctly suspected, came almost instantly.

To put things into perspective here, allow me to digress and interject that Adam was not a "car-dude." Unlike many of his peers, he was not the guy who did burnouts in the high school parking lot, or smashed the gas pedal to the floor on some open stretch of highway to find out how fast his truck could go. In fact, Adam greatly preferred riding his bike to driving, and, if time allowed - which it most often did in his world - he favored the grounding modality of walking to either of them, since he could then enjoy the tranquil sights along the way. While driving his own vehicle, Adam was often the fellow plodding along in the slow lane, being passed by drivers who peered into his truck and were likely disappointed to see their suspicions were unfounded, as he was not a blue-haired old lady.

Anyway, back to the story.

The blaring siren jolted the young guard to attention, freeing him from all semblance of *tranquility*, and by golly, young Adam was about to enter into his first high-speed pursuit call (with no formal pursuit training mind you), embarking on an adventure that to him, would be tantamount to piloting the Space Shuttle.

Adam floored the gas pedal and the Cherokee sprang up to speed. The chase was on!

As they sped along the roadway, Loeffler began shouting out a cram course on the basic points of making a vehicle stop on a motorcycle.

"When he pulls over to the side of the road, you pull in front of him....making a 'T' which will block his path back onto the roadway...you understand?"

"Got it....make a 'T' – Block his path," replied the young lifeguard, obviously nervous.

Loeffler, not fully trusting his young trainee, and feeling the need to further solidify this important point, clarified, "So, to be clear, when the motorcycle pulls over, you will make a 'T' with him....He will be the POST of the T and you, pulling the truck in front of him, perpendicular to his path, will be the TOP of the 'T' blocking his escape route. You got it!?"

"Top of the T," reiterated Adam, clutching the wheel tightly.

Moments later, after negotiating a few turns, and locating a wide spot on the roadside, the biker, diligently pulled over.

Unfortunately, at this, the moment of truth, Adam, completely forgetting the recently provided directive from his supervisor, did not make a "T" but rather pulled up parallel to the motorcycle, forming more of an "=" sign with the biker, placing the Jeep in a far more congenial, "Hey, how are you doing?" sort of posture.

The confused motorcyclist, presumably unsure as to why he was being pulled over by a couple of *lifeguards*, then seeing the gun-wearing, 6' 10" giant getting out of the passenger side, instantly decided he wanted no part of whatever they were selling. With a clear escape path in front of him and his bike still running, he gunned the throttle, spewing a plume of gravel behind him and fled the scene, thereby breaking the "=" sign into a solitary "dash."

Loeffler jumped back in the Cherokee and the guards were immediately back in pursuit, with an added charge of evading an officer (and a Tap Dancer). The motorcyclist wove tight turns and accelerated along the straightaways, and the young, curly haired peacenik, flushed with a focused thrill he had never experienced before, swung the wheel back and forth, delivering the truck around a series of circuitous turns with an agility and sense of purpose he did not know he had in him. With Kurt yelling pointers, interspersed with plenty of chiding for *"NOT MAKING THE 'T'"* they flew past the familiar landmarks of Carmet Beach, Whale Point, Wrights Beach, and Duncans Landing, speeding southbound. Drivers, after being passed by the speeding motorcycle, and hearing their siren following, pulled onto the shoulder and allowed the hurtling lifeguards to pass. Loeffler requested the air support of Henry-I as well as all-points bulletin sent out over the airwaves for any officer in the area to intercept the law-breaking motorcyclist in Bodega Bay. And, with the adrenalin-pumping siren blaring overhead, Adam carried on in a frenzy, too focused on negotiating the turns in the roadway to even speak.

They carried on, at times losing sight of the rider, then catching a glimpse of him on some turn far ahead. The loud and staticky radio traffic added to the crazed confusion as responding units chimed in to ascertain the biker's description and direction of travel. On they flew, past the State Park Office, and Salmon Creek, before entering the small town of Bodega Bay.

It was there the motorcyclist eluded them, likely turning off on some side street.

Reluctantly, Loeffler switched off the lights and siren and, with a voice of resignation, directed Adam to slow down and pull into a small parking lot.

It was over.

Loeffler radioed the dispatcher to let all units know they had "Terminated the pursuit."

Adam sat there in the driver's seat breathing as heavy as if he had been chasing the motorcyclist on foot. His eyes danced around – struggling to reorient himself to the returning sounds of silence and the resumption of calm. He later confessed that at that moment, he was "As amped up as any time in my life."

Suffice to say that overcooking the quinoa, from now on, wouldn't carry quite the same level of excitement for him.

12-23-1991
POACHER'S GREED

Although it was McNulty who had already begun solidifying his role as the primary abalone poaching enforcer, occasionally the other officers got into the mix as well. In the early morning hours of December 23rd, Kurt Loeffler, Dave Schardt and two of the rangers, working off a tip, were able to surreptitiously monitor the actions of two suspicious scuba divers in the Fort Ross area. While watching them with binos from a covert spot in the bushes, they witnessed the two seedy-looking men - one quite overweight, and the other with a scraggly beard - exit the water with their scuba gear. Both men carried burlap bags which appeared to be filled with abalone. Because it was illegal to take abalone using scuba gear, the officers had them dead-to-right for poaching, but before they approached, they monitored their actions to see if they could tack on any additional charges. Sure enough, once the men reached shore, they began gathering several other burlap sacks (also filled with abalone) they had taken during the night, and had stashed under the cover of darkness. With a daily bag limit of four abalone, their greed was unconscionable.

Together with Schardt, the officers continued monitoring from a safe distance away as the vagrant-looking men, periodically scanning the area around them, began gathering their sacks and stashed them deep under one singular large rock. Then, with the light of day potentially exposing their escapade, each man grabbed a single bag, flung it over their shoulder, and began the first of several brisk trips to their truck to escape with the booty, collected over many hours the previous night.

During their short walk up the trail, the State Parks guys had enough time to return to their vehicle and drive over to the poacher's truck. Loeffler, flanked by the two rangers and Schardt, simply positioning themselves next to the beater truck, waiting for the poachers to come to them. As the two unsuspecting men approached, laughing and elated in celebration of their hard work and their glorious haul, they were greeted with the shocking sight of three uniformed officers, wearing badges and carrying guns who appeared to be waiting for *them*. Needless to say, their light-hearted banter shut off mid-sentence, and was immediately replaced with "*Oh Shit*" expressions, realizing that their planned festivities for the day were about to take a turn for the worse.

Loeffler greeting them with an opening line which removed any doubt that they were screwed.

"Hello there, gentlemen...may I ask what it is you have there in those bags?"

Standing before the officers, still decked in scuba gear, they had no defense. They fell silent as Loeffler hand-cuffed them, identified them, then sat them on a log next to their truck while they proceeded to search their bags. With the rangers assisting, Loeffler began methodically removing, measuring, counting, and photographing the abalone in full view of the two suspects. The face to face display, directly before them was the ultimate humiliation and Loeffler took his sweet time in exposing the violations to the men. To make matters worse, many of their take were under-sized. When the tallying was done, the sacks contained 32 abalone, which was 24 over limit. Additionally, almost half of them were under-sized, and all of them were taken on scuba, elevating the gravity of the offense to a gross-misdemeanor. The penalty, including the enhancements for the under-sized and scuba, was substantial and would likely cost the men in the neighborhood of $10,000 along with the permanent loss of their fishing licenses.

Although it was setting up to be a very costly day for the poachers, even at this seemingly low point in their lives, the men must have secretly felt like they had out-smarted these State Parks goons, since at least in their minds, the officers didn't know about the *other* bags which they had cleverly stashed away back by the water's edge. They would return later to retrieve the abalone and sell them off in San Francisco for $60 apiece, and still come away with a profit.

Loeffler then faced them squarely. "Are there any more?" he asked, knowing fully of their stash, yet giving the men a chance to come clean.

"No," the heavier man said defiantly.

"Do you agree with his statement, sir?" Loeffler offered, directing the question to the bearded man.

"No more," said the other poacher.

One can only imagine their devastation when Loeffler then stood them up, and began marching them, still handcuffed, back down the trail they had just come from. In what must have been the worst game of "hotter and colder" Loeffler didn't need any clues. He bee-lined the group directly to the rock where they had stashed their bags, sat them down and began retrieving the bags one by one.

"You should never lie to a Peace Officer," Loeffler said to them both. "We will add these to the charges."

At that point Loeffler called dispatch and requested a tow truck, explaining to the hand-cuffed men that their crime was now elevated to a felony; their truck would be impounded, and they would both be booked into county jail.

The officers, with Schardt assisting and the men watching, retrieved the bags and began the lengthy task of photographing them and documenting their sizes to the overall tally. Unfortunately, since the bulk of the abalone were taken many hours earlier in the night, most of them were no longer viable, which added yet another charge of "wasting game."

Dave Schardt with the illegally taken abalone (12/1991) – Photo: Loeffler

The men were done. The case was clean and they would eventually be prosecuted to the fullest extent of the law. With a gross take of 191 abalone, the arrest would be one of the largest abalone poaching busts ever in Sonoma County. The two men would endure tens of thousands of dollars in fines and spend years in jail. The loss of so many abalone was a grave disappointment, but the application of justice in sending the two men to jail in a bullet-proof case provided a rewarding finish to the year.

11

LIFEGUARD JOURNAL: 1992

Henry-I flies low to assess the scene

2-1-1992
GRACE ROCK – FISHERMEN

The winter brought the continuation of the bulky and fractured surf, along with the expectant rain and wind which would last for much of the season.

On a grey February morning, two lifelong friends, bonded by both the love of their children and fishing, ventured out to Grace Rock for a day of angling with their adult sons, who had grown up together. Having fished that coastline for many years, they knew to stay well above the breaking waves. The fishing was good, and they shared hot coffee from their thermos and reminisced, sharing stories of previous trips when the kids were young.

Perhaps it was the stories which distracted the men. Maybe it was a truly freak occurrence, but at some point a massive and unexpected set of waves appeared on the horizon. None of the four men noticed before it was too late.

The first of the huge waves exploded violently on Grace Rock engulfing them all in a wall of water. Both of the older men were immediately knocked off their feet and swept into the sea in the powerful receding backwash. As the first wave retreated, in preparation for the next assault, one of the elders was able to scratch and claw his way back up the barnacle-encrusted rocks, assisted by his son. But the other man had already been pulled into the deeper water. Floundering, he eventually was able to grab hold of a wash rock farther out, but unfortunately it was fully-exposed and utterly vulnerable to the oncoming surf.

Seeing the next huge wave approaching, his terrified son yelled to him, "Hold on, here comes another one!" In desperation the old man clung to the rock for his very life, but his human grip was no match for the intense power of the massive wave which completely engulfed the rock, ripping him off and thrusting him back into the churning seas.

In a gallant though foolhardy act of heroism, his son jumped in to try and rescue his father, who was already overwhelmed by the horrendous conditions, and floundering. The third wave, as large as the previous two, rolled over the man, submerging him from view for several seconds. When he re-appeared, the back wash was hauling him farther out to sea.

His lifelong friend, now safely on a higher ledge, watched in horror as his old friend was helplessly pulled out into the rough seas. The final wave of the set engulfed him and he quietly disappeared beneath the surface. Seconds later, he was gone.

Osh McNulty, along with rangers Stephenson, Wood, and Walton all responded to the scene and found the three remaining men gathered on the bluffs above the scene. The son had been pushed south by the swell, but was able to climb out to safety on his own, suffering numerous cuts to his hands. All three men were wet and cold.

With the surf running 10-12 feet, no serious rescue effort could be mounted to recover the father's body. The surviving elder sobbed uncontrollably. The victim's son stood silent. The survivors were evaluated for hypothermia by the arriving medics and eventually released. All three, including the son who jumped in, would recover from their nightmare. At least physically. Despite an hour long debrief with the State Parks staff, the elder man remained inconsolable.

The sheriff's helicopter was hailed in hopes of recovering the man's body. They performed several "fly overs" of the area, but the body of the old fisherman was not found.

2-2-1992
"WE DO GOOD THINGS"

The day after the Grace Rock tragedy, with the surf still running in the 10-12 foot range, the sun emerged, and although it was still brisk, the clear skies brought crowds of people to the South Sector, bundled up to enjoy the beauty of the coastline. Steve Franklin, working alone in the south, spent the bulk of his stressful day logging endless numbers of safety contacts at Goat Rock Beach.

In the afternoon, Franklin was confronted by a frantic man who had just come off Goat Rock.

"My friend just got swept off the rock!" he yelled.

Franklin sprang into action. Owing to the angry water on the windward side of Goat Rock, Steve knew this would be a heavy call. He radioed the location of the pending rescue and the need for Henry-I along with back up units. He quickly pulled on his wet suit and responded to the south side of Goat Rock to assess the conditions on the back side. What he saw frightened even the experienced waterman, as an endless train of waves exploded off the back of the rock, shooting white water 20 feet into the air. Worse yet, Steve could also see an absolutely monstrous rip current pulling at least a half-mile from shore, and although he couldn't see the victim, he feared the man might be in the powerful flow.

Morning before visitors at Goat Rock Beach – Photo: Bogdonovich

Franklin stashed his duty weapon, then locked the truck and tucked the keys behind the license plate. He left the overhead lights flashing to make it easier for the arriving helicopter to locate him. He then scampered down along the rocky shoreline and stopped to watch another huge set roll through. Steve would later confide that this particular entry would be the most terrifying of his entire career, as the waves just north of him, were exploding directly onto Goat Rock and those immediately before him broke spectacularly on the shoreline, shaking the ground and sending plumes of water skyward.

Timing his entry just after the last wave slammed into the wall of Goat Rock, he dove in "old school" armed with just fins and a rescue buoy.

He sprinted hard to get through the dangerous impact zone and avoid getting slammed back onto the dangerous rip rap. One wave, easily double-overhead, hit him hard and he was pummeled. But he quickly resumed his sprint to clear the impact zone. He dove under a following wave, holding his breath and diving to the bottom, feeling the mass of water roll over him. Kicking up, his head broke the surface and thankfully, there was a lull. He carried on, ascending and descending over large unbroken waves which thundered behind him as they broke. After making it though the worst section he now found himself in open water, though the ocean surface was disorganized from the competing energies of the oncoming swells and the refracted waves coming off Goat Rock, making it difficult to swim. Eventually, as he distanced himself from the rock, the ocean surface leveled out somewhat, and he fell into the natural rhythm of a distance swimmer.

The outside waves blocked his view farther out to sea, but each time he felt himself being pushed up to the crest, he raised his head to utilize the elevated vantage, and scanned the ocean surface in hopes of spotting the victim. Unfortunately, with each attempt, he saw nothing but open water. A quarter-mile from shore, he looked back to orient himself, and saw a group of climbers had ascended to the top of Goat Rock. Acting as spotters, they were waving to get his attention, and pointed even farther outside, attempting to direct him to the victim. With their confirmation, Steve carried on, swimming with the momentum of the powerful rip current, and realizing the victim had certainly been pulled in that same flow of water.

Gabriel Case, an accomplished local surfer, had been surfing south of the drama at Goat Rock, in the partially sheltered area of Blind Beach. From a considerable distance away, Case saw the commotion, and could see Franklin entering the water. A good-natured man, and the only surfer in the area, Case decided he would try to offer the lifeguard some help. Thus, as Steve was already far outside on his lengthy swim, he was shocked when Case paddled up alongside of him. Franklin briefly acknowledged the surfer, and together they continued moving off-shore in the pull of a massive rip. By the time he had reached Franklin, Case was admittedly nervous, as he was already farther outside in the ocean than he had ever paddled before. But the presence of Franklin gave him the courage to keep going. I would imagine the same might have been true for the lifeguard.

The overhead lights on Franklin's patrol vehicle attracted dozens of people to the scene. People lined the shore to witness the dramatic rescue unfolding before them. Curiosity and speculation spread amongst the growing crowd, but no one actually knew what it was the two men were swimming for. Occasionally someone would yell out, thinking they had spotted a victim far from shore, but no one could say for certain as the lifeguard and the surfer carried on a ridiculous distance from shore.

Case and Franklin fought feverishly to reach the drowning man in time. The spotters atop Goat Rock, who had been instrumental in directing him earlier, now stood still, unable to provide Franklin with any guidance. By then, they had lost sight of him and feared he had already drowned. Later, one of the men referred to his last sighting of the victim as "a little speck way out in the water." By then, the victim had already been pulled almost a half-mile from shore, and had turned south east of Goat Rock.

Then, as one of the large waves lifted them, Case pulled up to his knees for better vantage just as Franklin had stopped swimming. It was Case who shouted, "Dude, there he is!" Franklin, immediately behind him, also caught a glimpse of the victim's arm and the top of his head.

Steve closed the final 30 yards to the victim, but tragically, by the time they reached his location, he was no longer there. After Case confirmed they were in the right spot, Steve took a deep breath and dove down. Remarkably, Case's estimation was dead-on and in the clear water, Franklin spotted the pale whiteness of the man's bare chest, as earlier, the man had managed to shed both his shirt and his cowboy boots. Now, his body was suspended in the water table, just a few feet below the surface, facing skyward with his arms hanging uselessly at his side. Franklin could see the victim's eyes had rolled back in his head and saw a thin stream of bubbles pouring from his mouth.

Steve clutched the lifeless body and brought him to the surface.

Case, utterly astonished at the re-emergence of the victim from beneath the water, spontaneously yelled out, "Dude, you got him!"

The victim's eyes were open but his gaze was distant. White foam drained from his mouth. Franklin, confident he had been conscious only moments earlier, shook the man and yelled at him.

Getting no response, Franklin then tilted his head back to open his airway, preparing to deliver a rescue breath, and the man groaned. Franklin supported his head above the water and distinctly heard the man groan again. Seconds later Franklin heard an exhalation emerge from his mouth. He brought his ear closer to the victim's face to listen. Sure enough, the man was breathing on his own.

The two rescuers pulled the victim onto Case's longboard, and soon afterwards, Franklin heard in the distance, the familiar and comforting sound he and so many of his fellow rescuers had come to appreciate. Searching the skies above, he saw Henry-I approaching from the east. The pilot spotted the three men, circled once, then pulled directly overhead. Seconds later, they lowered one of their deputy/medics on the static line amidst a windstorm of downdraft.

Together the three men managed to get the victim into the rescue collar. Then, with a rotating hand signal from the medic, Franklin's victim ascended in the care of the deputy. Once the victim was aboard, the chopper turned and flew towards shore, leaving Case and Franklin behind. Steve thanked the smiling surfer for his help in saving the man's life. Case was both shocked and ecstatic in seeing what he would later refer to as a *"miracle rescue"* as well as *"the most insane thing I have ever been a part of."*

Far from shore, gently rising and falling with the passing swells, with nothing but the vastness of open water in all directions, they could see the chaotic scene in the distance. The rescue vehicles, with their brightly colored lights were tiny and silent, and a crowd of non-descript people lined the shore, watching in wonder as the victim, dangling below the helicopter, flew directly towards them to reach the awaiting medics in the parking lot. Despite the drama on shore, the two rescuers could hear nothing but the sound of the breaking waves in the distance. Franklin held onto the front of Case's board and the two men indulged themselves in a bit of laughter, basking in the gratifying luxury of knowing that together, they had just saved the life of a fellow human being.

The helicopter returned and Franklin offered Case the rare opportunity for a spectacular ride to shore, but Case, wanting to stay with his board, opted to paddle himself to shore. After confirming he was okay for the return paddle, Franklin swam to the deputy and grabbed the harness, putting him face to face with the medic for the lift off.

From their incredible vantage point 200' in the air, Steve could clearly see the huge rip current which had pulled them a half-mile from shore. He also had an incomparable birds-eye view of the surf pounding against Goat Rock. In the parking lot, he saw the spinning lights of fire trucks, sheriff's vehicles, State Parks trucks, CHP sedans, and a huge crowd of onlookers. It was a crazy scene, and he knew that he would soon be lowered into the epicenter of the hoopla and all eyes would be on him, like a rock star making a spectacular descent onto a stage. Yet just for those few moments, dangling high above it all, and despite the deafening noise of the rotors spinning direct above him, he felt oddly peaceful and content.

The officers in the lot had cleared the people from one area, forming an impromptu landing zone, and in that spot the pilot lowered the two men to the ground. Franklin had barely gotten out of the harness and cleared the area of rotor wash when the victim's girlfriend came running to him. She was crying with an unrestrained release of stress. She immediately gave Steve a huge hug, seemingly unconcerned that he was cold and wet. And, in a rare occurrence for any guards, but especially so on the North Coast, she thanked him repeatedly.

As Franklin walked through the crowd towards his vehicle carrying his fins and rescue buoy, all eyes were on him and he was greeted with a spontaneous outpouring of applause. Many of the people standing there had watched the entire event, and would no doubt retell this story in the coming weeks. Some stepped forward and shook his hand, but most of them seemed content to just be able to put a face to the previously anonymous lifeguard.

Because the rescue had taken over an hour to play out, an enterprising young reporter, who had been monitoring the police scanner and heard the rescue unfolding, raced to the scene and arrived in time to witness the culmination, with Henry-I hoisting the stricken victim from the sea, and the subsequent delivery of the guard back to shore. He approached Franklin while Steve was drying off, eager to get the details of the dramatic story from him directly.

Ironically, Franklin's day was far from over. There were more waves and more people, and he was *still* the only guard on duty in the South Sector. Thus, Franklin cut the interview short, excused himself, quickly changed out of his wet gear, threw his wetsuit into the truck bed, and resumed his patrol on that crazy coastline.

Steve Franklin had just experienced one of the most critical and successful rescues any guard could ever hope to accomplish. He had saved a man's life in the most dramatic fashion. Yet what made this particular rescue *truly unique* was the fact that *a reporter had witnessed the event with his own eyes.*

The Santa Rosa Press Democrat published the rescue story the following day. Contrary to the less flattering terms used to describe the lifeguards in the media thus far, the article ended with a quote from the victim referring to the guard as "a hero." The article also mentioned the death of the fisherman who had been washed off the rocks in a similar incident at Salt Point, which shed light on the guards' larger scope of responsibility. That victim had not been so fortunate and the reporter correctly stated the lifeguards were still waiting for his body to surface.

Articles detailing Franklin's rescue were printed in various publications on Monday, Tuesday, Wednesday and Thursday. The articles served as a powerful validation for the lifeguards and a testament to their skills and service to the community. In the Napa Register, the victim recounted the traumatic nature of the event, saying, *"I was climbing on dry rocks when the wall of water hit me and swept me up like a huge waterslide,"* and, *"I was sucking water into my lungs and they were burning."*

Another complimentary article highlighting Franklin and the lifeguard service came out in the February 28th edition of the Sacramento Bee, including a quote from the victim confirming that he had submerged. *"I was so cold and tired, I was just praying to God for a couple minutes more...but then I slipped below the water and I just didn't have the strength to get back up to the surface."*

The articles were a revelation. They captured an undeniable and heroic rescue which would serve as a bright spot toward redemption, documenting the gravity of an event similar to the other successful rescues his fellow guards had already made. The Press Democrat, the largest local newspaper in the county, ran their own article which ended with a statement from Franklin himself which hinted at the undercurrent of frustration all of the guards felt. In his quote, one can hear him imploring the public to recognize the lifeguard's valuable service to the community.

Rescue

ifeguards defy dds on coast

noma Coast's elite lifeguards do the impossible

"We started lifeguarding here at the end of 1990 and we were greeted with criticism. I think it's important that people are shown what we can do....We lifeguards do good things."

To say the guards felt a sense of vindication by Franklin's rescue and the subsequent positive press would be an understatement. They all shared a swell of professional pride in Steve's rescue, and hoped the bickering over whether they were a waste of taxpayer money would finally come to an end.

For Franklin personally, as one might imagine, the rescue would be the most dramatic of his career. He later described it as a sports analogy. *"It was like that amazing catch you make in a baseball game when the culmination of practice, timing, and sheer luck all came together."*

In retrospect, the circumstances surrounding the rescue played out perfectly on several fronts. Occurring on a crowded day, it was witnessed by hundreds of people. In Gabriel Case, they had the validation and statement of a first-hand witness who was actually on scene. And above all, the victim, having survived, added the most compelling and unbiased perspective of all; that of the benefactor, whose life was saved. Finally, they had the all-important documentation and validation from the press, whose beat writer, striving to capture the story, was able to witness the final dramatic act of Steve Franklin's performance.

Franklin, it seemed, was content. True to his word, he had made good on his promise to Hickey that he would provide him with that *"One Great Rescue"* and pulled it off in dramatic fashion. For a few weeks, the guards rode high on the wave of validation that they had delivered on their claims. Finally, in their minds, they would be accepted by the community as a valuable and integral force in saving lives.

But such a hope would prove to be too much to ask for, and their acceptance by the community would remain elusive. Although Franklin's rescue had brought a respite from the criticism, the interlude turned out to be short-lived. Eventually the muted voices of the dissenters once again rose above the din of their supporters, and the guards were relegated back into their familiar roles in defense of their very existence.

Apparently, *"One Great Rescue"* would not be enough to appease the stubborn public, and eventually the guards were forced to accept that bitter pill. But as the great collection of dedicated lifesavers they were, quietly and assiduously, they carried on, ready to make *ONE*

MORE great rescue, or *TWENTY MORE* if necessary, to turn the tide of opposition.

The final tragedy of Franklin's rescue was that it occurred squarely in the midst of the lifeguard's personnel squabbles, and for whatever reason, despite the undeniable gravity, danger, and heroic measures that Franklin had personified in saving the man's life, none of the managers ever thought to submit it to the United States Lifesaving Association for Medal of Valor consideration.

THE POOL CAPER

While the North Sector guys had a decent place to do ocean swims in Gerstle Cove, the South Sector guys had nothing of the kind. Needing to keep their gills wet, Martino arranged for them to use the community swimming complex in Sebastopol before work. Although it was over 20 miles from the coast, the trip was worth it, since they all knew that their commitment to fitness might one day save their lives. Martino, who had previous experience as a swim coach, devised a series of elaborate and challenging 4,000-yard workouts which included hypoxic sets – designed to improve the guards' abilities to tolerate potential hold-downs under massive waves.

The opportunity for the lifeguards to commune in the familiar element of water also served to bond them closer as friends.

And so it was, on an otherwise uneventful cold and rainy morning that Adam and Loeffler showed up to do their pre-shift workout at the pool. With the steam rising from the pool in the 40 degree air, they stripped down to their speedos on the deck, and stashed their gear under a bench to keep it dry. Adam tucked his curly hair under a white swim cap, and the two guards grabbed their goggles and pranced across the cold wet cement deck to begin their workout.

Not more than 100 yards into their swim, Adam noticed a transient-looking guy who had wandered in through the gate. Not thinking much of him, he continued swimming, but after two more laps he looked up and saw the transient was digging into Loeffler's bag.

Adam immediately yelled out to him.

Realizing he had been spotted, the man turned and ran toward the exit gate. Meanwhile, Loeffler, suddenly realizing what had happened, pulled himself from the water, and with Adam only slightly behind him, entered into a hot pursuit of the fleeing transient.

Not having time to dry off or even grab a towel, the two lifeguards sprinted through the gate and onto the city streets wearing nothing but their speedos and a thin sheen of chlorinated water. As if they didn't look ridiculous enough, in their haste, both men still had their goggles on, and Adam was still wearing his swim cap.

Once outside the gate, Loeffler spotted the man, briskly crossing the busy four-lane street, and the two guards, running barefoot, darted between the cars in a frenzied chase. Drivers stopped to watch, no doubt entertained by the curious sight of these two seemingly fit, and near-naked goggle-men, whose height disparity and circumstance suggested that perhaps the circus might be in town.

Thankfully, the pursuit ended just a few blocks away, and after questioning the man, it was determined he hadn't in fact taken anything.

The guards were then forced to begin their rather embarrassing return walk along the streets of Sebastopol. Coming across a red light, they were obligated to stand and awkwardly wait at the intersection, looking absolutely ridiculous in the rain.

Just then, a car window rolled down and two women, who couldn't help themselves, yelled out *"Hey you guys – you wanna come for a swim with us?!"* after which the girls began laughing hysterically.

The guards offered a sheepish smile, and a paltry wave in acknowledgment.

Looking back, at least the lifeguard's impromptu dash through town served to put a little joy and humor into the morning commute for a handful of drivers who no doubt had a pretty good story to bring into work that day.

4-1-1992
OPENING DAY - 1992

The abalone season for 1992 kicked off on Wednesday, April 1st. The memory of the single drowning death the previous year still lingered as a blemish on an otherwise stellar Opening Day performance.

The guards had enjoyed plenty of success in their 19 months patrolling the coastline and had most certainly saved several lives, but no matter how many rescues they had logged, and how many victims they had plucked from the seas, the guards knew the truest measure of their worth would be found in the only objective statistic which truly mattered; the undeniable and quantifiable tally of *deaths by drowning*. For the next 12 hours, hundreds of divers from across the state would arrive, suit up and waste no time making awful and foolhardy decisions, entering the ocean in God-awful spots, and place themselves in situations so dangerous that one would be left wondering if they were *intentionally* searching for new and creative ways to kill themselves.

The statistics bore this out, as least *one diver had drowned on every opening day for four years straight.*

It was a disastrous streak they desperately wanted to end. Thus, their goal for the day, as simple as it sounded, was for all of the divers to leave the park *alive* at the end of the day.

The crew was at full staff, adding a newcomer from Huntington, in veteran guard Mike Thomas. Thomas had started back in '76, but had left guarding for some time to pursue a law degree. When that didn't work out, he was drawn back by the reward and the thrill of the lifeguarding, and was eagerly accepted into the fold. Like the others, Thomas would quickly realize the unique challenge posed by working the North Coast. With no time for any familiarization to the operations or procedures, the Opening Day Extravaganza would serve as his "orientation."

The supplies were loaded in the trucks, the oxygen tanks were full, and the boat was gassed. On that day alone, the sheriffs would launch their own rescue boat as well, and Henry-I would be staged in the Salt Point maintenance yard, poised for a speedy deployment.

An incredibly thick fog bank clung to the coastline for most of the morning, which both assisted and hindered the guards. The fog made it impossible to see the areas off-shore, but the sound of waves, like rolling bands of thunder set an ominous tone, and dissuaded most of the inexperienced divers from going out. In a seeming paradox, the wind blew early and strong, yet was unable to clear the tenacious fog which swirled around yet stubbornly resettled. The melding of the chilly winds and tenacious fog painted a mood over the coastline that was bleak and eerie. The arriving divers, emerging from the warm cabs of their trucks, stood on the bluffs to assess the ocean and were rudely greeted by the pervasive wind, chilling them with a frigid wetness which permeated through their clothes, and into their bones. Many of the divers resigned themselves to cash it in, choosing instead to set up their campsites, have a morning beer, puff a cigarette or two and to wait to see if things improved. But of course, there were plenty of eager souls who were dead-set on going out and weren't the kind of men who would let a little wind and fog stand between them and their pursuit of glory.

The guards worked their magic, locating disoriented divers in the fog by whistling and isolating their cries for help. They staged the IRB at the head of known rip currents and waited for the divers to be delivered to them via the rips. Utilizing their compass, and orienting themselves by the sounds of the breaking waves, they even ventured inside to check on novices, making several more rudimentary rescues near rocks. By noon, the guards had logged close to 400 safety contacts and would log another 200 in the afternoon.

As the sun set, and the divers retreated to the campgrounds or had begun their return trip to Sacramento or Fresno, there was cause for celebration. For the first time in four years, no one had managed to die along the Sonoma Coast on Opening Day.

The guards held an impromptu debrief session at Salt Point. Leaning on a patrol truck, they were finally able to let their guard down. Loeffler led the celebration, breaking the tension with some of his patented hilarity and good natured ribbing. For half an hour they reviewed the calls and swapped details among themselves. It had been a great day...a great day to be a State Lifeguard.

The opener was covered by several Northern California newspapers. The Bodega Bay Signal led with the headline "No Fatalities for 1992 Abalone Opener," but the narrative gave more credit to the wind than the guards, adding, "*Winds that gusted to 45 miles an hour on the Sonoma Coast last weekend may have been responsible for this being the safest abalone opener in the last four years, the first in that time to register no fatalities.*"

Regardless, the guards, riding high on the momentum of the opener, carried their passion through to the following weekend which expectantly brought droves of divers. Over the two days, an estimated

242 | ONE GUARD OUT

2,000 divers entered the water in search of abalone, many of them rock pickers who took advantage of the concurrent negative low tides.

The guards performed many rescues, led by newcomer Mike Thomas, along with Loeffler, and Straub. Jon Gulick single-handedly rescued four divers by himself; a fitting finale in his last save before transferring south to work the beaches of San Clemente for the summer.

The undeniable fact remained - not a single life was lost in the first week of the abalone season.

In fact, no lives were lost in the entire month of April, and the crew found themselves riding on the proverbial wave of their success.

5-2-1992
TRAGEDY TIMES THREE

Two days after their month-long hiatus from any fatalities on land or sea, the guards were dispatched to High Point for a report of a vehicle over the side of the cliff. Straub and Loeffler responded and came upon several people waving them down. Peering over the side, the scene was utterly horrible. A Volkswagen van had somehow driven off the cliff in a particularly steep area and tumbled at least 800' below the roadway. Unfortunately, there was nothing they could do. The terrain was too steep to reach on foot, and there was no possibility of anyone surviving the crash. The guards stood by on the roadway as Henry-I was summoned to extricate the bodies of an elderly couple from what remained of the van. Just as the deputies were lifting the last victim to the roadway, the guards were diverted to another emergent call at Fort Ross.

A newly certified SCUBA diver had accompanied two of his free-diving buddies who were hunting for abalone in the calm waters of Fort Ross Cove. Their intent was to stay together, but as was often the case while diving, they soon became separated.

One of the free divers was kicking along the bottom searching around rocks for any legal abalone when he happened to come across the scuba diver's spear gun laying on the bottom. Immediately concerned, he ascended and began scanning the entire cove area, yelling out for his friend. Eventually, he spotted the scuba diver's lifeless body washing against the rocks. The two divers were able to pull their friend onto shore and frantically tried to revive him.

Loeffler, Schardt, Straub, and Thomas responded and took over the CPR, but unfortunately they were unsuccessful in their attempts to revive the 41-year old man. No one knew how he had gotten into trouble, or if he had suffered some medical emergency while under water.

Three deaths in a single hour signaled an ominous beginning to May. Despite the fact none of the fatalities were preventable, from the perspective of the rescuers, like all deaths on their watch, they added to the emotional burden they carried.

5-31-1992
STRAUB'S EPIPHANY

North Coast Lifeguard sizing up breaking waves – The Face (1996) – Photo: McNulty

It would be a bold statement to say that any single rescue could meaningfully alter the path of a lifeguard's life. But on a spring day in 1992, there's little doubt that's exactly what happened.

A significant factor directly affecting the guard's lives on the North

Coast was their paygrade. The wage made by Seasonals at the time was paltry compared to their fellow lifeguards working for agencies like LA County. Back then, County Seasonals with their EMT certification and five years of experience working the beaches of Manhattan, Santa Monica, or Zuma were earning noticeably more (over 35% more - by my unofficial estimation) than the veteran State Seasonals with comparative skills working in Sonoma. Considering the challenges that the North Coast crew endured, it's mind boggling to realize how grossly underpaid they were. Unfortunately it's a fact which is still true today.

One might assume, commensurate with other lifeguard agencies, that their paltry base salary might be augmented by the fact that they had certified as EMTs (at their own expense) allowing them to perform with increased skills and responsibilities. Nope. Same for hazard pay; there was no such thing. And common sense might suggest that some stipend would be offered to offset their living costs in that remote location. Similarly, no such bonus existed. Admittedly, the Perms made a decent wage, with health benefits and the supplementary lure of a pension if they persisted long enough, but the Seasonals had nothing of the sort.

It should be noted that every one of those Seasonal guards was creative and talented, and could have landed a lucrative job in any number of different sectors of the workforce, but each one *chose* to work there as lifeguards. Their incentive to relocate and work that coastline was rooted heavily in their sense of altruism which, last I checked, provided no financial reward. As a consolation, they may have believed they were etching their names into some storied chapter in lifeguard lore. The truth is, I fear that within 50 years or so they would likely have been forgotten had they not shared their stories and allowed them to be printed in the collection of pages you now hold.

Although lifeguards tend to be keenly resourceful, and the crew adapted their lifestyles to make ends meet, Straub's station in life was unique among them. Not only did he have a life-partner in Pam, but he also had a small child to provide for. They were a traditional family in many ways, except for the fact that he and Pam were not married. Don was not opposed to marriage in general - he just had reservations about the institution as an endeavor *for himself.* Regardless, when they sat down at the kitchen table two years earlier, Pam listened intently as

Don, brimming with excitement, first spoke about the wild North Coast, and the fact that people were unnecessarily dying there in great numbers. He explained that they were starting a lifeguard rescue service and had asked him to come work there. He tried to convey the significance and the gravity of this once-in-a-lifetime opportunity to do something truly remarkable – to be a lifeguard in a place where his skills could make a significant difference and save lives. Pam, in support of her talented lifeguard/partner, and always up for a new adventure, jumped on board with his crazy dream.

"Where the lifeguard goes...the lifeguard's family will follow," she said.

Her statement was prophetic in both a literal and figurative sense. In retrospect, many career guards who are married and/or have children would concur. The various aspects of the job and the lifestyle have a way of permeating into family life like no other career I am aware of.

Pam, with baby Tiana in tow, agreed to follow Don in his quest to "save people from drowning" and to change a small part of the world. They would join forces and do their best to support each other in this alternative and unconventional lifestyle somewhere north of San Francisco in a place they referred to as the "North Coast."

As a man of unfailing pride, Don was determined to succeed in establishing this lifeguard service, but he was also committed to his responsibilities as a father, and trying to reconcile both with limited resources would prove to be a continual challenge. Don used his skills as a diver to supplement the family's diet with plenty of abalone, Uni and fresh fish. In the winter months, they foraged for wild mushrooms. Don also did side jobs in construction on his days off. And living within the margins of frugality and ingenuity, after 18 months, Don somehow managed to save enough money to purchase a new trailer for the family. Finally, he was able to free them from the isolation of Arky Camp and "move them up" (albeit it a small step), into the employee residence area at Salt Point. There, the three settled into their life with Don continuing to navigate his disparate roles as the cornerstone of his family, as well as the cornerstone of the lifeguard service.

It was Sunday...and also happened to be Memorial Day. Across the country Americans from Maine to San Diego were honoring the heroism and bravery their soldiers endured for the country's collective benefit. Coincidentally, at Salt Point, a different kind of heroism would play out in real time to a far more modest audience.

The off-shore buoy readings the previous day had heightened the guard's concern. Offshore swell readings registered 15' at 22 second intervals - unusually large for that late in the winter season. Off-shore buoy readings of 15' with long intervals translated to 20'+ breaking waves on shore. There was little doubt that an imposing long-period swell would greet the Memorial Day divers.

Just before dawn, Straub went on-duty as the solo lifeguard on the early shift. Arriving in the patrol truck in the main lot at Salt Point, at first glance Don was relieved – as the ocean displayed only the remnants of the local wind-swell, generating evenly spaced, head-high waves breaking along the inside. The low-lying fog had partially lifted and stabilized about 40' above the ocean surface like a suspended blanket, filtering the light and shading the coastline in grey.

As Don scanned the horizon, he was surprised to see a group of unmistakable lines rolling in from far off-shore. Eventually, the rogue set arrived in dramatic fashion, with three solitary waves, spaced almost 40 seconds apart - thundered down some 400 yards from shore, then rumbling onward in a trio of well-separated 15' walls of white water.

A dozen vehicles were parked in the lot belonging to rock pickers, who had arrived before dawn to take advantage of the concurrent low tides, completely ignorant of the arriving swell. The huge waves broke far outside in shapeless walls and rolled towards shore, gradually disintegrating after being dragged over the rocky bottom. The pickers, having scurried out among the tide pools to try and find a few abalone during the long lull, were caught off-guard by the large waves and Don was treated to an aquatic slapstick show as frightened wetsuit-clad men stumbled across the slippery rocks in full-retreat from the unexpected set. By the time the waves had reached them, they were shoulder-high remnants of their former glory, but they still possessed enough force to tumble the men clear from the tidal area and unceremoniously dump them back on shore.

Then, just as suddenly as the set had appeared, another long lull followed and the ocean returned to an eerily calm.

Like all lifeguards who spend decades scrutinizing the whims of the ocean's swells and breaking waves to detect changes, Don was attuned to the subtleties of swell direction, size, and the influence of tidal shifting on the breaking waves. He was also well-aware of the long lulls that often accompanied the arrival of large swells. The impressive set served as a bold declaration that the expected swell was making her dramatic entrance on the Sonoma Coast.

Scanning the ocean with binos to make sure all of the pickers had escaped safely, Don's heart dropped. A small group of wetsuit-clad men standing on the shoreline were waving in his direction – never a good sign. Initially Don thought it might be a medical issue on shore – then he spotted a lone diver caught in the flow of the infamous "Salt Point Rip." Having kicked out before the set arrived, the diver was now squarely in the flow of powerful rip, fueled by the retreating waters from the set. Terrified, his screaming had caught the attention of those on shore.

The rip was a recurring phenomenon and a notorious culprit in snatching divers when swells grew formidable. The current was growing rapidly and the counter flow of the water against the dominant direction of the waves created a swirling and choppy mess, with the floundering free-diver's head bobbing in the very vortex of it. Fueled by the additional back flow from the massive set, the diver was being pulled off-shore at a healthy clip. Having already been struck by several waves, his abalone float, as well as his mask and both fins had already been stripped from him.

With no other guards on duty, no boat in the water, and Henry-I unavailable, Don would be alone on this one. He quickly stripped down and pulled on his wetsuit. Running towards shore, he scrutinized the victim one last time and grew concerned seeing that the man's head was low in the water, suggesting that he might already be losing his battle to stay afloat.

In order to reach his victim, Straub needed to traverse the vast expanse of exposed rocks in the inter-tidal area, then swim across an equally wide swath of water to reach the convergence of the rip current and the impact zone, an area to which the victim was being rapidly delivered.

The lifeguards knew the drill. The "rock dance" across the inter-tidal zone was the ultimate obstacle course, with wet kelp covering the sharp rocks in layers of slippery ribbons, causing them to slip and slide with almost every step. Between the rocks, narrow tide pool channels of water allowed the guards short sections where they could swim before resuming the awkward rock dance.

Straub made his way through the channels, alternating between pulling himself along the bottom, swimming and stumbling into the next pool. Eventually he was able to reach waist-deep water and began swimming towards the feeder of the rip which would propel him out faster.

Swimming head-up, the lines of white water blocked his view to the victim, but despite the white-noise rumbling of the surf, and his wetsuit hood muffling his hearing, occasionally he could hear the random high pitched screams for help from his anonymous victim, flailing out beyond the waves. Unknown to Straub at the time, the victim had not thought to drop his weight belt, and had endured a succession of sizable waves with the added burden of 20 pounds of lead strapped to his waist. As a result, each wave had submerged him and held him under the surface long enough to intensify his panic, evident by the escalating volume of his screams.

To the veteran lifeguard, who certainly realized the critical nature of the situation, the resumption of his screaming was actually a good thing – as evidence that the man had not yet drowned.

Don began a series of short sprints, separated by repeated descents under the incoming head-high walls of white water. He made progress, but as with all rescues on the North Coast, the cold water and restrictive wetsuit hindered his natural swimming stroke, causing it to become stiff and choppy. After diving under several dozen waves, each progressively larger than the previous one, he finally reached deeper water.

There, Don stopped momentarily and lifted his head. The arduous series of sprints had left him breathless, and the sensation of his own respirations were amplified by the wetsuit hood covering his ears; muffling out the external sounds. Resting on his buoy, he pulled off his hood and held his breath momentarily to silence his respirations and strained to hear the victim's screams.

Don heard nothing but the rumbling white noise of the waves, a realization that immediately caused him to suspect the worst. The most likely scenario was that the victim (conscious or not) had been delivered even farther from shore by the powerful rip, out past the surf line, and into the open ocean, clear of even the largest of the breaking waves. In his mind, Don began a silent conversation with God, praying that the diver was still floating on the surface far off-shore – still conscious – still alive - and that the 7-mm of rubber he was wearing would keep him afloat long enough for Don to reach him.

Seeing a new and larger set approaching outside, he pulled his hood back on and continued off-shore.

Having reached the deep green water, an area normally outside of the breaking waves, the sight of even larger waves building outside was remarkable. The ocean was moving the goal posts, and pushing the impact zone farther out. Straub carried on swimming head-up to monitor the impressive wave building before him. From the perspective of sea level the slow rise above the ocean surface was impressive. Knowing he would be caught inside by the huge wave, yet confident in his skills to navigate under, he paused for a moment to behold the majesty of this wonder of nature and magnificent show of force, as the double-overhead wave toppled and crashed down well-outside of him with a resounding boom. Don was gassed from his swim, but in preparation of his descent, he took several deep and exaggerated breaths. The 10' wall of white water propelled towards him with speed and power. Timing his convergence conservatively, Don dove down early and deep to avoid the brunt of the wave's energy, then felt the tug on his harness as his buoy tombstoned at the surface. While the wave passed over him, Don maintained a well-practiced and Zen-like calm to preserve his oxygen – knowing that this would likely be the first wave of a new set, and that the next ones would likely be larger, forcing him to dive earlier, descend deeper, and stay down longer.

Attempting to remain calm, Don repeated his descents under several more tumbling walls of water, each slightly larger than the previous one. Surfacing from beneath what he had hoped would be the set wave, his heart dropped. The final wave was building outside, with a face that would exceed double-overhead, matching any wave he has ever had to contend with before. Don took several exaggerated deep breaths, grasped the buoy – turned it streamline with his body, bent at the waist and dove down, pushing the buoy under and actively kicking to descend. With eyes closed, he descended deep under the surface to avoid the majority of the moving water, then turned horizontal under the water to streamline himself and offer the wave less surface area to pull him. A long shadow of darkness rolled over him accompanied instantly by a violent wave of energy which swept over him, as if the ocean was establishing her dominance. The feeling to Don was a blending of an ultimate thrill coupled with a profound vulnerability. Even before he surfaced Don shuddered, realizing that his victim was likely being struck by this same set – and wondering if he could survive.

Don rode the buoy back to the surface, released it to trail behind him and immediately resumed swimming, head up and eyes open, breathing deep and scanning for the possibility of another. And just as he had expected, there on the horizon, already beginning to rise, the next challenger was forming.

There is no doubt that it would be larger than the previous one – and solidified the fact that this was the largest surf he had ever been in before.

Straub knew, above all else, that he must avoid the cascading wall of the impact area, and position himself either inside or outside of the narrow landing zone of the crashing wave. Feeling that he had a chance to make it over the top, and avoid further abuse, Don put his head down to maximize power and committed to sprint directly into the teeth of this massive wave. The decision was crucial, and he knew that if he came up short and was unable to crest the lip, that he would be pulled backwards over the falls – and dropped directly into the waterfall, enduring the full force of thousands of pounds of cascading water – then being held down for God-knows how long.

Stroking directly into the core of the peaking wave, Don felt his body rising as the wave lifted him into her belly. Riding up the face, he felt a surge of confidence as his momentum quickened and he was thrust upwards towards the peak. Still stroking, yet feeling victorious, he reached the crest. And at that moment, at the very crux of the conquest, Don couldn't help but peek back over his shoulder to behold the daunting drop down to the ocean surface, a distance of three stories below him. In the next instant he turned back and shot over the lip, followed by his buoy, successfully "breaking through to the other side" as the ocean exploded behind him in a reverberating boom.

Don's sense of relief was further enhanced when he looked up and saw before him - a blessed lull.

The ocean surface was chewed up and rough, but there, another 100 yards outside and slightly to his north, Don spotted his elusive victim. Owing far more to luck than skill, the Salt Point Rip had fortuitously pulled the hapless diver a ridiculous distance from shore, depositing him safely outside of the impact area before the massive set of waves had rolled through. Ironically, the deadly and formidable rip had almost certainly saved his life.

Don yelled out and the victim turned toward him and began screaming and waving wildly, not unlike a man adrift in the vast Pacific, trying to gain the attention of a passing plane. Don swam towards him, feeling a blend of both wonder and elation that he was alive.

The man had been pulled past the terminal head of the massive rip which had finally dissipated, no less than a half-mile from shore. That significant distance, under normal circumstances, would have brought him well-clear of danger and Don could have relaxed. But as Straub continued his swim toward the victim, he gazed toward the horizon and witnessed a sight that shot a dose of adrenalin through his arteries...as still farther outside, though barely perceptible yet, a wall of water was beginning to rise some 250 yards *farther outside*.

The wave would be substantial, and Don knew there was no way he could deliver the victim outside in time to safely ascend over it. The beating would be unlike anything Don had ever experienced before, and the realization quickly came over him that he would have to endure it with the additional burden of tending to his victim.

The diver, facing Don with his back to the horizon, was oblivious to the fact that the river of luck had been riding along was about to run dry.

The victim's head was low in the water, despite the buoyancy of his thick wetsuit, and only when Don got closer did he realize the rather incredible fact that the man had survived thus far in these horrendous conditions, with his *weight belt still synched to his waist!*

With the massive wave approaching, and some 50 yards left to reach the victim, Don began yelling at him repeatedly "DROP YOUR WEIGHT BELT!"

The victim, either confused, hypothermic, or crazy, yelled back with a series of panicked and disorganized statements - but did NOT drop his belt.

Some 30 minutes into this rescue ordeal, Straub finally came face to face with the previously anonymous victim. Their exchange was raw. The victim's face, seen through a six-inch opening in his hood, revealed a shell-shocked individual, fearful and pleading, muttering loudly despite the fact that the lifeguard was immediately before him.

Again Don yelled at him to "drop your belt" but the man seemed oblivious. Glancing over his shoulder at the building wave, Don knew that if the diver was struck by that wall of water with the added ballast of the weight, he would have no chance of reaching the surface and would most assuredly drown. Not getting compliance, Don grabbed him forcefully by the shoulders, spun him in the opposite direction, reached around him and released the buckle. Instantly the man's body rose in the water.

Don then swung the rescue buoy around him and clipped him in. Normally this would be a moment of some relief, as the victim was now secured in the lifeguard's care. At that point it would simply be a matter of logistics to negotiate his safe return swim to shore. In other rescues at the head of that rip, Don had swam his victims out farther, rounded Salt Point proper, and delivered them safely into protected waters of Gerstle Cove. But this time, in the path of the monstrous wave, there was no way to get outside and nowhere to escape.

While the wave continued its slow build, Don tried to prepare the man for the impact, giving him specific instructions to take a huge breath and dive as deeply as possible. But by then the man has become a basilar version of himself – stripped of all pretense and façade, and seemingly incapable of comprehending Don's instructions.

Swimmers getting rescued are often scared, and lifeguards are generally sympathetic to those fears. Over the years, veteran guards learn a variety of techniques and verbal rhetoric to calm their victims before, during, and after the rescue is completed. But this guy was different. His fear had rendered him thoroughly petrified. Despite Don's attempts to placate him, the man remained inconsolable. To this victim, the vast distance from shore created in him, a persistent and alarming sensation of being separated from life itself, and he began yelling, "*I want to get back in now!!*"

Dealing with challenging divers was not uncommon on the North Coast, but absolutely unheard of *while in the process of being rescued.* This was a truly unique situation, and one Straub was not prepared for. The guy desperately needed Don's help and was in no position to debate, yet like a stubborn child, the victim was unable to follow the lifeguard's instructions.

In an unforeseen twist, when the man finally looked off-shore and witnessed the immense wall of water building outside of them, he fell silent... Apparently even a man crazed with fear, when faced with the means by which he might die, falls silent before his God.

Don knew that the wave held no ill will towards him, yet at the same time, he realized that he had entered into sacred ground and placed his corporal body on a collision course with this majestic and awe-inspiring phenomenon of nature. He was squarely in the path of this monster, and it was far too late to turn back. Every decision he had made on this rescue had brought him to this very place. He was well-aware the wave might kill them both, but he wasn't going to go down without fighting like hell to avoid that eventuality for them both. Pragmatically, he also knew that if they survived the beating from this wave, there would likely be more behind it.

And he was right.

The wave was substantial - growing in immense magnitude. In his time on the North Coast, the veteran lifeguard had seen plenty of waves this large before, and even larger, but he had never witnessed their immensity from the perspective of the water line, knowing that he would have to contend with it. Worse yet, while facing this looming threat, he knew that the compromised state of his victim would compound the situation significantly.

The sight of this awesome display of nature was both mesmerizing and daunting. This was not a place for human beings. The ascending liquid wall, pulling vast amounts of water from the trough, rose up as if in slow motion, continually substantiating its immense height and loading up for a great release. The landing zone before it, having fed the towering wave, dropped lower, further distancing the trough from the eventual peak.

Had he been alone, there was a chance that Don could have made it safely over the monster, but towing the dead weight of the victim eradicated that option. Their only choice was to hold their position and brace for impact and the separate lives of the lifeguard and the diver would soon be joined in a monumental moment of common fate.

The view from shore was daunting. Even terrifying. A dozen rock pickers would be the only witnesses of this spectacular event, and they watched in disbelief and vicarious fear. Having seen the lifeguard swim past them long ago, they stood in awe realizing that he *chose* to enter the ocean in conditions such as these. Collectively they watched in silence, struggling to keep the two small heads in view, so very far from shore. The wave, rising outside, was larger than anything any of them has ever seen before, and they continued to watch, some with their hands over their mouths, certain that they were about to witness the imminent death of both men.

The two men had a prime vantage of nature's majesty and immense power not more than 70 yards away and closing fast, and their reactions were revealing. While the victim turned away from the oncoming wave, Don stared directly into the maw of it. As the wall advanced and continued to rise towards them, specific details came into view...the white foam ascending up the face, the murky green texture and thickness of the body, and above all, the commanding sense of incredible mass. The velocity caused a spattering of water to blow back off the lip as the wave gained height.

A final attempt to prepare the victim was of no use...he had seemingly checked out.

The moment had come. In accordance with the laws of nature, the energy of this majestic marvel, generated in some hellacious storm in the Gulf of Alaska, had completed its traverse across a large swath of the Northern Pacific Ocean. Reaching its ultimate destiny on this shoreline, it would explode in a violent and spectacular crescendo.

As the wave entered into 30' of water, it dragged along the bottom and slowed while the upper section continued to move ahead without resistance, thereby leaning it forward. Then, at some magical point, the angle of repose was exceeded and the weighty top half of the wave pitched forward in a mighty heave. For one magnificent moment, the massive lip became air-born in a suspended silence before the explosion.

The deafening collision of water on water detonated in a thunderous boom, resonating with an imposing power unlike anything else in nature. In theory it was a simple phenomenon - but in that setting and on that scale - this was something truly magnificent as thousands of pounds of falling water instantaneously collapsed with the focused force of a crumbling warehouse wall. The resultant plume of spray shot in the air some 40' or more, followed by a jumbled chaos of water struggling to coalesce and organize into a rolling barrage of water at least 20' thick.

Don knew they needed to descend as deeply as possible to avoid the major brunt of impact. Knowing they would be held down for a long while, Don yelled at the diver to *"Take a huge breath"* then wrapped his arms around the man, dipped his head toward the bottom, and forcefully drove him under the surface. Had Don been alone, he could have descended much deeper to avoid the brunt of the wave's impact, but having to wrestle with the victim and fighting the combined buoyancy of the victim's wetsuit along with his own rescue buoy, posed an added challenge.

The moment of impact was horrendous. Their world went black as the enormous bombardment of water engulfed them. Fully submerged, the noise surrounding them was deafening. Don's death grip on the diver was resolute, despite the fact that they were being pummeled violently in a fierce vortex of turbulence, driven down and held under by the dominating wall of white water. In that fierce tumbling darkness, suspended in the barrage of aerated water, both men were rendered utterly helpless. Not knowing which direction was up, there was no way to kick to the surface. Despite the turmoil, Don had managed to maintain his hold of the victim, and eventually their collective buoyancy guided them to the surface. In an act of valor, Don then lifted the man's body so his head could reach above the white water and take in several breaths. Unfortunately their reprieve was short-lived.

Although the tumbling had transported the men some distance under water, they were still far from shore and a second wave was bearing down on them, forcing them to brace for another onslaught. The victim, gasping deeply was too exhausted to scream.

The lifeguards' well-established methods of rescue off the face usually involved swimming the victim off-shore to be picked up by the boat, or by Henry-I, or swimming them around the point and into

Gerstle Cove. The idea of bringing a victim *in through the surf line* was frowned upon, owing to fact that the waves would propel them with force into a virtual minefield of protruding sharp rocks.

But this massive rogue set of waves has eradicated the safer plan, and Don's newly adopted goal had been stripped down to simply surviving at any cost. After enduring the first wave of the set, Straub had hoped they would have been washed further inside, but because their initial distance from shore was substantial, the wave had only moved them into a no-man's-land, fully vulnerable to the next wave. Don grabbed his victim and again dove him down as deeply as possible to avoid the brunt of the impact. Again they were beaten cruelly by the huge wave, and again Don eventually guided the man back to the surface and supported him so he could breathe. But Don's efforts to save his victim had greatly compromised himself and he soon realized he was running on empty.

Then, with a third wave approaching, the diver, desperate to claw his way above the white wash to reach the life-giving air, snatched Don in a death-grip of fear, forcing him under while arching his head to breathe. By then Straub had reached his breaking point. With his lungs throbbing in oxygen debt, he had nothing left to give. In that instant of revelation, Don's identity as a *lifeguard* was vaporized by his own desperate and primitive instinct to survive. After fiercely clinging to his victim to avoid losing him through the onslaught of massive waves, he had reached the point where he now needed to ditch the victim in order to save himself.

In one powerful thrust, he broke the man's hold. Finally free from the smothering victim, Don was able to take in several breaths of air. Then, still hyperventilating from oxygen debt and fearful for his own life, Don reached to his shoulder and pulled the loop of his rescue strap over his head, holding it in his hand. It was a moment of reckoning for Don. In his desperate struggle for his own survival, simply letting go of the strap would sever his connection with the victim, casting him off to fend for himself in the continuing maelstrom.

In that instant, time stood still.

Among the thousands of rescues in the lifeguard's storied career, it would be this moment that would ultimately define him. Free from the burden of the buoyed diver, Don would be able to descend deeper and avoid the bulk of the continuing abuse, preserving what little oxygen was left in his tissues, and saving himself. But he also knew that abandoning the man in those tumultuous seas would almost assuredly cause him to drown. There was not a man alive who would blame him for the decision, nor many who would even question the choice to save himself in a situation so grave.

With the third wave bearing down on them both, mere seconds before impact, Don shoved the strap back over his head and grabbed the diver one last time. By then he was so exhausted that he was unable to submerge at all, thus the two men were struck broadside and completely annihilated with the full force of a 15-foot barrage of white water. During the turmoil, Don's head was slammed onto the bottom, causing him to "see stars" and further disorient him while the wave continued to tumble both men into the rocky minefield of rocks inside.

Eventually the two heads surfaced together in 10' of water, tangled by the rope of the buoy line. In truth, it was unlikely that either man would have been able to remain conscious for another beating, but mercifully, they didn't have to. The ocean too had surrendered. The truce was evident by a forgiving lull, and not long after, the cumulative push of the dissipating surf delivered them inside, and out of harm's way.

Laying on their backs in the shallow inside water, both men breathed heavily, slowly ducking under waist-high white-water waves rolling over them. Initially, neither man was able to stand. Despite their life-threatening tribulation, no words were exchanged between them. Eventually Straub rose to his feet and assisted the victim to stand, and together, on wobbly legs, the two men began stumbling over the slippery rocks until they were finally free from the sea. Don sat the diver on a large rock. Confident that he was okay, in an uncharacteristic move, he left his patient alone to wait for the medics, while he walked away in the direction of the parking lot.

The chance meeting between lifeguard and victim became one of the most monumental events for both men. Having been immersed in those hellacious conditions, the ultimate victory for the diver amounted to nothing more than the simple resumption of "normal." He was still alive.

Don began the walk back to this truck, his legs stiff from the cold.

Passing the rock pickers, they called out random praises – but their compliments went unacknowledged. For the lifeguard the usual rush of fulfillment and elation in pulling off a critical rescue, this time, would not come.

Don reached his truck and hailed the dispatcher to let her know that he was clear of the rescue and requested a land-based medical crew to come and evaluate his patient, who was obviously shaken up from the ordeal. The dispatch log revealed that Don had been involved with the rescue for a full-hour.

Straub had been battered soundly on the rocks. His shoulder was throbbing, his left hip was badly bruised, and he was bleeding from several areas on his scalp and hands. But a much deeper blow had been inflicted in his soul. He dropped his fins and his unwrapped buoy on the ground next to his truck and sat alone on the tailgate staring at the ground. Exhausted and shivering, he felt his heart pounding under his wetsuit, and in that poignant moment, he experienced a profound revelation that he had not known before. The gravity and depth of the insight came not in the form of words, but rather in the ethereal realm of emotion. It was the honest realization of his advancing age and the recognition of his own mortality.

Beyond the gift of saving his victim's life, he had willingly dispatched his own being into the ocean during the most horrendous conditions imaginable. But unlike all of the previous rescues of his career, this time, he had exceeded the safe zone of control. After delivering so many victims back from the brink of death, and flirting with the seas in times of crazed conditions, on this occasion, his peek beyond the curtain of death extended too deep and he had stayed there too long. The bitter taste of death lingered in his mouth.

Here and now, having been returned from the "other side," his station in life, his defining role, his value system, and all of his defining guideposts had been torn to the ground. His confidence and skill in the surf line had found their limits, as he was no longer impervious to the perils which threatened those with lesser skills. His aging body, the years of abuse, and the many times he had tempted fate had finally succeeded in eroding through the thin cracks in his armor. And that vulnerability, like an insidious venom would continue to seep into his soul.

His blank stare at the ground continued. The salt water, pink with his own blood, trickled from his hair and dripped onto the concrete below. Each red drop of his life bounced in the same spot, gradually forming a small puddle of darkening red on the grey background. His gaze transfixed, he made no attempt to stop the flow.

The revelation hit him hard. There were many people in his life who depended on him, and while sitting on that tailgate he allowed his mind to ponder the ramifications to all of them if he had died. On that rescue, only the slightest alterations would have been necessary for him to fail in both of his cornerstone roles, and for *all of their lives* to be affected greatly. Being unmarried, Pam would have no legal right to any of his death benefits and his young daughter would grow up without a father. In all likelihood, she would only vaguely remember him by the time she reached adulthood, and the only significant influence he would have on her entire life would be genetic.

The volunteer fire department arrived and Don looked up without speaking and simply pointed in the direction of the small crowd, now huddled around the victim. The EMTs rambled off with their gear bags, winding their way down the small trail to the water's edge. No one thought to ask Don how he was doing. The lifeguards are *always* okay.

At the end of his shift Don drove home and, without the embellishment of decorum or ceremony, he asked Pam if she would marry him. She glowingly accepted his offer. The following day they drove to Santa Rosa to pull a marriage license.

When you get down to it, a lifeguard's love and dedication for their job translates to a desire to protect the all-inclusive populace known as "mankind." In my mind, that is an undeniable expression of love. Don Straub was wholly invested in his role as a lifeguard and he was damn good at it. In his years as a guard he had an unedited and unbiased view of the fragility of life, and the agony of demise. On many occasions, *his actions alone* had been instrumental in snatching victims from the jaws of death, and returning them safely to their families to live on. But Don's dedication to protecting *everyone* ultimately hindered his similarly noble commitment to protect *his own*.

Cognitively he had always known that he had his limits, but on that day he faced the grave and sobering reality that this job could *actually kill him*...and ultimately, gallantly dying in the line of duty would guarantee his failure as a father.

"Where the lifeguard goes...the lifeguard's family will follow."

After the minimum seven day compulsory waiting period, he and Pam returned to Santa Rosa the following week and were legally married on the steps of the courthouse. On the long drive home, Don confessed the details of the rescue which had precipitated his change of heart. With the ink barely dry on the marriage certificate laying on the back seat, he explained to Pam that in the event that he was killed in the line of duty, she and Tiana would have full access to his Social Security and death benefits.

Don's family had faithfully followed him away from their conventional world, in support of his altruistic desire to provide for the safety of the nebulous collection of anonymous humans known as "mankind." And while garnering undeniable success in that goal, ultimately Straub also made good on his more direct commitment to provide for two very special individuals within that group of "mankind" who mattered the most to him.

In *both* circumstances, I believe that those are manifestations of love.

Don and Pam with Tiana (1992)

8-1-1992
THE FALLEN BIRD

The narrow and precarious roadway which traverses the Sonoma Coast has always been prone to vehicle accidents. It winds and bends, climbs steeply and descends precipitously. When slick with rain, it becomes exponentially more dangerous.

So it was on a rare rainy day in August, when Straub and Loeffler were dispatched to a motorcycle accident near what was arguably the most dangerous section of the entire run; the precarious crest of High Point. The rider had been racing, slalom-style around the curves when he hit a slick spot, lost control of his bike, veered into the opposite lane and struck an on-coming car.

Straub and Loeffler raced up the High Point grade, and eventually came upon several cars stopped in the roadway. They slowed, taking in the scene, trying to piece together the clues that would reveal the recent violent interaction - and the kinetics of hardened steel versus delicate human bodies.

A deputy waved to them from behind the car. The motorcyclist's momentum had tumbled him up and over the roof of the car. The patient laid in the roadway – his body curled, shaking slightly and moaning. The guards' main concern was for his head and neck - the most vulnerable areas of his spinal cord. His right lower leg was obviously fractured. Methodically, they applied a cervical collar, and ran through the well-honed steps of securing him to their backboard to be ready for transport.

By the time Henry-I appeared overhead, the guards have the patient fully immobilized on a backboard. They have also splinted the fractured leg and dressed his wounds. State Parks Rangers, working with the Sheriff's Deputy closed off the roadway on both ends, allowing the emergency response teams to work without having to contend with vehicles entering into the scene. They had also established a landing zone in the roadway, but the pilot, Tom McConnell, after circling the entire scene once, chose instead to land in an adjacent grassy area.

The rotor wash caused the customary wind-whipped havoc and the guards had pre-emptively warned the patient to expect the loud noise and strong winds generated by the bird. They did their best to shield the patient's eyes from the sand and debris flying about and to keep him calm for his unplanned flight to the ER.

With the rotor blades cut back to half-speed, the deputy got out and helped the guards load the victim in through the starboard side of the craft. Once the patient was securely locked in, the guards turned and shuffled away from the helo. Straub and Loeffler had seen this movie before and knew enough to seek the sheltered solace inside of their truck to avoid a repeat sandblasting from the rotor wash.

Although the chopper had landed close to their vehicle, once they had slammed the doors closed, they were insulated from the deafening noise and the onslaught of sand and debris. The sight of a helicopter ascending off the ground, and knowing their patient was safely nestled in the back compartment was one of those spectacles which never failed to stimulate a sense of astonishment for the guards. It was a feeling of pride that they could, at any time, summon this miraculous flying machine, and hand off patient care to the medics to expedite transport for their critically injured patients, thereby giving them every chance of a favorable outcome. By then, there was also an accompanying sense of validation the sheriffs, at least in the North Sector, had begun to show them some respect. After working with them on so many calls, the separate crews had come to know each other as individuals, and the previously frigid relationship had begun to thaw. Although no one voiced it out loud, both sides, at least, had finally developed a mutual admiration for their truly unique skill sets. If pressed, both sides would have admitted that no one on either side could perform the others' job worth a damn.

In the narrow roadway, the guards watched from the security of the protected cab just 30' away as McConnell began juicing up the rotor velocity in preparation for their liftoff. The lone deputy, who hadn't thought to seek refuge in his patrol vehicle, stood just outside, preparing to watch the dramatic lift-off from close range. Loeffler remembered "*I was watching McConnell in Henry-I. We were in the truck with the windows up so it was like watching a movie through our windshield. I even mentioned to Don at that moment that there were aspects of the job I dearly loved. Being able to summon a helicopter, then work with them to package our patient. That was amazing.*"

The pilot had landed the helo between the guardrail of the roadway and an innocuous 4 x 4 post sticking up out of the ground, likely a remnant from an old sign. As he started to ascend, McConnell attempted to drift out sideways towards the ocean, but hadn't yet cleared the height of the post, and the chopper's skid began pressing against it.

In a rare act of inattention, the veteran pilot never saw the post.

Instead of ascending, he continued to push the helo westward, still pressing against the unseen post, which held tight in the ground. The added pressure on the post caused the bird to lean slightly, then lean even more. Seconds later the helo began to tilt precipitously from the normal horizontal orientation. Eventually, the main rotor had angled down so far that the blades suddenly began slapping the ground with explosive force. They chewed into the earth in a ghastly scene, hurling large divots of earth along with a barrage of rocks which began pelting the guards' patrol truck. The lone deputy standing outside immediately "hit the deck" and even inside the cab, both Loeffler and Straub instinctively ducked.

After the astonishingly powerful gouging of the earth, the bird continued to bend sideways, and the massive blade penetrated deeper into the ground until it impaled itself in the solid earth. At that moment, all of the torque normally delivered to the massive rotor was transferred back into the cockpit. In full view of the horrified guards, the entire cab then started spinning wildly with the two deputies, and the patient trapped inside. The violent catastrophe was horrific, as the aircraft then began breaking itself into pieces which were then flung haphazardly into the air in all directions and orientations in a scene of utter chaos. The truck was pelted by random parts of the bird with sporadic thuds which made it sound as though they were getting hit by gunfire. Unidentifiable pieces of fiberglass and metal were bouncing off their windshield and spiraling in the air around them.

Then the scene, already apocalyptic, got even worse.

Because the chopper had been perched so close to the steep drop, when the body of the cab was pitched westward, it began to tumble down the hillside, gaining momentum until it slid out of sight from the crew on the roadway.

In a matter of 20 seconds the previously sleek and agile engineering marvel which was Henry-I had been battered to hundreds of broken pieces.

Instantly, Loeffler grabbed the mic and every staff member working that day heard the unforgettable radio call from the normally subdued Loeffler, as he frantically reported the emergent message which would begin a full-scale, multi-agency response:

" *Henry-1 HAS CRASHED AT HIGH POINT!!! Henry-1 HAS CRASHED AT HIGH POINT!!!* "

Carter, patrolling Goat Rock at the time, later referred to Loeffler's radio call as *"The single most bone-chilling radio transmission of my career."*

Straub and Loeffler bolted from the truck and ran to the precipice along with the others. There, far below the roadway, they could see the battered cockpit, with the passengers still aboard. It had slid a considerable distance down the hillside before coming to rest near the edge of an unimaginable drop.

The remnant of the cockpit, as if stopped by the hand of God himself, laid perilously close to the edge of the bluff and a 300' descent to certain death. One more complete roll, or a slide of another 12 feet and the remnants of the copter would have plunged down the vertical cliff and smashed on the rocks below.

Seeing the precarious location of the bird, Don ran back up and re-positioned the patrol truck close to the edge of the roadway. He then grabbed the end of the winch cable and released the free spool to allow the line to feed out. Then, as Loeffler raced down the hillside with their medical supplies, Don followed with the cable hook, praying that his 150' of winch cable was long enough to reach the cab. It was. The path to the helo was a horrendous sight, with parts of the fresh wreckage strewn far and wide. Permeating the air was the oily smell of jet fuel which had been sprayed liberally across the hillside.

The guards descended down, continuing through the debris field. As they approached the cab, Loeffler looked down and noticed a miraculous reality; the only reason the helo did not slip over the edge of the bluff was because one of the skids had been stopped by a single rock, no larger than a basketball.

Don felt a rapidly growing fear that the entire hillside might, at any moment, explode into a fireball and engulf them all. Regardless, he attached the hook to one of the skids, thereby preventing it from slipping over the edge of the bluff. Then the guards cautiously approached the cockpit together, not knowing what to expect, yet fearing the possibility of finding three fatalities inside.

Instead, they found the pilot, Tom McConnell, alive and still strapped into his seat, hanging upside down with blood covering his face. Without hesitating, McConnell, concerned for his passengers said, "Get a line on this thing! Secure the helicopter!" and Straub assured him they had already accomplished that. McConnell, shocky and somewhat disoriented, was muttering that he had just "Killed the helicopter program," and it was Loeffler, who by then had been on many accident scenes with the famed pilot, who tried to orient and comfort him repeating, "You're alive, Tom. You're alive."

Working together, the guards were then able to extricate him out of the mangled cockpit and onto the ground outside the craft.

Meanwhile, on the other side of the cab, the deputy had managed to free himself and began staggering away from the remnants of the bird before collapsing to his knees while guarding his right shoulder. His arm was obviously fractured, and his shoulder was dislocated. Straub approached him, and the deputy, moaning in pain looked up at Don with a distant gaze.

"My service weapon," uttered the deputy.

"What about it?" answered Don.

"Take it!" commanded the officer, "I'm about to pass out."

Dutifully, Don pulled the weapon from the deputy's holster and to no one in particular, looked up and shouted the rather memorable line, *"What the fuck do I do with this!?"*

The deputy was pale and diaphoretic. In a normal setting he would have been laid down and treated for shock. But the issue of being surrounded by jet fuel caused Straub to freak out, finding himself in the uncharted territory normally left for fire fighters and hazmat specialists to deal with. He was a lifeguard. We don't do fires or HAZMAT. Yet, there he found himself on a dry grassy hillside liberally splattered with a hundred gallons of the stuff, which by then, had also soaked into his overalls. He wondered if, at any instant, the entire hillside might explode into flames around him. With no evidence to the contrary, and no one else in charge, Don decided they all needed to evacuate the scene. And that meant *everyone...right now!*

To complicate matters, people who had been stopped on the

roadway had left their cars and ran toward the scene to get a better view of this insane event. The lone deputy, also aware of the jet fuel issue, had been forced to stay up top to keep the bystanders from entering the scene.

In later discussions, Don admitted, "*I didn't have a clue what the safety protocols was for a jet fuel spill...Only later, when we were back up on top of the bluff did someone explain that jet fuel was only as combustible as kerosene. But I didn't know that!!!*" Hell, I was ready to clear the world from that scene!!!"

In retrospect, it might not have been the best choice in terms of patient care, but Don explained to the injured deputy that they needed to walk up the hill. The officer was momentarily confused, but Straub explained sternly, "Do you smell all of this jet fuel? We need to get you out of here!" Don stuffed the officer's gun in the pocket of his overalls, and assisted the deputy to stand, then draped the officer's "good arm" over his shoulder. Using his own body as a splint, he took much of the officer's weight and, using a lot more muscle than finesse, and no doubt jostling the officer's injuries more than was ideal, they began an awkward ascent back up the steep hill. Thankfully, the other officer met them part way up and Straub was able to pass off both the deputy and his gun.

Back at the helicopter, Loeffler approached the original patient who was still in the patient hold of the cabin. He too was alive, though understandably hysterical from the event. Assessing the victim, Loeffler immediately noticed a piece of shrapnel had caused an additional avulsion on his previously fractured leg, which was bleeding badly, but treatable. Amazingly, the patient was still securely strapped to the backboard, with his wrists still tied together, which likely saved him from further injuries. Slowly, amid the patient's cries, Straub assisted Loeffler in extricating the patient from the twisted wreckage. In the most unlikely and unfortunate chain of events imaginable, this seemingly cursed motorcyclist had been involved *in two potentially deadly accidents in the course of 30 minutes*. The guards attempted to evaluate his lesser injuries, but it was impossible to determine which of his wounds were from which event. Regardless, after enduring two major accidents, he most definitely was lucky to be alive.

Emotionally though, the man was a wreck. Hysterical and crazed, and still strapped to the backboard, he wanted nothing more than to escape from the madness of the incident. As the guards began hauling him back up to the roadway, Loeffler's portable radio delivered the confirmation that the REACH helicopter they had requested was indeed enroute to fly the patients out. Immediately after over-hearing the radio call, the victim began pleading with them, *"DON'T PUT ME ON ANOTHER HELICOPTER!"* which he repeated incessantly. The guards, understanding his fears, but at the same time realizing his injuries were significant, knew that getting him to the ER quickly was in his best interest. They apologized and tried unsuccessfully to rationalize with him. But attempting to allay his fears by touting the safety of the helicopters was an argument neither of them had the audacity to proclaim. Regardless, the REACH chopper landed on the highway and they loaded up the motorcyclist, who was still protesting wildly. The flight medic then started a line and provided some well needed morphine. Minutes later, they lifted off into the clouds with their heavily sedated patient safely stowed aboard.

The deputy on the other hand, obviously traumatized as well, adamantly refused to be flown out and as a professional courtesy, his request was honored. A land-based unit was summoned and he rode with them along the circuitous route to Santa Rosa General, gladly accepting the 45-minute delay in getting pain meds on board in exchange for not having to board another chopper.

Miraculously, despite being beaten around the cab as well, McConnell escaped from the ordeal with non-life-threatening injuries. He too, was transported in a medic unit via roadway to Santa Rosa.

The Coast Highway remained closed for the next six hours, while dozens of uniformed personnel arrived to investigate the accident, gather the debris, and retrieve what was left of the cockpit. If their intent was to account for every piece of wreckage to re-construct the bird, they would later find they were one piece short. Before they had arrived, Loeffler had grabbed an 18-inch section of the rotor wing and hid it under his gear bag in the back of the truck. He would later take it home as a souvenir from the most insane event he would ever witness, viewed from his first row vantage, less than 50-feet from where the helicopter exploded into fragments before his eyes.

The aftermath of the crash brought a revelation to all emergency personnel who had ever worked with Henry-I. This was the third Sonoma County rescue helicopter destroyed in dramatic fashion. In both of the other two crashes, the pilots had been killed. In this disaster, three people narrowly escaped a similar fate. That sobering realization was clear to all of them; the very nature of their rescue work exposed them to an ongoing level of inherent risk they themselves were certainly not immune from.

Clearing the call, Loeffler "held it together" for the remainder of the shift, swallowing back all emotions related to the event until he got home. But once free from the insulation of his uniform and the façade of his role as an officer, the gravity of the event hit him hard and the emotions poured from him. Watching that horrific crash, he had fully expected to confront the grizzly deaths of two of his colleagues as well as his patient. But miraculously, as if placed by God himself, a single isolated rock embedded into the hillside, kept the cab from sliding off the edge of the cliff and killing all three people aboard.

The crash forced him to face the reality of human frailty. He summarized the event succinctly, "*One moment you are alive, and then you are dead.*"

For Loeffler, some things which once seemed important suddenly were no longer so, and the experience of life itself, of fully participating and enjoying the time allotted, became significantly more important.

To say everyone on scene that day experienced a similar epiphany would be untrue, but the crash, if nothing else, added another highlight to the intense nature of their jobs, and the fact that on any given day, any rescuer on the rugged Sonoma Coast might pay the ultimate price in their service of others.

~

On the second anniversary of their existence as a lifeguard service, in addition to the treatment of numerous medical aids, the North Sector Lifeguards had logged 225 aquatic rescues and numbers of safety contacts which reached well into the thousands. Collectively, they enjoyed a quiet sense of reward for their notable success.

The big news for the South Sector was the State Parks' capitulation in their dubious struggle to implement day use fees on their beaches.

The perseverance and ultimate victory of the locals' "Free the Beaches" campaign gave them a genuine cause for celebration, which they did with fervor.

Interestingly, while the South Sector guards had managed to eke out *some* credibility with the EMS personnel, their relationship with the larger citizenry was tenuous at best, and the locals' victory in the fee issue did little to soften their opinions of guards. One lifeguard admitted, "They still viewed us on par with rehabilitated felons which had been relocated into their back yard."

Despite all of their good deeds, many of the locals still didn't trust them, and given a vote, would have gladly banished them back to Huntington Beach (or whatever beach they came from) without a second thought.

∿

The advent of fall brought the anticipated seasonal changes along the coast. The inland temperatures cooled, allowing the seemingly ever-present fog to melt away, revealing china-blue skies and a refreshing crispness in the air. School was back in session, pulling kids from the districts beaches and relocating them back in the classrooms. This created a partial respite from the crowds along the coast.

And yet the rescues continued.

Straub and Thomas rescued a diver in 15-foot surf off of Salt Point.

Martino saved a 14-year old special needs child from a rip at Salmon Creek.

Details of both rescues were scant, but the guards admitted in both cases that the victims involved would likely have been fatalities.

Within a week it would be Straub and Thomas again who rescued four divers in dramatic fashion after they tempted fate in large surf, foolishly entering the tumultuous waters at Horseshoe Cove. Earlier, the two guards had been forced to abort their boat patrol since the swells were too big and too consistent to allow them to gain access to the inside water along much of the coastline. It would turn out to be a dubious decision, as an hour later the guards came upon the four divers in serious trouble, and with Henry-I out of commission, Thomas and Straub had no alternative but to swim out "old school" with fins and buoy and begin the arduous task of hauling all four (two apiece – with gear) to shore. Thomas later speculated that at least two of the divers would never have made it back to shore on their own.

None of these rescues generated even a word of recognition from the press.

※

Unfortunately, despite the guards' performances, the undercurrent of unrest continued to brew amongst the ranks. That original crew were a veritable all-star team, each one chosen based on personal attributes which would give the collective team the best chance of success. They were aquatically skilled, intelligent, and dedicated individuals who had distinguished themselves in their home districts. But along with their stellar attributes as pure lifeguards, a few of them also carried bold personalities which made them almost impossible to lead. The hard-driving Franklin and Loeffler were the two whose names came up most often, and eventually they became the main players leading a slow but destructive internal opposition movement.

Obviously, within the structure of any work environment, people are brought to together who differ in innumerable ways, and they may disagree on a myriad of topics; sometimes emphatically so. Lifeguarding is no different. I've known guards who hated each other, and were forced to work together; even riding in units together. That's just part of the social work experiment we all have to live with. Yet, despite their differences, those guards somehow found a way to be cordial, put their scorn aside for those 8-hours, and find common ground in their discussions while consciously avoiding the incendiary issues. It might not have been pleasant, but they were able to successfully work together toward the common goal of providing public safety and service to the community.

Conversely, the opposition movement on the North Coast was seemingly unable to rise to that challenge.

By his own admission, Bud found himself in a job too big for him. According to McNulty, "Bud was a great guy, but he was in way over his head...he did his best, but really he was put in a position in which he was doomed to fail." And instead of working to help him improve, the oppositionists seemed hell-bent on wanting him gone, and overtly worked toward that goal, spreading bold opinions regarding his shortcomings with the rest of the guards. Hickey felt that there were those who "purposefully fanned the flames of animosity," systematically and successfully eroding Bud Brown's positional authority. Most of the younger guards attempted to steer clear of the conflicts. Regardless, slowly but surely, the destructive cracks of discontentment in the façade of workplace harmony began to widen.

Two caveats to this issue are worth noting. The first is the realization that every one of those guards were experiencing unimaginable stress within the course of their job. By now, you've read their stories, so you might have gained some empathy and understanding for what they were going through. Looking back, through the larger lens of history, perhaps we can cut them some slack, understanding how they might not have been functioning as their "truest optimal selves" in those years.

The second point, universally agreed upon by the guards, is that they *NEVER* allowed their differences to compromise their ultimate duties as guards, and their solemn dedication to "having each other's backs" on rescues. When ANY guard swam out, they knew emphatically their partners were covering them and prepared to back them if necessary. In that regard, they never faltered.

~

The North Coast crew had now entered what would prove to be the darkest time of their young existence as an agency. Bud remembers his work life was "a living hell" in those years. Eventually, as he put it, "Every day was a fight." He fought with the sheriffs, and fought with the public. The press continually ignored his staff's accomplishments and were reluctant to support his program publically.

Like his subordinates, he was forced to contend with horrendous incidents and occasionally he too swam out on rescues in huge surf. And, living in a State Residence near Goat Rock, he was often woken up and dispatched to call-outs involving various water-related emergencies, law-enforcement issues, and motor-vehicle accidents. After returning home from these calls, he often laid awake for hours, unable to calm down. Soon he found himself in a continual fog all day.

And through it all, just as his father had prophesized, he was reminded every day he was *"A black man living in white world."* After several phone conversations with a local reporter, Bud agreed to meet with him in person. Realizing Bud was black, the reporter's opening greeting, assumedly intended to be a compliment, was, *"You speak really well for a black guy."* Later the same week, his visiting mother entered a local store in Bodega Bay and the woman behind the counter, seeing she was black, asked if she was the mother of the Lifeguard Supervisor. Expecting to hear praise from the clerk, she readily admitted that yes, in fact he was her son. Shockingly, the shop owner then scowled and spewed, *"I hope you realize we are planning on running your son out of town!"* Indeed, living in that small community, it was impossible for Bud Brown to assimilate or hide and soon he became an even more obvious target than the 6'10" Loeffler.

Bud Brown extricating an accident victim (1992) – Photo: Loeffler

The fatigue, the oppressive calls, the lack of respect from the community and the racism were enough to drive anyone from that job, but the coup de grace for Bud Brown came in the escalating internal scorn he endured from his own staff. He could tolerate everything else, but the perceived disdain he felt from his partners was like a stab in the back which was slowly rotting him inside. Driven by his father's invocation to prove himself beyond doubt, Bud felt the added shame of failing him as well.

Wholly aware of his staff's dissatisfaction, Bud felt cornered. In his previously charmed work-life he had ascended, almost effortlessly up the ranks, propelled to ever-loftier heights by virtue of his gifts of gab and charm. Yet now, amidst the unshrouded real-world drama of the North Coast, playing to an unforgiving band of hardened front-line warriors, his bevy of previously reliable skills proved to be worthless. The simple reality for Bud was that he had no method to appease their high standards, nor any viable strategy to cope with their disdain.

With no viable option for salvation, Bud walked into Hickey's office and confessed that he couldn't stand it anymore. He offered few details to support his decision beyond his admission that the oppression and the stress had now reached the point of being unbearable. He wanted out. He confided he had already researched alternative careers, and decided he wanted to enroll in a Culinary Institute.

Surprisingly, Hickey admitted that he had expected this day to come and, having witnessed the unfair treatment the young supervisor had endured, was actually surprised Bud had lasted as long as he did.

But Hickey, who had personally chosen Brown and was thoroughly invested in his young supervisor's ultimate fate, still held out hope he might eventually redeem himself and persuaded him to delay any rash decision to bail out. He suggested, then later *implored* Bud to seek the services of a therapist in Santa Rosa, something Bud had never considered before. The idea provided Bud with a glimmer of hope that he might salvage his job. The two men then reached an agreement that any resignation would come only after he had attended a set of counselling sessions.

In his first meeting, Bud released an uninterrupted, 2-hour long monologue the therapist seemed unprepared for. He detailed the gut-wrenching cumulative effects of terrifying rescues, call-outs in the middle of the night, challenging law enforcement confrontations, strained domestic violence calls, various heart-wrenching issues involving human suffering, his persistent feelings of anxiety and lack of sleep, the stings of public scorn, the realities of abject racism in the community, the ever-present shadow of death, the self-realization of his own frailty as a lifeguard, and ultimately the animosity he was dealt from his staff.

When Bud finally exhausted his list, the therapist, obviously ill-prepared to deal with this magnitude of stressors, admitted as much and offered little in the way of therapeutic measures to help him. Zeroing in on the low-hanging fruit of his issue with *insomnia,* and without thinking it through, she leaned forward in her chair and said, *"Perhaps you might sleep better if you buy a sound machine and played some soothing sounds of the ocean waves at night."* Bud looked at her in a state of shocked disbelief, and immediately the therapist, realizing that the ocean formed the most foundational part of his stress, corrected herself and admitted, *"I'm sorry sir, but I don't think I am the right therapist for you. I think you might be better off seeing someone who specializes in issues like yours."*

The second therapist didn't offer much help either.

Regardless, Hickey asked if he could stay on a bit longer, and Bud, feeling a mild sense of peace in finally sharing his burden out loud, agreed to stay.

LIFEGUARD JOURNAL: 1993

Onlookers watch from the safety of the bluff top as 12' waves roll to shore (1992)

4-1-1993
OPENING DAY - 1993

After an unusually quiet winter, and perfectly timed for Opening Day in '93, the fickle ocean mounted a swell as angry and ugly as any opener in 20 years. Mike Thomas described them not merely as big but as, "Big, big, big waves." Formidable storms had been swirling around the Gulf of Alaska for weeks, generating significant waves of energy which exploded in glorious 18' crescendos on the Sonoma shoreline. Despite a series of ominous warnings left on the recorded dive line for days, divers arrived anyway. Just after dawn, vehicles started showing up at the usual spots, and like lemmings, the men got out and, with steam rising from their breath into the chilly air, began suiting up and preparing to kick out.

The staff, as usual, was at full force and included several rangers, coastal deputies, Henry-I, a team of Search and Rescue staff clad in orange vests, as well as volunteer spotters and the Sea Ranch Firefighters.

As the sun rose, the guards raced between the popular dive spots. They implored every diver they came across to abort their plans, adding that if they absolutely MUST dive, to seek the sheltered coves of Fisk Mill or, better yet, Fort Ross. The booming waves in the background added a powerful deterrent in support of their grave warnings, and thankfully most divers heeded their advice. The guards fully realized these preventative tactics were paying dividends in averting recues and possibly saving lives.

By then, after thousands of face-to-face contacts, some of the regular divers now recognized the lifeguards and greeted them by name. Many of them had witnessed those same guards making high profile rescues and word of those rescues had begun to spread through the dive community. Thus, the North Sector crew had finally begun to establish a reputation. The reward for the guards came as the vast majority of divers they contacted (though certainly not all) now heeded their warnings without much contention. And on that particular opener, rescue tallies which normally would have reached into the dozens, were instead held to a minimum.

Most importantly, the official total of drownings for the day, despite the tumultuous ocean conditions, once again totaled *zero*.

AN EPIC OPENING WEEKEND

Although "Opening Day" always received the bulk of the attention, in 1993, as was often the case, the auspicious date fell on a weekday - Thursday. Since most divers were blue collar guys who held regular jobs, many of them couldn't always get there for the opener. Thus, it was actually the first *weekend* of the abalone season which often attracted the largest numbers of divers to the coast. That was certainly true for 1993. The weekend surf showed no respite from the extraordinary display on the opener, and as expected, the crowds of divers started arriving before dawn. Even the full complement of guards was insufficient to adequately cover all of the areas, and many divers slipped past them and dispersed into the various coves and secret spots unwarned.

The big surprise was that for the first time anyone could remember, reporters from several local newspapers showed up and were seen darting between various locations, interviewing divers as they prepared to go out. As a result, those same reporters would be on scene to witness a few of the guards' rescues first hand.

The rescues started almost immediately. Schardt made the first on a single free-diver at Fisk Mill Cove before 7:00 am. McNulty followed moments later by pulling three divers to safety at a little known dive spot they simply called "42.15," named for the mile marker adjacent to the its closest access point. An hour later it was McNulty again rescuing three more from a rip outside Gerstle Cove. With the radio alerting all of the guards of these rescues, they were running at a heightened sense of vigilance, eager to join in the fray. But amazingly it was McNulty, showing up his Seasonals yet again, who then pulled two more divers to safety at South Gerstle. After the third consecutive rescue from the elder lifeguard, the teasing began on the radio and the guards frantically searched for victims so as not to let Osh "snake them" yet again.

The press, using Salt Point as their base, happened to witness several of the rescues, and were able to interview a few of the victims immediately after they had been delivered to shore. Understandably, with their egos crushed into shame, none were willing to provide their name, but most of them were more than happy to explain how they had gotten into trouble, and to acknowledge the incredible power of the ocean.

Just after noon, a call rang out over the radio of another rescue in progress at Gerstle, and yet again it was Osh who brought the lone diver to shore.

Finally, it would be Carter who would strike, pulling a female free-diver in at Fisk Mill Cove while at the same time, Bud Brown, working with Straub on the boat, pulled in two at Ocean Cove.

An hour later Carter and McNulty swam out together on a two-victim rescue at Salt Point proper. As they were pulling the divers into the safety of Gerstle Cove, Straub responded on the boat to assist them, only to find the two guards, swimming backstroke side by side, were laughing so loudly that he could hear them from 100 yards away. It was a moment to savor...as Carter and McNulty, in the prime of their lives, were flushed with joy, performing at the absolute pinnacle of their game.

With the tide dropping and numbers of divers still arriving after long drives from distant locations, the afternoon was shaping up to be one of the most prolific days in the short history of lifeguarding on the North Coast.

And as expected, the ocean delivered. By late afternoon the flood gates opened with another frenzy of activity. Within two hours, virtually all of the guards had made multiple rescues. Just two years earlier, every rescue they performed was viewed as an illustrious event, which would be documented and discussed at the end of the day. But by '93, those same rescues had become routine, and their earlier collective drive to document and immortalize their work by way of tallying rescue statistics had faded. The guards still loved making the rescues, they just didn't care much for writing about them afterwards.

The net result was that by sunset, the memories of the dozens of excellent rescues, became muddled in the general chaos of the hectic day, and much to the dismay of Hickey, the final rescue count submitted was a "best guess." While the actual number of rescues performed was likely 30 or more, the "official" tally of rescue cards amounted to 12. Although they all knew the actual number was far greater, no one could be bothered to try to recount them all. Nevertheless, even the adversarial Bodega Bay Navigator credited the guards with "rescuing at least 18."

In retrospect, it would seem rather obvious that capturing those rescue statistics would help to provide an empirical cornerstone justifying their existence, thus one might immediately infer their cavalier attitudes in failing to document their work was a manifestation of irresponsibility. But one has to remember that these guards (like most lifeguards) were guys who lived squarely in the moment. In *their* minds, their successes and rewards were experienced first-hand, on the shoreline, while they were still wet and cold and breathing heavy, when their victim reached out and shook their hand. The value of scratching out rescue cards after the fact, and sending them off to Sacramento added nothing to that reward. When the rescue was over, they shared a high-five with their partners and immediately headed off in search of another. At the time, their short-term perspective offered little global insight that what they were doing there and then might one day be appreciated when seen through the wider lens of history.

To the guards, to the press, to the State Park managers, and most importantly to the divers and their families, the only statistic which really mattered at the close of that epic weekend, was the drowning tally, which, once again shone brightly at the undeniable number of *zero*.

For the remainder of the week the surf refused to back off and the crew carried on in stride with their stellar performance. Ultimately, thousands of divers had arrived for their annual pilgrimage and were dealt a formidable challenge with the surf reaching harrowing heights. Yet this small band of dedicated guards were able to exact their mission just as they had been brought there to do and prevented anyone from dying on their watch.

The same article which gave the lifeguards credit for 18 rescues on opening weekend, also credited them with making safety contacts on "over 2,000 divers" during the first week.

After the years spent bargaining, planning, and finagling to get this lifeguard service established on the North Coast, Brian Hickey could finally sit back and feel a well-earned sense of accomplishment. The guards were succeeding. By God, his guards had even received a subtle nod from the local newspaper. Imagine that. Having a glowing article on the cover of the New York Times would not have given Hickey more joy than the realization that the 300 individuals on the circulation list of the Bodega Bay Navigator were reading the first words of praise for his guards.

With the opening week in the books, the volunteers left. The Henry-I crew flew back to the hanger and the fire department staff returned to their stations. The guards were once again left alone to fend for themselves on the front lines to care for their visitors. And there would be many more weekends, and many more divers. As Martino remembered, "*The weeks lined up to the horizon like sets of waves on the ocean. When one looked out at what lay ahead, the incoming wave of humanity seemed endless. If nothing else, we felt a sense of job security.*"

Dare anyone admit it, when the foam had settled on opening week of the 1993 abalone season, and the North Sector guards had rinsed the salt water from their wetsuits, if any of them would have pulled back to see the bigger picture, they might have noticed that they had become a respected, and dare I say it, *vital* part of the EMS community.

Unfortunately, the South Sector guards still had a ways to go.

4-1993
FOUNTAIN of SORROW

I am not one to proclaim any deep understanding of the human mind and its many moods. But it seems to me, after living with my own simple mind for over 60 years, and some insights made during the course of my travels, along with 40 years of well-intentioned, yet sporadic meditation practice, the emotions of happiness and anger share the common traits of being fleeting and transitory. They both can erupt reactively and sometimes boldly, yet both, at least for me, tend to fade quickly.

Sorrow, on the other hand, tends to linger and infuse itself into one's entire being, coloring every aspect of our perspectives in dull aching shades which persist in a slower fade. I once heard a Buddhist master explain that the mind could be viewed as a colored cloth. Joy and anger could be viewed as distinct spots on the cloth, whereas sorrow is represented as the color of the cloth itself, permeating the fabric entirely.

In my conversations with the members of the original crew, it became readily clear that none of them anticipated, nor were adequately prepared to deal with the amount of *sorrow* they would encounter while working on the North Coast. Soldiers going off to war undoubtedly had realistic expectations that they would face death and sorrow, and likely prepared themselves as much as anyone can, for their exposure to that trauma.

Conversely, every one of those original guards endured more than their share of emotionally devastating trauma, and whether it was a case of ignorance or apathy, no such preparations were offered to the lifeguards; they were seemingly blindsided by the realities of human suffering and pain. Worse yet, no methodologies, therapies, or counselling services - besides Bud's last ditch visit with a counselor - were offered to them afterwards. They were left to grapple with it on their own.

In writing out the narratives of the following stories, I was continually reminded of Jackson Browne's soulful and moody ballad, "Fountain of Sorrow." Using words as his medium, Jackson masterfully paints the emotions of his sorrowful failed love, coloring his mourning with his distinctive down-to-earth phrasings and approachable imagery. For me personally, the melody lifts the message into the realm of the divine. Delivered with the grounded tone and earnestness of Jackson's voice, his grieving is raw and honest. The minor chord phrasings envelope the message in tones of sadness; forming the perfect mood to deliver his imploring admission that the wonderful love he once shared with this woman has failed.

I've always viewed the expressive musical imagery in that song as a metaphor for death and rebirth. *Fountain of Sorrow* has always haunted me and drives me to a deep and centered place of introspection where I can somehow connect with sorrow more genuinely.

On the heels of their successful opening week, the Sonoma Coast crew would justly celebrate their great performances, completely unprepared for the unspeakable tragedies lurking in the shadows. They would soon experience their own "Fountain of Sorrow" with a string of unimaginable and heartbreaking deaths delivered in succession, as if the fickle ocean, now turned vengeful, had intentionally released her wrath on them.

4-17-1993
LOSING GRIP

The first of these tragedies occurred on April 17ᵗʰ just north of Wright's Beach, at a spot called "Whale Point." A large family had come to the beach and were marveling at the colossal waves, which Loeffler and Franklin later confirmed were 15' or more.

While the family played in the wet sand, as was the typical scenario, an enormous wave slammed onto the shore, engulfing them all, and washing the entire group into the frigid ocean. Instantly, all of them found themselves struggling for their lives in the violent turbulence of the shore pounding waves. The 4-year old boy among them was, by far, the weakest. While the other family members struggled to pull themselves from the sea, the father instead swam farther out to save his son. Despite subsequent waves slamming over them both, amazingly the father *was* eventually able to reach the boy, and momentarily grabbed hold of the boy's hand. Just then, another wave engulfed them in a massive wall of water, hammering them with violent force and bouncing them on the bottom. The father was no match for the incredible power of the ocean, and the unimaginable force of the wave broke his grip, snatching his son away from him.

Seconds later, the boy was swallowed into the depths of the sea.

Loeffler and Franklin arrived soon after, and theoretically had a chance to save the boy if they could spot his body quickly. Loeffler, already in his wetsuit, ran towards the water's edge and stood before the thundering waves, poised for the daunting task of entering the violent ocean. Meanwhile Franklin, positioned on the vantage point of the bluff above, scanned the water with binos, searching for any sign of the boy's body – ready to dispatch Loeffler if he spotted him.

Loeffler, ready to explode into action, diligently waited for Franklin to pull the binos from his face, point in the direction of the body and yell for him to go!

With the young boy's life quickly slipping away with the elapsing of time, Franklin scanned the water feverishly...praying for the ocean to raise the boy's body to the surface to reveal his location, even just for a second, so he might catch a glimpse and direct Loeffler where to enter, and possibly save him.

For Loeffler, waiting on the shore of this raging sea was agony. The signal from Franklin never came.

Dozens of units arrived on scene and staged on the bluff – joining Franklin in the search. Henry-1 appeared in the skies overhead and scanned a half-mile area, searching for any sign of the young boy. But after an hour, with the sun getting low, they called it.

The family was gutted with remorse and disbelief. As darkness approached, Franklin and Loeffler, their souls bleeding with empathy for the family, met with them and offered their sincere condolences. As was customary after a tragedy of this magnitude, Loeffler then asked if there was anything the staff could do to help the family. Having been dropped off at the beach, they asked him for a ride to Monte Rio and Loeffler agreed. While the family began gathering their belongings, hidden from view behind their patrol truck, Loeffler and Franklin did a somber session of Rock-Paper-Scissors to see who would be tasked with the unenviable job of transporting them, immersed in an all-consuming grief, on the 40-minute ride to Monte Rio. Loeffler lost.

It is doubtful *any lifeguard on the planet* could have provided any measure of solace to that family at what was undoubtedly the worst moment of their collective lives. Loeffler admittedly was ill-equipped and ill-prepared for that role. Thus, as the family filled the patrol car with wails and crying, Loeffler said little during the entire drive, and struggled not to make eye contact with the father, seated next to him, for fear of "losing it" himself. In a subsequent interview, he later said that drive was likely the hardest thing he had ever done in his career as a lifeguard.

While all loss of life by means of drowning was devastating for the guards, the death of this innocent child shattered them all. Although no lifeguard was in the area at the time, Whale Point was part of their patrol pattern, and Loeffler and Franklin had checked in at that location just 40 minutes before the fateful tragedy. Thus it was entirely possible they *could* have been there and prevented the boy's death with a simple safety contact. Hence, the incessant and soul-crushing *"what if"* questions surfaced again like old demons.

The family's unimaginable grief radiated outward to the boy's friends, school mates, and extended throughout their local community.

As was usually the case, no one thought to include the lifeguards among the grieving.

The father's lost grip on his son's hand would haunt him for the rest of his life.

It would haunt the lifeguards too.

The boy's body was never found.

~

The drowning hit Franklin particularly hard. Scanning through the events log, the boy's death was the last event in which his name appears in the records.

After handling more than his share of heavy calls, and citing insurmountable personal stress issues which no one doubted, Franklin requested a transfer and was offered an opportunity to leave the North Coast to assume a position at Huntington Beach. Following Melvin's lead, Steve abandoned what he considered to be a sinking ship.

Around the same time, Jon Gulick also left, though his reasons had little to do with politics or a lack of faith in supervision. He had been accepted into nursing school and would leave to pursue a career as a Registered Nurse.

With their departure, the original crew of 11 guards had been whittled down to a hearty 7.

4-24-1993
UNIMAGINABLE LOSS

In some instances, a lifeguard's most difficult rescue was the one they failed to make. For Don Straub, that was exactly the case. Seven days after the loss of the young boy, a family arrived to camp at Salt Point. The father was an avid abalone diver and like so many other families, he had planned to retrieve several abalone and bring them back to the campsite to have a celebratory feast with his wife and his seven-year-old son.

He donned his wetsuit and gathered his dive gear, and the whole family walked down to an area just south of the reserve. While his wife and his son sat excitedly watching from their vantage point on the bluff immediately above, the diver made his way down a small trail to the waterline.

Unfortunately, a powerful long-period swell had been battering the coastline. The buoy readings were a staggering 20 feet at 17 seconds, and although the area was partially sheltered from the direct impact of the huge swell, plenty of residual wave energy wrapped around Salt Point proper, and pounded the shoreline with solid 10-foot waves, punctuated by an occasional massive set every 30 minutes or so which brought a dozen waves in the 12 to 15 foot range. The conditions were so bad, in fact, no other divers had dared to venture out all day.

Fixated on the idea of bringing abalone to his family, the diver walked down to a large sloping rock just south of Gerstle Cove in an area which quickly dropped off into 15 feet of water. Without taking the time to watch the ocean for a full cycle, he jumped in during a lull, unknowingly placing himself directly into the impact zone.

His hope was to get in and out quickly, in a little pocket area the guards knew well. It was an area we would later refer to as "*The Frozen Food Section*" because of the ease and speed in which you could hop in and grab a couple of abalone on a single dive with a minimum of effort.

But not with the surf running like that.

His timing was awful. Immediately after his entry, a massive set barreled towards shore. The first wave of the set was estimated to be double-overhead. It lifted the diver into the air and slammed him back onto the sloping rock with such ferocity – that he was instantly rendered unconscious. The backwash then cruelly dragged his limp body back down into the trough where, after a brief pause, it was picked up by the next wave and slammed *again* onto the same rock. Several more waves continued battering his body against the boulders at the foot of the bluff. As each receded, he was again rolled in the backwash, with his lifeless arms flailing horrifically, before being dumped back into the trough. As if the ocean had some sadistic desire to punish the dead man further, the final wave of the set repeated the abuse with even more intensity. After the water had collected for a moment, a final massive backwash rolled him back with added speed and intensity, then submerged him into the deep trough.

His wife screamed in terror, while both she and their young son watched the horrific ordeal from the rocks above, not more than 25 yards away.

Straub and Carter were ten minutes out when the "diver down" came across the radio.

They arrived at the bluff top scene and found the victim's frantic wife. Her son stood next to her, expressionless. The woman, now fully consumed in hysterics, began describing the horrendous details of the ocean's beating on her husband. As she spoke, Carter pulled on his wetsuit and his eyes danced back and forth between her and the hellacious surf beating against the rocks below them. In his mind he was weighing out his options, trying to determine if he should go. He vacillated. His heart, bleeding for the woman and her young son pushed him to challenge the ocean, while his mind yelled to him - that entering that ocean would be an act of utter insanity. There was no Perm on scene to assert the correct decision to stand down. He looked back at Don who was wearing a grave expression, his teeth clenched. Unable to speak in the presence of the victim's wife, Don said nothing but slowly shook his head side to side – indicating "no" in an effort to dissuade Carter, yet knowing that the ultimate decision would be Carter's alone.

Carter looked back at the death zone just as a massive wall of water slammed against the rocky shoreline and felt a cold flush of adrenaline surge through his veins.

Then, mid-sentence in the woman's continuing explanation, Carter had heard enough. He took off, sprinting for the top of the goat trail. Scampering down the steep makeshift trail he made it about halfway down, then slipped and fell hard on his right flank. As if God himself was protecting him from his foolish gallantry, his injury abruptly ended any attempt at making the rescue. It was a relief for both him and Don, as it would have been an act of sheer insanity to dive into the maelstrom to try and retrieve the man's body. Carter slowly hobbled back up with the waves crashing below him. The very real possibility of an additional disaster was averted.

Back on the bluff top, the guards conferred and quickly agreed any endeavor to retrieve the man's body would risk the lives of the guards for no viable reason. The man's wife stood on the bluff sobbing, holding her young son in her arms. Seemingly not fully understanding what was happening, the boy stared at the ocean vacantly. Don walked over to her and calmly informed her that because of the heavy surf, there was nothing else they could do.

Straub drove the mother and son up to the park office in the patrol truck. She was inconsolable but requested to use the phone to notify her family. Don sat her at the ranger's desk and slid the phone towards her. He left momentarily and returned with a blanket which he wrapped over her shoulders, more for a sense of comfort than for warmth. The boy, still dazed, stood next to her. Don felt it might be best to pull the kid away from the despondent mother and offered to take him outside for a walk. The mother agreed it would be best if he didn't have to listen to her phone calls.

Having no script to work from, yet knowing this would be the worst day in his entire life, Don took the young boy by the hand and walked him into the service yard and simply began showing him the equipment and the emergency vehicles. The right words did not come to him, so he said little. At some point it was the boy who broke the awkward silence. He looked up at the uniformed lifeguard and asked the simple question which would replay in Don's mind and haunt him for decades...

"Will I ever see my dad again?"

Don pursed his lips. His eyes welled up with tears. Realizing he needed to be honest, after a pause, he simply said "No. I'm so sorry." And in that moment, the heart of the heroic lifeguard "bad ass" had been ripped apart. Then and there, Straub lost it. While they continued to walk, Don was unable to conceal his grief and the tears poured down his face.

Those tears conveyed everything to the young boy that he was unable to express in words.

TEARS in the OCEAN

In physics they say every action has an equal and opposite reaction. In the world of lifeguarding, the reactions to major loss and death often manifest themselves in an internal angst to assimilate and comprehend the events into the guards' personal philosophical beliefs regarding life and death itself. If the physicists are right, the anguish and pain they felt should balance with "equal and opposite" levels of peace and joy, or even simply a sense of understanding. But in the world of the North Coast Lifeguard, that balance can be elusive, and in reality, rarely comes.

For many years, the image of the young boy's face would randomly appear in Don's mind. It was the face of innocence, suffering the most devastating loss imaginable. Every human being who has ever loved their father can empathize. And any lifeguard worth their salt would have risked their own life to bring the boy's father back if there had been any viable chance at all to rescue him.

And, as always, the questions arose. How could this have happened? How could it have been prevented? How will the boy fare without his father? Was this really God's will? After such an irreconcilable loss, there were no acceptable answers.

While holding the small hand of that young boy and grieving with him for the loss of his father, it was impossible for Don to absolve himself of guilt. Despite his dedication to this job, a pervasive feeling of regret gnawed at his soul, admonishing him for *not being there* to prevent that tragedy, and reminding him of the grave ramifications of his perceived failure. For weeks after, Don was overwhelmed by feelings of futility. Like tears falling into the ocean, despite his best efforts, he realized they would never be able to save everyone.

But his reticence always stopped short of acquiescence of the fact that people died in accordance with God's will. Ultimately, they were put there to deny the rationalization that *any death* on that coast was "*God's will.*" Their unified response was, "*Not if we can help it.*" They were lifeguards, whose core mission was to provide for the public's safety and he knew in his soul they did exactly that with remarkable success. They had accepted the responsibilities of keeping the public safe from the violent ocean and their ultimate ideal; of making sure *everyone* would go home alive was still a noble, though not always tenable goal. Cognitively he knew the notion that anything less amounted to *failure* was unnecessarily pejorative, and any single death on their coastline was not a condemnation of their overall worth.

But that one rocked him to his core.

4-25-1993
HORSESHOE COVE

After the second drowning in seven days, every member of the crew was understandably shaken. A grey fog of despair and hopelessness descended over the coastline, as if Mozart's Requiem played in the background.

The following day, the North Sector guards patrolled as diligently as they ever had, hiking out to every vantage point with binos, leaving little to chance, and searching the water for any sign the ocean was ready to return the missing father to the terrestrial world.

And sure enough, just before noon the guards received the call they were expecting; of an *"unconscious diver"* at Secrets. Realizing the body had washed up overnight, Dave Schardt and ranger Karen Broderick responded to the area. They parked their patrol vehicles, grabbed a body bag, and left all of their medical supplies in their trucks to be as light as possible for the unpleasant job of carrying the deceased diver back up to the top of the bluff.

One can only imagine their disbelief when they arrived on the shoreline and discovered the body lying on the rocks was *not* that of the deceased diver who had drowned the previous day, but rather a *different diver* who had just been pulled to shore by a surfer, and up until an hour earlier, was very much alive. The rescuers were caught in the unenviable position of having to initiate CPR without any of their rescue gear. Thus, Schardt was forced to deliver respirations on the dead diver utilizing the *mouth-to-mouth* technique.

Despite the best efforts from the rescuers, Henry-I landed and after further assessment, pronounced the diver deceased.

WHEN RATIONIZATIONS FAIL

Disastrously, the ocean had claimed three lives in the course of a mere 8 days.

Of course they had no way of knowing it, but mercifully, their *"Fountain of Sorrow"* would finally run dry and provide a three-week respite to their battered souls.

The surfer who had reported the 3rd death at Secrets was so shaken by the experience, he was quoted in a newspaper article asking the rhetorical question lifeguards have always asked: *"Why should people be dying in the ocean?"*

For three solid weeks the surf had been running in the 8-12' range. But with divers' obsession with procuring abalone, coupled with their arduous drives to get there, many were determined to dive at all costs, and were intoxicated with the thrill of challenging themselves in those rugged conditions. The definitive answers to the question of why people push their limits and die in the ocean are as varied as the individuals themselves, but the one thread linking all of those tragedies was undeniable...

They failed to respect the power of the ocean.

Three deaths in eight days.

In that same timeframe, they had warned hundreds of divers, recorded 23 swimming rescues and made plenty of other aquatic saves they simply didn't have time to record, bringing the conservative total quoted in the newspaper to 40. They had also humbly provided safeguards to the ocean community and for the previous 11 months, not a single life was lost by drowning in their water. Yet in just eight days the ocean delivered them three cataclysmic blows, completely overshadowing all of their good work.

In each of those three events, *as with all drowning events*, a series of actions played out which allowed the drowning to occur. Punctuated along the path of their misfortune, opportunities for *someone to intervene* existed in the form of a conservative parent, a well-meaning bystander, a fellow diver, or even the potential victim's sudden realization that *"this might not be a good idea."* But in all three instances no one stepped forward to change the tragic course of events. When viewed within the totality of these events, the lifeguard's role in rescuing the victim from the ocean is essentially the *last resort* in the chain. And in all three of these events, they were elsewhere monitoring others in similar circumstances.

To the lay person, the lifeguards would have been exonerated from blame, and in fact heralded for the many rescues they had performed that week. But in the minds of the guards themselves, and not subject to debate, the tally of *failures* for the week on their watch amounted to *three*.

Rescue statistics are nebulous. Although they document an act of intervention, in essence each rescue card was a reflection of an awful event which *didn't happen*. The victim *didn't drown*. They were rescued. They dried off and quickly recovered from some harrowing interaction with the ocean. They drove home and resumed their lives right where they had left off. There were few if any residual effects. No funeral. No mourning. No ongoing suffering or sorrow. Side-stepping the tragedy, an almost instantaneous return to "normal" began anew. And with it began the gradual fading of the event from their memory.

But owing to the simplest twists of fate, three people drowned. And *all drownings leave deep scars*. Those three people were more than statistics. They left behind grieving families. Wreaths were tossed into the water at Wright's Beach, South Gerstle, and Horseshoe Cove, marking the place where the lives of their beloved son, father, husband, or brother came to an end. In the subsequent years their family members would somberly reconvene in those same places on the anniversary of their death to remember them...until eventually the memories of their existence would gradually fade into oblivion with the next generation, or perhaps the one following.

5-1993
KAYAK STRIKE

The mouth of the Russian River at Goat Rock Beach is a veritable cafeteria. Along with pairs of sunglasses fallen from the heads of stoned kayakers in Guerneville, the river drains a constant supply of nutrients and various life forms collected along a circuitous 100-mile journey from its origin in the Redwood Valley.

The terminus is like a conveyer belt delivering a steady stream (pardon the pun) of delicacies to various sizes and species of fish and invertebrates. The sandy beach serves as a permanent settlement for a healthy population of harbor seals who, when hungry, need not travel far for their next meal. They simply jiggle over to the water's edge and fall in to see what varieties of treats are being delivered to their table. Life is good for the harbor seals at Goat Rock.

Except for one small issue.

Moving one last rung higher on the food chain, the waters just off-shore are also home to the ultimate predator, The Landlord, The Man in the Grey Suit, El Tiburon, Great Whitey. While the seals forage on the smorgasbord of healthy fish, the Great White sharks feast on the smorgasbord of plump harbor seals, thereby ensuring their numbers are kept in check.

And like the spider who ate the fly, and the frog who ate the spider, the ecosystem at the Russian River outlet goes 'round and 'round and maintains a healthy balance.

Normally.

But every so often, one of the Great Whites, perhaps one of the dumb ones, makes a mistake and chomps onto a human. And all hell breaks loose.

Dr. Peter Kimley, a Professor at UC Davis, is one of the most well-respected shark authorities in the world. He is a disciple of the school of thought that *sharks don't eat people*. But, even he admits that occasionally they do bite. Sensing our relatively low fat content compared to pudgy harbor seals, they generally spit us out like a mouthful of stale Doritos, but still that initial bite can sometimes be a doozy.

In the '90s Kimley spent a considerable amount of time studying sharks on the Sonoma Coast. As troubling as it sounds, he rarely had much trouble finding them. Occasionally a seal carcass would wash up on shore at Goat Rock with a crescent-shaped, two-foot wide section of its torso curiously missing. Upon finding the mangled remains, Kimley always felt obligated to inform the State Parks managers there was *"evidence of shark activity"* in the area. For the record, *decapitated* harbor seals also qualified as similar *"evidence of shark activity."*

Managers, armed with this seemingly important piece of information now had a decision to make. Do they notify the public of potential *"shark activity"* along the Sonoma Coast? That would seemingly accomplish little besides confirming the rather obvious fact that sharks do, in fact, live in the ocean. Or should they just place their hands behind their backs, look up and whistle? Most often, they decided the safest practice to avoid litigation would be to print up a bunch of *Shark Warning* signs and assign the lifeguards the task of posting them at various junctures along the beach.

In theory, this practice might seem like a good idea, but in reality, it didn't pan out too well. For one thing, *"shark memorabilia"* of any kind tended to maintain a healthy collectible value in the *teen surfer* demographic, and within 24 hours of their posting, *ALL* of them would be snatched from the beach and relocated onto the walls of teen bedrooms, dorm rooms and frat houses. (I have two by the way).

The second issue was that older surfers, who had been rolling the dice and surfing North Coast waters for decades, wondered what all the fuss was about, since they had long since accepted the fact that sharks lived there anyway.

Which sets the stage for a spring day in 1993. Loeffler and Martino found themselves on patrol at Goat Rock when a woman in a wetsuit, physically shaking and obviously distraught, approached the guards and proclaimed, "I don't know how to tell you this, but I just got attacked by a shark!"

Seeing no blood and quickly accounting for all four of the woman's limbs, the guards were initially confused. They led her to the back of the truck and let her sit on the tailgate. Martino then wrapped her in a blanket and allowed her to calm down a bit before asking for clarification.

The woman stated, "I was kayaking with my friends, when I thought I had hit a rock. I got pitched out of my kayak and landed on a sand bar. I tried to get back in my kayak but it filled with water and tipped over. I couldn't stay in the thing and ended up back in the water again. That's when I heard my friends yelling, 'SHARK SHARK!!!' Then one of my friends picked me up in his kayak and brought me to shore."

At that moment in her story, her friends arrived and were able to piece the events together a little more clearly.

The woman had been kayaking with her friends when a massive grayish black shark emerged from the depths below and violently struck her kayak *hard*. One witness stated "We could clearly see it was a shark, and about 10 feet of its body was exposed just as it bit the kayak. The force of the impact threw the woman at least six feet into the air – a significant distance from her boat...then remarkably, she actually *landed on the shark's back* (which *she thought* was a sand bar) before it descended into the murky water and disappeared, leaving her swimming next to her damaged kayak."

The woman futilely tried to climb back onto the kayak, but was unable to do so. While the rest of the group, infused with a new sense of vigor, began paddling briskly towards shore, one member of the group had a two-person kayak, so after seeing the shark descend, he gallantly paddled over and helped haul her aboard his boat, while another friend towed the damaged boat to the beach.

The guards walked over to inspect the boat.

"Holy shit," said Loeffler, not hiding his amazement.

On the bottom was an almost perfectly oval bite mark. Pulling out a tape measure, the bite measured 20 inches from top to bottom and 15 inches across. The deeply gouged edges were triangular, suggesting the serration marks from very large teeth. Cracks radiated outward from the bite indicated an incredible amount of crushing pressure.

The small group stood there for a moment in silence, all staring at the partially destroyed kayak. The incident was a staggering jolt of reality for all of them. With her initial confusion faded away, the full reality of her intimate and violent encounter with a massive predator became clear. By all accounts, she narrowly avoided being killed in the most savage way imaginable. The guards too pondered the incident from the scope of a larger lens. Although they always knew these monstrous animals patrolled these waters, this encounter brought home the sobering reality that if they would attack a 12' bright orange kayak, they could most certainly attack a 6' dude dressed in a wetsuit. It was a particularly sobering reality since these guys entered that same ocean almost every day.

The guards shifted into compassion-mode and eventually, the victim began to settle down. Someone brought her belongings and she toweled off and changed into dry clothes. Photos were taken and measurements were re-done and documented.

Upon hearing word of the incident, Supervisor Brown left his office and arrived on scene, immediately assuming the lead role in addressing the gathered crowd of gawking visitors. Having seemingly transformed himself into the role of a wildlife biologist, he shared a series of bold assertions regarding shark behavior which the public eagerly consumed.

In the background, the two guards repeatedly glanced at each other with raised eyebrows, viewing some of his emphatic claims with skepticism. But seeing the man in his element, they certainly had to admit he could "entertain a crowd" like no one else.

Dr. Kimley was summoned and provided a more accurate analysis of the bite marks, estimating the shark to be a stunning 15-feet long and weighing upwards of 1,500 pounds.

LOEFFLER'S NIGHT BOAT RESCUE

Less than a week after the shark incident, after completing his shift, Loeffler and his wife Lisa invited Dave Schardt over to the house for a late dinner.

They were relaxing after a nice meal when Loeffler got a phone call from the sheriffs requesting his response for an emergency boat rescue at Timber Cove. Receiving a call directly from the sheriffs – requesting help from the *lifeguards* - was a reflection of how far they had come. That call would *never* have been made two years earlier, and represented the symbolic beginnings of the lifeguards' acceptance.

Kurt threw his gear bag into the patrol truck and sped off.

With no city lights in that rural community, Loeffler pulled out of his driveway and on to the darkened roadway. Hoping to have some ambient light from the moon to guide him on the rescue, instead he encountered ominous thick clouds which choked almost all of the residual moon light.

While enroute, his lights and siren pierced through both the darkness and the silence along the Coast Highway, likely waking up the neighbors in their dormant houses along the way. For the entire seven mile run to Timber Cove he saw no other cars, and in fact his patrol truck was probably the only vehicle which had traversed that stretch of roadway for hours. Unknown to Kurt at the time, ten minutes behind him, Lisa and Dave were speeding toward Timber Cove in her orange VW Squareback to "back him up."

Timber Cove was a protected area, largely sheltered from the majority of the winter swells. The roadway along that private stretch of land was lined with a few dozen trailers. The owners assumedly paid some nominal fees in exchange for the privilege of keeping their trailers parked there. But the harsh environment was not kind to those trailers, and most of the rigs were in sad shape, giving the place the lonely look of an abandoned shanty-town.

Kurt pulled into the cove and began suiting up. Reports indicated the stricken boat was a 20' inboard with a small cabin, actively sinking a half-mile off Timber Cove. Kurt peered through his binos and was able to spot a single faint light. There was no way to confirm for sure that the light belonged to the sinking vessel, but he felt confident it was, based solely on the fact there were no other lights visible in any direction.

Every Ocean Lifeguard has a few intriguing memories tucked away which involve their immersion in the great Pacific Ocean in the darkness of night. Free diving for lobster with spotlights at Crystal Cove. Surfing at San Onofre by the light of a full moon with a group of semi-buzzed off-duty lifeguards. Better yet, frolicking with their 20-year old giggling girlfriend (or boyfriend) in the waters of Costa Rica or the Yucatan. But this night was different. His entry into the cold and ominous ocean was most certainly not by his choosing.

On most nights, the moon light shines down on the water and splinters into thousands of glimmering reflections on the surface. But not on that night. Along the entire coastline the clouds hung dense and low, successfully choking out all of the residual light, and casting a pall of utter blackness over the ocean.

Kurt unstrapped the paddleboard, grabbed his mini-dive light, and with the paddleboard over his head, made his way to the water's edge. The ocean laid before him was bleak and foreboding. He directed the beam from the light out into the water – and like some magic trick, the futile little beam was swallowed up in the darkness.

He began the awkward "rock dance" across the inside rocks to reach the water. Needing both arms to paddle, he stuck the little dive light in his mouth, jumped on his board, and shoved off into the icy water, embarking on a half-mile paddle in the direction of the faint light.

His dive light was utterly inadequate. As he paddled on his knees, the beam, moving up and down with every stroke, was only powerful enough to illuminate the bright yellow surface of the front of the board and his hands repeatedly dipping into the black water. Yet, he carried on out to sea on a course into the dark night praying to God this event would end well and the batteries in his feeble light would not give out.

He paced himself on the long paddle from shore. As he carried on, his thoughts were his only companion, continually reminding him this was not his place. Heck, this wasn't a place for *any* man. In that vast ocean, greatly obscured under the cover of night, he felt small, painfully vulnerable, and utterly insignificant. For Lisa and Dave, now standing on the shoreline, Kurt had already disappeared into the abyss where the combined blackness of the sky and water merged.

Making progress, in his fragile state of mind, the memory of the previous week's shark attack crept into his thoughts. The bite width, the torn edges, the tremendous jaw strength which had crushed that kayak. The predator was out there somewhere, and could easily target him. He tried to block it out, trying to focus only on his paddling rhythm, but it was impossible. With the little light in his mouth, he felt like a human lure, trolling along as potential bait for the massive predator lurking somewhere below. His senses were peaked, aware of every ripple on the surface, every sound around him. And every time he put his hands in the water, he imagined the massive white head with jaws open, exploding from the darkness to grab it.

He did his best to maintain a sense of calm in an attempt to instill hope and strength.

The fear he experienced was so profound that he would distinctly remember it 30 years later, and admitted that thinking about that night paddle still gave him the creeps. For Loeffler, this half-mile paddle in total darkness would be the most emotionally intense rescue of his career.

Loeffler reached the boat and surprised the two men aboard. By then the vessel was already partially sunk, riding extremely low in the water. One man was working feverishly to stem the leak and get his bilge pump working, while the other man was bailing with a small bucket.

Loeffler immediately confirmed they had already summoned the Coast Guard. Seeing their radio was still working, he took the mic and hailed them directly, discovering they had dispatched their helicopter. Unsure where they were, Kurt was able to contact the pilot directly, and was given their location in Latitude-Longitude coordinates. These meant little to the lifeguards who preferred using physical landmarks for their local calls with the Henry-I pilot. Regardless, Loeffler scanned the skies and soon spotted the helo far to the north, already well-past the boat. Using simple commands of north-south, then left-right he was able to guide the helo to their location. Soon the skies above the boat were awash in the blinding lights, rotor noise, and strong downwash winds generated by the huge helicopter.

The view from shore was dramatic as hell. Watching through the binos, Schardt surveyed the scene, now brightly illuminated by the powerful lights from the helo, and he clearly identified Loeffler on board, wearing the bright neon state-issued wetsuit. And soon, like animals crawling from their dens after hibernation, awoken by the noise and the lights, the residents of the local "community" began emerging from their trailers to witness the drama.

The Coast Guard helo lowered a crewman onto the stricken vessel, followed by a portable bilge pump. He fired up the high powered pump and within minutes the boat began to rise. Eventually the operator was able to find and repair the leak and within half an hour, the potential tragedy was averted.

Loeffler had hoped to make the paddle back to shore while the lights from the helo lit up the night sky, but unfortunately, with the boat now safely under way, they hoisted their crew man and cleared the scene. Shortly afterwards, the repaired boat fired up the engines and were ready to head off towards Bodega Bay.

Thus Kurt found himself alone once again, greeted by the enveloping darkness. He jumped back on his board, placed the small dive light back in his mouth, and began his return paddle for shore. Although the distance and menacing conditions were the same, the shoreline was now faintly illuminated by the residents, and he was further bolstered by the knowledge that on this paddle, instead of heading off into the unknown, he was heading home.

Reaching shore, a small contingent of trailer-dwellers greeted him, curious to hear the details of his dramatic rescue. Kurt appeased them with a brief overview of the call. In the back of the crowd he spotted Lisa and Dave and gave them a nod and a knowing smile, realizing perhaps he wasn't quite as alone as he had originally thought.

LOEFFLER TAPS OUT

Whether by his own doing or not is a matter of debate, but it could be argued that the North Coast dished out a set of challenges to Loeffler which far exceeded those thrust onto the other guards.

Along with the perpetual stress which all of the guards faced, and the frustrations the perms faced in their perceived shortcomings of their leader, Loeffler had managed to forge his public persona into that of a tyrant. Although his citations were valid, the public often contended they should have been given "verbal warnings" for their violations, as had been the practice before his arrival. Loeffler, while writing the citations, simply pointed to the relevant signs which were usually posted within eyesight, and countered, "That sign was your warning."

When people started showing up to the beaches with hand-made poster board signs that read "FIRE KURT LOEFFLER" and accused him of being a Nazi, Loeffler, never one to back down from a fight, doubled-down and wrote even MORE citations. Of course this only embroiled him deeper into the chasm of public hatred. Loeffler, as adroit with clever banter as any officer, admittedly took a measure of pride in "pushing the buttons" of violators who challenged him, and often toyed with them "just to get a reaction" as he put it. Clearly this was not a tactic condoned by any agency, and likely damned him even deeper in the opinions of the local constituency.

Right or wrong, it's not pleasant being openly hated by the very people you are trying to serve. Loeffler once walked into a shop in Bodega Bay, and was promptly advised by the owner, "It costs five dollars to enter the store." When Loeffler asked if the policy was true for everyone, the man boldly stared him down, adding, "Nope. Only for you."

Kurt's acerbic wit, coupled with his 6' 10" frame made it impossible - both literally and figuratively - for him to successfully assimilate into a crowd. That was especially so in Loeffler's role as a lifeguard. With no place to hide during his patrols, Loeffler was easy to locate and was often harassed relentlessly by many of the locals. Being on the receiving end of their belligerence, he felt he had to be continually on guard for the possibility that the verbal attacks could escalate into a physical confrontation. And since he lived in a state residence and was part of the community, there was no escape from the public's wrath, and he was forced to maintain a heightened sense of vigilance through his days off as well. He never went into any local bars in Bodega Bay, knowing that it if he did, like some old western movie, all beers would have stopped half-way to the drinkers' mouths in dead silence.

In the end, whether you support him or damn him, the cumulative turmoil of the North Coast experience took a heavy toll on the health and well-being of Kurt Loeffler. His marriage, too, had begun to suffer. At the end of every shift, he arrived home dragging the heavy burdens of conflict, hatred, and seemingly never-ending stress. Those stories colored their lives in shades of sorrow and pain. Despite his best efforts, it wasn't long before their young marriage was on the ropes and soon dissolved.

Contrary to the poor coping methods of his peers, Loeffler actually sought counseling and regularly met with a therapist. Remarkably, both he and his therapist reached the same conclusion - Loeffler's ship had listed too far from center to correct. Loeffler had reached his emotional end. Despite the love he had for pure lifeguarding, the combination of negative factors on the North Coast were slowly killing him. After responding to innumerable heavy calls, the one which finally pushed him "over the edge" was a vehicle roll-over near Bodega Bay. Inside the crushed cab of the Chevy Blazer Kurt discovered the body of a drunk driver along with the mangled remains of his three dogs. The call had come directly on the heels of a suicide in the park, in which the stiffened pale body of a woman in her early 30s was found crumpled in the driver's seat of her car. As Loeffler opened the car door to assess her, he noticed her dashboard was adorned with a collection of mementoes and photographs of her loved ones.

His decision made, Loeffler drew up his resignation paperwork based on the undeniable and irreconcilable effects of cumulative stress. Immersed and sinking in the quicksand of anxiety, he had not even considered any possible alternatives for gainful employment, yet he was willing to leave the job he once loved with no plan for his future. He just knew he needed to get out of there.

Sitting across from District Superintendent Bob LaBelle, with his resignation paperwork in a manila folder on his lap, Loeffler began explaining how the job was slowly killing him. LaBelle, a gentleman of compassion and empathy, understood full-well what he was going through. Loeffler then reached the point in his confession where he admitted he was "not fit for duty." He placed his gun and his badge on the table and slid them toward LaBelle, explaining he would not be coming into work the following day.

LaBelle sat back, ever the diplomat, and considered Loeffler's admission and sudden resignation.

Then, in a move which surprised them both, LaBelle slid the gun back to Loeffler.

"You have to come to work tomorrow, Kurt, but I will do what I can to get you transferred out of here so you can keep your job."

Feeling like the back door of his prison cell was now open, after pondering LaBelle's counter proposal for several minutes, Kurt reached over and took the gun back. The envelope in his lap, containing his resignation paperwork, never made it into LaBelle's hands.

Two days later, Loeffler was offered a transfer to Candlestick Park in San Francisco, where he would remain a Law Enforcement Officer. There would be no huge surf, no divers, no harrowing ocean rescues. And in the course of his work day, he wouldn't see a single sign with his name on it - damning him or demanding that he be fired.

The new job would represent an opportunity for Kurt Loeffler to re-create himself.

He accepted the position on the spot.

NORTH COAST SEDITION

According to most members of his staff, Bud's ultimate undoing came by virtue of his own hands. Whether his blunder was intentional or not is a matter of debate.

By then, every guard had certainly realized their overall victories as a whole. But the human mind works in peculiar ways, and although statistics and personal harrowing rescues were clear and irrefutable validation of their cumulative accomplishments as a lifeguard service, as any great manager can attest, the mind of the average adult male is often motivated on a reward system based on *acknowledgment* for their individual successes. In that realm they were shamelessly lacking. These guys were performing crazy rescues in ungodly conditions and besides a high-five from their partners, were provided with little or no recognition at all. It would not have taken much to keep them happy, but what they were provided was essentially nothing. After a while, they were left to wonder if anyone out there was even aware of what they were doing.

Carter and Straub, having garnered the *Medal of Valor* award from the United States Lifesaving Association, were the only exception, as their rescue had been canonized by the ultimate entity in our profession. But by then, *every North Coast guard* had endangered themselves in similar conditions, rescuing divers from 15' seas, rappelling down cliffs to retrieve bodies, and pounded out CPR compressions on remote rocky shorelines with the surf crashing at their backs...and for them, there was seemingly no acknowledgement of those efforts. No thanks from the local EMS community, no professional awards, no commendation from the District Superintendent, and certainly no recognition from the public. A true travesty, Franklin's rescue, undoubtedly worthy of the Medal of Valor, was *never even submitted for consideration*. Nor were a series of other unpublicized, yet similarly dramatic rescues performed by the other guards.

Despite the recent bylines from the press, the disregard and disdain from those same publications for the previous three years had created deep wounds which still festered. Those periodicals had neither apologized, nor admitted they were wrong, and truth be told, that mattered to those guards.

Another potential source of appreciation could have been given by Bud Brown himself, but after enduring months of disrespect from Franklin and Loeffler, any praise Bud gave them would likely have been seen as disingenuous and robustly rejected.

As for the local citizens, the idea they might publicly *praise* the lifeguards was a pipe dream. They too had long memories, populated by unpleasant encounters and hefty citations received from the men in blue. Many of them still clung to their appalling opinions of the lifeguards and still would have loved nothing more than to see them jettisoned from the county entirely. It's safe to say they were not arranging any honorary parades for them either.

Then a remarkable present arrived at their door.

The bureaucrats in Sacramento had taken notice of their accomplishments.

In an unexpected, though greatly appreciated gesture of recognition, they called the Lifeguard Supervisor to notify him his crew would be granted the *Governor's Award for Public Safety*. Granted, it was an accolade presented by a panel of individuals in Sacramento, none of whom had likely ever been to the Sonoma Coast, let alone *seen* what the lifeguards did. Nonetheless, this was *Big Smoke* to those guards and a profound acknowledgment of success in their overarching mission as lifeguards, bestowed by the Governor of California himself.

It's impossible to predict the feelings of self-actualization and confirmation the award *could have* provided to the crew, and perhaps it might not have been a panacea to "right the ship" and finally bond them as brothers in their common cause, but we will never know. Because, in a strange twist which no one saw coming, the award, along with all of the associated recognition and glory, was issued to Bud Brown himself - *with no mention of his crew*.

It's hard to overestimate the damage incurred, but in interviews with the crew, when judged against all of the perceived wounds they suffered; the early disrespect from the press, the struggles assimilating with the sheriffs, and even the public hatred they endured, the exclusion of the crew from the *Governor's Safety Award* was generally agreed to be the most egregious insult they had endured. Clearly, the award was a team effort and all resultant honor and recognition should have been shared by them all.

It isn't known how or why the award was issued solely to the supervisor, and perhaps Bud could have called the committee and lobbied to have their names added, but for whatever reason, that didn't happen. And with the omission, any remaining chance Bud had of redeeming himself was demolished.

The guards began mocking their supervisor on calls. One of the Perms admitted that while treating an unconscious patient, his partner stated, *"Don't worry sir, you are in good hands, my boss just won the Governor's Award for Public Safety."* The statement highlights the level of scorn they felt for their supervisor and it bears mention that his contempt was so extreme, he was willing to compromise his own professionalism just to slander his boss. At that point, all of the gains they all had worked so hard to establish, now ran the risk of being destroyed in an implosion of anarchy if he stayed.

Jilting the crew from the Governor's Award supplied them with a unified justification to hammer the final nail in Bud's coffin. The crew coalesced and began formulating plans for a silent mutiny in the form of a unanimous "vote of no confidence."

Bud, hearing the rumblings and seeing no way out, returned to Hickey's office and admitted failure. This time, his decision to leave - by whatever means necessary - would be final. Hickey, well-aware of his tremendous potential, committed himself to arrange for his re-classification into a non-peace officer positon.

Despite later describing this period as *"The darkest time of my life,"* Bud refused to admit the deck was stacked against him. To him, despite the inordinate challenges thrust in his face, he remained steadfast in his opinion that he should have succeeded. Worse yet, on a deeply personal level, he felt he had failed to live up to his father's faith in him.

Bud Brown was relocated from the wild coastline of the Sonoma Coast some 500 miles south to Silverwood Lake, located on the west fork of the Mojave River. The quiet pace of this lovely mountain lake, surrounded by forests of Douglas Fir, and Black Oak, would offer Bud, an avid fisherman, a veritable sanctuary to recover from his *"dark time,"* enjoying carefree days, fishing for striped bass and trout on his days off. His new position, as an *"Interpretive Specialist"* would be a dream assignment which matched his skill-set perfectly, as he would study Bald Eagles and offer presentations to various groups of all ages.

It should be noted that his vacant Lifeguard Supervisor position on the North Coast would remain vacant for over ten years.

For Loeffler, who made no secret of his struggles with Brown, there was little cause to celebrate. Even with his own approved transfer, his well-being had already been crushed under the oppression of his failed marriage, and the never-ending struggle to keep people alive along that coastline. He left the coast an emotionally damaged man, yet hopeful of resurrecting his career as a law enforcement officer in a new district.

In correspondence with Loeffler, decades after his departure from the Sonoma Coast, it was clear his disdain for the citizens of Bodega Bay had not faded at all. To those who openly hated him, he offered no apology and remained defiant. In one of his letters to me he wrote: *"Like most people who visit the Sonoma Coast for the first time, I found the quaint village and long miles of rugged, unexploited coastline a refreshing change from the smoggy, overcrowded, traffic jam of Southern California. However, by the time I left, years later, I was convinced all the inbreeding God had commanded Adam and Eve and their children to employ in populating the earth had actually begun in Bodega Bay - and was still going on."*

It is safe to assume that upon his departure, somewhere in Bodega Bay, a group of locals gathered together and celebrated his exodus in grand fashion.

~~~

Conversely, in further proof the karmic wheel rolls both ways, amidst the turmoil and departures of two key figures in the crew, a beautiful and easy-going woman from Sweden named *Barbro* happened to be touring through California and crossed paths with the lovable and perennially jovial Dave Schardt. Their chance meeting would be one of those *"love at first sight"* moments for them both, and despite the fact she returned to Sweden, the cosmic pull of love between them remained strong. Schardt, a true believer in the old adage, *"When you meet the right girl, never let her go,"* accepted the phrase as gospel, even if *the right girl* lived some 5,000 miles away. Their mutual love proved strong enough to justify the purchase of a series of round trip plane tickets between San Francisco and Stockholm, and eventually, in accordance with the adage, Dave would pull stakes from California and relocate to Sweden where they would eventually wed.

Dave's farewell party with the guards was only slightly more difficult to face than having to say good bye in his alternate role as "Dave Shark" to his most loyal and ardent fan in Bodega Bay.

6-1993
TIM HARVEY and FRANK CERCOS

Within three years, the original crew of 11 had been decimated. They had lost Melvin (to Fish and Game), Haug (to the Academy),

Gulick (to nursing school), Franklin (transferred to Huntington), Schardt (moved to Sweden), Loeffler (to Candlestick Park), and now Brown (re-assigned to Silverwood Lake). Martino (to the Academy) and Carter (to LA County) would be gone the following year, leaving Straub and McNulty as the last men standing.

But the stories involving the original crew and their exploits guarding the wild North Coast continued to leak out to the other districts, and the crew would replenish and rejuvenate itself with fresh rescuers who brought in their own skills and experience, along with their unique humor and spirit.

The most notable to arrive was the legendary Tim Harvey. Harvey had won more National lifeguard championships for the State Guards than anyone - until he handed off the torch to Mitch Kahn. Living in San Francisco and pursuing a career in photography, he made himself available to work the Sonoma Coast. He would have already been around 40 at the time and well-past his prime, but was still the strongest swimmer on the crew. He was also a phenomenal free-diver, excellent medical practitioner, and seemingly impervious to the cold water. Above all, Harvey was an easy-going and gregarious breath of fresh air to a crew who was in desperate need of a respite from the drama. He quickly assimilated himself into the system and happily joined in the rescue derby almost immediately. Records indicate his first documented rescue was in June of '93 saving two divers with McNulty at Moon Rock. The thought of *those* two legends of lifeguarding joining forces on a rescue is pretty damned cool.

Tim Harvey (early '80s)

But wait, there's more.

As if the managers had searched an honor role of retired lifeguards in an effort to create an all-star crew, Frank Cercos miraculously showed up inquiring about the possibility of returning to lifeguarding to work the North Coast. Cercos had been a State Guard in the '60s in the Santa

Barbara area. He had logged a few years on the beaches and made a name for himself before beginning a career in the fire service, where eventually the poised leader would become a Deputy Chief with the San Francisco Fire Department. Amazingly, he too had gotten wind of the emerging Sonoma Coast Lifeguard Service, and despite being out of the profession for 25 years, he wanted back in.

His quarter century hiatus from guarding meant that he would have to complete the Rookie Lifeguard Training Academy in Huntington with a classroom of kids who were less than half his age. True to his nature, Frank spent most of the 8-day session helping his fellow trainees who were struggling with the first aid skills and scenarios. To his credit, he was able to hold his own on the swims, and ended up finishing in the top ten.

One can only imagine the reaction of the local EMS crews when they received the first patient hand-off from the "new lifeguard" and discovered he

Frank Cercos – Salt Point (1993)

was a Deputy Chief of SFFD. As one might imagine, his presence there quickly reverberated through the community and having "Chief Cercos" on staff gave the guards an instant boost in status amongst the various Fire and EMS agencies.

Frank was a humble man who rarely spoke about his exploits, despite leading one of the nation's largest Fire Departments. But when Martino prodded him to explain his stature in the fire world, Frank, wearing a huge smile, wryly proclaimed, "Martino, you guys couldn't lick my boots."

Obviously Frank was a wealth of information and skills; not to mention an even-keeled leader who was confident and capable of handling virtually every conceivable type of emergency. The crew immediately adopted him and began referring to him simply and deferentially as "Chief."

11-27-1993
THE GREAT SALT POINT FIRE

This account of the Salt Point Fire, lightly edited, was generously provided by Mike Martino.

Two days after Thanksgiving in 1993, Dave Carter was on patrol at Goat Rock when, around 10:30, he noticed a plume of smoke rising in the air far off in the North Sector. Shortly thereafter, the radio crackled with a request for firefighters to come help with a *"small fire at Salt Point State Park."* Apparently the rangers were struggling to contain the blaze that started when a careless camper left a fire unattended at one of the ecological campsites.

Initially only a dozen firefighters were dispatched with the hope the favorable winds blowing gently from the south and east would push the fire towards the cove at Salt Point and keep the damage to a minimum.

Then, as Carter continued to watch the rising smoke, a stillness settled which got his attention. An eerie silence followed, and the guard, attuned to the variations in weather, immediately noticed it.

"Oh shit," said Carter as he stepped out of the vehicle, looking at the dune grass. "The wind's changing."

Suddenly twelve men were not enough. Twenty were not enough, nor thirty. The call for help went out and the chaos of the blaze shattered what had been a tranquil day.

Carter watched the column of smoke as it expanded into an ever-increasing black cloud. He heard the calls for evacuation and the request for more and more firefighting units. As the blaze picked up strength, the flames jumped from tree top to tree top. Soon those flames spanned the campground roadways as if they didn't exist. Burning vapors leapt from one area to another and the fire began generating its own howling wind which urged the flames forward with the singular message to burn, burn, burn!

With the park ablaze, Carter immediately worried about the fate of his lifeguard brothers in the middle of the maelstrom.

Coincidentally, Adam Wright had been involved in a lengthy rescue just outside Gerstle Cove when the blaze started, and had missed all of the emergency radio traffic. As he emerged from the ocean, dried off and put his uniform back on, he could see the entire hillside ablaze east of him. For several moments he sat in the patrol truck, confused as to what he should do. Soon the flames were rolling toward him like giant fiery waves. Feeling the heat, at one point Adam contemplated abandoning the truck and swimming back out into the ocean to escape. From the panoramic perspective of water he would be safe to watch as the destructive fury incinerated the land, the visitor's center, and eventually the patrol truck as well. Alternatively, he could make a "run for it" and try to save the patrol truck by racing up the road and out of the park.

Adam got on the radio, questioning if the park road and the Coast Highway were still passable. The response was an unsettling and vague *"Probably."*

He slammed the door closed, fired up the truck, and sped off towards the half-mile long park road. When he reached the foot of the steep roadway, the smoke was so thick he couldn't see more than a few feet around the truck, restricting him to slow to a crawl. As he drove up through the grey haze, he felt an ever-increasing sense of regret with his decision. Flames were jumping the road from the treetop to treetop directly over him. Summoning the courage to continue, he felt as if he had grabbed the hand of Dante himself, who might well be leading him straight into Hell.

The intense heat permeated through the closed windows, as the blaze completely surrounded him. Looking to either side, he saw only walls of flame, and above, the racing flames of a ceiling of more fire. He pushed forward almost blindly along the roadway. It was a path he had driven countless times, but now had to navigate partly by memory. One slip to either side would put him in a ditch and the flames could easily engulf the truck - with him in it.

Only a surfer or a lifeguard could experience such a situation, with the swirling chaos of fire surrounding him and describe it as Adam did. *"I was totally in the barrel...and I shot through the tube of fire!"*

Indeed, happily for Adam and his crew, he maintained his composure, kept the "board" on the road, and in a moment which stretched to infinity, he shot through that "barrel of fire." Approaching the crest, suddenly more of the roadway came into view, and he picked up speed, punching through the raging vaporous flames. The flames gave way to smoke, and the roadway cleared further. He accelerated more. Now in the clear of the active flames, the scene began to open around him and he drove onward through the blackened landscape and the skeletal remains of the smoking trees which the fire had just decimated. Adam had survived the ordeal and like a triumphant surfer on a huge day, he couldn't help but feel the exhilaration of having come face to face with elemental nature and somehow, through luck and skill, managed to emerge from the ocean of fire unscathed, saving the lifeguard truck in the process.

Osh McNulty was well north of the fire when it started, intently watching two divers who were poaching abalone. As was his method, Osh meticulously noted every dive in his notebook and documented each time one of the men placed an abalone in their float. Word of the fire had been flickering over the radio, but the diver's violations were egregious and Osh didn't want to lose the bust. Thus, contrary to most people's basic instincts, his attention stayed with the divers. He sat comfortably ensconced in the bushes stalking his prey but he too noticed the shifting of the wind and uttered the same *"Oh Shit"* response as Carter.

Soon the divers were out of the water and the hunter sprang into action. Osh had heard the call for the evacuation come over the radio so he had pre-written out most of the details on the citations for the poaching violations he had observed. Calm and composed, Osh radioed that he would be en route to help as soon as he finished writing the citations. One can only wonder what the abalone poachers were thinking as the dark clouds of smoke continued to thicken, eventually obscuring the sun, while this lifeguard/officer quietly continued writing out their citations, seemingly unaffected as the park around them was burning to the ground.

Osh instructed both divers to sign their citations, then carefully tore them from his cite book and handed them their copies. Only then, looking up to the blackening sky, did he instruct the two men that it might be a good idea to evacuate the park immediately, via the northern route. As large amounts of glowing ash descended on them like snow, the errant divers didn't need to be told twice.

In the early stages of the fire, a small corps of firefighters with two engines and six smaller trucks seemed adequate enough to control the blaze, since the fire was moving slowly toward the ocean bluffs where the lack of fuel would eventually cause the fire to die.

They requested air support but unfortunately, the few aircraft which might have been able to help were already engaged in fighting fires in other parts of the state. The only aircraft available was Henry-I, but it wasn't equipped to fight fire. Still, pilot Tom McConnell hovered above the firefighters and offered what help he could in relaying observations from the air.

The firefighters worked hard, and during the early going it appeared they would succeed in their suppression efforts. That is, until the wind shifted. From above, McConnell watched as the winds went silent then picked up again, this time blowing the heat and flames directly *back* at the firefighters. McConnell later described that moment, *"It just took off...and I watched in awe as a huge part of the park exploded into flame and was gone in twenty minutes."*

Down below, the overwhelmed firefighters scrambled back to their trucks and retreated as quickly as they had arrived, calling for more support and as many fire fighters as could be spared. By then the fire had turned the sharp corner from a "routine call" - for those who fight fires - to an extreme emergency for everyone in the area. Rangers drove through the park announcing on the P.A. system, *"There is a fire, please evacuate as quickly and calmly as possible."*

In that emergent situation, one might expect the campers to panic and mirror the chaotic movements of the fire itself, but by most accounts the campers evacuated safely. With limited escape paths and circuitous roadways, it is a fitting tribute to the firefighters and the rangers in charge of the evacuations that no one died.

In all, 250 firefighters from twenty-two local fire departments and CDF stations would respond, and the residents of Guerneville and Jenner watched the steady stream of fire trucks roll through their town, enroute to the blaze. Crews arrived from Jenner, Fort Ross, Sea Ranch, Timber Cove, Forestville, Cazadero, Monte Rio, Camp Meeker, Guerneville, Occidental, Rincon Valley, Gold Ridge, Sebastopol, Graton, Bodega Bay, Cotati, Penngrove, Rohnert Park, as well as CDF units from Sonoma, Mendocino, Napa and San Mateo Counties.

Almost 500 acres of the park were decimated. In addition to the forest burned, the state lost an old barn at Salt Point where at least

$100,000 of virgin redwood and maintenance equipment had been stored. In the Gerstle Cove area, crews *were* able to save the A-frame visitors center, the ranger's residence, and the maintenance yard with all of the supplies, vehicles and structures, including the shoddy (though quaint) lifeguard trailer.

As the sun began its descent into the ocean the winds shifted back, and the heavens brought a most welcomed rain. This blessing provided the firefighters with their final advantage over the fire. Throughout the night crews continued to work, making sure the blaze did not rekindle. They doused the flames, contained the hotspots, and by morning most of the crews were able to return to their stations.

The *Great Salt Point State Park Fire* of 1993 would put the exclamation point on yet another dramatic year of death and destruction along Sonoma Coast.

Mercifully, no more fatalities would be recorded for the final month of the year. In fact, no major events would mar the month of December at all. It was as if both Nature and Man, having spent so much energy in creating and fighting the blaze, decided to invoke an unspoken truce, a cease fire where Man agreed not to do stupid things in the ocean, and Nature agreed not to snatch anyone who violated that agreement.

13

LIFEGUARD JOURNAL: 1994

Lifeguards retrieve body from vehicle over bluff

3-1994
THE ARRIVAL of REX GRADY

Rex Grady arrived in early 1994. The future attorney and law professor had been a long time guard at San Diego Coast as well as an academic with double Master's Degrees. Even before college, Grady carried himself with a professorial demeanor, and definitely didn't ascribe himself to the stereotypical image of a Southern California surfer-lifeguard. But he was a rocket in the water, and arrived ready to challenge himself. Grady, almost instantly, would make a significant contribution to the operation.

Rex Grady (1995)

3-26-1994
MANUEL

In truth, it would be difficult to find a more conscientious lifeguard than Rex Grady. Despite being faced with intimidating conditions, he showed no hesitation in answering the call of duty, joining in the fray and swimming shoulder to shoulder with the other guards on rescues. As a student of both the practice and the history of lifeguarding, Grady methodically studied the guards' strategies and approaches to making rescues and readily assimilated them into his own skill set. On land, as well, he listened to the guards' well-established warning speeches and preventative techniques and began utilizing them almost immediately.

Unfortunately the ocean offered little in the way of a probationary period for Grady, and within the first month, working almost exclusively in the South Sector, he logged an impressive tally of rescues. In addition to the saves, he had also pulled visitors off of wash rocks, treated several major medicals, enforced several dozen rules violations, and contacted hundreds of people who had unknowingly ventured into dangerous situations.

On the weekend of March 26th, in just his fourth week on the North

Coast, the ocean rose to test Rex Grady like no other time in his career, with solid sets of waves up to fifteen feet in height focusing squarely on the Sonoma Coast shoreline. As always, the ocean's choices in handing out the types and intensities of tragedies were indiscriminate, and this time it would be South Sector who would be the target of the ocean's wrath.

Grady and Adam Wright had posted up in the patrol truck at the Jenner overlook, just north of the Russian River outlet when an emergent call came over the radio reporting an *active drowning* taking place at Goat Rock Beach. From their vantage, with binos, they had a clear and unobstructed view of the entire beach to their south. They scrutinized every possible area on that beach and saw nothing but a few walkers. The radio was soon choked with voices from multiple agencies, reporting they were dispatching emergency units to Goat Rock.

In this unprecedented and disturbingly alarming situation, with an army of EMS personnel speeding to their home beach for someone who was *"fighting for their life"* in *their* water, and the fact they were already on scene; ready, willing and able to swim out to rescue the victim, they could see no one in their water.

To not know the *exact location* of their drowning victim was excruciating. Yet to drive to Goat Rock Beach from the Jenner Overlook would take them on a circuitous four-mile route inland in order to cross the Russian River Bridge, then another mile south to reach the Goat Rock entrance. Worse yet, from where they stood, they saw no reason to respond there at all.

Dave Carter, working one of his last days on the North Coast, began racing south from Fort Ross, but with a 30-minute run ahead of him, they all knew he would never make it there in time to make a difference.

Rex jumped out of the truck and ran to the bluff edge to get a better view of the north side of the river, in case the rescue was happening on the desolate beach directly below them. Adam stayed in the truck, steaming in indecision on where to go.

Moments later, Rex returned to the truck. "Adam, its north. It *has to be north!*" Rex's voice conveyed a confidence which broke the indecision. At that moment, rescue units from Bodega Bay Fire, Monte Rio Fire, volunteers from Jenner, Sheriff's Deputies on land and in the air, and State Park Rangers, were racing *south* to the reported location at

Goat Rock. After taking one last look at the river mouth below and seeing nothing, Rex made a bold and fateful decision. Still racked with uncertainty, and with a human life in the balance, they pulled back onto the roadway and turned *north*, driving into oblivion, in the *opposite direction* of the reported location. Rex knew that his decision in that very moment would be the most important of his career.

He switched on the lights and siren and doubled down, telling Adam to "*Step on it.*"

Thus, while every available rescue unit on the coast was racing *towards* Goat Rock for an aquatic emergency, the only two trained rescuers in the area capable of swimming out to save the drowning victim, were actually speeding *away* from it.

They continued on, further distancing themselves from the chaos of the arriving units which would soon descend onto Goat Rock. Heading north they began searching for an unknown victim in an unknown location. They both knew if they were wrong, the repercussions would be unimaginable, as life and death hung in the balance, as did their judgment and credibility.

With each passing mile, and each cove and desolate area revealing nothing, their tensions grew. By then, the first rescue units were arriving at Goat Rock. The guards listened intently to the radio with a sense of dread in anticipation of a call reporting they *had* found the victim there, thereby proving them wrong. Moments passed, and thus far, that call did not come.

Then, a white pickup truck, driven by an old fisherman sped toward them from the opposite direction. From the window, his hand could be seen, frantically waving for them to stop.

"Go north! Farther up the road!!! A little boy, he's in the water!"

That was it. That was the call. Grady was right!

The guards sped north along the winding roadway with a new sense of confidence. They rounded another turn and saw a group of people gathered at the side of the road frantically waving. Grady barked out the correct mile-marker to the dispatcher, some eight miles north of where the other units were converging. Their single radio call would immediately redirect an entire army of rescue personnel to their location.

The guards ran from the truck leaving the doors open and the lights spinning on the roof.

Rex ran down the goat trail and came upon a middle-aged couple. The man was standing. The woman was kneeling on the ground, sitting on her heels. At their feet laid the body of a young boy, lifeless.

Rex dropped to his knees, quickly checked for a pulse, and immediately began chest compressions and breaths. The parents backed away and watched in horror. Adam arrived and took over the ventilations. His last transmission from the portable radio was the tragic update, "CPR *in progress on a young child.*"

The two guards worked feverishly. Compressions and breaths. Compressions and breaths. Fifteen to two. Fifteen to two. But there was no sign of life. The cycles continued and still they carried on, completely absorbed in the task before them with a focused sense of resolve and determination. Time passed. Still no change.

The responding medics eventually arrived to relieve them, calling out that they were prepared to take over ventilations and compressions. By then Grady was utterly exhausted yet was reluctant to leave his victim. The medics repeated they were ready to take over, and Rex eventually backed away from the child and relinquished care to the medics.

Grady stood a short distance away, staring at the medics working on their patient. His expression was vacant and devoid of emotion. Not only was this the first CPR for both of the guards, additionally they were forced to endure the added grief that their victim was a young child.

Grady looked up and saw the familiar face of Dave Carter standing next to him. Having been deeply locked in his all-consuming task, and oblivious to how much time had actually passed, he was momentarily confused as to how Carter had gotten there. Grady stood in silence, as rescuers bustled around him barking out orders and carrying equipment. Slowly, the synapses in his mind began re-orienting him to the world around him and the larger realities of place and time.

Carter approached the distraught fisherman, who was the boy's father. In broken English, laced with the universal language of grief, the man explained that his son had fallen into the water and both he and the boy's uncle had tried to save him, but it took them too long to reach the boy. At that point, he broke down and was unable to finish the rest of the story.

Moments later, Henry-I arrived and whisked the young boy away.

At the time of transfer, the boy's condition was grave. Although there was a glimmer of hope, as his heart had resumed beating, he was still unconsciousness and not breathing, and a considerable amount of time had passed before CPR was initiated. The efforts of the guards and the medics had managed to keep him alive, but his very survival hung in the balance.

With the patient transported, Grady and Wright, along with the members of various rescue agencies, slowly and dejectedly carried their equipment back up the trail with their heads hung. No one spoke.

Back in the patrol truck, Rex sat in the passenger seat staring forward, expressionless.

Under his breath he softly said, *"Please God...Let him live."*

～

Young Manuel remained in critical condition at Children's Hospital in Oakland for several days, but he would never awake.

When his ultimate fate was solidified, in an act of benevolence, and a wish for part of their son to live on, the family decided to donate his organs in hopes others might benefit from his life. It was a remarkable gesture which proved to be the ultimate gift for seven different individuals who received gifts from their son. Even in his death, the little boy continued to give, and one can only hope that some small portion of his joy and love transferred to the recipients who received those gifts. The fact that the diligent efforts from the lifeguards allowed his organs to survive provided them no consolation.

On Friday, April 2, Manuel was buried at Petaluma Calvary Catholic Cemetery. With a communal gathering of his family, his teachers, and his classmates surrounding his little casket, Manuel was laid to rest. Those who spoke at the ceremony remembered him as a kind and happy little boy. Their shared grief was universal and absolutely soul-crushing.

News of the boy's death shook Grady to his core.

To this day, he is unable to speak about the event without a noticeable resurgence of sorrow.

I am told that Rex still visits the young boy's grave.

4-1-1994
OPENING DAY - 1994

It was McNulty who narrated the dive-line report for Opening Day in 1994. *"Buoy readings are 14' at 14 seconds resulting in 12 to 14 foot breaking waves along the coastline. There is NO SAFE PLACE to dive at Salt Point State Park. The surf is big, and is expected to stay big through tomorrow. If you were planning on coming up to dive, the lifeguards recommend you change your plans and stay home."*

On that particular morning, McNulty's blunt message did not mention the customary alternatives of diving at Fort Ross or Fisk Mill. That was not a mistake. By his estimation, there was *no safe place to dive anywhere on the Sonoma Coast that day.*

The crew of guards were "in for it" and they knew it. With McNulty leading the charge, the team which took the field in the North Sector included Straub, Mike Thomas, Carter, Harvey, and Adam Wright. Henry-I was staged in the maintenance yard as usual, and rangers Ashford Wood and Karen Broderick would be on patrol. Rex Grady would be the lone lifeguard left to cover the South Sector.

Most divers with any common sense heeded the warnings and stayed clear of the broiling mess of saltwater which battered the county shoreline. Most of those who did arrive smartly chose not to go out. Some of them sat on the tailgates of their trucks, smoking cigarettes and drinking beer, while watching the relentless surf hammer the coastline. The effects of the alcohol generated a predictable and ever-increasing sense of euphoria, and soon the men began cheering loudly at the crashing plumes of water rocketing high into the air like an inverse fireworks show. One guard theorized the main source of the divers' joy from the ocean's powerful display was the fact *they weren't in it.*

But of course there were some who tempted fate because there are *always* those who tempt fate, and divers arrived on the coast, suited up and attempted to kick out into a sea of insanity with solid and unrelenting 14' surf. The guards struggled to maintain the perspective that the diver's blatant disregard for their warnings was not a sign of disrespect, but rather a justification for their paycheck.

The North Sector guards would make several hundred contacts, but fortunately they only needed to rescue five divers from the heavy seas. The abalone hunkered down a bit tighter on the rocks and were left alone. On that Opening Day, their populations would remain intact....at least until the following weekend.

And, for the 3rd consecutive year, every diver who ventured out into the ocean on the Sonoma Coast on Opening Day emerged from that crazy ocean alive and well.

4-1-1994
THE SAMOAN BOY

Ironically, while all eyes were on the North Sector guards patrolling the abalone opener, it was Grady, guarding solo on the South Sector, who would make the most momentous rescue of the day. The same swell which battered the coastline at Salt Point was punishing the beaches down south as well. Preparing for the worst, Rex made a strategic decision his fellow guards had only reverted to when things were truly dicey. He put his wetsuit on in the morning and kept it on all day while on patrol, in order to save a potentially critical 40 seconds of time if faced with a timely rescue. The decision would prove fortuitous.

Seeing a group of four children playing in the wet sand at Goat Rock, and having already witnessed first-hand how their seemingly benign play could quickly transform into a tragedy, Grady started driving towards them to get them away from the ocean. The parents were some distance away, laying on a blanket on the dry sand.

Grady parked the truck and started walking in their direction. As he got closer, looking outside, he saw a line of huge waves approaching. Directing his gaze back and forth between the kids and the approaching waves, he began to jog, then run, and ultimately sprint towards them. As he crested the berm, the first wave of the set smashed against children waist high, knocking them all to the sand. They tumbled about clumsily, unable to stand or escape to the safety of high ground. In a now familiar scene which had played out on that beach hundreds of times, the powerful pull of the retreating water began dragging them down the berm, while the next huge wave was loading up for impact. Three of the children were able to right themselves and climb against the strong backflow of the receding wave, but the smallest boy was not. He cried out in fear for his parents who, until that moment, were oblivious of any danger.

Grady reached the boy just as his father, a large man of Samoan heritage, came over the top of the berm. Rex yelled to him to stop, not wanting to have two victims. By then, the boy had been pulled to the very cusp of the drop off, directly at the impact area as the second wave jacked up, ready to crush him. Rex fell on top of the child and wrapped his arms around him just as the wave pummeled them both into the sand. The massive wall of energy thrust them part way up the berm. Desperately holding onto the boy, Rex looked up and saw the father, who had witnessed the unexpected calamity, and was running down toward them.

A smattering of on-lookers stood watching, as the thigh-deep water began receding, pulling both rescuer and victim back down towards the impact area of the next wave. Rex, now laying on his back and partially submerged by the receding wave, lifted his head and yelled to the father, "Take him! Take him now!" and he extended the boy above the flow of water. The father then set his feet in the flowing sand and braced himself against the powerful rush of water. He grabbed his son from the extended arms of the lifeguard, lifted him to his chest, and began trudging up the steep berm. Free from the responsibility of keeping the boy safe, Rex allowed himself to be pulled by the retreating waters, then skillfully ducked under the brunt of the next breaking wave, which immediately thrust him back up onto the sand. From there, he was able to awkwardly crawl up the berm before regaining his feet and jogging clear of the next crush of white water.

The father, a man with a huge heart - consistent with his size, met him on the top of the berm with a world-melting smile and a powerful handshake. The small crowd of people on the beach were astonished. Realizing they had just witnessed their own private display of aquatic skill, and seeing all of the actors were now safe, they spontaneously erupted into a smattering of applause.

Unprompted, the young victim, still breathing heavily, approached Grady, who went down to one knee to greet him eye to eye. Without words or hesitation, and quite unexpectedly, the boy wrapped his arms around the guard and held him tightly around the neck. Grady, never one to delve too deeply into emotional situations, offered no words either. None were necessary.

The devastating blow in the death of Manuel, just two weeks earlier, had burrowed a deep wound in the lifeguard's soul which was still actively bleeding.

The rescued child could not have known it, but his heartfelt gesture of thanks to the anonymous lifeguard was both timely and profound. The young victim's genuine and innocent act of gratitude had unknowingly given Grady exactly what he so desperately needed at that moment; a sense of validation of his role as a lifeguard.

This boy, with his arms clinging around Grady's neck, was vibrant and healthy. There would be no helicopter. There would be no ascension of a young boy's body to the heavens amidst the noise and rotor wash of stinging sand and grieving parents. For the long drive home, he would take his place in the back seat of the family car with his brothers and sisters, and they would buckle his seat belt for safety, like they always did. Perhaps their father would surprise them on the way home, stopping for ice cream. The kids would cheer and indulge in a special treat, oblivious to the reason for the spontaneous celebration. But the parents would know. They would sit and watch all of their children, joyously licking the sweet concoction...but mostly they would stare at their youngest, allowing the reality to continue to soak in; he was *right there, still with them*, and very much alive.

After that rescue, Grady reported pulling sand from his scalp and ears for days.

5-2-1994
PLAYING HURT

On May 2nd, Straub was the first guard on duty in the North Sector, and as part of the early guard's responsibilities, he took the patrol vehicle down the hill to assess the visibility and surf conditions for the dive line.

While watching the breaking waves, he tuned in the scanner to the weather report to pick up the swell readings at the 200-mile buoy so he could predict the surf report for the next 24 to 48 hours.

But on that particular morning, Don had a very special partner accompanying him as he had invited his 4-year old daughter to jump into the patrol vehicle with him.

Don and little Tiana were sitting in the vehicle at Gerstle Cove, enjoying some silly daddy-daughter time while waiting for the sun to rise enough so he could assess the visibility in the shallow area of the cove. Don already knew the water clarity would be awful since the surf was large and an unusual early morning wind was already ruffling the ocean surface into whitecaps.

While they were parked, two guys pulled up in a black truck and began readying their dive gear. Don walked over to their truck and began a casual conversation which culminated with a warning not to attempt diving anywhere along the exposed areas due to the significant swell. As was often the case, the divers seemingly knew better and continuing to suit up, obviously undeterred in their decision to kick out. Don, now openly pissed off they had so boldly blown him off, confronted them again. This time, instead of *asking* them not to go in the water, he *told them* not to go in.

His lack of diplomacy may have hindered any chance of compliance. Without so much as acknowledging him, the two men walked right past him, heading in the direction of Salt Point proper, where solid 8-10' waves were breaking.

Don pulled the truck directly out to the point, a move which the lay person might assume had something to do with monitoring the divers' safety. But if we are being honest here, Don's *primary* motivation in bringing the truck so close to their entry point was to get a front row seat to watch the divers getting crudely and unceremoniously rejected back to shore by the huge sets of waves. Having the patrol truck well within their field of view also guaranteed the additional *"bonus humiliation"* of them knowing he was watching every second of their failure - and likely cheering.

Don and Tiana watched as the two men navigated their way over the inside rocks. Straub was certain that once they got close to the breaking waves they would come to their senses and admit defeat. He was wrong. On the contrary, both men, seemingly doubling down on their defiance, briskly hopped on their abalone floats and began kicking out into a substantial swell. With their terrible decision solidified, Don jumped out of the truck and began putting his wetsuit on.

Soon after they entered, the two divers became separated. One of them successfully made it over a few of the smaller waves on the inside before being utterly blasted by one of the larger sets. He was quickly and rather unceremoniously launched back to shore. Don, standing in the truck bed for optimum visibility, yelled out to him, then thrust both of his thumbs high above his head to ensure the man knew he had witnessed the whole thing. The man did not acknowledge the gesture.

The second diver had somehow managed to place himself directly into the neck of the Salt Point rip pulling off the face. In a matter of moments, he would need to be rescued.

Straub radioed McNulty, obviously upset, and notified him he was going to have to go out on this knucklehead.

After hearing the unfriendly conversation between her dad and the two men, and seeing how mad they had made him, his daughter grew quiet and seemed scared, not understanding what was happening.

Don was caught in a bind. He had thought the trip down the hill with his daughter would be a quick one and he would have her back at home in ten minutes. He hadn't planned on having to leave his young child unattended while he was tasked with making a rescue. Having no alternative, he faced her squarely and calmly explained, "Sweetie, everything is going to be okay, but daddy has to swim out and rescue that silly man out there." Looking at the emergency gear and the radios left on the bench seat he added, "Just don't touch anything sweetie." Tiana nodded in solemn understanding, and Don turned and ran for the point.

Struggling out over the slippery rocks was never easy or graceful, especially if it was in the haste of having to make a rescue. Don stumbled his way into waist deep water then turned his back towards the waves to put his fins on. After getting his right fin on, in what he would later describe as "one of my biggest bonehead maneuvers," he pushed the finned foot to the bottom just as a wave was coming. The fin slipped down between two rocks where it became solidly wedged, locking his foot in place just as a head-high wave smashed into him. The impact twisting his body 180 degrees with significant force and he felt his ankle crack, along with an instantaneous jolt of electricity which ran up his leg. He then fell backwards, writhing in pain.

When the wave passed, he was able to free his trapped fin from the rocks, but his ankle flopped uselessly. He reached down and pulled the fin from his freshly fractured ankle and heaved it towards shore.

Don then paused for a moment, contemplating his next move. Looking to the shoreline, he could see his white patrol truck parked at the point and knew it contained all of the necessary medical supplies to splint his fractured ankle. Then he turned his gaze off-shore and spotted the diver, still floundering. With no other guard close enough to respond, Don had no real choice. He dove forward, beneath the oncoming wave and began swimming out into the flow of the rip. He would have to make the rescue with one fin, dragging his freshly busted ankle behind him.

Just as he neared the victim, a large wave, well overhead, was cresting. Finding themselves in the worst possible spot, both men were thrown over the falls. Despite the numbing effects of the cold water, the tumbling of the wave torqued Don's ankle in every direction, causing his pain to triple. Don popped up to find his victim had been thrown so hard by the tumbling wave, he had been stripped of both of his fins as well as his dive mask. At that point, according to Don, the victim then began *"screaming like an idiot."*

Don completed his sprint to the diver and clipped him in the buoy. As per usual, the diver still had his weight belt on, which Straub immediately dropped, adding it to the tally of gear he would be donating to the sea. Jettisoning the weight, the man now floated high in the water. He would not drown. At least not today. The inside was nasty with relentless waves breaking over a mine field of boulders which Straub wanted no part of with his compromised ankle. So he decided to swim the victim offshore to the safety of the deeper water. Together they went under several waves, and were eventually clear of the surfline. By then McNulty was on scene and had called for Henry-I. Straub, knowing the helo would be coming, waited with his victim far offshore. He was tempted to give the man a piece of his mind, but he bit his tongue, knowing the ocean had already sufficiently scolded him. Together they floated amidst the whitecaps off Salt Point. Don had not taken the time to put on his booties, but in this case the cold water numbed his feet so completely, that at least for the time being, the pain was tolerable.

Soon after, Don spotted Henry-I flying in over the tree tops of the coast range and, under his breath said to the man, "Here's your ride."

"Are you kidding me?" demanded the victim. "I'm going to fly in that thing?!"

Don paused. "You won't be so much 'in it' as you will be 'under it' suspended from a line."

The diver was obviously terrified with this news, but he was not in a position to offer any resistance to the plan.

The helo circled once then lowered, engulfing them in a maelstrom of wind and whipping water. Don continued yelling instructions to the side of their diver's head, loud enough so he could hear through the hood of his wetsuit.

The helo lowered further and dropped their flight medic into the water. During the pickup, Don yelled to him that he had suffered an angulated ankle fracture on his entry, and for the first and only time in his North Coast tenure - he requested the medic return and pluck him out as well. The medic was stunned. His eyes widened and he boldly clarified, "*You just made that rescue with a fractured ankle!? Are you serious?!*"

McNulty arrived in time to witness the extrication by Henry-I. Just as the sun was coming up over the pine trees, Tiana watched as the helicopter hoisted the terrified diver from the water and flew him over the patrol truck to the safety of the parking lot. She then saw the chopper return to the scene. Moments later, she could see her dad in his familiar blue and yellow wetsuit, dangling precariously from the static line. Don, now in the role of an injured victim, was gingerly lowered down close to his truck.

Ironically, while making the rescue, Don's main concern was for his young daughter, who was watching all of the drama from the truck. He knew she would have seen the large surf, and was old enough to realize the significance in seeing her father getting thrown over the wave with the other man. In those horrendous conditions she probably didn't understand why her dad hadn't returned for so long, but she likely knew the situation was serious. Seeing the helicopter pulling the two men from the sea, perhaps she wondered if they were even alive. Like many guards, Don had always tried to shield his daughter from many of the harsh realities of his job. He reasoned there would be time to explain these things later, when she was older and could understand the nature of what her daddy did for a living.

McNulty had pulled out to the point and waited there while Don was gently lowered near his truck and the helo cleared the area. Osh could plainly see his ankle was fractured and wanted to splint it up and send him to Santa Rosa General for treatment. But first, Don needed to see Tiana. He stood up, dropped his buoy and his single fin, then hopped over to the truck to greet his daughter and hopefully alleviate her fears.

He reached the driver's door and there in the seat, dutifully *"not touching anything"* was his little girl, sitting with a very concerned look on her face. Seeing that she appeared to be traumatized by the event, Don, still in his wetsuit and dripping wet, questioned whether she had watched the whole rescue. She nodded *"Yes"* she had. He calmly explained the diver would be okay and that he too would be just fine after the doctors fixed his ankle.

Still seemingly concerned, Don eventually asked her what it was that was bothering her.

"I'm really sorry you spilled your coffee when you were getting out of the truck," she said.

Don looked down and saw that in fact he had knocked over his travel mug which was laying on the ground in a puddle of milky coffee. He laughed out loud. Apparently it was the spilled coffee which had caused her this grave concern. The dramatics of the spectacular rescue hadn't fazed her at all.

14

THE SCARS OF VALOR

Henry-I flight medic descends onto the scene

By the end of 1994, the original crew of the Sonoma Coast Lifeguard service had been decimated. The ocean had battered them far more than anyone would have expected, and nine of the originals had fled to safer pastures, licking their wounds and not daring to look back. Permanents Brown, Loeffler, Melvin, and Franklin were gone and the Seasonals had lost Carter, Schardt, Gulick, Haug and Martino - who had been accepted into the Peace Officer Academy, jumping ranks as a ranger. Only Straub and McNulty remained.

Don Straub would carry on for another year, then he too would depart to start his own construction company. His departure would end the unsurpassed and incomparable career of one of the most skilled and dynamic lifeguards to ever wear a pair of reds. With Don's departure, Osh McNulty would be the last man standing.

By then, new guards had arrived to fill the vacancies. Don and Osh trained them.

Coincidentally, around the same time, the sheriffs hired two new medics who were assigned to work with McConnell on Henry-I as the primary rescuers.

Although the two agencies always maintained a professional relationship in the field, a few of their elders still carried an undercurrent of ill-will from their early confrontations with the original crew and tainted opinions had been indoctrinated into new staff members on both sides. But the new medics, Eric Thompson and Robert DeLambert, happened to be gracious professionals who, not knowing any better, showed the guards a level of respect they were not accustomed to, providing a salve to heal old wounds they had no part in creating.

By then both sides had come to the realization they were joined in a common purpose and, working shoulder to shoulder, were essentially *fighting the same fight*. Before Thompson and DeLambert, no one had seemingly been able to swallow their pride long enough to admit it.

With their arrival, informal "debrief sessions" became common occurrences. After calls, they would land the chopper and hang out, leaning on the patrol truck to exchange a few stories. The sessions always ended in a handshake or a pat on the back. That might seem trivial to the outsider, but it was a huge gesture which was not wasted on the guards. The guards had finally received a measure of professional respect from the sheriffs they had craved since their inception. Without exaggeration, within months, DeLambert and Thompson helped to eradicate years of tension, and a solid bridge of camaraderie between the agencies was formed.

Flight crew and lifeguards "debrief" after a call – Salt Point (1996)

As if that was not enough, in an absolutely mind-blowing scenario, one of the guards jokingly suggested they attend the 8-day Lifeguard Academy in Huntington, adding that if they passed the curriculum, they could add *"Ocean Lifeguard"* to their pedigree. Despite the fact that neither of them had been competitive swimmers, they were given approval from their Sergeant and sure enough, they showed up at Huntington Beach the following June.

Entering the inner sanctum of the entity once viewed as the "competition" was the ultimate "olive branch" gesture and nothing short of historic. The two men trained diligently for six months and arrived as prepared as they could be. Despite their advanced medical skills well-beyond those of the instructor staff, they were humble and sat through all of the lectures. And despite not actually competing for a job, they participated in every aspect of the program.

In the evenings, they set up study groups and tutored the young rookies who were struggling with the medical skills. Then, each morning, with bold smiles on their faces, they were soundly smoked in the physical races and the ocean rescue drills by those young rookies.

In the end their deficiencies in the surf line, having never been competitive swimmers, torpedoed them, and they did not pass. Regardless, the greater gift lay in earning the guards' undying respect.

When they returned to Sonoma, they completely shot down the last of any lingering questions about the skill level of any State Guards, and both sides happily agreed to let bygones be bygones.

Henry-I dipping a wing to greet the lifeguards with a low fly-over

Thanks to DeLambert and Thompson, the relationship between the sheriffs and the guards would thrive. Their crew was invited to the State Parks events, and the guards were given free rides aboard Henry-I - in the cockpit as opposed to hanging on the static line below. From that point on, whenever a lifeguard was dealing with any kind of heavy rescue which necessitated Henry-I, they could be sure the paramedic being lowered to assist them viewed them not only as a peer, but also as a friend.

∽

Those 11 original guards arrived on the North Coast with the lofty goal of establishing a bonafide lifeguard service where there had never been one before.

After five long years of hardship, finding themselves embroiled in the combined distractions of the inter-personal struggles, the fracturing and exodus of their partners, the responsibilities of training the newly arriving guards, and the all-encompassing daily responsibilities of keeping people alive along the Sonoma Coast, no one, it seemed, had bothered to look up long enough to notice something truly remarkable...

They had succeeded.

There was no single day of proclamation or reverie etched onto the calendar which would become an annual celebration. No parade. No fireworks. No finish line with adoring crowds. In fact it was a fade so slow and subtle that few even took notice. But Hickey did.

Fittingly, only Straub and McNulty were left to enjoy it.

The five-year mark seems to be the benchmark by which they had firmly established themselves as the undisputed guardians of life in the ocean waters along the Sonoma Coast.

Although it's difficult to objectively evaluate the cumulative worth of any emergency response agency, by then, the crew had garnered the undeniable success for which they came. They had bolstered the boat program, purchasing a flashy bright orange 6-meter Hurricane Rigid-Hull Inflatable with twin 90-horse engines. The rescue vessel upgraded their response capabilities and made them

Osh McNulty and Don Straub (1994)

far more efficient to respond to off-shore events and work mutual aid calls with the Coast Guard.

Along with the new patrol vessel, the consequence of their proactive strategies and heroic acts in the overall provision of public safety were beyond reproach, and statistics relating to rescues and medical calls provided objective and undeniable proof of their value.

After performing hundreds of rescues, it was inevitable that stories of their exploits would spread throughout the community and eventually it was the rare local who chose to cling to their previous negative opinions of the lifeguards. Local reporters, hearing those same stories of daring rescues along their home coastline finally recognized those rescues made for captivating front page stories in their newspapers. With the fortification of the lifeguards' reputations as courageous and skilled watermen, any carry-over vilification of the guards in print would have seemed punitive and unjust.

And most importantly, at the 5-year mark of their existence, and despite the increased visitation and burgeoning popularity of abalone diving since their arrival, the appalling and fatalistic 40-year trend of ever-increasing drownings in their district, had decreased precipitously under their watch. In fact, a review of the statistics solidified an astounding reversal of the trends, with significant numbers which were immune to any anomaly. A theoretical continuation of the previous trend would have resulted in close to 50 ocean-related deaths during their first five years of existence. Instead the actual number of drownings amounted to just 18.

Undoubtedly, that number was still unacceptably high from the guards' perspective, but one important "qualifier" of those drownings shines an even greater light on the overall value of the lifeguards...

Every one of those 18 drownings occurred in "unguarded" water.

Considering the tens of thousands of swimmers, divers, and surfers which the lifeguards monitored directly for 5 full years, *not a single person drowned in their water.* Not one.

Pure and simple, by virtue of their proactive strategies, their public education, and their abilities to swim out and rescue people from the ocean when those first two measures failed, some 32 human beings are alive today who would have perished along the Sonoma Coast between 1990 and 1995 had it not been for the efforts of those guards. Brian Hickey's audacious plan, of bringing lifeguards to the North Coast to save lives, was realized.

Every one of those original North Coast Lifeguards had every right to sit back and acknowledge they had played a part in achieving their ultimate goal.

One of the monumental historical tragedies of the Sonoma Coast Lifeguard service - and yet another twist to their story - by the time their ultimate success had been realized, the vast majority of the original crew were already gone, thus there were precious few left to celebrate their ultimate success.

As mentioned near the outset of this book, many people in the greater circle of the North Coast populace expected the original crew would fail miserably in their endeavor to successfully guard their wild ocean, predicting they would escape in shame back to the beaches of Southern California with their tails between their legs.

On that account, the guards proved them wrong.

Where those locals were correct was in their assertion that the conditions on the North Coast would "kick their ass." Oddly though, the damage inflicted from that "ass-kicking" turned out to be of a manner no one had predicted. The terrorizations and graphic threats of the ocean's cold fury suggested the guards would not be able to withstand her raw power in making rescues. In that regard, the guards demonstrated in fact, *they could,* and they did make hundreds of rescues in those seas, including several dozen in conditions the sheriffs originally reported as being *"non-survivable."* But where the ocean most certainly over-powered the lifeguards was in her relentless and never-ending assault to their psyche. All of the guards seemingly did fine for several months - some, even for a year - but eventually the cumulative and all-encompassing effects of the job took a heavy toll on them....and while etching their names in the annals of lifeguarding history, I doubt any of them considered they would leave bearing a set of emotional scars they would carry for a lifetime.

In those formative years along the Sonoma Coast, the ocean proved to be a far more challenging adversary than they could ever have expected. Although the guards loved the bulk of their job, their job didn't love them back. As the guards began to bail, the district soon developed a well-earned reputation of chewing up lifeguards and spitting them out. The same enticing flames of challenging ocean conditions which lured them there and tested them with gripping rescues, were the same flames which ultimately burned them and drove them to leave. The pervasive fact that they could be killed in the course of making a rescue was a recurrent and eventually debilitating fear anytime those buoy readings exceeded 12', which, as stated, was quite often.

The isolation was another factor in their departure. The usual social diversions they had enjoyed in urban areas were simply not available to them. Winters were cold, damp and grey. The nights were long. In the winter, their wetsuits would not dry out for weeks. They contended with mold issues. Grocery shopping was a full-day undertaking to Santa Rosa which necessitated a drive over High Point. The prospects for dating were almost non-existent.

In addition to Martino, later arrivals who plied some of their Seasonal years on the North Coast would go on to become Perms. Among them were Griff Hutton, Kevin Craig, Todd Shanklin, Sean Homer, Tim Murphy, Brad Ewart, Levi Pior, and Ryan Peterson.

Beyond everything else, there's little doubt that a major factor in driving them away from the Sonoma Coast was the gruesome nature of drownings, body recoveries, suicides and the general carnage on land and sea. The cumulative effects eventually eroded through the defenses of even the most callous of lifeguards. Straub later admitted, *"People don't get it. They don't get what it takes to be in a situation where you deal with life and death over and over. We saw a lot of death. It took its toll on me. Emotionally. There's a part of me where compassion used to live that has been removed. I feel a certain disconnect from people. I rarely open up to people unless they are really close. Otherwise I keep my distance."*

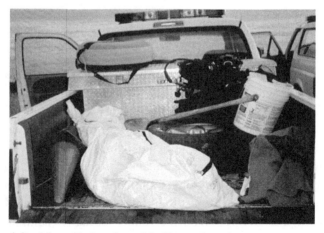

A diver's bagged body in the truck bed (year unknown)

Later in the same interview he further explained *"There's a part of me that's very jaded and removed. I have a hard time relating to people's perceived suffering and their 'first world' problems. When I hear them complaining about some inconsequential issue, sometimes I just want to yell at them to stop their bitching and tell them – Hey, you're alive!"*

A COASTLINE of SCARS

"...When lifeguards fail, people die. Fatal drownings have a way of becoming deeply etched into a lifeguard's memory. We lifeguards may not remember every heroic rescue we made, or every CPR we performed...but the drownings form deep scars which can stay with us for a lifetime...reminders of our failures which we will likely ponder on our death bed...."

— rookie graduation speech

Their universal doctrine to prevent drowning was the same one engrained into every man or woman who ever wore a pair of reds. When fate called on the ocean to snatch someone's father or son, or daughter or mother, and drag them to their death, it is the lifeguard who intercedes. In their actions the guard essentially declares "No" to Drowning. "Not on my watch. Not in my water." They intercede and perform the rescue, delivering the victim back to shore to reunite with their kin. That's what lifeguards do. In their world, swimmers aren't supposed to die.

And yet, in rare circumstances - which occurred more frequently on the North Coast - and despite the efforts and heroics of the lifeguards in saving most of them, 18 people still died. And although the guards arrived on the North Coast fully expecting to face those tragedies, with rare exception, they proved to be grossly ill-equipped to deal with the aftermath of those deaths.

～

The quantification and assessment of drownings can be grouped by year, location, cause, season, age, or any other number of demograhics.

Statisticians and bureaucrats utilize these groupings to view the larger picture in the realm of social health and accident prevention. In the course of these pages, I too am guilty of the same tactic to highlight the gravity of the issue of drowning along the Sonoma Coast.

But for the lifeguards there, lumping those drownings together in any grouping of statistical analytics feels repulsive. Each and every death involved a father, mother, son, or daughter who lost their life there, and left a loving family to grieve. Those guards were personally involved in every one of the tragedies and similarly, they grieved for those individuals too. They would remember their names and study their obituary photos in the newspapers to see what they looked like when they were alive. Long after the families, the medics, the Deputies and the bystanders left the heartbreaking scene of their death, the crew remained behind and continued to patrol there for the rest of the day, and then the following day, the following month, and the following year....because the victim had come to the *lifeguard's home* to die.

Every day they passed those ill-fated places, the powerful memories resurfaced. New tourists would arrive at those same majestic spots, piling out of their cars laughing, wholly oblivious to the tragedies which had occurred there, and eager to be inspired by the grandeur of the wild seascapes. But the guards viewed those same locations through the blackened lens of grief. As time went on, and the number of tragedies climbed, the coastline became tainted in an ever-expanding map of sorrow...The CPR on the diver at South Gerstle, the child drowning at Wright's Beach, the spot where the elderly couple drove off the road at High Point, and so many more.

And reminiscent of Hickey's orientation tour at the beginning of their time there, where he branded each location with harrowing stories of *past* tragedies, those guards now had experienced their own collection of calamities which created their own *coastline of scars*.

When the program started in 1990, there was little talk about PTSD. At that time I was entering my 15th year as a lifeguard and I had only heard the term used for military people coming home from wars. Like all guards, the North Coast crew of pioneers were expected to be tough, and after responding to yet another vehicle which had gone over the cliff with mangled bodies scattered on the bluffs, or recovering yet another dead diver from the bottom of the ocean while the family watched from shore, any confession these events somehow *affected them*, would have been seen as an admission of weakness.

With the exception of Audrey Haug (whom I was unable to track down), in my interviews with the original guards, every one of them admitted they left with varying degrees of emotional scars. In fact, three of the original crew were granted an early retirement as a result of significant cumulative stress issues incurred during their time on the Sonoma Coast. It was the first time any of us had ever heard of a lifeguard retiring as a result of the psychological damage from stress-related issues.

I have little doubt *all of the guards* suffered from various degrees of PTSD, yet those three were the only ones who were obligated to admit their issues as part of being granted a stress-related medical retirement. One member of the original crew had what many referred to as a "nervous breakdown" shortly after leaving. When the powers-that-be reviewed the specifics of the horrendous issues they had been forced to deal with, there was little doubt as to the veracity of their claims.

Many of the guards who followed them suffered a similar fate. Three of the guards I worked with in the late '90s, who will remain nameless, still admit to having recurrent nightmares of insane rescues on rocky shorelines in large surf. If I am being honest here, I do too.

Some 20 years after Martino had worked his last day on the Sonoma Coast, he returned to visit those familiar beaches while on a family road trip. While descending down the main road to Goat Rock, without warning he suddenly began having

Martino extricates a victim from his totaled vehicle (1993) – Photo: Loeffler

"flash backs" of sordid events he had experienced there. He could feel his heart rate climbing and his blood pressure rise. For God sakes, it had *been over two decades* since his last day working there, yet his sympathetic nervous system still jumped into a primal stress response just from *being there*. Simply put, the staggering consequence of working the Sonoma Coast furrowed deep and lasting scars into the psyche of the guards.

As further proof of cumulative scars associated with the North Coast; despite the intoxicating beauty and grandeur of the Sonoma Coastline and their varied levels of assimilation into the community, *not one of them* settle there. The painful memories haunting them in so many locations along that stretch of coastline eclipsed the inherent beauty. True. After having lived there in the prime chapters of their lives, and enduring some of the most spectacular moments of their careers there, few of them would ever return to the Sonoma Coast - even to visit. They rode off to other counties, other states and other countries and never looked back.

Working for a Department which spanned over 600 miles, the door had always been open for any of these proven guards to transfer back to their home beaches in Southern California to bask in the warm water, body surf without wetsuits, pursue their social lives, dine in restaurants, and enjoy the conveniences and luxuries of the urban lives they had missed for so long...all for the same paycheck. But strangely, after they had worked the North Coast, the only members of the crew to return to Southern California as lifeguards were Dave Carter and (much later) Mike Martino.

Furthermore, and rather astonishingly, upon leaving the North Coast, Bud Brown, Kurt Loeffler, Scott Melvin, Steve Franklin, Don Straub, Dave Schardt, Jon Gulick, and Audrey Haug never wore a pair of reds again.

After citing a bold fact like that, it's rather disappointing to me to admit I don't have the follow up answer as to "why."

Most assuredly, an element of social distance affected the crew as well. Most of them admitted feeling disconnected from the general population. Similar to the phenomenon of soldiers returning from war, many of them reported feeling a sense of being *misunderstood* and had difficulty *fitting in* to society on the whole.

I am no psychologist, but in scrutinizing the emotional fallout endured by the original crew, I found it interesting that despite the fact that 85% of Americans have children, *NONE of the original Permanents had kids*. In fact, only *three* of the eleven guards in total (Schardt, Carter and Gulick) had children after they had left the North Coast.

McNULTY'S LEGACY

And so it was, after weathering the collective barrage of Sonoma Coast drama; frightening rescues, isolation, processing hundreds of poacher's citations and arrests, responding to a myriad of atrocious land-based calamities, and having to witness the painful melodrama surrounding his supervisor's departure, Osh McNulty was still there, making the same heroic rescues and busting the same avaricious poachers. He had watched his original crew suffer through the anguish and stress which beat them down and ultimately took them out, yet after enduring the first five years of the craziness of the Sonoma Coast, remarkably *Osh McNulty carried on working there for another 14 years!*

Furthermore, despite enduring a tenure almost *four times longer* than any of the original crew, Osh had seemingly managed to insulate himself from the battery of abuse which had affected his peers so intensely. Beyond comprehension, McNulty emerged free from the dark tunnel of the Sonoma Coast Lifeguard experience largely unscathed.

This is not an inconsequential point. If Osh had tapped into some technique or spiritual practice, or some method which allowed him to cope with the ultimate stressors of his multi-faceted role of being a Peace Officer / Lifeguard on the North Coast, there was an army of fellow emergency response workers out there in the world who were eagerly awaiting to find out how he pulled it off, and ready to assimilate his methods into their own daily coping strategies.

Without exaggeration, I had pondered this for the entire seven years

I worked with Osh, and routinely questioned him about "*How he did it?*" Not one to elaborate on matters of the heart, Osh offered little explanation beyond a shrug of the shoulders.

Almost 20 years later, as I began my research for this book and began my interviews with the many characters which by now, you've undoubtedly come to know and love, I embarked on a deeper dive into the lives of those original guards; and clearly the emotional fall-out and scars were a large part of their story. It was then that Osh's mysterious method of coping reemerged into the forefront of my mind.

Each recalled many of their dramatic events and rescues with uncanny clarity and precision. This, of course, provided welcomed fodder as I sought to capture as many details as possible. As each one of them tapped into colorful details of some of the most profound memories of their lives, I feverishly scratched it all down in an ever-expanding treasure trove of notes that would eventually fill three spiral-bound notebooks.

Osh McNulty – his final year as a lifeguard (2009) – Photo: Tom Neth

Ironically, it was Osh, whom I had worked with the most, who proved to be the most difficult to interview. In a series of three phone calls, the amount of tangible material I got from him - despite his storied tenure - was *significantly less than any of the others.* I would prod him for stories and it was like the proverbial *pulling of teeth.* When I asked specifically about events he had been involved in, including some calls we had worked together, after pondering awhile, the most common response he gave was a rather unsatisfying, "*I can't remember.*" I should point out here that after working together for 7 years, I consider him among my closest friends, thus I know he was not trying to hide anything from me. He genuinely *could not remember the majority of his* rescues, some of which were dramatic as hell!

After each phone call, I resigned myself to the same obvious conclusion that McNulty, despite his brilliant and analytical mind, had the *worst memory of any of my peers.*

Then, in 2019, a week after one of those calls, I had my epiphany, discovering what I believe to be Osh McNulty's magic elixir. In the end, it was as obvious as could be. In fact, it was so obvious that he had already expressed it to me innumerable times already, but I had never chosen to listen. In trying to lead him back to re-visit those powerful moments and those awe-inspiring rescues, he continually responded with;

"I can't remember."

Osh McNulty couldn't remember.

Using the most conservative standards, I estimated McNulty had been involved with over 50 fatalities in both land and sea along the North Coast – though the actual number is likely significantly higher. That conservative fatality estimate would be among the most endured by any lifeguard working on the West Coast of the United States, if not the world. Additionally, with his small crew, he was often tasked with having to deal with many of those deaths *personally*, in all of their tragic forms, including the body recoveries of dead divers - some partially decomposed - from the bottom of the ocean which, as any veteran guard will tell you, is probably the most unpleasant part of the job. His tally of heroic rescues exceeded those of any other lifeguard who had ever worked in the district. In fact, no one was even close.

But looking back over his storied 20-year career there, he *couldn't remember much.*

One of the essential doctrines in Buddhism is the quest for *non-attachment.* I am certainly no expert on the subject, but as a lay-Buddhist I understand that concept involves the tendency for our minds to bind our sense of *self* to a myriad of objects, ideas, and emotions. We are inclined to *cling* to good things - which never last - and develop *aversions* to bad things - which also never last. In both examples, we tend to *dwell* on things.

On the North Coast, when "bad" things happened, the tendency for the guards involved - as it would be for most of us - was to ponder the event for days and months, clinging to the pain and the associated trauma by re-living the events in their minds....wondering why this had to happen and questioning their decisions, abilities, and even their worth.

But Osh was a man who lived squarely in the moment. His ultimate elixir in dealing with and coping with these events, as it turned out, was his uncanny ability to *let the events go*. No dwelling. No pondering. No re-living or questioning. No clinging. Once he cleared the scene, he would let the trauma wash away, making no attempt hold onto it.

This is not to suggest he was superficial or cold. He was, and still is a kind, generous and empathetic man with his friends and most certainly served his community with a generous spirit.

Osh performed to his best abilities on those calls, and many - though not all - ended favorably. Knowing he had done his best, he walked away from every call, and eventually his collective career, without regret...regardless of the outcomes of any specific call. Thus, without clinging or attachment, it was easy to forget them. Which he did. Apparently quite successfully.

Of course the down-side is that the details of many of his great rescues are lost. Thankfully, I was able to obtain many of Osh's stories from other guards who were on-scene with him for many of his calls, but one can only wonder how many other great stories had already passed from his recollection.

An old adage I once heard, in reference to Tim Harvey, was that he had *forgotten* more great rescues than the average veteran lifeguard would *ever make*. The sentiment most certainly was true for McNulty.

In retrospect, performing CPR on his first day of work was a fitting opening act for Osh's time on the North Coast, and was followed by 20 more years of drama until his eventual retirement in 2009. His farewell party at Fort Ross was attended by a large and enthusiastic crowd of his friends and coworkers who were thrilled to witness the departure of a true legend in the field of lifeguarding. The man who greeted them that night, still scrappy as hell, was still quite capable of performing the job at the highest level of competence. Only his salt and pepper hair (by then more salt than pepper) revealed his age, and on that night Osh fielded the compliments and praise from his peers, ever the humble warrior.

The following day, he and Karen loaded up their truck and headed off to Oregon.

They never looked back.

McNulty's retirement celebration (2009) – (Osh and Karen – behind their new dog)

Rewinding the clock back to 1994, in the fall, I made my humble entry onto the North Coast.

I was fortunate enough to work alongside both Straub and McNulty. Looking back, it was the perfect time to arrive as the earlier drama was over and we were in the process of rebuilding the crew, staffing it with easy-going yet dedicated guards who genuinely liked each other, and worked well together. Over the next few years we added stalwarts like Tom Neth, Paul "Pablo" Barnes, Mark James, Hoon Kim, Nate Buck and Brit Horn.

Many more would follow, immersing themselves in the operation and adding their names to the roster of the North Coast guards. With such a small and intertwined crew, each guard would contribute their personality and experiences to the overall flavor and reputation of the force. The new guards would develop their own style and methods, adding to the foundation which had been laid by their predecessors.

By the end of 1995, with the overhaul of the crew complete, the operation would find a sense of peace and stability the original crew had once thought impossible. The system was working. Following the playbook they had constructed, new guards patrolled proactively, making scores of contacts and performing skilled rescues with success. On almost every rescue, that "One Guard Out" could be assured a back-up guard was speeding to his location and would be covering him from shore, ready to swim out to assist, or call for Henry-I to bail them out.

The North Coast Crew: Paul Barnes, Vodrazka, Mark James, Hoon Kim, Nate Buck, McNulty, Tom Neth (1996)

While the next wave of lifeguards changed the vibe of the service, the ocean never relented, dishing out the same wrath for the new guards it had for the original crew. Those new guards came with the same fire in their bellies, eager to prove themselves, and to forge their skills.

Thus, with our story coming full-circle, you might assume the narrative of the original Sonoma Coast lifeguard pioneers has come to an end.

But not quite.

In order to truly understand the "end" of their "beginning", we need to carry on down the path of the original guards' history just one rescue further...

15

STRAUB'S FINAL RESCUE

The site of the Straub's rescue – on a calmer day in (1995) – Photo: Vodrazka

Over the course of a career, lifeguards make plenty of rescues. The majority of them tend to morph together, and the specifics are difficult to isolate or remember. The standards which make a rescue "memorable" tend to involve the critical nature of the event, or those which placed the rescuer in the greatest personal risk, and many variables come into play to bolster these elements. The ocean conditions and surf size are obvious factors, but so too are the number and age of the victims, the water temperature, the time of day/night, and of course, whether or not the victim survived.

As you have no doubt gathered by now, the North Coast is a fertile area for *phenomenal rescues*. And eventually, the larger lifeguard world took notice. Despite being the smallest agency on the West Coast - with an average crew of just of 6-8 individuals - and the fact that many of their great rescues were never submitted for consideration, in the first ten years of their existence, *the Sonoma Coast Lifeguards would be awarded more Medals of Valor for heroism than any lifeguard agency in the world.*

Feel free to pause a moment to reread that last statement and let it sink in.

I will close this final chapter with one last event which happened to occur during my second year on the North Coast. By then I had already made my share of rescues on ill-prepared scuba divers and rock pickers, and towed many exhausted free divers out of rips at Secrets, Windermere, Timber Cove, Fort Ross, Horseshoe Cove, and off the Face of Salt Point. I had also recovered the bodies of dead divers from Ocean Cove, South Gerstle, and Fisk Mill Cove. Yet, if I am being honest, I still felt a need to prove myself worthy as a North Coast Lifeguard.

On a Saturday morning in the fall, as usual, the divers arrived at Salt Point. Although the surf was a solid 8', the protective coves still offered passable conditions to dive. Unfortunately, the buoy readings foretold of an advancing swell of some significance, expected to reach the coastline that morning, and the breaking waves were expected to double in size. Many of the experienced divers, aware of the coming swell, arrived early to get in and out before the swell hit.

That morning we received an emergency call reporting a diver struggling in the ocean along the northern part of "The Face," south of Stump Beach. That expanse of coastline, as previously explained, was a mile long rocky stretch with no beach and limited access. With almost no protection from the northwest swell, it was an area seldom safe enough to dive, conversely it was one of the premier spots where veteran divers found trophy-sized abalone.

~~~

Two hours earlier, four experienced divers decided they would take their chances diving there. They hiked out with all their gear, walked out to a rocky ledge and jumped into the 50° water directly off the face. They knew their efforts to hike off the beaten path, coupled with their courage to dive off the exposed area would be worth it. The 8' surf was certainly challenging, but since the entire area was rocky, their plan was to kick far from shore and dive the deeper water, where the surge would be manageable and they would be rewarded with some trophy-sized abalone. All four of them made the jump, and safely kicked quite a distance from shore.

Their plan seemed sound, and diving in 30' of water, all four men filled their floats with limits of sizable abalone. Unfortunately, distracted by the thrill of the hunt, none of them realized that the predicted swell had arrived, and the large surf they had entered with some trepidation two hours earlier, had now doubled in size. Along with the swell, the rising tide had filled in as well. As they assessed the rocky shoreline, they could see their planned exit spot was getting soundly hammered by thick and ominous 10' walls of water crashing spectacularly onto the rocks.

Having dove there before in more favorable conditions, they knew their best down-current exit was at Gerstle Cove, but that meant kicking with their heavy game bags for upwards of a mile; easily an hour-long proposition. After their lengthy dive in the frigid water, they were not only exhausted, but also shivering with the onset of hypothermia, so the prospect of having to spend another hour in the water was not an option. The gravity of their situation quickly settled in. They needed to get out of that ocean...and they could see no viable option to escape.

Still short of panicking, they thought about summoning for help from the lifeguards, but in choosing to dive in that remote location, there was no one on shore to yell to. Floating together off-shore, the passing swells lifted and lowered them, and they could watch the waves roll and break in spectacular fashion on the rocky shoreline. Adding to their frustration, they could see the safe haven of solid ground, not more than 100 yards away, but in a practical sense, that refuge was a world away. Between them and safe solid earth, was an inaccessible 12' wall of dark, barnacle encrusted rocks, with imposing jagged prominences which extended in either direction as far as they could see, all of which was getting bombarded by a relentless barrage of waves.

They had no way out.

Just to their south was a large rock separated from shore by a channel. Like a narrow island, the massive rock was probably 40 yards long and 5 yards wide. The channel separating it from solid land was about 15' wide and probably 15' deep. Its orientation, size and structure created a most unique dynamic of hydrology with the incoming swells. Like blood being pushed into a constricted artery or hose water being sprayed through a high pressure nozzle, the breaking waves, rushing into the narrow gap from the north intensified the flow, raising the water level dramatically, and sending a powerful surge wave through the channel, purging out through the south end.

Additionally, the waves entered in from the southern end, causing a reverse surge, flowing in from the opposite direction. At times the two waves converged in the middle of the channel, dramatically raising the water level 15' or more. Worse yet, the larger swells washed over the entire structure, completely engulfing it with a 5' thick wall of water, and creating an enormous wide waterfall which dumped into the channel from above.

The men were trapped between two choices, both of which were bad. Reality quickly consumed them and their plan for an enjoyable outing of abalone diving had now morphed into a serious situation.

Still well off-shore, they gathered together to consider their options. The most experienced diver in the group was a 51-year old man who had over ten years of experience as a diver. The group looked to him for guidance, but he was unable to offer any viable plan. With their bodies already stiff and their minds somewhat confused from their worsening hypothermia, all of the men agreed that spending another hour in the water kicking south to Gerstle Cove was out of the question. Kicking north to Stump Beach would involve a substantial fight against the longshore current, which was now flowing stronger with the increasing swell, making it an incredible challenge at best, and more likely, impossible.

With no one to yell to for help, and no other option in sight, three of the men decided their only escape would be to kick directly in, towards a sloping rocky ledge they had seen when they entered. Fully expecting to get hammered and realizing the gravity of their predicament, they smartly ditched their weight belts and abalone irons. With their revised priority of simply getting out alive, and a desire to be as light as possible, they also released the prized abalone from their floats, letting them sink back to the bottom. Thus, they would attempt to escape wearing just mask and fins, riding on their abalone floats, which they hoped might buffer them from the rocks.

The elder diver was not at all comfortable with their plan. He felt the waves were far too big to "ride" directly onto the rocks and the men might be seriously hurt while getting slammed onto the jagged ledge. He decided he would wait outside and watch his partners from the water to see how they fared.

In a last minute decision, in order to traverse through the impact area more quickly the three divers ditched their float tubes as well. Thus, left with just mask and fins, they readied themselves for their attempt to traverse through the impact zone to reach land.

Waiting until just after a set had passed, and praying for a respite in the form of a lull, together they began kicking in a frenzy of energy hoping to escape from the ocean before the next set came.

They did not make it.

Halfway to shore, the men looked back and saw the imposing sight of a large set of waves approaching and they knew they could not escape. For several seconds they kicked on in futility, knowing the massive wave was chasing them down, poised to annihilate them.

The first of three huge walls of water lifted them and slammed them directly onto the rocky ledge, tearing their fins from their feet and beating them savagely on the rocky ledge. Then, as they were being pulled back towards the sea with an almost equal ferocity by the retreating backwash, the second wave crashed on them again, repeating the abuse and submerging them in a wall of water. The water soon retreated and the men struggled to breathe while they futilely grabbed for any structure to hold onto. Unable to grasp any kind of handhold, the water dragged them back over the rocks, cutting their wetsuits and exposed body parts on the sharp barnacles.

Subsequent waves pummeled them again, ripping off their masks, and pushing them farther up the rocky ledge. During the retreating wall of water, again they scrambled to grab hold of any prominence. Two of the men, fortuitously were eventually able to grab hold of the rocks and resist the pull of the receding wave, but the third man was then pulled completely off the rocks and back into the deeper water. As the backwash completed its retreat, the two who were able to hold on, like beaten animals, began crawling clumsily over the rocks, but mercifully they were able to climb high enough to reach safety.

The following wave, now carrying the body of the third diver, thrust him, yet again onto the rocks where he extended his hand to the others for assistance, but both men were still in the process of saving themselves and unable to help him. Luckily, his hands found a jagged outcropping which he clutched with all of his strength. Like the others, he resisted the profound and weighty pull of the retreating backwash and was able to maintain his grip until it passed. Bruised and thoroughly exhausted, he too crawled over the jagged rocks to reach the sanctuary of higher ground.

Between the three men, the ocean had stripped them of almost all of their remaining gear. But in the big picture, the loss of their gear was a small price to pay. The three men had essentially ridden a 10' wave directly onto a rock reef. Their wetsuits torn, they were bruised and bloody, but all three had survived the ordeal.

They gathered together and spontaneously embraced, celebrating their successful escape from the ocean. Moments later, they spotted a lone jogger and yelled at him to run to Gerstle to get the lifeguards to come rescue the last diver. The jogger dutifully ran off to summon help.

Separated from their partner by the sight and sound of the daunting impact zone of the breaking waves, the men yelled out over the breaking waves to let the elder diver know they had summoned help for him. But their cries were futile. Had he heard them, perhaps he could have held on for another 30 minutes until Henry-I arrived and plucked him free from the ocean. Unfortunately he heard nothing but the continued crashing of the waves.

From his vantage point in the ocean, the veteran diver had witnessed the disastrous extrication play out and decided he wanted no part of getting slammed onto the rocks. He would have remembered seeing the channel on his way out, and must have reasoned it might provide him with shelter from the direct impact of the surf.

Unfortunately he had no way of knowing how dramatically the surf had intensified inside the channel. With seemingly no other viable option, he made a decision that he would enter the channel, and once inside, would try to find a way out. It was a decision which would cost him dearly.

He yelled something out to his partners but they couldn't decipher what he said. Then the three divers stood on the edge and watched as he started kicking towards the channel from the north. As he got close, he was swept up by a large wave and thrust into the middle section of the channel. Another wave then greeted him from the south end spitting him back out of the mouth through the north end. By then he had placed himself in the no man's land of the impact zone. He was again swept back into the channel and only at that point did he realize the walls of the channel were vertical, offering no viable place to climb out. Worse yet, there was no way to escape from the relentless sets of waves entering from both ends.

He tried unsuccessfully to grab the rock wall, but he was hurtling far too fast and the buffering of the waves against the rocks prevented him for getting close enough to grab hold. His friends watched from the ledge directly above him. At times he washed past them so close that they could see the fear in his eyes, yet with no rope or any flotation to offer him, they were left to helplessly watch as he struggled to escape the channel on his own.

The elder diver soon realized he had ventured into an unescapable trap. As if the assaulting waves slamming him from either end weren't enough, the huge set waves rolled completely over the rock, fully engulfing it and creating a resultant waterfall which poured over him, driving him under and holding him down under the substantial weight of the water. Relentlessly, the ocean continued to punish the man with repeated blows; sending more waves from either end. Then, as if the ocean had intentionally positioned him in the most vulnerable position near the middle of the channel, another monstrous wave roared over the top of the rock and submerged him, yet again, under another massive wall of whitewater.

Time after time the diver held his breath as the waves pushed him down and held him under, and each time his friends watched in horror, waiting for his head to re-appear. The diver, strong and tenacious, fought valiantly to stay alive, but just as he had endured the deluge of the waterfall, the north swell would start again, reengaged in the battle with the opposing south swell. Between waves he repeatedly tried with futility to maintain a hold of the rock wall and climb out of this cauldron, but it was hopeless. With each new wave, he was once again peeled off with his arms extended, reaching helplessly in the direction of the rock while being pulled back into the maelstrom of watery hell.

After a lengthy battle, fighting for his very life, he must have come to the realization that it was only a matter of time before he would lose his struggle, and that this deadly channel would become his tomb.

And ultimately, with all three of his friends shouting encouragement while watching from less than 30' away, a massive rogue wave delivered a huge wall of water which poured over him from above, submerging him deeply. It proved to be the final beating from which he would not resurface. His partners, having witnessed him being swallowed whole by the ocean, stood in a collective disbelief.

By then the jogger had reached the main lot at Gerstle and notified Tom Neth and me of the situation. We sped off code-three down the rutted road, witnessing the huge surf crashing along the way and marveling that anyone would have gone into the ocean in those conditions. While Tom drove, I suited up in my wetsuit and pulled my fins out of my pack.

We ran the final 100-yards to the edge of the channel where we saw the three divers standing. One of the divers, obviously upset, yelled out that they had just watched their friend drown in the channel not more than 10-minutes earlier. I asked one of them where they last saw him, and the man pointed down into the churning waters, directly in front of where we were standing. With no plan, or even so much as a word of discussion with my partner, I sat on the ground and pulled on my fins, then yelled to one of the divers, "Throw me your mask!"

Then, in a moment which still gives me shudders as I write this almost 25 years later, I stood up, looked into the channel, took a deep breath, and jumped into the same turbulent waters which had just killed the man.

I made one surface dive in hopes of finding his body, but of course it was impossible to see anything in the tumultuous murky water. I tried a second dive, descending blindly in a mass of bubbles and debris, with my arms outstretched, blindly groping for an arm or a leg.

While I was near the bottom in 10' of water, an unseen wave from the south end jettisoned my body violently to the north. Disoriented, I surfaced, surprised to see I had been thrust under the water a solid 25-yards from where I had dove down. Worse yet, the surge had delivered me clear of the north end of the channel, and into the impact zone. Seconds later another wave came from the north, and having no control over the situation, I took a deep breath and tried to dive under it, bracing to see where it would take me. The wave shot me right back into the mouth of the channel, delivering me past my initial entry spot. Another wave then shot in from the south end which pushed me back into the middle of the channel. For a few moments, the competing swells from north and south pushed me back and forth. I felt utterly helpless amidst the powerful display of the ocean's whims. But the worst was yet come. A larger set arrived and huge waves washed completely over the top of the immense rock, pushing me below the surface under the weight of a massive wall of water, holding me down, and forcing me to hold my breath until the flow abated. Feeling the intensity and mass of the water, I suddenly realized how the diver had been killed.

Like him, I too had no control of my situation. The waves were relentless, and the ocean continued its game, playing with me like an insignificant toy being thrown back and forth by the power of the surging water. At one point I looked up and saw McNulty and Straub had arrived and were standing on the rocks far above me. Curiously, for a fleeting moment I felt an odd sense of pride, realizing these legends of lifeguarding were now witness to me risking my ass, fully invested in my predicament. One can imagine my surprise when, instead of yelling out words of support or praise for my efforts to try and recover the dead man's body, Osh screamed out the rather disconcerting question;

"WHAT THE HELL ARE YOU DOING IN THERE!???"

In retrospect it was a very good question for which I didn't have a ready answer.

In deed - What the hell was I doing in there????

Well, up until that very moment, I *thought* I was demonstrating the skills and daring qualities of a North Coast Lifeguard. But in light of his question, apparently I was f***ing up royally.

In my haste to recover the diver's body, I hadn't stopped to think things through. In those conditions the diver was already dead, and in that turbulence there was no way in hell I would find him. Even if I did, extricating him from the channel would have been impossible. Additionally, I had violated the golden rule of "Scene Safety" and my partners were now faced with the newly emerged challenge of rescuing *ME* from the same deadly predicament which had just killed the man, and I was now in the process of getting my ass *soundly kicked* by those same waves.

It was Straub who quickly pulled his wetsuit on and approached the edge of the channel wall. Feeling for, then establishing a solid handhold anchor with his right hand at the top of the ledge, he lowered his body over the side, testing then finding two decent footholds. He then faced the channel and extended his left hand out in hopes he could grab me as the ocean pushed me past. I could see Don's outstretched hand reaching for me and I understood what he was trying to do, but each time a surge of water pushed me towards him, just as quickly, having little influence over my trajectory, I was swept past him. Don saw that too, but he was not one to give up. Despite being hit by the intermittent brunt of the waves himself, he lowered himself *farther down* from the safety of the ledge, until the waves were breaking on him with some force. The obvious worry for all of us was that one of the larger waves would blast him off the rocks and dump him into the channel with me.

After several more close passes, a larger wave appeared which propelled me directly in Straub's direction. I had to overcome my natural instincts to avoid swimming directly into the jagged wall, but I stroked hard, and essentially rode the wave directly towards the rocks. As the wave crashed against the wall, engulfing Don, I extended my right hand in Straub's direction and felt Don snatch it, grabbing my wrist. He then held on while the water retreated, allowing me to grab onto the wall. I latched on to the rocks like a tree frog, and seconds later, both Don and I were able to scramble our way up the wall and crest the ledge with the help of Osh and Tom.

I shook Don's hand and offered a heart-felt thanks before fielding some good-natured ribbing from my partners.

Unfortunately for the victim, there was nothing more we could do. The three surviving divers stared into the cauldron for some time, all likely imagining his body being battered somewhere along the bottom. We all knew, with that amount of water moving, he could have been anywhere by then. Osh explained to the divers that no further rescue actions would be taken. As they processed the gravity of his statement and the reality that their buddy was gone, Osh answered the question they were likely pondering, explaining that we would now have to wait for his body to surface, which usually took at least three days.

Having seen our attempted rescue first hand, his friends understood. They thanked us. My sense of empathy for the loss of their friend was profound, and I apologized, adding that we were sorry we couldn't do more. Osh and Straub cleared, and eventually I sat on the rocks with them and made a futile attempt to console them. Neth gathered their information and explained that the family would be notified when his body was recovered. Henry-I arrived soon after and made several passes of the area in hopes of spotting the body, but were unsuccessful.

Four days later, the diver's body was seen by a fisherman, floating face-down in Fisk Mill Cove. Confounding all of our estimates, it had travelled a distance of over two miles, *against* the prevailing swell direction. Such is the power and mystery of the ocean. Straub was on duty and retrieved the diver's body by himself.

A week later I was on a routine patrol with Don on the rescue boat. The swell had tapered considerably and we were enjoying a rare calm and sunny day. With no active calls or any valid reason to burn fuel, we dropped anchor just outside Gerstle Cove and sat on the sponson, peeling our wetsuits down to our waists and enjoying the rare sensation of the warm sun on our skin. We entertained ourselves narrating the antics of the beginning scuba students in the protected cove and shared a laugh. From my first days there Don had shown me a sense of respect I wasn't sure I deserved, but most certainly appreciated. I think the mutual esteem we felt for each was rooted in elements of our lives which extended far beyond lifeguarding. By then, over the dozens of shifts riding together in the boat and the patrol truck, Don and I had already delved into many of the deeper topics of life and become close.

The mood was light, and there, while bantering in the random topics of conversation, I tried to find the words to thank him for pulling me out of that precarious situation in the channel the week before. I fumbled over the impromptu speech, and the words didn't adequately express exactly what I was trying to say. In the end, I joked that without his efforts, I would likely still be caught in that cauldron and we both laughed. But Don understood. If nothing else, Don Straub was a soulful guy who understood matters of life and death. He may have passed it off as "no big deal" to graciously forgive my debt to him, but we both knew that *it was a big deal.*

After the channel rescue - and probably because of it - Don and I became tighter. By then, his days as a guard were numbered, as he had already started his construction company in Cloverdale.

For those original guards, accepting their position as a lifeguard on the North Coast came with a critical and unquestionable responsibility to protect and cover for each other. And every time that need arose, those lifeguards proved worthy and answered that call without hesitation. Instances of their teamwork and camaraderie flourished in those first five years; whether swimming out to back each other on rescues, belaying each other on cliff rescues, pulling each other onto the boat, or coordinated their partner's extrication from outside the surf line.

And it wasn't until months later, when Don was already gone, that I had the rather profound realization that after focusing on the hundreds of rescues he had made along the North Coast, Don's "Last Great Rescue" was not on an anonymous member of the public, but rather in hoisting a *fellow lifeguard* out of a truly sketchy situation. To say that Don saved my life that day might be an exaggeration, but if so, it wasn't by much.

The colorful Don Straub certainly had his share of foibles, and there were those who never allowed him into their inner circle, but I was not one of them. After sharing in the camaraderie of lifesaving on the Sonoma Coast, I miss all of the lifeguards I worked with, but I will always hold a special place in my soul for Don Straub.

"It's a Great Day....to be a State Lifeguard"

EPILOGUE

The patrol truck on a beautiful spring day – North Sector (1995)

Like any good story, questions naturally arise regarding the guard's eventual careers, families, assorted exploits, and ultimate landing zones. After peeking into the prime years of their lives some 30 year ago, when they were young and fearless ocean gladiators, then delving into their successes and failures, this book would seem incomplete if we didn't know where they ended up.

To that end...

BUD BROWN

Bud Brown reported for duty at Silverwood Lake, embarking on a completely new journey in a novel role as an *Interpretive Specialist*. In this new position, he would be free from law enforcement duties, there would be no surf to contend with, nor the responsibilities of managing gut-wrenching medical aids and rescues. Additionally, he would have no defiant staff to administer to, and for the bulk of his work days, he would be spending more time in the company of bald eagles than human beings.

Unfortunately, by then a detrimental toll had already been inflicted on his psyche and he arrived there rattled and scarred. Although the undeniable beauty of the outside world surrounded him in peace and quietude, the inside world of his mind was still reeling. The depth of those wounds "to his soul" - as he put it - manifested themselves in bouts of chronic anxiety, and proved to be resistant to the tranquility surrounding him. It didn't take long for Bud to realize this new assignment was not the panacea he had hoped for.

Although the duty statement for this new position specified far fewer responsibilities, seemingly guaranteeing him an opportunity to heal and recover, every day he pulled his uniform from the hanger, he saw the same State Parks' logo on the patch which stirred a bitter reminder of the collective anguish he had endured on the Sonoma Coast. In the end, even this seemingly idyllic position could not tip the scales of the collective darkness which continuing to work for the State Parks created.

Seeing no viable method to mitigate the ongoing stress, in a surprisingly bold move, Bud not only resigned from this dream job, but walked away from the State Parks entirely.

Yet no one could have foreseen the extent to which Bud Brown would escape from the life he had worked so hard to carve out for himself. After resigning his position and walking away from his pension, Bud fled from every peripheral aspect of his work life as well, severing ties with all of the friends and acquaintances he had made in the decade he had worked as a lifeguard, including those who were once dear to him.

His name came up often in the early years after his departure, but attempts by several guards to locate him proved unsuccessful, and it soon became clear that he was a man hell-bent on vaporizing himself clear from anything associated with lifeguarding, the ocean, State Parks, swimming, and even California.

Bud Brown simply vanished.

Eventually, rumors surfaced he had returned to Kansas, and some 20 years after he had left, while searching on Facebook, I found a realtor in Leavenworth (Bud's home town) named "Norman Brown" who looked like he could be an aged version of Bud. I made several attempts to connect with him but got no response.

Then an amazing thing happened...

In the summer of 2021, I retired from my own lifeguard career with the California State Parks and some friends began planning an elaborate retirement reunion back at my home beach of San Clemente. Invitations went out to lifeguards from multiple agencies in an attempt to reach anyone who might want to attend. And somehow, word of the reunion reached a distant connection in New Zealand; a woman I had barely known, who had visited California and hung out with the guards some 40 years prior. She, as it turned out, had maintained a connection with Bud Brown and told him about the retirement party.

Bud and I had developed a solid friendship in those six years we guarded together at San Clemente, and although Bud had successfully obliterated his physical connections with his original crew, his departure did little to purge the fond memories he still carried of our formative years, living the dream lifestyle of Ocean Lifeguards on the idyllic beaches of San Clemente.

The night before the occasion, after a self-imposed 35-year exile from our home beach town, Bud returned to San Clemente for the first time since 1986. As he drove through town, he was surprised to see the once wild hillsides were now covered with homes and mature trees. He checked into a hotel room at the south end of town and soon began feeling a profound sense of apprehension, imagining what it would be like to face not one, but 150 *people*, all of whom were linked to the State Parks family he had purged as part of his personal recovery.

Walking into the event, he later admitted, "*I was nervous as hell to come back. As I approached the check-in table, I felt myself trembling....and I fought the urge to turn and run. Then I saw the smiling face of Debbie Friedman, a woman I had swam with and guarded with and shared many soulful conversations with. She immediately wrapped her arms around me in the hugest welcome, and I confided that I wasn't sure I could do this....but she was so great. She convinced me that I could....and pointed out her daughter Clare, then Danny Lineback - both of whom had seen me and were coming over to greet me...they were smiling!...and so began one of the most magical nights, revisiting with my old friends...laughing and joking and sharing memories I had not spoken of for over 30 years. And then there was Don Straub...he came over and gave me a huge hug – so did Dave Carter and Mike Martino. And somewhere in that wild night I had returned home....and home was a good and happy place...I was back to my roots as a lifeguard...as part of my old band of friends. It was magical....purely magical.*"

Not long after, Bud and I embarked on a series of phone conversations, originally intended to uncover some of the details of his time on the North Coast. But over the course of 10 very productive hours, in addition to re-living plenty of stories, we also rekindled our friendship. Bud was amazingly candid as we unearthed a lot of the issues he was never able to honestly face. It was a powerful adventure for us both, and I will admit that each of us cried several times. Bud was frank and open about his short-comings and his mistakes, and he openly shared the devastating hurt he had carried from the cumulative pressures of working there, and the condescension from his staff.

What was likely the most poignant moment in all of those hours came when I confided to him that in my interviews with the other guards, they too had suffered deep and lasting emotional scars from their years working the North Coast. Bud was stunned at this revelation.

Amazingly, for all of those decades, he had thought he was the only one who was unable to reconcile the suffering and anxiety from his time there.

It was striking to me too, realizing they had never reached out to each other to offer much in the way of empathy or compassion, or even to simply commiserate together to mitigate the universal suffering they all shared.

That fact, it would seem, was the ultimate tragedy for them all.

Bud eventually moved back to California and now lives near San Bernardino. He works with troubled inner city kids. He remains unmarried with no children.

Bud Brown (sporting a vest) with family. Father bottom right (2020)

KURT LOEFFLER

The circumstances of Kurt's departure from lifeguarding bore an uncanny similarity to those of Bud Brown.

Like Bud, Loeffler's exodus included an almost complete severing of the ties he once shared with his lifeguard partners. The rumor, which had been circulating in the ranks since his departure from the Sonoma Coast, was that shortly after his transfer to Candlestick Park in San Francisco, in search of a more peaceful existence, he was witness to a violent gang-related killing. The scene was reportedly so gruesome it "pushed him over the edge" and he was granted an early retirement from State Parks citing stress disability from the cumulative effects of both the shooting and his North Coast experience.

Loeffler, again like Bud, proved to be almost impossible to trace down. After exhausting almost all of my leads, I eventually was referred to an old high school friend with whom he was still in contact and located him in Colorado.

Kurt, too, was surprisingly candid in our series of interviews. A man of intelligence and eloquence, Loeffler was not only able to recall events with impressive specificity, but was also able to rekindle the vague particulars back to life utilizing his unique perspective and style.

He was neither apologetic nor elitist in self-appraisal of his time on the Sonoma Coast, and was rightly proud of his accomplishments.

I eventually breached the subject of the shooting at Candlestick, and he confirmed the thumb nail sketch was true, and in fact, was the tipping point which forced him into his early retirement. It had been over 20 years since the event occurred and Kurt confessed the rather staggering truth that he had only spoken about the harrowing specifics of the shooting *one time* since it had occurred. That single admission was to his therapist, shortly after the event occurred.

Ironically, working predominantly in the ghetto of Hunter's Point, Loeffler stated that initially, he felt more at peace there than he had on the Sonoma Coast, clarifying *"It was a heavy place to work, but at least I wasn't hated, and I didn't have to worry about the potential of risking my life every day."*

While in the course of our interviews, Kurt shared the details of the shooting. While he narrated the shocking events in detail, I feverishly took notes and eventually wrote them up in a second-hand summary of the event. I sent it to him for review then quickly realized a story of this magnitude would be much better told by Kurt himself. I knew it was probably a longshot, but asked Kurt if he would be willing to write up an account of the tragedy to be used in this book as part of his overall legacy and to my surprise, a few days later, he sent me his first-hand narrative of the event.

Thus, with Loeffler's permission, the account below provides us with his honest and frank recounting of the awful event from the officer's perspective and in his own words:

"Candlestick State Recreation Area is a narrow stretch of grassy landfill with walking trails, picnic sites, a dilapidated pier, and a few struggling trees trying to maintain their hold in a mixture of dirt, sand, and industrial rubble. The park runs along the shore in the Bay View,

Hunters Point district of San Francisco, adjacent to where the historic ballpark of the same name used to exist.

At that time the crack epidemic was fueling crime and addiction, especially in the housing projects. The collateral footprint of violence it spawned reached every corner of Hunters Point. And a series of unsolved, gang related murders fostered community frustration with the police.

The Candlestick Park office on Carroll Ave is a fortress, a cement cube right across the street from one of the most notorious projects in San Francisco, the Alice Griffith Housing Development, commonly referred to as Double Rock or Two Rock. The police called it the Kill Zone, because a year prior, six people were murdered there in a single night.

It had rained on and off for six weeks. Then the clouds parted, and on that particular morning, bristling with sunny optimism, I was on my way to do a bank drop, driving north on 3rd Street. As I approached Newcomb Avenue I heard the sound of a fully automatic weapon unloading a burst of at least 30 rounds, but I wasn't immediately sure where. Up ahead I saw a white van speeding toward me that turned quickly onto Newcomb. Half a block past Newcomb people were scattering from the sidewalk. I saw a yellow compact car parked against the curb, the windows blown out of it and spent shell casings scattered on the ground around it. I had dispatch clear the channel and expedite PD and medical. Three men were in the car, all of them slumped over with significant gunshot wounds to their head, face, chest and neck. The front passenger door was open, the seat empty.

American cinema may have desensitized us to the sight of a single gunshot wound to the arm or body, but seeing multiple gunshots to the head and face is an extremely disturbing sight. As I worked my way around the car checking each man for a pulse, I felt the sobering reality of violence gnawing at me. The shattered illusion of control that brings one into perfect harmony with the fragile and unpredictable nature of existence - which at that moment was three dead men.

An older gentleman called to me from the doorway of a nearby liquor store. I noticed a thick blood trail on the sidewalk from the car to where he was standing. He said there was another victim inside, and that he had dragged him there. A few feet inside the door, lying on faded red and green floor tiles, was a young boy no more than 15 years old. He was on his back in a thin pool of blood, gasping for air. Two women knelt on either side of him working methodically with wads of paper towels, determined to stem the bleeding from bullet wounds to his face, neck, and upper chest. Between the two of them they had established decent pressure on all of the wounds. I encouraged them to stay with it, as there was nothing in my first aid kit that could have made a difference.

As I updated dispatch, that young man looked up at me helplessly. Unable to speak, unable to move and struggling to breathe with a punctured lung, he searched my eyes with a desperate vulnerability that I had never seen before and I will never forget. I heard an approaching siren. I hoped it was medical, and stepped outside to meet them. In the short time I was inside the liquor store, the street and sidewalk had filled with a large number of people that swallowed the crime scene.

The siren was a solo San Francisco police officer. As I briefed him, the swelling crowd encompassed our vehicles. As much as we tried to protect the crime scene, it was completely out of our control.

Now a captive audience of two in a sea of rising uncertainty, we were spectators to the grief and outrage pouring from the people around us. Shouting, wailing and angry outbursts of disbelief. One man pounded on the hood of the car with both fists, screaming in despair at the top of his lungs.

There is a temperamental, aimless quality to anger. Like lightning it can start out in one place and end in another with very little effort. Knowing the degree of tension that already existed between the community and law enforcement in Hunters Point, I wondered if their collective frustration would turn on me and the SF officer.

We were grossly outnumbered. We couldn't retreat or advance. That's what eats away at you. The powerlessness. Not knowing if it's coming. That's when I considered the 18 rounds of ammunition on my belt. It was a pitiful thought, but there you are. That's the nature of uncertainty.

We stood in front of our vehicles like chess pieces, maybe ten feet apart, exchanging occasional looks of concern. Both our heads on a swivel, constantly scanning the crowd. Neither of us uttered a word in the escalating emotional momentum.

You can't believe how long two minutes can last. That's how long it took before the cavalry arrived, before I was finally able to hustle the *paramedics into the liquor store, before I and the other officer could take a deep breath.*

The young boy would survive, albeit in a wheelchair as a quadriplegic.

That was the end of my career. No gold watch, no retirement party. Just the weightless misery of a trap door opening."

Kurt left Law Enforcement entirely. For a short time, he remained in the Bay Area, working on fabrication, installation, and repair of neon signs.

Loeffler then left California for good, settling in Great Falls, Montana.

He too never re-married nor had any children.

Kurt Loeffler – repairing the neon sign of the Chancellor Hotel (1996)

SCOTT MELVIN

Scott Melvin (2021)

Although he most certainly made a contribution to the overall success of the original North Coast guards, the perceptive Scott was one of the first to realize the combined effects of stress and frustration which came with the job were having a deleterious effect on him. Seeking a tangible way out, he was able to land a highly sought-after position as a Fish and Game Warden with the state, thus becoming the first of the Perms to bail out.

Scott would eventually become a well-respected warden, and was able to ply a fruitful and rewarding career in that role until his eventual full-retirement.

Melvin married a ranger, Connie Breakfield, whom he met in the

Peace Officer Academy. They too decided not to have children. They currently reside in Watsonville, California.

OSH McNULTY

In his time on the Sonoma Coast, Osh would make hundreds of ocean rescues - dozens of which were dazzling and heroic - he would perform hundreds of medical aids, write over 1,000 citations to abalone poachers, arrest violent criminals, and rescue people from every situation imaginable: huge surf, cliff falls, vehicle accidents, fallen trees, being lost in the woods, and a host of other events too numerous to mention.

While other guards worked the North Coast for 2 or 3 years, Osh would forge an entire career at Salt Point. Just short of 20 years of service, his tenure on the North Coast *quadrupled* that of all of his original partenrs.

McNulty quietly and humbly reached legendary status, not just in the State Lifeguards' history, but in the global annals of lifeguarding. If the "powers that be" ever created a Lifeguard Hall of Fame, his name would most certainly be on the first ballot.

In an oversight and injustice which would have greatly upset any other guard, after two full decades of service on the Sonoma Coast, and despite performing hundreds of staggering and awe-inspiring rescues and being personally responsible for saving dozens of lives in the process, Osh McNulty was never nominated for a Medal of Valor. Without a doubt, many of his rescues could have (and should have) been considered for the honor, but the sad truth is that no one bothered to submit them for consideration. In some ways, he was a victim of the philosophy which he helped create; that making rescues on the North Coast was "simply part of your job." He saw no need for hoopla or grand acknowledgment. When the rescue was done, you wrapped up your tube, threw your fins in the back of the truck and drove off to look for another. For those of us who worked with him, it hurts us that he never received more recognition, but I doubt it hurt him.

Osh guarded in the most remote and awe-inspiring outpost on the West Coast, blissfully distanced from the politics of the powerful lifeguard agencies in Southern California. But that isolation also distanced him from knowing 70 of his brethren California State Lifeguard Peace Officers, and remarkably, even at the end of his stellar career, the majority of them had never even heard of him. In some ways, that's even more of a travesty. One of my sincere hopes in sharing these stories with the lifeguard community and the general populace (written not by a member of the press – but rather a fellow lifeguard) is for Osh McNulty and Don Straub, as well as the rest of the original crew, to finally get their due recognition.

Osh McNulty and Karen Broderick (2022) – Hood River, Oregon

Together with his wife, ranger Karen Broderick, Osh retired from State Parks service on the rather auspicious date of the 4th of July, in 2009. They moved to Hood River, Oregon where they designed and built their dream home with a view of the Columbia River.

As with the other Perms, they too never had children.

STEVE FRANKLIN

Of his time on the North Coast, Franklin wrote, *"I was very proud of being a part of history...I loved that job and I was good at it. It was what I was meant to do. The things we did were truly unbelievable, but they were true. We were the lifeguards with the greatest stories, based solely on the true facts that happened while we were there. I loved those guys. I was God-damned proud of it. We were the first lifeguards ever that far north in California. We were a hard core group of dedicated watermen. We suffered the cold wind and giant surf. We dealt with shark attacks, a crashed rescue helicopter, cliff rescues on cars plunged hundreds of feet down rocky cliffs to wave-battered rocks below. We swam out to retrieve dead bodies in the freezing, rocky surf.*

We were lifeguards. We are genetically pre-determined. We are the guys who, in the eighteenth century, would have been out on whale boats searching for Moby Dick."

According to his friends, Franklin had always been a high-strung guy, but his time on the North Coast seemed to exacerbate his anxiety quite profoundly. Citing a need to "get

Franklin with his friend, legendary singer Herb Jeffries (date unknown)

out of there," in less than three years he transferred back to Southern California, eventually accepting a position as a ranger in San Clemente. I worked with him there and although I loved and admired the guy, I can attest to the fact he struggled with stress. In his short career, he had been embroiled in several high-profile confrontations with various entities in the State Parks and claimed vehemently he had been grossly mistreated, a claim that may well be true. Regardless, the transfer to Huntington – then San Clemente did little to alleviate his burden, and within a few years he too retired from state service on stress disability.

In a situation uncannily similar scenario to those Brown and Loeffler, shortly after leaving the State Parks in the late '90s Franklin too severed ties with his lifeguard brethren and seemingly dropped off the face of the earth.

Some 20 years later, after pursuing a myriad of dead-end leads, I finally discovered Franklin had not only withdrawn from the lifeguard community and State Parks in general, but had distanced himself even farther than Loeffler or Brown. While Brown and Loeffler had essentially removed themselves from their previous lives, bolting from California in the process, Franklin took it one step further, and actually succeeded in

Steve Franklin and Luz (2022)

dropping out of Western society entirely, settling in a tiny farming village outside of Medellin, Colombia.

There he met a beautiful woman named Luz Marina Franco. They fell in love and eventually wed. Steve has been adopted into the local community, about as far from his previous life (literally) as is humanly possible. In my correspondence with him, he claimed he hadn't spoken English in over 10 years.

I am pleased to report the hard-driving Franklin, it seems, has finally found his peace.

Completing the statistical anomaly, as with all four of the other Perms, Franklin too never had children.

DON STRAUB

Reaching legendary status in the lifeguard world might do wonders for one's self-actualization but unfortunately everyone has to pay the bills. Financially, Don tried diligently to parlay the role of a lifeguard into a bonafide career, but had limited success. I can think of no one who would have been more deserving. But having been arrested early in life, he burned any chance he had of ever becoming a Permanent.

For a time he was able to scratch out a living on the North Coast and even managed to coerce the state to provide a trailer pad for him. He then proudly went out and bought a new trailer and made it a home for years, but eventually the increasing needs of his family outgrew his lifeguard paycheck.

Don Straub (2020)

That said, his tenure on the Sonoma Coast was one of the longest of any Seasonal Lifeguard, and he distinguished himself as one of the true legends. Don may have made some questionable decisions in his life, but no one could ever question his abilities as a guard. Personally, I loved the guy, and look back at our year working together as one of the fondest of my entire career. I consider him to be a close friend and credit him as a mentor on the North Coast. In fact, let it be known if necessary, I would hold his beer if some guy needed to be throttled.

Straub's achievements and heroics would place him on anyone's short list of the ultimate North Coast Lifeguards, joining the likes of true legends Brit Horn, Osh McNulty, and Nate Buck and Tim Harvey. He ruled over the ocean with a sense of reckless abandon which would likely have brought disciplinary action elsewhere, but on the North Coast, was viewed and respected as sheer gallantry.

His fractured ankle was bad - no doubt exacerbated by the additional thrashing on that rescue. Don underwent several surgeries to repair it, but it never healed correctly. Limited physically by the ankle, and seeking financial stability, Don would eventually leave the ocean where he had so ably served. Hanging up his reds for good, he started his own construction company in Cloverdale. Entering the construction world already in his 40s, making ends meet was initially a challenge.

But utilizing his cowboy-construction skills, his work ethic, and plenty of continued referrals, his company eventually thrived. He ultimately sold the business for a hefty profit and retired relatively young.

AUDREY HAUG

Not many details are known regarding the woman who is credited with making the first rescue of the fledgling lifeguard service. Despite many attempts to locate her, she was the one guard who remained elusive.

The thumbnail sketch of her work history shows she left the Sonoma Coast to attend the State Park Peace Officer Academy and accepted her initial position at Lake Elsinore.

She eventually left the State Parks and became a Sheriff's Deputy with Riverside County where she distinguished herself and was eventually promoted to Sergeant. She then transferred to the Contra Costa Sheriff's Department, then got hired on with the Elk Grove Police Department where she retired as a detective in 2018.

MIKE MARTINO

Mike gathered up experiences and recognition from his four years working the Sonoma Coast then was chosen to enter the State Parks' Peace Officer Academy as a ranger candidate. Finishing well, he was assigned a position back in his home district at San Diego Coast. He then reverted back to lifeguard status, transferring to work the San Luis Reservoir, where he started their fledgling lifeguard program. Mike eventually returned to the ocean as a Lifeguard Supervisor at Silver

Strand, near the Mexican border. There he helped to solidify the aquatics operation and served as its leader for many years.

But Mike's clever mind and skills as an orator continued to propel him up the ranks and eventually would land him at the apex of the State Lifeguard ladder in the lofty role of the *Aquatic Specialist*, overseeing all of the State Parks aquatics operations from Mexico to Oregon.

Utilizing his combined passions for lifeguarding and writing, he was commissioned by the San Diego City Lifeguard Service to compile and chronicle their history. The first third of his endeavor, chronicling their existence from their beginnings until World War II has already been released under the title *"Help – San Diego Lifeguards to the Rescue."* The book has been well-received and critically praised. As I write these words, Martino is well on his way to completing the 2nd volume covering World War II through the early 1970s.

Mike eventually married a kind and supportive spouse, Angie. They live in a modest home in Imperial Beach, California. As with the Perms, they too do not have children.

After a distinguished career, Martino retired from service on Angie's birthday in December of 2016. His future plans include joining forces

Mike Martino – Mainland Mexico (2022)

with fellow lifeguard-scholar Rex Grady, to write the history of the California State Lifeguard service as well. Needless to say, there are scores of people out there eagerly awaiting its release. Martino is still a rocket in the water, an avid surfer, body-surfer, and cyclist

DAVE SCHARDT

The great mystery is how long the affable Dave Schardt would have continued working the North Coast had it not been for his chance encounter with the beautiful and charming Swedish traveler who happened to be passing through Northern California and swept him off his feet. But leave it to Schardt to have that fairy-tale *"Lifeguard meets Gorgeous Swedish Traveler"* story. No one blamed him. After racking up truckloads of good karma, he so deserved meeting the lovely Barbro - and she deserved him.

Schardt's son Ross appears stunned to meet Kurt Loeffler

Schardt worked the North Coast for just over three years and most certainly left his mark on the State Parks.

Interestingly enough, the park left its mark on Dave's future as well. During his final year on the Sonoma Coast, he and Barbro traded many overseas visits between Stockholm and San Francisco. In her visits to California, she spent plenty of time touring, which included the Sonoma Coast. In fact, their first son "Ross" was named after the location where he was conceived at Fort Ross. You can work out the details on your own.

Schardt moved to Stockholm with his lovely bride, learned to speak Swedish and planted himself squarely in the Swedish lifestyle and culture. They live as a traditional Swedish family with two kids. I haven't heard a single complaint from Dave.

He still swims regularly and has distinguished himself as one of the premier members of the Masters' Swim program in Stockholm.

60 years young and in his element

DAVE CARTER

Certainly one of the most beloved lifeguard personalities to ever work the Sonoma Coast, Carter stayed on for four years before leaving to take a job with the Los Angeles County guards, necessitating a move back to the South Bay of LA.

The charming Carter would eventually become a full-time Ocean Lifeguard Specialist there, and for several years served as the Program Director for the largest Junior Lifeguard program on the planet, overseeing thousands of JGs.

Grandpa Carter (2021)

At press time, Carter, in the twilight of his distinguished career, is working 24 hour shifts in the "Call Car" on the South Bay beaches of Manhattan, Hermosa, and Redondo.

Yet, Dave still credits his four year stint as a North Coast Lifeguard as the most challenging assignment of his career.

JON GULICK

Jon would eventually leave lifeguarding to become a registered nurse, accepting a position near Sacramento.

Jon married a decorated NCAA swimmer who also became an Ocean Lifeguard, as well as a Smoke Jumper in Oregon. Gretchen and Jon would move their young family to the big Island of Hawaii to soak into the lifestyle and ocean community. Then, seeking an ever more substantial change and alternative lifestyle, along with uncrowded waves, they moved the entire family to New Zealand, where they still live today.

Immersed in both the ocean and lifeguard worlds, both of their children (Noah and Mikayla) also became guards in New Zealand.

Still very much a surfer and forever a guard, his family has seemingly adopted the unofficial role of *"New Zealand Ambassadors to the California Lifeguards."*

Jon and Gretchen Gulick – Whangarei, New Zealand (2022)

In the summer months, their home is a virtual youth hostel, housing a steady stream of wayward traveling lifeguards from various agencies in California.

They are absolutely great that way.

BRIAN HICKEY

Brian Hickey – Touring the Mosel River in Germany (2021)

Hickey's career with the California State Parks was impressive. He started in 1967 as a Seasonal Lifeguard at San Diego Coast, then after promoting through the various ranks on the blue lifeguard ladder, he jumped ship and continued his climb on the green ranger ladder. His tenure on the Sonoma Coast lasted 13 years and his efforts to help establish the Sonoma Coast Lifeguard service would go down as his proudest accomplishment. In 2000, with the program firmly established, he accepted a final promotion and transferred to the highly desirable Sierra District to complete his career as a Ranger-5. There, he plied the final six years of his State Park service, retiring in 2006 after logging 39-years of service.

Hickey now lives a peaceful existence, far from the ocean's roar, in Oakhurst, California near the entrance to Yosemite.

MICHAEL STEPHENSON

Michael quietly served the Sonoma Coast in the capacity of a Supervising Ranger for over 20 years. Despite not being given the position which would allow him to lead the fledgling lifeguard program, no one ever heard him voice any complaint nor criticize the program in any way. Quietly and humbly he continued to serve a vast populace of beach goers and, when necessary, adeptly tapped back into his aquatic roots to swim out and effect rescues or perform body recoveries.

One of those rescues was a night call-out in which he and Seasonal Lifeguard Tim Murphy spent several hours in a dark ocean in 12' seas to rescue a stranded surfer from a wash-rock over a half-mile from shore. With no back-up from boat or helo, the two men were left no option but to swim the exhausted, hypothermic patient to shore "old school" and deliver him through the 12' shore break. The rescue was one of legendary status and was honored by the United States

Stephenson – never far from the water – sailing San Juan Islands (2021)

Lifesaving Association with the Medal of Valor for both Stephenson and Murphy.

Stephenson retired young. He and wife Mary Jane are living a humble existence in Hood River, Oregon.

They too decided not to have children.

Two of their neighbors are retired ranger Karen Broderick and some guy named Osh McNulty.

ADAM WRIGHT

Adam lasted on the North Coast for about two years before moving back down to San Clemente to work the warm home waters of San Onofre, San Clemente, and Doheny. For many years he was one of the stalwart vagabond guards, continuing on the tradition of living in his truck to save money.

Eventually, he acquired his teaching credential and is now a full-time 2nd grade teacher in the San Clemente area, though he still works his fair share of shifts at San Onofre and San Clemente each summer.

He is also the drummer in the famed San Clemente all-lifeguard band - *The Knotty Knees*.

Adam is married and lives in San Clemente with his wife Jody and their two children (Willow and River)

Adam – banging the skins

And yes, he still drives painfully slowly.

REX GRADY

Rex retired from lifeguarding around the year 2001. He became a successful attorney in the Santa Rosa area and is now a well-respected Law Professor in the county.

Grady goofing around with Tom Neth (1995)

TIM HARVEY

Harvey worked part-time on the Sonoma Coast for about five years, before moving back to Southern California to work at Leo Carrillo in the Angeles District, where he became the Junior Lifeguard Coordinator, a position he held for over 15 years.

In a shocking twist, in 2020, already in his late '60s, Harvey pulled stakes from the position which had made him a local celebrity and *moved back to the Sonoma Coast* to start their first Junior Lifeguard program. By then the program had lost considerable support and on most days, alarmingly Harvey found himself in the unenviable position of being the ONLY lifeguard patrolling the entire district.

It is my sincere hope that those State Park managers, who have been awarded a position of authority, will realize that it is their supreme responsibility to keep the public safe along the Sonoma Coast. Perhaps this book will shed some light on the sacrifices and dedication the lifeguards invested to establish the service on the North Coast - and inspire those

Tim Harvey visits with a couple of Junior Lifeguards (2021)

managers to do the right thing and rebuild the lifeguard program before any more lives are lost unnecessarily.

FRANK CERCOS

Frank hung around for a few years filling in part-time shifts until he slowly faded off the schedule. I am told he is enjoying a well-earned retirement living in the Santa Barbara area.

THE SECOND WAVE

The Crew: McNulty, Buck, Neth, Kim, Shoaf, Shanklin, James (2004)

THE SONOMA COAST LIFEGUARD ROSTER (1995-2022)

In closing, I wish to acknowledge and pay my respects to all of the great guards who carried on the traditions and followed the trailblazing path left by the original lifeguard pioneers chronicled in this book. Every one of these guards answered the call of duty on the North Coast and added their name to the fabric of the Sonoma Coast.

Paul Barnes	Griff Hutton	Blake Nogleberg
David Birdwell	Sean Homer	Aaron Pendergraft
Steve Bourget	Dominic Horath	Ryan Petersen
Jordan Boyce	Mark James	Levi Pior
Nate Buck	Lexi Jones	Michael Porter
Dillon Cleavenger	Hoon Kim	Chad Sambell
Kevin Craig	Myles Koczera	Tom Schatz
Chris Emery	Greg Knapp	Todd Shanklin
Raul Escobar	Scott Kwon	Doug Shoaf
Brad Ewart	Derek Laub	Jake Snyder
Mat Fuzie	Caspian Morast	Joe Stoffers
Christian Guinness	Tim Murphy	Orion Walton
Clark Hale	Malcolm Muter	Luke Walton
Brit Horn	Tom Neth	Ryan Wilson

ABOUT ED VODRAZKA

Ed Vodrazka became an Ocean Lifeguard in 1976 and has managed to maintain that role, in assorted variations, for the past 46 years. In celebration of his career, in 2021 he was asked to throw out the ceremonial first pitch at the San Diego Padres home opener. Honoring him as a lifeguard, according to Vodrazka, was *like praising someone for winning the lottery* adding, *"this job has provided me with a rewarding and colorful life that far exceeds anything I could have ever hoped for. When I consider the many blessings I have been given – my mentors, my friends, my lifestyle, my connection with the ocean, diving, surfing, my travels, my home, my band, my wife and my children, along with maybe saving a few lives along the way - the rather astonishing fact is that every one of these wonderful gifts came to me through lifeguarding."*

In his 20s, Vodrazka spent over three years venturing through South-East Asia, the South Pacific, India, Nepal, and China. He credits his years on the road (along with the guidance of his mentors) as the major influence on his spirituality, his values, and his overall outlook on life.

His first book, *"Stories from Sea Level,"* released in 2021, is a collection of some of the most heroic and humorous rescues performed by his fellow lifeguards on the California Coast over the past 50 years.

Vodrazka currently lives near Del Mar, California with his wife Jennifer and children, Jade and Charlie.

He can be reached via email at *ezlifeguard@juno.com*

Made in the USA
Las Vegas, NV
09 May 2024

89718531R00223